An Illustrated History of Hull & Barnsley Railway Locomotives

Kirtley 2-4-0 rebuilt as Class H, in typical livery. The prominent letter 'A' reveals it to be on the duplicate list - hence, this picture was taken after 1910.

An Illustrated
History of
Hull & Barnsley
Railway
Locomotives

Volume 1.

The Locomotive Classes

by

Martin A. Barker

CHALLENGER PUBLICATIONS

ISBN 1 899624 09 0

Dedicated to my dear Mother,
for her care and understanding
during the last eight years.

First published in the United Kingdom by
CHALLENGER PUBLICATIONS
15 Lovers Lane, Grasscroft, Oldham, OL4 4DP
Printed and bound by The Amadeus Press Ltd, Huddersfield

Contents

ACKNOWLEDGEMENTS.

Like all similar works, this book would have been a much poorer effort without the input and assistance from a considerable number of individuals. Thus thanks are due largely to three groups of people: from the enthusiast fraternity, from one-time employees of the Hull & Barnsley Railway, and from personal friends - although the three groups have frequently overlapped!

First and foremost must be mentioned Mick Nicholson, Willie Yeadon and Mike Lake for their meticulous checking of the text, which has benefitted greatly from their constructive criticisms and input of extra information. Willie gave freely and generously of his time, knowledge, information, advice and encouragement, as did Mick, who furthermore assumed the mantle of "Chief Draughtsman", redrawing several of the tank locomotive drawings. Especial thanks must also go to Nick Fleetwood, who allowed me the extensive use of his great researches into H&BR boiler repairs, Springhead Works and the Locomotive Department. This book is theirs as much as mine.

Invaluable contributions have come from Derek Charlton of Ashington; Gordon Coltas of Lancashire; Ted Dodsworth; C.T.Goode; Steve Goodhand and Hull Museums; Geoff Horsman and Armley Museum, Leeds; John Hooper of Challenger Publications for his help and encouragement; the Yorkshire Farming Museum at Murton, near York; the late Laurie Ward; Malcolm Parker of the South Eastern Coast Railway Society; Mr. Tom Norfolk (boyhood friend of Matthew Stirling Junior), and staff of the Institute of Chartered Accountants. Thanks must also go to the staff in Hull Central Library for uncomplainingly exhuming some incredibly heavy volumes, on which the dust of ages lay thick and undisturbed! David R. Smith of Cardiff and Jim Proud of Hull Society of Model and Experimental Engineers deserve particular mention, as does Bob Goodyear for help with various locomotive drawings and in particular for permission to use his splendid drawings of Classes A, H1 and J.

Other members of Hull S.M.&E.E. deserve acknowledgement, having cheered this project to completion from the sidelines, and in this context I have not forgotten the good wishes and interest shown by my ex-colleagues and the pupils of my last class at David Lister School, Hull; appropriately enough sited close by the H&BR's link to the Joint line, which leads down to King George V Dock.

Several ex-H&BR staff have contributed to this work, albeit posthumously in some cases. These include the late Laurie Featherstone, Draughtsman; the late J.George Gregory, Springhead Shed Foreman, and the late Matthew Stirling, Locomotive Superintendent. These three contributed much by way of drawings, notes, internal correspondence and other more extensive writings and photographs. Footplate staff included William Westoby, the late Bob Sedman and the late Sammy Lucas. Staff from other departments also helped: the late Alfred Dee spoke up for the Carriage & Wagon Department, as did the late S.H.Jackson; the late Jim Stork (a lifelong H&BR enthusiast), represented the Signals & Telegraph Department, whilst the late Ted Oliver of Little Weighton's Station staff gave insights into the workings of "his" railway in the period either side of World War I.

North Eastern Railway Association members Colin Foster and Ron Prattley gave invaluable help, as did members of the Hull & Barnsley Railway Stock Fund, notably Brian Crowther, Allan Halman, Peter Sargeson and the late John Wright.

Finally, a mention must be made of the late Ken Hoole, who was planning his own book on H&BR locomotives in 1987. His untimely death early in 1989 left the present author pondering the question as to whether such a book would ever be written, hence this attempt to fill the largest remaining gap in our knowledge of LNER Constituent locomotive history. Now that he has done so, he can but hope that Ken would have approved of the result!

The Hull & Barnsley Railway.

Preface

The Hull, Barnsley & West Riding Junction Railway & Dock Company scheme was mooted in May 1879 by Hull merchants and West Riding coal owners as a reaction against the perceived baleful monopoly of rail access into Hull by the North Eastern Railway.

The truth of the matter was that so much traffic was offering that it swamped the existing arrangements, but the real bottleneck was the outmoded state of the Hull Docks - the owners of which seemed to lack the will to modernise their property or sell out to the North Eastern, which had both the capital and desire to make the required improvements. So local opinion felt that the best way out of the impasse was to become totally independent of both the North Eastern and the Hull Dock Company and establish a new, through trunk-route from the heart of the Yorkshire coalfield near Barnsley, to Hull, at which town a splendid, new deep - water dock was to be built.

Suffice to say here that construction started in January 1881 in a blizzard: a possible portent of stormy times ahead, for due to constructional difficulties encountered in the Yorkshire Wolds plus shortages of funds, leading to suspension of work for five months in 1884 by the contractors, capital expended totalled £6 millions upon completion.

By the time opening of the HB&WRJR&DCo. took place in 1885 it was substantially as outlined above; schemes to extend westwards to Halifax although passed by Parliament, proved stillborn. Upon opening, the HB&WRJR&DCo. fulfilled the hopes of Yorkshire's traders by undercutting the existing cartage tariffs, thus sparking off a three-cornered rate war which only the North Eastern could hope to survive unscathed. The results were a foregone conclusion: the Hull Dock Company was eventually taken over by the North Eastern (which immediately invested some £2 millions in updating the docks), whilst the HB&WJR&DCo. had to call in the Receiver. The 1880's had proved to be a disappointment to the Company, for traffic was painfully slow to build up, and shareholders' meetings became increasingly acrimonious since London shareholders (subscribers of the largest part of the capital), became increasingly frustrated at having no prospects of any dividend returns because the Hull factions were (as they saw it), enjoying the benefits of cheap transport at their expense.

Amalgamation with a larger company was either torpedoed by the unwillingness of other companies to risk the enmity of the provincial but massively powerful North Eastern, or the intransigence of Hull Corporation which held (and exercised), a veto regarding absorption of the HB&WRJR&DCo.

The corner was turned in the 1890's however, following the indulgence of Parliament in allowing a reorganisation of the HB&WRJR capital; the opening of a branch in West Yorkshire (Wrangbrook to Denaby opened in 1894), an extension to Alexandra Dock (opened 1899), and the agreement with the North Eastern in 1899 to construct jointly a new deep water dock in Hull, immediately east of the HB&WRJR's Alexandra Dock (ultimately opened as King George V Dock in 1914). Further consolidatory moves came with the opening of the Wrangbrook -Wath branch in 1902, and the through Hull - Sheffield express service over Midland Railway metals from the HB&WRJR's terminus at Cudworth; the part - share in the short Great Central, Hull & Barnsley, and Midland Joint Railway, and the much longer Hull & Barnsley and Great Central Joint Railway. Also of importance was the 1905 appointment of Edward Watkin (nephew of the eminent Sir Edward Watkin of the Great Central), as General Manager of the HB&WRJR. Under his careful hand, a rapprochement with the North Eastern came about in the form of a mutual co-operation agreement: by 1914 it was not unrealistic to describe the HB&WRJR as a prosperous concern.

Sadly, the HB&WRJR never really recovered from World War I; it was deeply ironic that as a prelude to the 1923 Railway Grouping the Company was amalgamated with the North Eastern Railway in April 1922. The H&B Section (as it became under the London & North Eastern Railway in 1923), suffered along with the rest of that system due to the effects of the great slump and the depression years of the Thirties. Tonnages carried rose due to World War II, but the decline afterwards was swift and severe. Passenger traffic (already cut back from Cudworth to Howden as early as January 1932, and even earlier on the branches), was abandoned completely from August 1955 and through coal traffic struggled on for a little longer, the last through coal train having arrived in Hull on the evening of 29th November 1958. The rest of the line died by inches, being closed piecemeal throughout the 1960's until only the section around Hull on the embankments and about three miles through Carlton to serve Drax power station remain at the time of writing. Even the HB&WRJR's most profitable asset, Alexandra Dock, was closed for some nine years throughout the 1980's but has happily been returned to useful life once again.

However, as much of an enigma as the HB&WRJR&DCo's own history is that of the Company's locomotive stock, to which we will now turn forthwith.

Martin A. Barker, Hull 1996.

Cab view of Hull, Barnsley & West Riding Junction Railway Kirtley 0-6-0 Goods No.32. Built by Beyer, Peacock & Co., 1885.

INTRODUCTION

The Hull, Barnsley & West Riding Junction Railway & Dock Company, (or to use its more familiar title as adopted officially in 1905, the Hull & Barnsley Railway), became the last large - scale, independent railway scheme of Victorian times to come to completion. Other, more doubtful distinctions were that it was the most expensive line built in Britain (at an average cost of £58,911 per mile); it was additionally unfortunate enough to be the first of the Pre - Grouping companies to have its main line closed; lastly, (and of more relevance for the purposes of this book), the only sizeable, independent, constituent company of the London & North Eastern Railway group to have no representative of its locomotive stock preserved.

Being a provincial company and generally at a distance from centres of population, the H&BR has been largely overlooked by historian and enthusiast alike, yet in numbers of locomotive stock it compared not unfavourably with several other (and better-known), companies. In 1915 the H&BR operated a total of 186 locomotives: a greater number than the Furness, the Highland, and Great North of Scotland, the Rhymney or the Barry Railways, and only half a dozen engines less than the North Staffordshire.

As lacking in recognition as the H&BR's locomotives was the man responsible for them, namely Matthew Stirling. A son of the illustrious Patrick Stirling of Great Northern Railway fame, Matthew Stirling served the H&BR from May 1885 (before train services began), to Amalgamation with the North Eastern Railway in April 1922, establishing a record for length of service with one company broken only by Marriott on the Midland & Great Northern Railway due to the much later absorption of that concern.

Reference has already been made to the fact that the H&BR was a latecomer on the railway scene. This however, brought two major benefits as far as the establishment of a locomotive department was concerned.

Firstly, by the 1880's Great Britain had established the World's first and foremost locomotive building industry; with over fifty years' experience, Britain's locomotive engineers could virtually guarantee that anything reasonably orthodox which they cared to put on rails would perform its duties satisfactorily (and for an astonishingly long time in many cases).

Secondly, the sixty years between the opening of the pioneering Stockton & Darlington Railway and the Hull & Barnsley saw methods of railway working and management come to maturity, along with the emergence of a body of competent engineers, designers and administrators. Of no lesser importance, the crafts of locomotive management and maintenance had also become established on a sound basis, so the H&BR was in the position of being able to fill its locomotive department vacancies with experienced manpower. The days of hiring and firing as circumstances (frequently of the economic variety), dictated, from the semi-literate, displaced masses of largely agricultural background as had been the case a half-century earlier were a matter of history by the mid-1880's, at least as far as the railway companies were concerned.

On the other hand, the H&BR was hardly large enough to attract the very best candidates for senior managerial positions, and if so it could hardly expect to retain them for long: by the 1880's a considerable 'reserve' of able railway officials had become established, many of whom would rise to occupy important positions 'behind the scenes' with the bigger companies, although being largely unrecognised by history. The more ambitious young men would inevitably tend to move around in order to gain promotion, rising relatively quickly to positions of eminence within the smaller companies at home, or in the Colonies - the Irish railways in particular became almost a nursery for future Chief Mechanical Engineers of the mainland companies!

Another factor working against the H&BR was that its awesome neighbour the North Eastern was not only its most serious enemy for many years, but was also widely recognised as

N13 No. 2410 (ex-H&BR F3 No 18), at the east end of Springhead shed in the 1930's. J.George Gregory, Springhead shedmaster *(wearing cap),* **is pictured showing a young enthusiast, W.B. Yeadon** *(visible to the right of J.G.G),* **around. J. George Gregory's father was one who followed Matthew Stirling from the GN to the H&BR, in due course getting young George employment on the H&B. Willie Yeadon became a good friend of J.G.G, inheriting his notebooks and records, which he put to good use when helping compile** *Locomotives of the LNER* **for the R.C.T.S., and also in checking through this work on behalf of the author.** *W.B.Y coll.*

being probably the best-run system in Britain, one which (certainly by the 20th century), had trained and selected a pool of management talent second to none. Yet despite these two powerful influences a surprising number of able staff found the atmosphere of working for the H&BR congenial enough to settle permanently in Hull, devoting much of their working lives to the Company - the prime example being Matthew Stirling himself.

Although Stirling was the only Locomotive Superintendent throughout the H&BR's entire independent operating life, the three classes of locomotives ordered for the opening owed nothing to him, originating in 1883 from William Kirtley, Locomotive Superintendent of the London, Chatham & Dover Railway. A seemingly inexplicable candidate for the job as Consulting Engineer, albeit on a temporary basis, he was most likely recommended as a result of the influence of James Staats Forbes. Not only was Forbes a member of the H&BR Board, he was also Chairman and General Manager of the London, Chatham & Dover Railway. (Coincidentally the LC&DR like the H&BR, spent much of its existence in a state of deadly rivalry with an older-established neighbour, in this case the South Eastern Railway. Further coincidences were that the South Eastern's Locomotive Superintendent was James Stirling - Matthew's uncle; and finally, the feud between the LC&DR and the SER was ended by what was in effect if not in fact, amalgamation - broadly similar to the ending of H&BR/NER hostilities!)

James Staats Forbes had been associated with the H&BR from its earliest days, and largely at his insistence it had been laid out to first - rate standards as a passenger line, at greater expense than would otherwise have been incurred and leaving the H&BR with a legacy of lavish over - provision for the relatively few passenger for which it catered. (The reason for this attitude on Forbes' part is probably not too hard to uncover: the LC&DR was for many years little short of ramshackle. Its permanent way was among the poorest in the country, having been largely built down to a price. Passenger accommodation regarding stations was at best indifferent; regarding carriage stock appallingly bad. The vendetta with the South Eastern had led to the mutual impoverishment of both concerns, and with about a sidingful each of shining exceptions, both companies marshalled the most dismal, poky, fly - blown throwbacks to the stagecoach to be proffered anywhere to the hapless travelling public! Regarding the locomotive department, it need only be said that the average age of LC&DR locomotives in December 1885 was some 15$z\x$ years - including two new express locomotives whose ages could best be noted in days rather than years. Clearly, although Forbes couldn't be held responsible for the state of affairs before his appearance on the LC&DR scene, he wouldn't have wanted to start from scratch in such a manner: hence he saw his chance to turn out a quality product with the H&B!)

William Kirtley had been established for some eleven years on the LC&DR at the time of his H&BR commission; it should come as no surprise to find that his three H&BR designs were in effect developments of existing LC&DR types, and also to some extent harbingers of future developments of that railway's motive power. The three H&BR locomotive classes totalling 42 engines, were all built by Beyer, Peacock & Company of the Gorton Foundry, Manchester. Curiously, after this substantial initial order they received no more custom from the H&BR, except for a few orders for new boilers; another odd fact is that they never constructed any locomotives for the LC&DR. With the exceptions

of a small order for 0-6-0's from the Vulcan Foundry, Newton-le-Willows, the three G2 Class tank engines from Robert Stephenson & Co. of Newcastle and the ten Class F3 0-6-2 tanks from Hawthorn, Leslie & Co., also on Tyneside, the H&BR never went outside Yorkshire for new locomotives; they invariably patronised either Kitson & Co. of Leeds, or the Yorkshire Engine Co. at Meadow Hall, Sheffield.

These later orders were naturally to the specifications of Matthew Stirling, and again students of locomotive history will not be surprised to find that they generally conformed with the styles associated with the Stirling family: father Patrick on the Glasgow & South Western Railway at Kilmarnock up to 1866 had established the style, then gone on to develop it further at Doncaster Works on the Great Northern. Uncle James, upon taking over from his elder brother at Kilmarnock continued in the same style, and again continued to develop it at Ashford on the South Eastern after 1878. A Stirling locomotive with its domeless boiler, round-topped, short-roofed cab, dished smokebox door and generally austerely-plain but harmonious outline was unmistakable, no matter with which of the trio it had originated. Despite these apparent constraints however, Matthew Stirling contrived to achieve the stamp of individuality on his works, tending to follow his uncle's styling variations rather than his father's. For example, the Great Northern's brass trumpet-like, safety-valve cover was eschewed in favour of South Eastern-style, open Ramsbottom safety-valves. Similarly whereas Patrick Stirling's GNR six-coupled shunting locomotives were inevitably given saddle tanks, their South Eastern cousins were graced with side tanks and Matthew Stirling followed that example, although he differed from his uncle regarding the styling of the aforesaid side tanks; thus the H&BR never owned any saddle tank engines.

However, Matthew showed a totally independent streak in producing the only Stirling family 0-6-2 tanks, and with the massively imposing Class A goods locomotives of 1907 he turned out the biggest Stirling locomotive, the only eight-coupled engine to originate from the Stirlings, the biggest Stirling boiler type, and the only Stirling boiler with a Belpaire firebox - all in one fell swoop! As the last of the dynasty, in Great Britain at any rate, it fell to Matthew to produce the last Stirling express locomotives, and the only Stirling types to be built with superheaters. Finally, he even produced that Stirling rarity, an ugly engine - in the form of the five L1 0-6-0's of 1911 with Phoenix superheaters; although some may also place the Kirtley 2-4-0's reboilered to Class H1 by Stirling in the 'ugly' category, the author considers them to have acquired a somewhat 'roly-poly' appearance!

Due to the H&BR only having the services of two Locomotive Superintendents, the majority of its engines could be classified under two broad headings: Kirtley's and Stirling's. For ease of reference however, it is considered expedient to divide the locomotive stock into four groups: Kirtleys; Kitson designs; early Stirling classes (introduced 1889 to 1907); and later Sirling classes (introduced 1907 to 1915); along with, in an Appendix volume to be published later, separate sections covering details of construction, fittings, and so on. Furthermore, although the H&BR employed three systems of locomotive class-designations by letter at various times in its history, for reasons of clarity reference will be largely made to the final scheme introduced in 1908, since it covered all eighteen classes and variations in use from then until the 1923 Grouping.

Part 1. THE KIRTLEY LOCOMOTIVES

Very few locomotive superintendents found themselves in the position of William Kirtley, being given carte-blanche to provide a new railway company with a complete stock of locomotives as he saw fit. Quite a number of Victorian railway companies had built up their locomotive stocks on a piecemeal basis, all too frequently being short of capital by the time they were ready for opening. (Kirtley's 'own' LC&DR was a prime example of this: financial constraints meant that for the first five or so years after its 1857 opening, trains were worked by a motley collection of undersized, unsuitable or well-worn, second-hand locomotives. They all possessed but two common virtues: they were available, and cheap. Even after Kirtley took charge in 1874, by which date the LC&DR had achieved a position of financial stability, he never had the resources to embark on a policy of 'scrap-and-build'. Instead, he relied on judicious rebuilding to attempt to keep various old crocks in a position where they at least had a hope of maintaining timetabled services, whilst simultaneously 'topping up' the locomotive stock with modern designs by degrees (as and when opportunities arose).

Although the dates of William Kirtley's first tentative contacts with the H&BR seem lost in the mists of time, we do know that he was appointed as the H&BR's Consultant on 19th February 1883. With the permission of the LC&DR Board of Directors, he produced drawings and specifications of his proposed H&BR designs for approval by the H&BR Board on 30th March. At first glance it would appear that Kirtley took around 35 working-days to do this. However, a moment's reflection leads one to the inescapable conclusion that this was an impossibly short time for one individual to produce complete, detailed drawings of three classes of locomotive as well as keeping on top of LC&DR matters. It is doubtful whether the indulgence of the Chatham's Directors extended so far as allowing the entire resources of Longhedge Works' Drawing Office to be devoted to Kirtley's extra-mural activities for over a month, so clearly there must be another explanation.

Fully detailed locomotive drawings and blueprints can appear quite formidable to the untutored eye, so it would seem likely that Kirtley produced simple, basic outline drawings, backed up by tables, figures and/or calculations. (Later generations of locomotive engineers would tend to refer to such simple drawings as 'Weight Diagrams'). Of all the members of the H&BR Board of Directors, only James Staats Forbes had any training in locomotive engineering - a considerable number of years before, under Brunel and Gooch on the Great Western. Since he had most likely put forward Kirtley to the H&BR Board, he would hardly proffer any doubts as to the work of his protégé! (Some criticism could indeed be levelled at Kirtley's work, but this will be dealt with at a later stage). So it would seem that Kirtley used various LC&DR locomotive component drawings with which to put flesh on the bones of his diagrams. More probably, the detailed designing was included in the work put out as part of the contract.

In any event, Beyer, Peacock & Co. was one British builder to maintain a large and active drawing-office: such work as that given to them by the H&BR was their bread and butter. Further clues as to the lineage of the Kirtley locomotives are in the three

relevant Beyer, Peacock general arrangement drawings: none bear William Kirtley's signature, simply that of the draughtsman responsible. They are also liberally sprinkled with references to other drawings, covering parts and sub-assemblies. Presumably many if not all such items were parts conforming to standards already established by Beyer, Peacock, if not in fact widely recognised throughout the industry by the majority of manufacturers. What should also put the matter beyond all reasonable doubt is that Beyer, Peacock's General Arrangement drawings are dated well after March 1883: 9th November 1883 being the earliest date, for the 0-6-0 shunting tank locomotives. (It should also be borne in mind that there are several instances of Locomotive Superintendents or Chief Mechanical Engineers having nothing to do with the actual design of certain locomotives for which they were nominally responsible. The classic example of this occurred with the design and construction of the London, Midland & Scottish Railway "Duchess" Pacifics in 1937: although the C.M.E. William Stanier received the credit, the responsibility for them was that of the Chief Draughtsman, Tom Coleman, for Stanier was at the time occupied as a member of the committee investigating the poor riding of other Pacifics - in India!)

To return to the H&BR, William Pintler and Vincent Hill of the Rolling Stock Committee (presumably with some input from William Kirtley), arrived at probable numbers of locomotives and other rolling stock required by the empirical method of studying numbers of vehicles per mile on other railways. They achieved a measure of success, since the H&BR found it unnecessary to augment its motive power until nearly four years after the opening. (The additional early purchase of six four-coupled shunters from Kitsons was necessitated by the peculiar operating conditions on Alexandra Dock, as explained in Part Two).

The Rolling Stock Committee wisely did not blindly copy the LC&DR regarding types of locomotives and numbers. In December 1885 (by which time all 42 Kirtley locomotives were in service with the H&BR), the LC&DR had 177 locomotives in service, of which 74 were of Kirtley origin. Those 177 could be placed in four groups, as tabulated below:

Table 1. LC&DR Locomotive Types

	Express Passenger	Passenger Tank	Goods Tender	Shunting Tanks	Totals
Nos. of Locos	76	72	25	4	177
% of loco stock	42.9	40.8	14.1	2.2	100

The numbers in the first group reflect the considerable prestige Continental boat train traffic and seaside excursion workings from the Capital. Hordes of smaller locomotives in the second group highlight the substantial residential traffic which had already arisen on the LC&DR's network of lines, radiating southwards from Victoria and Ludgate Hill. The much smaller numbers in the third group indicate that either the Chatham had little goods traffic; utilised numbers of passenger engines on various goods workings, or didn't over-exert themselves in catering for goods traffic. The final group of only four engines was composed of two geriatrics which had been rebuilt as saddle tanks as early as 1865, plus two Kirtley side-tanks of 1879, and the direct ancestors of the H&BR's first locomotive class. Both Kirtley and his predecessor William Martley had recognised the need for purpose-built shunting locomotives, but had received insufficient resources to do much towards remedying the situation. Consequently, too much use was made of tender engines in varying states of well-being, according to how long they had been out of Longhedge Works: to the intense frustration of all directly concerned with shunting. (A large, main line tender locomotive is a most unwieldy tool for goods yard work, the driver inevitably having a restricted view being further away from the ends of the locomotive, and almost invariably having to use screw reverse gear instead of the much handier lever reverse).

Fortunately for the H&BR, those responsible for its early motive power policy decided upon a different balance of motive power. Despite the optimistic claims in the H&B's Prospectus of 1880, anticipating the growth of substantial residential traffic to the west of Hull, the fact that no passenger tank locomotives ever appeared on the H&BR shopping list would suggest a more axiomatic attitude on the part of Kirtley and his collaborators than the H&BR's promoters! In the event, the first 42 H&BR locomotives were in the following proportions, as tabulated in *Table 2* opposite for ease of comparison with *Table 1*:

Table 2. H&BR Locomotive Types.

	Express Passenger	Passenger Tanks	Goods Tender	Shunting Tanks	Totals
Nos. of locos	10	nil	20	12	42
% of loco stock	23.8	0	47.6	28.6	100

The considerable percentages in the third and fourth groups reveal that the H&BR anticipated a plentiful goods and mineral traffic: not surprisingly since the railway had been promoted largely as a competitive route for the export of coal from West Yorkshire. The ten passenger locomotives comprising the first group proved in the event to be more than adequate, since twenty-five years were to pass before it became necessary to augment their numbers.

It only remains to note here that William Kirtley did not oversee the entry into service of his H&BR designs - that task fell to Matthew Stirling from his appointment by the H&BR on 13th May 1885, some two months before the railway opened fully to traffic. Despite his relative youthfulness, being aged 28 at the time of his appointment, this did not prevent him from some slight criticism of Kirtley's work and with an amount of justification, as we shall see.

No.12 posing for Beyer, Peacock's works photograph. *Hull & Barnsley Stock Fund collection.*

KIRTLEY CLASS G1 0-6-0 SIDE TANKS
(Originally Class A of 1885)

As stated earlier, these twelve locomotives had direct ancestors on the London, Chatham & Dover Railway. Although only two of these were in service at the same time their H&BR cousins were designed, another eight (slightly modified), entered LC&DR service between 1889 and 1893. All became LC&DR Class T, and took the numbers 141 to 150.

The H&BR engines formed virtually an intermediate stage in the development of the two groups of Class T's. Most differences between the three variations were not readily apparent, save for one detail: the cab and bunker assembly. The LC&DR's initial pair had cabs of around 5ft 4in from front to back - an adequate size, until consideration of the throw of the reversing lever is made. This, standing some five feet above footplate level with the engine in mid-gear, needed considerable strength to heave over. A clear space of just over a foot between lever top and cab backplate was quite inadequate, and would call for an amount of gymnastic prowess on the part of the driver to put the engine in full back gear without almost impaling himself on the lever. Kirtley must have recognised this, for he took the opportunity to increase the space in the H&BR cabs to 6ft 0in, and also increased the bunker capacity by half a ton, to a total of 1¼ tons. This latter figure was retained for the last eight Chatham T's, along with a further increase in cab size to 6ft 3ins, necessitating an increase in the length of frame plates of 6¼ ins compared with the first pair. The effect of the lengthening was visible in the different proportions of the lower cab sidesheets, for on all the LC&DR engines, the doorway was positioned towards the back of the cab cutout; this meant that most (if not all), of the extra 6ins length of the last eight was made up on the cab sides in front of the doors. Oddly enough, the doors on the H&BR engines were centrally placed within the cutouts!

The first two T's and the dozen H&BR G1's were built at the very end of what could well be termed the Second Iron Age, having two-ring iron boilers, iron wheels and some motion parts. A mere four years on from the entry into service of the H&BR's engines, Kirtley had joined the growing band of engineers who had resolved their last remaining doubts regarding the quality of steel, for the last eight Chatham T's had steel boilers, wheels and frame plates. As it was, steel made its appearance in various components on the H&BR G1's, such as the piston rods, slidebars, axles, horn guides and wedges, wheel tyres and coupling rods. Extensive use of steel was made in the frames: the frame plates, of 1 inch thickness, planed on the inside, were of Siemens - Martin

steel, and the motion plate was a substantial steel casting. That modern rarity, 'proper' wrought iron, was used for the crossheads, small end pins, valve buckles, valve gear links and dies, the reversing shaft, eccentric straps and rods, crankpins and spring buckles. Each connecting rod was hammer forged from a single wrought iron billet of substantial size, since the finished rods measured 5ft 3¾ in between the butt ends. The cylinders and valve chests were of cast iron of close-grained quality, without liners in the bores. Other substantial valve gear and engine parts were also of cast iron, except for the slide valves. These were of best gunmetal, and the steam pressure upon their backs exerted a force of 24,045 lb, a figure which should come as no surprise to anyone who has tried to put a (stationary), slide valve locomotive with lever reverse into full gear with the steam chest still full! However, due to the areas of the valves the pressure on them turned out to be 29.7 lb/sq in. Stirling reported in October 1891 that a set of valves recently removed had been reduced ⅝ ins in thickness, after running 242,000 miles. The cavity of the valves when new was two inches deep (154 cubic inches).

A big difference between the Chatham and the Barnsley engines lay in the boilers. It was not readily noticeable, but the H&BR engines had boilers of 4ft 3ins diameter (over the back ring), as compared with a maximum diameter two inches less on the Chatham engines. Thanks to their bigger diameter, the H&BR engines carried 199 tubes compared with thirty less on the LC&DR Class T's. All other boiler dimensions were common: boiler barrels were 10ft 0ins long, fireboxes 5ft 2ins long outside, and grate areas 15 sq.ft. All three varieties shared the same common 7ft 4ins + 7ft 8ins wheelbase. Possibly in order to preserve appearances as much as to increase water capacity, for like most Victorian locomotive engineers William Kirtley had an eye for proportion and neatness of outline, the side tanks on the H&BR engines were slightly taller. Not only did this have the effect of hiding the increase in boiler diameter, it also increased the tank capacity by 20 gallons over the 830 gallons capacity of the Chatham engines. Oddly enough, despite the bigger water capacity of the boilers and tanks on the G1's, this was not fully reflected in the weights - 42 tons 3cwt 2qtr compared

No.2 as built. Note the Westinghouse pump on the cabside, and numberplate on the tank side. Beyer, Peacock's worksplate is behind the fireman, who is striking a pose in front of the bunker whilst the driver tries to look busy. Even the railway constabulary have got in on the act. *Hull Museums collection.*

No.2 again some years on, displays changes brought about by Matthew Stirling. Note that the Westinghouse pump has gone, although the engine has been given vacuum brakes. No.2 has also acquired a cast-iron Stirling chimney and plated-in coal-rails; also the numberplate has been moved to the bunker, displacing the works plate to the front sandbox. The initials "H&BR" appear in block capitals on the side tanks. *Hull Museums collection.*

No.5 shunting at Alexandra Dock, Hull. The original print clearly shows guard rails over the rear cab spectacle windows, consisting of two vertical and two horizontal bars. No.5 was eventually sold to the C.W.S. colliery at South Shilbottle, Northumberland. *Driver 'Cookie' Robson, York.*

A later photograph of No.5. Although of indifferent quality it is of great interest in showing the acquisition of a rerailing jack on the footplating, plus a new injector fitted immediately below the left-hand boiler clack-valve. Just in front of the shed at Alexandra Dock are two Class K well-tanks, the leading one with a good head of steam.

with the exact 42 tons of the first T's and 42 tons 15 cwt of the last eight. Virtually all other measurements were identical between the two railways' locomotives; for further information regarding valves, valve gears and boiler construction, the reader is referred to the relevant sections towards the end of the book, in Part 5.

From signing the contract to build the H&BR tanks on 24th April 1883, Beyer, Peacock wasted little time, since their General Arrangement Drawing is dated 9 November that year. They were Beyer, Peacock's Engine Order No.6400, and ultimately took up Works Nos.2430 - 2434, 2436 - 2441, and 2614. The contract price was to have been £2,170 each, but it was decided to equip the first six engines with Westinghouse Air Brakes, which increased the cost of each of those so fitted to £2,259. (The others remained as specified, with steam brake only). The Chatham's first pair had been priced at £1,930 each, the last eight were costed at £1,840 apiece - clearly their Longhedge Works had made some progress in gearing up for the manufacture of locomotives in the ten years between 1879 and 1889!

Beyer, Peacock undertook to deliver six locomotives in May 1884 and the remainder in the month following, but as ever with delivery dates things didn't quite work out like that!

The first six, (Works Nos.2430 - 2434 and 2436), duly appeared more or less as agreed, and took up their H&BR Nos.1 to 6. It seems that H&BR Nos.7 to 11, (Works Nos.2437 to 2441), followed without undue delay, but No.12 apparently appeared late in 1885; for in the meantime Beyer, Peacock not only completed the H&BR orders for thirty tender locomotives, but also went on to complete a further 106 locomotives before remembering that they still owed the H&BR one engine, since No.12 carried Works No.2614.

The earliest engines to be delivered helped in the construction of the railway itself since lengthy sections of it were complete by 1884, with considerable mileages of permanent way in situ (as opposed to the more rickety temporary way which the contractors put down for their own use).

Before the H&BR opened to traffic it was found that the 15 ft wheelbase of the G1 tanks did not take kindly to the sharper curves on Alexandra Dock (where most of them were to spend the greater parts of their working lives), so in the summer of 1885 an order was sent to Kitson & Co. of the Airedale Foundry, Leeds, for six four-wheeled, shunting tank engines. (These locomotives are detailed under Class K - see *Part 2: Kitson-Designed Tanks*).

Despite the fairly widespread use of the LC&DR Class T's on inner suburban services, there is no record of similar, short-distance passenger use of the six Westinghouse-fitted G1's on

the H&BR, although it would have made operational sense to have worked emigrant specials from Alexandra Dock to Springhead with a Westinghouse fitted tank, before handing over to a tender engine. However, the Hull terminus at Cannon Street required the use of two 'pilot' engines (due to the layout of the station and yards one was probably the West side pilot, the other for the East side), and most certainly carriage stock shunting was included in this work, so a locomotive fitted with continuous brake equipment may have had some use. It would also seem that an amount of transfer trip working from Alexandra Dock in the east to yards in the west (and vice-versa), was undertaken until the advent of the 0-6-2 tanks in 1900. Otherwise, with the exception of presumable forays by the odd one into the nether regions of deepest and darkest West Yorkshire, they remained at Alexandra Dock shed. Photographic evidence tends to support the non-migratory habits of the G1's, since all the classic photographs of them in H&BR days are invariably on the dock estate or at Springhead Works, in West Hull. Under the H&BR's brake conversion programme of 1892 the first six G1's were converted from Air to Automatic Vacuum Brake, but in time this was found to be a luxury and eventually removed, thus rendering them all identical.

As Kirtley-pattern fittings wore out (items such as smokebox doors and chimneys especially), they were replaced with items of Stirling design. Coal rails were also added to the bunkers,

No.9 piloting at Hull (Cannon Street) station, shunts a van of Kirtley origin at the north end of the goods shed; the houses along Lockwood Street form the background. It is to be hoped that No.9's driver did not trip over the shunter's pole, threaded through the cab handrails! *W.B.Yeadon coll.*

giving a useful increase in coal capacity. Stirling also modified the livery (as dealt with under that heading), and made their ownership more clearly visible. Whereas Kirtley had decreed that the G1's should coyly hide their owner's initials from all but the closest inspection of their tankside plates, Stirling had these moved to the rear cab/bunker sides, and the initials 'H & B R' emblazoned along the tanks. The oval Beyer, Peacock's Works plates were displaced from the rear cabsides to the sides of the front splasher/sandboxes.

1st April 1922 saw the North Eastern and Hull & Barnsley amalgamate, as a prelude to the much bigger Grouping of

No.3 at Springhead on 19th September 1904. The engine still retains its vacuum brake but the coal-rails are not yet plated in. The efforts of the cleaners on the tank tops only serve to emphasise the general griminess of the engine.

January 1923, so for a few months the H&BR acquired something of a North Eastern flavour as all sorts of alien influences percolated throughout Springhead Works. Sadly, such things as plans for the future were not to include the G1's, for the Kirtley engines were becoming life-expired. The H&BR itself had started to withdraw the tender engines from 1917, so it was no surprise that the G1's were soon put to the sword. One can readily imagine the comments of the North Eastern's inspectors upon learning that the G1's still carried their original boilers and outer firebox shells: tributes to the designers, builders, and quality of the materials from which they were made, helped by the moderate boiler pressures. Yet despite the fact that the North Eastern lost no time in condemning them, they were in no great rush to scrap them. The NER were the biggest disposers of their old engines of all the pre-Grouping companies, finding ready purchasers especially in the North-East coalfields. Following in the noble tradition of second-hand locomotive salesmen, the London & North Eastern Railway was able to dispose of five G1's for further use in 1923. On 27th March 1923, Nos.2, 3 and 4 were sold to the Ashington Coal Company and on 4th May, No.8 was also bought by them. Finally, No.5 was sold to the Co-operative Colliery at Shilbottle, Northumberland on 18th May 1923. It called in at Hawthorn, Leslie & Co. of Newcastle for overhaul as it made its way northwards to its new home. (Although Dr. Parkes gives Nos.3, 4, 9 and 12 as being the Ashington disposals, the numbers given earlier are from the LNER's own records). Either way, the locomotives sent to Ashington became their Nos.16, 17, 19 and 18; the purchasers paid £350 for each engine. Presumably, an already-existing No.18 had been withdrawn unexpectedly about that time at Ashington, so they lost no time in getting another H&BR

locomotive to take its place. Those unlucky enough not to be given a reprieve ended their lives at Springhead Works, a few months later.

Curiously enough, two of the LC&DR Class T's were also sold for industrial service in the North: No.149 of 1889 was sold via a dealer to the Wallsend & Hebburn Coal Company in July 1937 and worked for them until August 1948, being broken up for scrap some three years later by Bowrans of Newcastle. More remarkable still was the disposal via the same dealer of No.141 of 1879. This, the first Kirtley tank engine, was acquired by Richard Evans & Co. of St. Helens and put to work at Haydock Colliery, adjacent to the Liverpool & Manchester Railway, serving from March 1940 to September 1958. British Railways took over three other Class T's from the Southern in 1948, the last of which was condemned by the summer of 1951.

Stirling tells us little about the everyday mundanities of work for the G1's, except to say that a bunkerful of coal (1¼ tons), was enough for a day's work: a shift of some 12 to 14 hours. However, the author can perhaps offer some clue as to how well the G1 tanks performed their duties by relating the following incident, which took place at Ashington Colliery in September 1968, nearly thirty years after their last G1 tank was withdrawn. A glorious late summer's day saw the Author and three friends embark on a tour of the North East coalfields to view the remaining steam locomotives. Three of the party had a soft spot for the H&BR, the loyalties of the fourth member (as he frequently proclaimed throughout the day), lay most emphatically with the Great Western Railway; to such an extent that he had headed a successful effort to preserve an ex-GWR saddle tank sold by them for further use at Ashington. "Stoker" Redfern (our guide around Ashington Colliery), and ourselves

No.2 was fortunate enough to be sold to the Ashington Coal Co. by the LNER. As A.C.C. No.16, it became the last H&BR Kirtley engine in service, being scrapped in July 1939. Worthy of note are the new injector fitted immediately below the boiler clack and the extended bunker - and also the ex-Great Western Railway pannier tank lurking in the background, also sold into industrial service. *D.G.Charlton.*

were frequently reminded of the importance of the ex-GW shunters to the Ashington Coal Company, until one of our long-suffering trio found his tolerance exhausted.

"Didn't you have some ex-Hull & Barnsley engines here, too?" he asked.

"Oh aye," replied Mr. Redfern. He stopped, and added, "They were good engines."

Loyal to the end, our friend again took up the cudgels on behalf of Brunel, Dean, Churchward and Collett, et al:

"But weren't the Great Western engines good ones too?" Mr. Redfern faced us.

"Yes, very good engines," he agreed, then stabbing the air emphatically with a forefinger he added, "but they weren't as good as the Hull & Barnsley ones! Now they were the best!!"

(The result of that remark is best summed up in the manner of a Victorian cartoon caption, to whit: "Collapse of stout party...!").

Summary: Class G1 (1885 Class A) 0-6-0 Tanks.

H&BR No.	Works No.	Delivered	Disposals	Private Owner's Nos./Withdrawal dates
1	2430	5/1884	Cut up Springhead ?/1923	-
2	2431	5/1884	Sold 23/3/1923	Ashington Coal Co. No.16. Wdn 7/1939*
3	2432	5/1884	Sold 23/3/1923	Ashington Coal Co. No.17. Wdn ?/1934
4	2433	5/1884	Sold 23/3/1923	Ashington Coal Co. No.19. Wdn 4/1937**
5	2434	5/1884	Sold 4/5/1923	Co-operative Colliery, South Shilbottle. Wdn ?/1938
6	2436	5/1884	Cut up Springhead ?/1923	-
7	2437	6/1885	Cut up Springhead ?/1923	-
8	2438	6/1885	Sold 18/5/1923	Ashington Coal Co. No.18. Wdn ?/1934$
9	2439	6/1885	Cut up Springhead ?/1923	-
10	2440	6/1885	Cut up Springhead ?/1923	-
11	2441	6/1885	Cut up Springhead ?/1923	-
12	2614	?/1885	Cut up Springhead ?/1923	-

Notes:

* Coal bunker extended at Ashington; **Stovepipe chimney fitted at Ashington; $ Never repainted at Ashington, retained its H&BR livery. All engines given new, copper inner fireboxes by H&BR., circa 1905; Beyer, Peacock Order No.6400. Cost per locomotive £2,170; Works No.2435 diverted at short notice to Rhondda & Swansea Bay Rly., eventually became GWR property.

A.C.C. No.17 (H&BR No.3) in profile. The cab roof ventilator would appear to be unique to this engine, and possibly fitted at Ashington. *D.G.Charlton.*

Ashington Coal Co. No.19 displays signs of heavy bodgery by Linton shops - note patched smokebox door and extended bunker. The "bodgery" was more extensive than is evident in the photograph - Nos.17 and 18 (H&BR 3 and 8), were cannibalised in order to keep No.19 in service until 1937. *D.G.Charlton.*

Class G1 Dimensions.

Cylinders: 2, inside. 17" x 24".
Motion: Stephenson with slide valves.
Boiler: Domed.
Max. diameter outside: 4' 3".
Barrel length: 10' 0" (10' 4½" between tubeplates).
Firebox length outside: 5' 2".
Pitch: 6' 10".
Heating surface:
  Firebox Stirling100 sq.ft; Parkes 96½ sq.ft.
  Tubes 199 @ 1¾" dia. - Stirling 940 sq.ft; Parkes 936½ sq.ft.
  Total Stirling 1,040 sq.ft.; Parkes 1,033 sq.ft.
Grate area: 15 sq.ft.
Ratio of grate area to heating surface: 1 to 69.
Boiler pressure: 140 lb/sq.in.
Wheel diameter: 4' 6".
Wheelbase: 7' 4" + 7' 8".
Length over buffers: 28' 11".
Weight in full working order: 42 tons 3 cwt 2 qtr.
Axleloads:
L - 12 tons 9 cwt 1 qtr; D - 14 tons 19cwt; T - 14 tons 15cwt 1 qtr.
Tractive effort @ 85% of boiler pressure: 15,284 lb.
Ratio of blast nozzle to cylinder diameter: 1 to 3.57.
Water capacity: 850 gallons.
Coal capacity: 1¼ tons, 52 cu.ft (new).

Note: Both Stirling and Parkes give different figures for some boiler dimensions; both are given.
Coal rails were fitted to all the locomotives under Stirling's superintendency, which would increase the bunker capacity. The H&BR's last diagram book gives a figure of 2½ tons after modification. Discrepancies between Dr.Parkes' and Stirling's figures are probably explained by the fact that Parkes was a knowledgeable enthusiast quoting the exact figures, whereas Stirling rounded his statistics off since he realised that exact accuracy in heating surface figures can be simply over-pedantic, and of little real value in the final outcome (i.e. generating steam). Another possible explanation could be that Stirling was describing the locomotives as built, whereas Parkes was writing about matters as they were by the middle to late 1900's: it is feasible that the new inner fireboxes fitted by the H&BR had a couple of tubes less than the originals, and that new front tubeplates were fitted at the same time. Unfortunately Parkes does not give the numbers of tubes, but the discrepancies between his figures and those of Stirling would be roughly accounted for by two tubes, and easing of the top corner firebox radii which Stirling had criticised, would have entailed a loss of heating surface commensurate with the differences in those figures. Finally, the H&BR Diagram Book figures support Stirling - but maybe the diagram for the G1 tanks remained unaltered: such things sometimes happened on far more "respectable" railways than the H&B!!

(top right) **Ex-H&BR No.3 as Ashington No.17 looks rather cleaner than on the H&BR in 1904! Note the Stirling smokebox door with two dog-clamps, and the new injector. The hole in the bufferbeam to the left of the driver's elbow is a reminder of the extended wooden block dumb-buffers fitted by the H&BR for shunting timber bogies. The crew seem to be quite satisfied with their engine - they have even gone to the extent of adding decorations to the smokebox door.** *D.G.Charlton.*

Ashington No.18, with a heart-shape cut out of the paint on the smokebox door, then kept brightly polished. No.18 has also acquired an odd lubricator plus new injector, unlike No.19, which retained its original injector below the footplating. No.18 was scrapped in 1934, still carrying its H&BR livery. *D.G.Charlton.*

Kirtley Class B No.32 posed for Beyer, Peacock's works photograph: note the monogram "HB & WRJR" on the tender-descriptive if somewhat illegible! *Hull & Barnsley Stock Fund collection.*

Class B No.14 at Alexandra Dock, Hull, on the morning of 28th May 1885. Several aspects arising from the occasion of this photograph are worthy of comment - firstly, it was some two months before the opening of the dock and railway, and the train depicted was the first which the company ran. Secondly, although it was brand-new, No.14 only got as far as South Cave before breaking down, causing two of the contractor's tank engines to be purloined. Absence of continuous brake equipment meant that the train, although carrying passengers consisting of officials and invited guests, was running "unfitted", although the engine's steam-brake and two brake vehicles provided adequate means of stopping. The party was to halt at Ouse Bridge to watch it being tested by means of six other Class B's (coupled in threes, one group per track), running back and forth over it. Having accomplished this satisfactorily, all made their way in due course to Cudworth. Kirtley's old-fashioned rolling-stock is noteworthy: No.14's train consisted of a luggage brake van; seven 1st/2nd class composites and another luggage brake or brake-third. For the first few weeks of the passenger services the H&BR's trains looked exactly as this one since the 2-4-0 engines had not then been delivered. Finally, the young man on the right in the Billycock hat is Matthew Stirling; this was his first public duty for the HB & WRJR, since he had only arrived in Hull a fortnight before. *Laurie Ward.*

KIRTLEY CLASS D/E 0-6-0 GOODS ENGINES.
(Originally Class B of 1885.)

When considering the specifications of this class in comparison with Kirtley's LC&DR 0-6-0's one comes to the inescapable conclusion that he had not really considered to any great extent the probable conditions under which goods traffic would be worked on the H&BR.

A glance at the gradient profile and system maps in the Appendices at the end of the book reveal that the railway was laid out "back to front" regarding haulage of coal trains in as much as the gradients did not especially favour them.

From the western end of the main line, at Cudworth Yard North, came an immediate climb at 1 in 110 for 2½ miles with odd lengths at 1 in 264 to a summit west of Brierley Tunnel. The next 9½ miles were generally downhill, followed by a largely level stretch of 22 miles punctuated by short climbs to cross other lines, rivers and canals. A last short, favourable stretch from Newport soon gave way to a gruelling climb of 7 miles at 1 in 150, up through Drewton Tunnel to a summit at its east end, and a glorious and well-earned coast with only a breath of steam on for the next six miles downhill, to the western outskirts of Hull at Springhead. At this point not only were the Company's main workshops and running shed situated, but also extensive arrays of sidings and yards for sorting and forwarding traffic onwards to local yards, depots and Alexandra Dock, via numerous trip and pilot workings around Hull. Coal export traffic, in due course continued eastwards over changeable gradients, which Ahrons likened to those of the more lighthearted kind of railway more usually found in amusement parks, until Alexandra Dock hove into view. (The climb at Newport commenced some 25 feet above sea level, and the summit at Drewton, at some 262 feet, was reached in seven miles: a tough job by any standards and considerably more gruelling than anything found on the LC&DR!)

The twenty locomotives which Kirtley provided for heavy goods haulage on the H&BR bore a striking visual resemblance to their 1876 LC&DR predecessors, the B1 Class, although in actual fact they had more in common dimensionally with an 1861 design by Martley, Kirtley's predecessor. (These were the 'Acis' class engines, designated as H Class under Kirtley's system).

These, and the H&BR 0-6-0's had coupled wheels of 5ft 0ins diameter with 17ins x 24ins cylinders, and with the new Kirtley boilers (all fitted by 1881), these components too were remarkably similar. For example, common boiler dimensions were diameters at 4ft 3ins, grate areas of 16.25 sq.ft and boiler tubes - 199 at 1¾ ins diameter. Similarities stopped there though, for the H&BR 0-6-0's shared boiler barrel lengths with the G1 tanks rather than the Chatham B1's or H Class.

Curiously, when the work the LC&DR engines had to do was considerably easier than that facing the H&BR locomotives, the Chatham B1's had cylinders ½ inch bigger in diameter with a two inch longer stroke, plus wheels two inches less in diameter than the H&BR B's. Effectively, this meant that the Chatham had a more powerful engine, whereas those of the H&BR might have proved marginally faster and therefore of somewhat more use on occasional passenger work. (Possibly Kirtley himself came to consider this as a greater virtue, for his LC&DR Class B2 of

1891 had 5ft 0ins diameter wheels, but with bigger cylinders still - of 18ins diameter. Clearly, his H&BR design could be regarded to some degree as having formed an intermediate stage in that process of development).

In retrospect, the H&BR's Class B could have filled a useful niche as far as the Chatham's motive power requirements were concerned, whereas their B1 and B2 Classes could have been marginally more useful on the H&BR; but whatever the validity of speculating on Kirtley's thought - processes, Beyer, Peacock & Co. agreed to turn out twenty Class B's, on 19th July 1883. Nos.13 to 22 were priced at £2,748-15s, the intention being to fit them with Westinghouse Air Brakes, with Nos.23 to 28 being rather more expensive at £2,775 being proposed for dual - fitting with both air and vacuum brakes. Finally, Nos.29 to 32 were fitted with steam brakes only, so consequently were cheaper, being priced at £2,695 each.

Although the class took Beyer, Peacock Works numbers 2489 to 2508, they had Works Order Number 6438 - rather curiously in view of the fact that the 2-4-0's (H&BR Nos.33 to 42 and Beyer, Peacock's Works Nos.2479 to 2488), had Works Order No.6436!

The builders completed design work on 7th January 1885 and so did commendably well to deliver at least seven by the end of June 1885. By the date of the H&BR's full opening on 27th July, several more had appeared, including three or four of the Westinghouse - fitted ones. None of the passenger engines were delivered until some three weeks after the opening, which meant that the H&BR had initially insufficient engines with continuous brakes to cover its passenger train diagrams unless some of the G1 tank engines were used, and they could hardly be regarded as suitable motive power for a fast working to Cudworth! However, legislation prohibiting the working of non-continuously braked passenger trains was not passed until 1889, so it is probable that some workings relied on locomotive steam - brake and guard's hand - brake in the carefree, time - honoured manner of old! A precedent had possibly been set for this - the H&BR's first passenger train, a nine-coach special for officers, directors and guests ran on 28th May 1885, hauled by No.14; although supposedly a Westinghouse fitted locomotive, a photograph of the event shows no sign of such fittings on the engine in question: i.e. bufferbeam hose connection. Also despite the fact that Beyer, Peacock's General Arrangement Drawing refers to the first six engines as being Westinghouse fitted, Ahrons was emphatic about the initial shortage of such locomotives. Examination of photographs would also indicate that Nos.13 and 17 were unfitted; but that No.16 received vacuum brakes, certainly after receiving a Stirling boiler if not before. Probably the specifications for types of brakes and the numbers fitted were altered at some stage between the initial orders and their deliveries at short notice by the H&BR; Ken Hoole gives Nos.23 to 28 as being air-braked, at £2,745 each, the others costing £2,695 apiece. They may well have realised that Kirtley only specified Westinghouse brakes due to its established use on the LC&DR, and that the biggest user of the Westinghouse brake was in fact the North Eastern: a concern hardly predisposed to hand over or share traffic, or agree to any joint workings with

Class B No.20 at Springhead. Note the Stirling cast-iron chimney and re-railing jack on the footplating. *Hull Museums collection.*

the upstart now in their midst! Consequently, the H&BR would be relying on developing trading links with companies out to the west - all users of the vacuum brake. (In passing, the initial train of May 1885 was notable for two events: firstly, it was the first public occasion which saw Matthew Stirling's attendance, having only taken up his post on 13th May; secondly, the train only got as far as South Cave before No.14 broke down, causing two of the contractor's tank engines to be 'requisitioned' before further progress was possible - a portent of unsettled times ahead regarding the H&BR's passenger services!).

Whatever the details of delivery dates and brake systems, all twenty were in service by the end of 1885; No.32 posed for the Works official photograph and presumably also for the cab view, since that shows a tender locomotive equipped with steam brake only.

Footplate crews would have appreciated that, mechanically, the B's were very similar to the A's, with two exceptions - the fireboxes were 4ins longer on the B's, being 5ft 6ins long outside. This gave the B's a grate area of 16¼ sq.ft, an increase of 1¼ sq.ft. Secondly, instead of lever reverse the B Class had screw reverse, with a left-hand, double-thread of 1 inch pitch. The reversing wheel of six spokes could be secured in eight different positions per revolution, and eight full turns of the wheel effected full forward to full reverse - so 32 different lengths of valve - travel (cut-off), could be set. From mid-gear, a full turn gave valve cut-off at 26% of the piston stroke; the second turn gave 46.2% cut-off; a third turn set cut-offs of 60%, and the fourth and final turn

gave a fixed, full-gear cut-off of 72%. Working the reverser from fore to back gear moved the die-blocks 8 ins in their links, and with an eccentric throw of 6½ ins, full-gear gave the valves a maximum travel of 4 ins. Travel in mid-gear was approximately 2¼ ins, and the valves had a 1 inch lap, (⅞ inch on the G1's), the valve cavities being 5½ inches by 14 inches and two inches deep: sufficient to provide a very free exhaust. Externally, the valves measured 16¾ ins x 11 ins. Lead in all cases was ⅛ inch, with no inside lap or clearance, in other words 'line for line'. The ports were 1⅜ ins x 14ins, and exhaust ports were 3½ ins x 14 ins: 2.54 times wider. Port areas measured 19¼ sq.ins and 48 sq.ins respectively. The bridges between the ports were 1 inch wide.

Stirling gave considerable information about the workings of the goods engines, for in his own words, "The goods locomotives command most of my attention, as the goods and mineral workings are the staple trade of the Hull & Barnsley Railway."

At 5 mph with a heavy load being hauled at 22.4 RPM, (with wheels of 5ft diameter, equivalent to 4mph), driven at full regulator and at a cut-off of 75% (in other words, flat out!), they used 4,000 cubic ins of steam per revolution, the steam flowing at a rate of 10 ft per second through the 4 inch diameter main steam-pipe. Indicator Diagrams (see *vol. 2, Appendix*), show the Class B's to have given their best work at 56 RPM, or 10mph, although the pair of cylinders were developing 267 Indicated Horse-Power at the highest speed, 31 mph. The diagrams, presented in 1891, were taken on a Hull-Cudworth train of 274 tons gross, although Stirling had stated in 1889 that average loads (including engine and tender weights), were 284 tons or 22 loaded wagons, averaging speeds of 25 mph. To accomplish this, the Class B's were consuming 787.5 lb of coal per hour, an average of 31.5 lb /train - mile. This worked out at around 48.5 lb /sq.ft of grate area per hour. Later generations used to seeing large eight or ten - coupled locomotives moving upward of some thirteen hundred tons at considerably higher speeds may be inclined to smile condescendingly upon the moderate speeds and featherweight trains of the H&BR, but their work should not be under-estimated.

Class B No.13 at Springhead; largely as built, but with Stirling cast-iron chimney.

No.17 rebuilt with 4ft 3in. diameter boiler to become Class E. These rebuilds retained their original footstep-mounted injectors, as can be seen from the boiler-mounted clack valves. The buildings in the background were put up in the 1890's - when No.17 arrived in Hull in 1885, Springhead was still largely a greenfield site. *J.B.Stork collection.*

The Class B's must have made the welkin ring as they blasted uphill to Little Weighton, for Stirling reported that chimneys were having to be replaced even before November 1889. Kirtley chimneys were made in three parts: a cast-iron top, flanged base of best Yorkshire iron, and middle section of best Staffordshire iron plate. The softer plates of the middle sections were suffering from severe erosion caused by cinder - cutting from part-burnt products of combustion pulled through the tubes and ejected from the chimneys of the hard-worked engines. This was despite the fitting of spark arresters in the form of $\frac{1}{4}$ inch thick wrought iron plate, affixed across the smokebox, level with the blastpipe top. The plate had 3,830 holes of $\frac{3}{8}$ inch diameter, at $\frac{5}{8}$ inch pitch, drilled in it. The replacement chimneys were of typical Stirling form, owing much to Doncaster outlines, and not surprisingly were of much tougher cast-iron.

Another feature to cause Stirling some concern was the tightness of the radii in the firebox inner plates. This was formed at only $2\frac{1}{2}$ inches radius, a figure which Stirling considered to be too little: "Too square a head," was the way he graphically put it, before going on to quote a figure of 6 inches as being a more usual radius. (It should perhaps be pointed out that tight curves in firebox plates were apt to suffer from cracking due to stresses set up through heating and cooling. Obviously it was highly desirable to avoid such a situation, hence the move towards larger radii, which could cope better with the various stresses).

Fortunately, other items were more durable; for example, in October 1891, Stirling reported that no wheel tyres on any Class B had by that time worn out, although the G1 tank engines had lasted for 148,000 miles. (Not only would the smaller wheels

make more revolutions per mile than larger ones, but the tight curves on the Alexandra Dock estate may well have exacerbated wear on the flanges rather than the treads). He also stated that the Class B wheels were put in a wheel lathe and the tyres turned to profile after an average of 46,030 miles: maximum mileage between turnings for a Class B was 67,279 miles.

Despite the pressures on the backs of the slide valves (the same as quoted for the Class G1's), valve wear was very slight. One set which Stirling had recently removed had reduced in thickness by $\frac{5}{8}$ inch after running 242,000 miles.

No crank axles had needed renewing by 1891 despite reaching mileages of 300,000 and having to endure considerable stresses. Stirling pointed out that the twisting moments due to steam pressure on the crankshaft (a force better known today as 'torque'), amounted to some 400,000 inch/lb. Not only that but the crank axles also had to take around 13 tons of the locomotive's own weight. Not surprisingly, hoops of best Yorkshire iron were shrunk around each crank-web. (Before getting bogged down in esoteric discussions of the stresses and strains in machinery with floating crankshafts and flexible beds, i.e. the steam railway locomotive, it is as well to bear in mind Matthew Stirling's words on the subject: "Strains on locomotives are many and various, and have never been calculated with any degree of accuracy.").

With regard to everyday maintenance features, Stirling pointed out that the cast gunmetal axle-boxes had adjustable, tapered wedges fitted to the back legs of the horns. These were adjusted by a screw at the bottom of the wedge, and locked by a bolt at the back. (Adjustment had to be done with an amount of

One for the modelmakers! The other side of Class E No.17, just for comparison; once again at Springhead works, as rebuilt with 4ft 3in. diameter domeless boiler in 1899. Note that the tender has acquired coal-rails and had the toolboxes moved forward, modifications which had started before reboilering, as can be made out on the photograph of No.20. Boiler-mounted clacks show these boilers to have retained the original footstep injectors. The manhole cover under the boiler can be seen between the leading and driving wheel splashers. Note the angle of the reversing lever reach rod.

circumspection - too little would not do anything to prevent the locomotive from knocking itself to pieces, whereas too much was liable to jam the axlebox in the horns, which in turn could lead to the risk of overheating or even derailment in certain circumstances).

Another unglamorous but essential job which was apt to be overlooked (and not only by the enthusiast fraternity!), was the regular repacking of valve and piston glands. The stuffing boxes for the valve spindles took ⅝in. diameter "Loco" packing, whereas the piston rod glands took four rounds apiece of ⅞ in. diameter packing, which cost around 5d. per pound. Average costs of packing per locomotive per annum came to 38/-, plus unquantifiable amounts of what may best be termed "Heavy Industrial English".

As the years of hard work gradually took their toll on the

Class B's their appearance gradually changed. At first, the tenders lost their monogram initials in exchange for "H & B R" in block letters, obviously due to Stirling's influence and of Great Northern Railway derivation, although in point of fact the monogram "HB&WRJR" was a more accurate description of the Company's official title, albeit at the expense of clarity and visual impact! (Further details regarding Liveries are given in *Appendix 1, vol.2*).

Probably around the time of the chimney renewals (1887 onwards), the smokebox doors were also replaced, most likely because of distortion caused by overheating. This was set up by the accumulations of part-burnt coal and cinders which had not been blasted skywards, having settled in the bottom of the smokebox and continuing to burn. At best this would scorch the paint off the door bottom; at worst it could so distort the

No.13 at Springhead Works, but as rebuilt to Class D in 1902 with 5ft diameter domeless boiler and Stirling cab. Note that the tender has acquired coal-rails and had the tool boxes moved forward, modifications which had started before reboilering, as can be made out on the photograph of No.20. Absence of boiler mounted clacks show these big boilers to have been fed via backhead mounted injectors. The manhole cover under the boiler can be seen between the leading and driving wheel splashers; the resemblance to Stirling's Class B may be noted.

An immaculate Class D, No.28, standing in Springhead yard on 19th September 1904. Class E No.31 can be made out lurking in the background, in equally spotless condition. *Hull Museums collection.*

door that the all-important air seal would be destroyed, which in turn allowed the 'char' to burn ever more strongly, ultimately making the smokebox door red-hot. In fairness to Kirtley though, it should be stressed that such problems were not confined to the H&BR: an old friend of the author could recall from boyhood memories in Lincolnshire how some of the older, smaller Great Northern locomotives could be seen at night initially by the brilliance of the glow from an overheated smokebox door, rather than the brilliance of the front lamps!

Tender toolboxes were also moved forward to a more accessible position across the front of the tender, simultaneously creating more shelter in this area, and around this time too the tender coal-spaces were enlarged by three coal rails around the sides, and across the back end.

The Brake Conversion Programme of 1892 saw Nos.13 to 22 presumably fitted with vacuum brakes (the enigma surrounding their initial braking systems has been referred to, and certainly at least No.16 was vacuum braked at some stage in its career). If in fact Nos.23 to 28 were dual-fitted or only equipped with Westinghouse brakes, then some may have retained such fittings for some time longer, for use on emigrant trains. These workings, heavily-loaded but not having to maintain express timings, were ideal for utilising six-coupled goods locomotives with wheels around 5ft diameter.

By 1897, boilers were starting to wear out, so a reboilering programme was instigated by Stirling. That year saw a start made with Nos.16, 30 and 31 passing through Springhead Works; the year after they dealt with Nos.14, 18 and 19. Nos.17, 24 and 25 took their turn in 1899 and there matters rested for some three years since similar work on the 2-4-0's had become necessary. (For those details, see next Chapter). The new boilers were of typical Stirling inspiration being domeless, but retained a diameter of 4ft 3ins. Heating surface totals were marginally reduced, to 1,027 sq.ft, but the fireboxes were enlarged slightly and boiler pressures increased to 150lb/sq.in. In addition, cylinders were bored out to 17½ins diameter, a measure probably having more to do with increasing power than correcting wear. The original cabs were retained, producing something of a hybrid combination of two design schools: Kirtley's Derby-inspired style and Stirling's 'Neo-Doncastrian' look. (Kirtley had commenced his railway career under his uncle Matthew Kirtley at the Midland Railway's Derby Works).

Under a Classification Scheme introduced in 1905 the 4ft 3ins diameter, domeless boilered variants became redesignated as Class D, but three years later under the H&BR's final scheme they became Class E, and as such will be referred to hereafter.

Class D was then allotted to the remaining Kirtley 0-6-0's, which had undergone a metamorphosis even more drastic than their fellows! Although initial reboilerings of the 2-4-0's had commenced in 1899 with 4ft 3ins diameter boilers, 1901 saw

others of that type pioneer the use of domeless boilers of the prodigious diameter of 5ft 0ins. Similar boilers appeared on Class B's rebuilt from 1902 onwards; initially on Nos.13, 15, 23 and 27, followed by Nos.22 and 28 in 1904, then No.20 in 1905 and finally Nos.21, 26 and 29 in 1907. No.32 was also rebuilt with a 5ft 0in diameter boiler, but at what date is not certain. These boilers were pressed at 170lb/sq.in.

The considerably-increased diameter of the new boilers meant that the cabs (6ft 7ins outside width), were too narrow, for in addition an extra 3ins each side had to be taken into account for boiler lagging, which would have left a mere 7ins each side between cabside and firebox sides. Consequently Stirling provided new cabs, wider than the originals and needless to say, of Doncastrian appearance! With their new large boilers and Stirling cabs, these rebuilds were at first glance very similar to his Class A 0-6-0's introduced in 1900 (see Early Stirling Classes C and B). However, the heavy brass casting with Beyer, Peacock's name, which lined the centre splashers, plus the absence of sandboxes either side of the same provided a ready means for the observer to distinguish between the two classes. The large Kirtley rebuilds were designated Class C in 1905, but reclassified as D in 1908.

At a similar time to the reboilerings, the Kirtley engines were provided with hand-operated, traversing screw-jacks of 20 tons capacity. These were carried on the footplating alongside the firebox, just in front of the cab on the left-hand (fireman's), side. The author cannot but express the feeling that it was not the intention that crews should strive nobly to rerail a stricken engine: it may have been a reasonably easy proposition to get the jack from footplate to ground level, but having had personal experience of having to move and operate the self-same jacks many years later, he is of the opinion that no two men could readily carry one let alone replace it on the footplate, not even on pain of instant dismissal! Still, having a jack readily to hand could have been of considerable help to a rerailing gang, and may have helped to avoid numerous full-scale call-outs of the breakdown train from Springhead to the further-flung outposts of the H&BR system in darkest South Yorkshire! Most likely the jack carried by No.19 was found to be of use at South Cave on 11th May 1910: platelayers engaged in changing a rail gave No.19's driver insufficient warning when working an empty mineral train, leading to its derailment.

Not all the Kirtley goods engines spent their lives mainly on goods workings: No.16 for example, was photographed at Wath on the branch passenger train, after reboilering but before 1911.

Class E No.16 standing at Wath with the branch passenger train and about to leave for Kirk Smeaton. This photograph was taken between the engine's rebuilding with a domeless boiler in 1897 and its transfer to the duplicate list in 1911. Kirtley's carriages are still doing sterling service, and have been vacuum-braked, as too has No.16.

The latter date was crucial, for it marked the transfer of No.16 to the Duplicate List. This was due to the delivery that year of replacement 0-6-0's in the form of Stirling Class L1 engines. The H&BR were unable to withdraw the older Kirtleys immediately due to constraints of traffic requirements and financial restrictions. Companies in a similar position marked out their demoted engines with a zero before the number, or letter 'A' or 'B' used as a prefix or suffix thereto. The H&BR used the letter 'A', possibly behind the number on the cabsides of those engines with Stirling cabs, but below the cast numberplates retained on the Kirtley cabs, as depicted in some later photographs of the 2-4-0's. Curiously, no photographs of the D's and E's showing their duplicate list numbers seem to have survived, but Company records plus delivery dates of new locomotives show when various engines were transferred. 1911 saw Nos.16, 17, 19, 24 and 31 displaced by five new L1's, and further deliveries of that type the following year caused the transfer of Nos.14, 25, 29, 30 and 32. Deliveries of Class F3 0-6-2 tanks in 1913 cleared Nos.13, 15, 18, 23 and 27 from the Capital List and 1915 saw Nos.20, 21, 22, 26 and 28 follow them, due to deliveries of Class LS 0-6-0's.

Doubtless the introduction of the fifteen massive Class A eight-coupled mineral engines in 1907 accelerated the downgrading of the D and E Classes. A possible indication of the downturn in their fortunes may be found in the fact that on 24th June 1907, Stirling Class B No.96 ran into a rockfall on the Denaby Branch, and a Kirtley Class E headed the Breakdown Train from Springhead to attend at the scene: even the most ignorant observer would instantly grasp the fact that considerably more hardware than a twenty-ton jack would have to be deployed!

The job of Breakdown Train engine was a somewhat lowly one on any railway, being traditionally part of the duties of the shed pilot engine, but since both Springhead Shed and Works purloined any suitable locomotive in steam for shunting, the use of a Class E on the Breakdown Train may just have been coincidental.

The First World War certainly had a detrimental effect upon the locomotive stock, the older ones in particular tending to suffer the most. Consequently it came as no surprise to find that No.17A was withdrawn by the H&BR some time in 1917, followed in June 1920 by Nos.14, 21A, and 31A. Most of these were small-boilered Class E's; the others soldiered on, presumably spending increasingly lengthy periods in a state of disuse although No.32A at least had been worked until the very last days of the H&BR's existence: a sad little memo. dating from March 1922 reported it as having "failed".

Between 5th June and 27th October 1922 the North Eastern Railway withdrew the remaining twenty six which it inherited. Nos.22A and 28A were broken up at Springhead in August 1922, the others were sent via Hull Dairycoates Shed to Darlington for scrapping, although Nos.15A, 23A and 30A were observed passing through Newcastle Central Station in the midsummer of 1922, en route to Percy Main for cutting up.

The last sizeable reminder of the Kirtley 0-6-0's lingered on for another two years in the form of No.28A's boiler. As a temporary expedient, Springhead Works had fitted it to Stirling Class B No.3055 in May 1923. This boiler had entered service in July 1904, and saw No.3055's entry into LNER service, before being replaced in its turn in 1924, just four years before 3055 itself was sent to the scrapyard.

Summary: Classes D, E (1885 Class B) 0-6-0.

H&BR No.	Works No.	Delivered	Withdrawn	Rebuilt to Class/Date	Notes
13	2489	1885	?/1920	D, 1902	To Duplicate List 1913 - F3
14	2490	1885	6/1920	E, 1898	To Duplicate List 1912 - L1. Cut up Springhead.
15	2491	1885	8/1922	D, 1902	To Duplicate List 1913 - F3. Cut up Percy Main.
16	2492	1885	8/1922	E, 1897	To Duplicate List 1911 - L1.
17	2493	1885	?/1917	E, 1899	To Duplicate List 1911 - L1. Cut up Springhead.
18	2494	1885	8/1922	D, 1898	To Duplicate List 1913 - F3.
19	2495	1885	8/1922	E, 1898	To Duplicate List 1911 - L1.
20	2496	1885	8/1922	D, 1905	To Duplicate List 1915 - LS.
21	2497	1885	6/1920	D, 1907	To Duplicate List 1915 - LS. Cut up Springhead.
22	2498	1885	8/1922	D, 1904	To Duplicate List 1915 - LS. Cut up Springhead, Aug 1922
23*	2499	1885	8/1922	D, 1902	To Duplicate List 1913 - F3. Cut up Percy Main.
24*	2500	1885	8/1922	E, 1899	To Duplicate List 1911 - L1.
25*	2501	1885	8/1922	E, 1899	To Duplicate List 1912 - L1.
26*	2502	1885	8/1922	D, 1907	To Duplicate List 1915 - LS.
27*	2503	1885	8/1922	D, 1902	To Duplicate List 1913 - F3.
28*	2504	1885	8/1922	D, 1904	To Duplicate List 1915 - LS. Cut up Springhead, Aug 1922
29	2505	1885	8/1922	D, 1907	To Duplicate List 1912 - L1.
30	2506	1885	8/1922	E, 1897	To Duplicate List 1912 - L1. Cut up Percy Main.
31	2507	1885	6/1920	E, 1897	To Duplicate List 1911 - L1.
32	2508	1885	8/1922	D, 190?	To Duplicate List 1912 - L1.

Notes:

Beyer, Peacock Order No.6438. Cost of each engine - £2,695.
* Nos. 23-28 Westinghouse braked, all others steam-braked.
The second column gives Beyer, Peacock works numbers: not to be confused with LNER numbers given to H&BR engines after 1924.

Dimensions Class B as built, 1885.

Cylinders: 2, inside. 17" x 24".
Motion: Stephenson with slide valves.
Boiler: Domed.
Max. diameter outside: 4' 3".
Barrel length: 10' 0" (10' 4¼" between tubeplates).
Firebox length outside: 5' 6".
Pitch: 6' 11".
Heating surface:
  Firebox Stirling - 100 sq.ft; Parkes - 101 sq.ft.
  Tubes 199 @ 1¾" dia. Stirling - 940 sq.ft; Parkes 936½ sq.ft.
  Total Stirling - 1,040 sq.ft; Parkes - 1,037½ sq.ft.
Grate area: 16.25 sq.ft.
Ratio of grate area to heating surface: 1 to 61.8.
Boiler pressure: 140 lb/sq.in.
Wheel diameter: 5' 0".
Wheelbase:
  Engine - 7' 4" + 8' 0" = 15' 4".
  Tender - 6' 0" + 6' 0" = 12' 0".
  Overall - 34' 11½".
Length over buffers: 47' 10½".
Weights:
  Engine 35 tons 19cwt (full).
  Tender 28 tons 3cwt (later given as 30 tons, possibly due to increased coal capacity after fitting of coal   rails).
  Total 64 tons 2cwt.
Axle loads:
  Engine L 12 tons 5 cwt; D 13 tons 0 cwt; T 10 tons 4 cwt.
  Tender L 9 tons 13 cwt; M 9 tons 8 cwt; T 9 tons 2 cwt.
Tender water capacity: 2,000 gallons.
Coal capacity: 3½ tons or 120 cu.ft.(later given as 5 tons).

Tractive effort @ 85% of boiler pressure: 13,756 lb.
Load limit: 25 wagons.
Ratio of blast nozzle to cylinder diameter: 1 to 3.57.

Note: Stirling and Parkes give different figures for some boiler dimensions; both are shown.

Dimensions Class D Rebuilds introduced 1902.

Cylinders: 2, inside. 17½" x 24".
Boiler: Domeless.
Max. diameter outside: 5' 0".
Firebox length outside: 5' 6".
Heating surface:
  Firebox 100 sq.ft.
  Tubes 209 @ 1¾" dia. - 988 sq.ft.
  Total 1,088 sq.ft.
Grate area: 16.25 sq.ft.
Boiler pressure: 170 lb/sq.in.
Weights:
  Engine 37 tons 18 cwt (full); 34 tons 8 cwt (empty).
  Totals 67 tons 18 cwt (full); 52 tons 8 cwt (empty).
Axleloads:
  Engine L - 13 tons 3 cwt; D - 13 tons 15 cwt; T - 11 tons.
  Tender L - 10 tons; M - 10 tons; T - 10 tons.
Tractive effort @ 85% of boiler pressure: 17,701 lb.
Load limit: 28 wagons.

Note: With the exception of the increase in cylinder diameter, little was changed below footplate level, so dimensions given earlier would apply.

Dimensions Class E Rebuilds introduced 1897.

Cylinders: 2, inside. 17½" x 24".
Boiler: Domeless.
Max. diameter outside: 4' 3".
Barrel length: 10' 0".
Firebox length outside: 5' 6".
Pitch: 6' 11".
Heating surface:
　Firebox 114.04 sq.ft.
　Tubes 194 @ 1¾" dia. - 912.96 sq.ft.
　Total 1,027 sq.ft.
Grate area: 16.25 sq.ft.
Boiler pressure: 150 lb/sq.in.

Weights:
　Engine 35 tons 19cwt (full)　33 tons 5cwt 1 qtr (empty).
　Totals 65 tons 19 cwt (full)　51 tons 5 cwt 1qtr (empty).
Axleload: L - 12 tons 5 cwt; D - 13 tons; T - 10 tons 14 cwt.
Tractive effort @ 85% of boiler pressure: 15,618 lb.
Load limit: 25 wagons.

Note: Dr. G.D.Parkes was a keen H&BR enthusiast, who chronicled the railway's history in 1946. This work was based on a paper he delivered to Oxford University Railway Society on 28th October 1936. It is not known where he took his figures from: they were certainly not those used by the H&BR on its official diagrams.

Class E No.30 on the Wath branch train at Hickleton & Thurnscoe station. The train consists of old Kirtley carriages - an all-third, a composite and a luggage brake. *W.B.Yeadon collection.*

An unidentified Class E in the twilight of its life, standing at the west end of Springhead shed; the shed staff carrying out disposal duties are actually engaged in cleaning 'char' from the smokebox - a filthy job at the best of times, and downright unpleasant when a strong wind was blowing! It was also the stuff which had eroded the original Kirtley chimneys thirty years earlier. *Hull Museums collection.*

KIRTLEY CLASS H/H1 2-4-0 EXPRESS ENGINES.
(Originally Class C of 1885.)

Although Kirtley's H&BR Class B design clearly formed an intermediate stage in his developments of such locomotives for the London, Chatham & Dover Railway, his design for H&BR passenger workings was to be something of a dead end, if viewed in a similar light. Put simply, this was because his H&BR design was the only locomotive type with the 2-4-0 wheel arrangement which originated with him, although he had inherited (and rebuilt), considerable numbers of that wheel arrangement on the Chatham. His own designs for the latter's passenger workings were entirely of the leading bogie, 4-4-0 wheel arrangement.

Amongst the Chatham's motley collection of ten classes of 2-4-0 representing 71 locomotives, were the Martley "Europas", or Class C under the Kirtley classification system. (the coincidental designation of the H&BR engines is worthy of note!) The four "Europa" Class engines which appeared in 1873 were, in their day, amongst the very best express engines south of the Thames, good enough in fact for Kirtley to pay his predecessor the compliment of adding two more to their number in 1876.

The "Europas" were Martley's last design, and were turned out with the Government Continental Mail traffic especially in mind, for the LC&DR had gained that contract in preference to the South Eastern Railway upon the ending of the Franco - Prussian War. In order to retain the contract, fast, punctual running was a "sine qua non"; the nickname "Mail Engines" bestowed upon the "Europas" by the Chatham's operating staff and regular travellers was but a reflection of their purpose in life.

The "Europas" remained on the Dover Boat Expresses and the services for Flushing via Queenborough Pier into the 1890's, despite the fact that Kirtley had introduced his own heavier and more powerful 4-4-0 express engines in 1877. Being a fairly pragmatic individual, Kirtley probably considered it more sensible to leave the fast but comparatively lightweight Mail trains with the capable "Europas" and deploy his new, heavier engines on the slower but heavier semi-fast express workings, for here the motive power picture was nowhere near so perfect!

Pragmatism probably led Kirtley also to consider something similar to the "Europas" as being suitable for the H&BR

passenger services, although an inconsistency in his approach may be noted in comparison with the H&BR Class B 0-6-0's. This is due to the fact that it should have been obvious that the H&BR was to be primarily a goods line (whatever delusions to the contrary may have been nurtured by James Staats - Forbes!), yet the locomotives provided by Kirtley for moving its anticipated staple traffic (i.e: coal), were not as powerful as their Chatham predecessors. (The lines south of the Thames were never known for the density of their goods traffic: "The Southern's goods train always runs to time" was an old jibe, heard occasionally into BR days).

The effects of bigger wheels and smaller cylinders on the H&BR B Class in comparison with the Chatham B1's have already been noted, but with the H&BR Class C's Kirtley did exactly the opposite for he specified driving wheels of 6ft diameter; 6ins less than on the "Europas". On the face of it, Kirtley underestimated them for passenger trains, although his actions could be explained on the grounds that his experience as a Locomotive Superintendent was on a line where passenger traffic was paramount - although it still leaves him open to the charge of not really having 'done his homework' too thoroughly regarding the H&BR!

A useful side-effect of all this as far as the Hull &Barnsley Class C's were concerned was that they were able to share in the workings of fast goods trains, such as fish, meat and other perishables; conversely, the H&BR 0-6-0's frequently took part in hauling secondary passenger workings: excursion trains, emigrant specials and latterly at any rate, branch line passenger trains.

The contract with Beyer, Peacock & Co. for the construction of the ten Class C 2-4-0's was signed on 19th July 1883, at the same time as that for the Class B 0-6-0's. They were to Works Order No.6436, and as noted earlier, although apparently ordered earlier than the Class B's, they appeared later: a fact borne out by their Works Numbers of 2479 to 2488; their H&BR running numbers of 33 to 42; and Ahrons' recollections that none were delivered to the H&BR until some three weeks or so after the full opening of the line to all traffic.

Beyer, Peacock chose No.42 to do the honours for their works photograph. *Hull & Barnsley Stock Fund collection.*

A superb study of Class C No.36 at Springhead in its original condition, complete with Westinghouse brake-pump and built-up Kirtley chimney. The photograph predates 1892 when the H&BR changed to vacuum brakes, although some engines may have kept Westinghouse brake equipment for some time afterwards. *Eddie Holland.*

As built, the Class C's bore considerable dimensional similarities to the "Europas", especially after the latter were reboilered by Kirtley from 1890 onwards.

Both classes had wheelbases of 7ft 9ins + 8ft 3ins; cylinders of 17ins x 24ins, firebox lengths of 5ft 6ins, grate areas of 16¼ sq.ft and boiler pressures of 140 lb/sq.in were also common to the two classes. Barrel lengths differed between the two classes: at 10ft 10ins, the "Europas" had boiler barrels 5ins longer than on the six-coupled engines, although the two H&BR tender locomotive types had identical fireboxes. Weights for both the "Europas" and the H&BR Class C's were remarkably similar, at 36 tons 16 cwts and 36 tons 13 cwts respectively. The extra weight of the "Europas" could be accounted for by their somewhat larger diameter leading wheels - 4ft 6ins as compared with 3ft 9ins - and their outside frames, which would necessitate longer and heavier frame stretchers than were needed for the Class C's; although oddly enough the "Europas" weight decreased by some 6 cwts apiece after they were rebuilt with Kirtley's standard pattern of boiler. Again, a possible explanation for this is not too hard to come by: the new boilers were of steel and consequently used thinner plates than the old, wrought-iron, Martley boilers.

The outside frames of the "Europas" imparted the appearance of harking back to an earlier age of locomotive technology, whereas the Class C's assumed a tidier, more 'modern' aspect due to their inside mainframes, although this statement should in no way be taken to imply that the "Europas" were in any way inferior!

For constructional details and performances, once again we have to turn to Matthew Stirling. Many items were common to all three Kirtley locomotive classes, so little purpose will be served by reiterating them again here, although it may perhaps be worth pointing out that even on smallish railways such as the Chatham or the H&BR, considerable degrees of standardisation were the norm, even as early as the 1880's. Indeed, the whole question of 'standardisation' had two sides: locomotives of different types could have many parts in common (as on the Great Western Railway); whereas conversely, a "standard" type built over an extended period of time could through development, end up with several variants (as with the 842 London, Midland & Scottish Railway "Black Fives", built from 1933 to 1951).

Bearings on all the Kirtley H&BR engines were identical, being a generous 8 ins long x 7¼ ins diameter, but the leading axles on the 2-4-0's were 9 ins x 6¼ ins. The leading wheel tyres on the 2-4-0's had an average life of 258,000 miles, requiring to be reprofiled in a wheel lathe every 56,412 miles on average; the coupled wheel tyres lasted for some 100,000 miles, although some had achieved maximum mileages of just over half as much again.

It would seem that Kirtley was conducting some kind of comparative trials (albeit of an informal and subjective nature), with the springing of his various passenger designs, for Stirling informs us that the H&BR 2-4-0's had Timmis section, spiral springs fitted below each driving axle journal, with leaf springs on all other axles. This was an arrangement which Kirtley had arrived at in 1880 with his Class M1 4-4-0's on the LC&DR, having previously used leaf springs throughout on his initial essay into designing a 4-4-0; namely Class M of 1877. He went on to try the reverse arrangement of Class M1 in 1884 with Class M2, but immediately after their introduction reverted to the M1 arrangement for the H&BR 2-4-0's, retaining it for Class M3, his last 4-4-0 design for the Chatham, and introduced in 1891. Oddly enough, the M3's had the same length boiler as the H&BR Class C's.

All the Class C's were equipped from new with the Westinghouse Air Brake, operating on all wheels except the leading pair, which had enough work to do already in guiding the locomotive at speed around curves (not that there were any especially sharp ones on the Hull & Barnsley, especially where the higher speeds were likely to be reached).

Stirling reported in 1889 that the 2-4-0's were averaging speeds of around 45mph on express workings whereas on stopping trains, progress was made at a much more sedate average of 33mph. Train weights were 145 tons, which figure also included the engine and tender; the usual make-up of the passenger trains consisted of eight four-wheeled carriages. (All the original H&BR rolling stock save for the locomotives and the breakdown crane were four-wheeled, and all were to William Kirtley's specifications).

To accomplish their work, the C's consumed 932.5lb of coal per hour, at a rate of some 57.4lb per sq.ft of grate area per hour. In terms of coal consumption per train mile, the 2-4-0's averaged 23.9lb, an improvement on the Class B 0-6-0's figure of 31.5lb, although doubtlessly that amount was somewhat increased by time spent waiting in yards or loops whilst their more fleet-footed shedmates dashed past on more glamorous workings.

Crews stepping on to the footplates of the Class C's would find them indistinguishable from the Westinghouse-fitted Class B 0-6-0's, for both classes had identical backhead fittings; both had wheel and screw reverse; and the tenders were common to both classes. The only likely give-away would have been the rear splashers; but even these were hidden away since they were combined with the rear sandboxes, built up to the same heights and provided with wooden tops to provide somewhere to sit: at least when the locomotive was not moving.

A point which may not have concerned the crews overmuch, but which could be taken as indicative of the H&BR's acute financial position at the time of opening was that the Class C's were paid for in instalments, and at £2,745 each, were the most expensive of the three Kirtley H&BR locomotive types; although the prices quoted for Class B Nos.13 to 28 were higher, as noted earlier there is some doubt as to which of these engines were in fact produced with air brakes or were dual-fitted (air and vacuum brakes).

Various spares to the value of £40-19s-0d were also supplied (presumably by Beyer, Peacock), with the 2-4-0's, and with the delivery of the last engine (probably in October or November 1885), Kirtley's involvement in H&BR locomotive matters came to an end: for his work, he received remuneration at the rate of approximately 2% of the cost of the 42 engines - a payment of £2,174-1s-7d being made.

The Class C's careers largely mirrored those of the Class B's: chimneys and smokebox doors suffered similarly and were replaced; tender toolboxes were moved, and three coal rails appeared around tender sides and ends. Under the H&BR Brake Conversion Programme, the 2-4-0's were changed from Westinghouse Air Brake to the Automatic Vacuum Brake in 1892. Stirling also instigated changes in their livery, as dealt with in the relevant section of this book. Photographs also show Nos.33, 39 and 40 to have been fitted with a large toolbox (probably of wood), alongside the firebox on the left-hand (fireman's), side of the engine, between the driving wheel splasher and the cab front. No.33 carried its toolbox or chest after acquiring a 4ft 3ins diameter domeless boiler in 1899, but by the time it was put on the duplicate list eleven years later, the box had been removed and replaced by a rerailing jack. Presumably other locomotives carried toolboxes at a similar time, but no example of a toolbox on a 2-4-0 rebuilt with a 5ft diameter boiler has yet come to light.

The reboilering of the Class C's commenced in 1899 with Nos.33 and 41 receiving 4ft 3ins diameter domeless boilers, followed a year later by similar rebuildings of Nos.35, 38 and 42. These boilers had slightly smaller heating surfaces than the

Class C No.37 at Hull (Cannon Street) station before reboilering in 1901. W.Heath Robinson obviously worked for the H&BR's Signal & Telegraph department, judging by the piles of old brake blocks, an oil drum and old rail chairs holding up the stay-post for the bracket signal....!

No.39 acquired a Stirling chimney, smokebox door and toolbox. The vacuum brake connection reveals this photograph to have been taken after 1892, and before rebuilding with a 5ft 0in. diameter domeless boiler in April 1903.

Class C No.40 at Springhead: the vacuum brake connection, and extensive building works in the left background date this photograph at around 1893. *Laurie Ward.*

originals, but the boiler pressure was increased to 150lb/sq.in and the cylinders bored out to 17½ins diameter, thus making as much use as possible of the potential extra boiler power. As with the Class B's similarly reboilered, the original Kirtley cabs were retained.

The remaining five Class C's were destined to make history, although their place in the Hall (or perhaps more accurately the Roundhouse), of Locomotive Fame has been largely overlooked. This was because Nos.34, 36, 37, 39 and 40 were turned out from Springhead Works between 1901 and 1903 with boilers of the exceptional diameter of 5ft 0ins.

These were the largest diameter boilers in use in Britain and furthermore, being parallel there was no tapering downwards to a considerably lesser diameter at the smokebox end. From 1901 onwards, no H&BR tender locomotive would receive a boiler of lesser diameter throughout the remainder of the Company's independent existence. The 5ft diameter boilers were in due course fitted to Nos.38 and 42, thus ultimately leaving only Nos.33, 35 and 41 as small-boilered variants.

The rebuilding with 5ft diameter boilers entailed considerable additional work: the fitting of new cabs of increased width in order to accommodate the reversing wheel and screw alongside the much wider backhead was a most obvious change, and once again the new cabs were of Stirling outline rather than Kirtley! A less noticeable change would have been required in the running gear: when reboilering the Class C 0-6-0's (introduced from 1889 onwards), to Class B (for details, see 'Stirling Class C' and 'Stirling Class B', later), new springs with an additional leaf in each were fitted, in order to accommodate the increased weight of both steel and water, so presumably something along the same lines was done with the 2-4-0's. The Timmis spiral springs on the driving axles could readily have been changed for others of the same length but heavier section, which would stiffen them up.

Like the earlier rebuilds with smaller boilers, the cylinders were bored out an extra half-inch, but the new, bigger boilers were pressed to carry 170lb/sq.in in this instance. Due to the combinations of larger cylinders, higher pressure and greater weight, the 2-4-0's became amongst the most powerful of their type in the country, but at some cost to their appearance. Gone was the rather quaint, 'drawing room ornament' look of the Kirtley original, to be supplanted by pot-bellied corpulence, transforming them into Falstaffs of the locomotive world!

(Before departing from the matter of bigger boilers, it is tantalising to speculate as to the factors which led Stirling to march along that road. It has been J.F.McIntosh of the Caledonian Railway who has popularly been given the credit for setting Britain's locomotive engineers along the route to large boilers with his series of developments of the 'Dunalastair' 4-4-0's, in four parts from 1896 to 1904. Legend has it that this was the result of a suggestion from Robert Urie, his Manager at St. Rollox Works, to the effect that all they needed were the same engines which had served satisfactorily for some years, but that an increase

in steaming capacity wouldn't come amiss. Another, apparently unconnected fact was that when one aspiring young locomotive engineer was seeking membership of the Association of Railway Locomotive Engineers, he was proposed as a member by McIntosh and seconded by Matthew Stirling. Two inferences may be drawn from this: firstly, that Stirling was on good terms with his fellow-Scot, and secondly, that his name carried considerable influence within the august ranks of the ARLE membership. A further, and more tenuous speculation may also be made: did McIntosh and Stirling collaborate - even if only on an informal, after-dinner discussion basis - over the development of larger boilers? Did each encourage the other, or was there an element of friendly, one-upmanship at work? The young engineer whose successful sponsorship was undertaken by the two Scotsmen was, incidentally, one Herbert Nigel Gresley, a name which will reappear not infrequently later within these pages! As an admirer of Patrick Stirling's locomotives, it must have been highly gratifying to Gresley to have his hero's own son as one of his sponsors!)

To return to the H&BR 2-4-0's, however: under the 1908 Classification Scheme, the small boilered variety became Class H, whilst their more rotund brethren assumed the designation of H1. Their duties after reboilering did not initially change, for they still ambled back and forth between Hull and Cudworth, or over the Lancashire & Yorkshire Railway from Hensall to Knottingley, with the occasional foray down the newly-opened branch lines on local passenger workings, when nothing more lowly was forthcoming from the Locomotive Department. There were also excursions which took them further afield, for example to Llandudno or Blackpool; even the Lake District and the Peak District, thanks to the Midland Rly; to Aintree on Grand National Day, and more frequently to Leeds on excursions for the theatre or football matches.

No distinctions appear to have been made between the large-boiled H1's or the smaller H's when being rostered for such work: for example, photographs exist of H1 No. 34 at Leeds on excursion duties, and of H No.41 on a football excursion at Lightcliffe on the Lancashire & Yorkshire Railway.

Both H and H1 variants saw considerably more of the countryside south of Cudworth after 1905, for thanks to steady pressure and agitating by the H&BR Board over the years, the Midland Railway granted running powers for H&BR passenger trains from Cudworth over their lines to Sheffield. The through

No.33 as rebuilt to Class H in 1899 with 4ft 3in. diameter domeless boiler.

Driver Jack Hudson (right) and fireman Walter Kirkwood (centre) with No.33 at Cannon Street signal-box. Driver Hudson regularly worked the night mail train, and in 1916 was credited with the highest speed recorded on the H&BR - 80 mph, reached between Kirk Smeaton and Carlton. His nickname, "Jarman Jack", would tend to indicate that he participated wholeheartedly in impromptu social events held on an informal but frequent basis by various members of H&BR staff when off-duty....!

Hull (Cannon Street) to Sheffield (Midland) service commenced on 2nd October 1905, and the Midland even lent the H&BR a number of their older (but comfortable!), six-wheeled, Clayton arc-roofed carriages: apparently the two train sets provided consisted each of three Midland six-wheelers (most probably lavatory composites), with an H&BR four-wheeled luggage brake van at either end. Although modern bogie carriages were on order from R.& Y. Pickering of Wishaw for the new H&BR prestige service, deliveries of these were delayed until February 1907. Meanwhile, the Midland required the return of their carriages by the end of April 1906, so the H&BR was forced to use their ancient four-wheelers for some 9 or 10 months before the first Pickering bogie carriages were delivered. It is perhaps worthwhile pointing out that by 1907, there were few

opportunities for the more masochistic amongst the railway enthusiast fraternity to indulge themselves in travelling by prominent express trains composed of wooden, four-wheeled carriages over twenty years old and still sporting gas lighting; and moreover, with the only 'amenity' in the heating department being provided by the obsolete tin footwarmer. The historically-inclined amongst the H&BR's clientele may well have mused upon the quaintness of the motive-power also, but it is doubtful whether this would have done much to mollify the more average representatives of the Company's customers! Indeed, it is hard to decide who is more deserving of sympathy: the H&BR's unfortunate patrons, or the H&BR Board themselves, embarrassed and humiliated at having to resort to utilising their antique passenger stock on their showpiece services! What the Midland Railway thought about having such relics disporting themselves along their main line has (fortunately), gone unrecorded.

No.34 at Springhead in August 1910, as rebuilt to Class H1, in October 1903, with a 5ft 0in. diameter boiler. By judicious rebuilding, Matthew Stirling had turned the old Kirtley engines into some of the most powerful 2-4-0's in the country. *Laurie Ward.*

Nevertheless, the new bogie stock did appear in due course and was well-received by the railway technical press, and one trusts, by the H&B's clientele, also! The H&BR were so proud that they may well have commissioned the photograph of H1 No.36 on a train of the new stock at Hull Cannon Street. The photograph has a rather 'posed' appearance, and although it has been reproduced a number of times elsewhere, the Author offers no apologies for reproducing it again!

The new carriages involved the fitting of steam heating equipment to the H and H1's, although possibly this had already been done to some of them for use with the borrowed Midland six-wheelers. Whether steam heating was extended to all the 2-4-0's is unknown; but photographs reveal that by the time of withdrawal, H No.33A and H1's 37 and 40 had received the necessary equipment; H1 No.34 was also fitted up by 1919, but not before December 1904.

Assuming that some 2-4-0's remained unfitted, then an amount of juggling with locomotive availabilities to ensure sufficient steam-heat equipped locomotives were useable in the winter would have been required; although the situation would have eased with the delivery of the five Class J 4-4-0's in 1910. Until that time however, the old Kirtley engines ruled supreme, both H and H1 varieties being used indiscriminately on main line services.

With the deliveries of the Class J's, Class H Nos.33 and 41 together with H1's Nos.35, 38 and 42 were transferred to the duplicate list. Photographs show some of the locomotives concerned after their demotion, with a letter 'A' painted below the number on each cabside. Such loss of rank did not necessarily bar those engines from important duties: No.33A was regularly rostered on the Night Mail train from 1912 to 1914, for example.

Cut-backs in passenger services as a result of World War I hastened the end of the 2-4-0's. H1 No.38A became the first Hull & Barnsley locomotive withdrawn, being dismantled at Springhead in 1917. The others were increasingly displaced on to the branch line services: for example, No.34 (an H1), was hauling the Denaby Branch workmen's train in 1919 - along with three of the old four-wheeled carriages, also living on borrowed time.

The remaining H and H1's spent increasingly lengthy periods on "Cargill's Sidings" at Springhead, becoming more and more shabby. Odd ones were exhumed and put to steam at moments of crisis in the Motive Power Department until 1922, when the North Eastern Railway inspected them all and promptly condemned them; withdrawing the nine survivors between April and October 1922. Nos.40 and 41A were despatched at Springhead before June 1922; Nos.33A to 37, 39 and 42A went via Dairycoates for scrapping at Darlington, although 33A at least was sent on for disposal at Percy Main, graveyard of so many tired old engines.

No.34 had been lucky to survive to 1922, being a casualty in the H&BR's worst accident involving a passenger train. On 23rd December 1903, No.34 and its train of five four-wheeled carriages and a fish-van, had left Cudworth at 4.50pm., but at Locomotive Junction on the outskirts of Hull some 2 hours later, a broken coupling resulted in a brake van and eleven loaded wagons from the preceding coal train being left in its path. Into this obstruction, which had gone unnoticed by the Junction signalman as the leading part of the Down mineral train passed him, the hapless No.34 ran at full tilt. Not only had the bad weather handicapped the signalman, it had also made footplate conditions difficult for the passenger train's crew, visibility being down to some 180 feet. The unfortunate driver was very seriously injured, his career on the footplate terminating from the moment that his engine came to rest across the Up line, on its side. Fortunately, only three passengers gave notice of slight injuries; the goods guard had jumped clear immediately before the smash, and No.34's fireman was able to go forward to warn the Junction signalman. No.34 suffered extensive damage but was judged worthy of salvage, and since at that time the H&BR was rather short of motive power and Springhead Works and shed were adjacent to Locomotive Junction, little time was lost by the breakdown gang in rescuing the unfortunate engine.

The Kirtley 2-4-0's had served the Company well, and considering that they were William Kirtley's only essay into that type, they can but be regarded as a success. Mr. William Westoby, who commenced his footplate career on the H&BR in 1919, had been very impressed with them albeit in the twilight of their existence, recalling years later that they were, "Very quick off the mark", and notably so in comparison with the Stirling Class J's of 1910.

But perhaps we should leave it to Matthew Stirling, the man directly concerned with keeping Kirtley's engines in order, to sum them up: "The whole of the locomotives... described were designed by Mr. William Kirtley, Locomotive Superintendent of the London, Chatham & Dover Railway, and were built by Messrs. Beyer, Peacock & Co. Ltd., Gorton Foundry, Manchester. They were all delivered and put to work in the year 1885 and have done good service."

Summary: Classes H, H1 (1885 Class C) 2-4-0.

H&BR No.	Works No.	Delivered	Withdrawn	Rebuilt to Class/Date	*Notes*
33	2479	8/1885	6/1922	H, 1899	To Duplicate List 1910 - J. Cut up Percy Main.
34	2480	8/1885	?/1922	H1, 10/1903	In Springhead collision - 23/12/1903.
35	2481	8/1885	?/1922	H, 1900	To Duplicate List 1910 - J.
36	2482	?/1885	?/1922	H1, 1/1902	-
37	2483	?/1885	?/1922	H1, 9/1901	-
38	2484	?/1885	?/1917	H, 1900; later to H1	To Duplicate List 1910 - J.
39	2485	?/1885	?/1922	H1, 4/1903	-
40	2486	?/1885	5/1922	H1, 12/1903	Cut up Springhead.
41	2487	?/1885	5/1922	H, 1899	To Duplicate List 1910 - J. Cut up Springhead.
42	2488	?/1885	?/1922	H, 1900; later to H1	To Duplicate List 1910 - J.

Notes: All built with Westinghouse brakes; converted to vacuum in 1892.
Built to Beyer, Peacock Order No.6436. Cost £2,745 per engine.

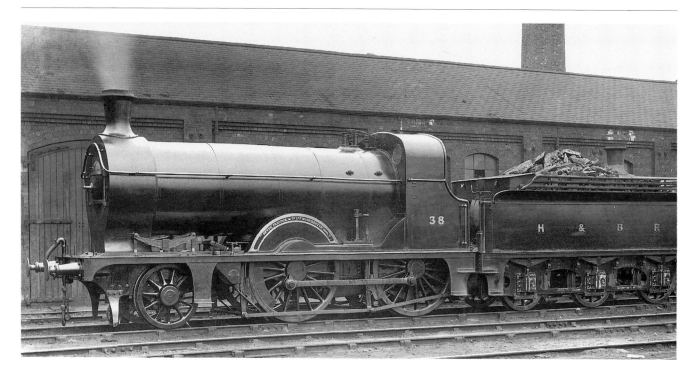

Class C Dimensions as built 1885.

Cylinders: 2, inside. 17" x 24".
Motion: Stephenson with slide valves.
Boiler: Domed.
Max. diameter outside: 4' 3".
Barrel length: 10' 5" (10" 9³/₁₆" between tubeplates).
Firebox length outside: 5' 6".
Pitch: 7' 0".
Heating surface:
  Firebox 100 sq.ft.
  Tubes 199 @ 1³/₄" dia. - 977 sq.ft.
  Total: Stirling - 1,077 sq.ft; Parkes - 1,075 sq.ft.
Grate area: 16.25 sq.ft.
Ratio of grate area to heating surface: 1 to 62.
Boiler pressure: 140 lb/sq.in.
Wheel diameters: leading 3' 9"; coupled 5' 0"; tender 3' 9".
Wheelbase:
  Engine 7' 9" + 8' 3" = 16' 0".
  Tender 6' 0" + 6' 0" = 12' 0".
  Overall 36' 7½".
Length over buffers: 47' 9⁷/₈".
Weights:
  Engine - 36 tons 13cwt 1qrt. (full)
  Tender - 28 tons 3cwt (later given as 30 tons, possibly due to increased coal capacity after fitting of coal rails).
  Total 64 tons 16 cwt 1 qrt.
Axle loads:
  Engine: L - 10 tons 5 cwt 3 qrt; D - 13 tons 14 cwt 2 qrt;
       T - 12 tons 13 cwt.
  Tender: L - 9 tons 13 cwt; M - 9 tons 8 cwt; T - 9 tons 2 cwt.
Tractive effort @ 85% of boiler pressure: 11,463 lb.
Ratio of blast nozzle to cylinder diameter: 1 to 3.57.
Tender water capacity: 2,000 gallons.
Coal capacity: 3½ tons, or 120 cu.ft (later given as 5 tons).

Note: Stirling and Parkes give different figures for total heating surfaces; both are given.

Dimensions Class H Rebuilds introduced 1899.

Cylinders: 2, inside. 17½" x 24".
Boiler: Domeless.
Max. diameter outside: 4' 3".
Barrel length: 10' 5".
Firebox length outside: 5' 6".
Pitch: 7' 0".
Heating surface:
  Tubes 194 @ 1³/₄" dia.
  Total 1,064 sq.ft.
Grate area: 16.25 sq.ft.
Boiler pressure: 150 lb/sq.in.
Tractive effort @ 85% of boiler pressure: 13,015 lb.

Dimensions Class H1 Rebuilds introduced 1901.

Cylinders: 2, inside. 17½" x 24".
Boiler: Domeless.
Max. diameter outside: 5' 0".
Barrel length: 10' 5".
Firebox length outside: 5' 6".
Heating surface:
  Tubes 209 @ 1³/₄" dia.
Boiler pressure: 170 lb/sq.in.
Weights:
  Engine - 39 tons 17 cwt (full) 36 tons 6 cwt (empty).
  Tender - 30 tons (full) 18 tons (empty).
  Total - 69 tons 17 cwt (full) 54 tons 6 cwt (empty).
Axleloads:
  Engine - L 10 tons 14 cwt; D 17 tons 11 cwt; T 11 tons 12 cwt.
Tractive effort @ 85% of boiler pressure: 14,751 lb.

Note: With the exception of the increase in cylinder diameter, little was changed below the locomotive footplate level, so other dimensions given earlier would apply. Dimensions such as heating surfaces are not known.

(above) **H1 No.38** standing at the west end of Springhead yard, glinting in the sunlight as one of Matthew Stirling's men strides purposefully to work: he's not losing any bonus payment for some bloke with a camera....

(opposite) **A classic study of Class H1 No.38** at Springhead in the 1900's - after rebuilding with a domeless boiler of 5ft 0in. diameter in 1900 but before relegation to the duplicate list in 1910. No.38, along with Class E No.17, was one of the first H&BR engines withdrawn, in 1917.

(centre right) **Class H No.42** standing at the north end of Sheffield (Midland) station, with the Sheffield-Hull through train, in 1905. Note the H&BR clerestory meat van (a Stirling design, based closely on the GNR's type); the Midland Railway water-crane with gas light on top, just visible above No.42's cab; the Midland six-wheel carriages in No.42's train. These were on loan to the H&BR in 1905 - thus giving a date for this photograph. The handrails and difference in height reveal that No.42 was also running with a Stirling tender - why and for how long is unknown. *J.B. Stork collection.*

(right) **By mid-1907, R&Y Pickering had** finally delivered the bogie carriages ordered by the H&BR, and No.36 poses at Hull (Cannon Street) with the "Sheffield Set". Driver J.Wheatley and his fireman glance at the camera from around the cab sidesheet. *J.B. Stork.*

H1 No.34 in Springhead works yard after the collision at Locomotive Junction on 23rd December 1904. Although extensively damaged, No.34 was de-bent and gave a further seventeen years' service. Nobody was killed, although the career of No.34's driver finished at the instant his engine turned over, such were the serious nature of his injuries. The towering edifice in the background is the water softening plant.

Thoroughly down-at-heel, Class H No.33A stands on "Cargill's Sidings" at Springhead in 1922. (Who the enigmatic Mr.Cargill was remains a mystery - probably some long-forgotten foreman whose domains included these reception sidings for the works).

At the end of its thirty-seven year life, Class H1 No.40 reposes in "Cargill's Sidings" at Springhead. Note the chimney windjabber, a fitting which had also appeared on No.34 by 1918, and possibly other engines of Class H1.

Part 2. THE KITSON DESIGNS.

This section deals with a mere eleven locomotives of two types, which owing nothing to H&BR influences in their inspiration, the author has chosen to refer to as "Kitson Designs" (for want of a better title).

The first group were six small, four-coupled, well-tank locomotives, ordered specially for shunting on Alexandra Dock and designated as Class K in 1908. They were delivered from 1886 to 1889 and were little more than enlarged tram-engines, de-frocked and de-bagged, since they were without the enclosed bodywork and side-skirting around the wheels: features inseparable from the tram-engine. (It is probably needless to point out that those other essential but less prominent tram-engine accessories, to whit: rooftop condensers, automatic speed governors and duplicate controls for either-end operation, were also missing from the H&BR engines).

The six Class K's were unique on the Hull & Barnsley in as much as they were the H&BR's smallest locomotives; their only four-wheeled type; and the only class the Company had with outside cylinders and valve-gear, albeit much of the latter was decently hidden away from curious gaze behind steel panels (which for all the world made them look like side-tank rather than well-tank engines). All served until withdrawn by the North Eastern Railway in 1922.

The second group consisted of five heavy, 0-6-2 tank locomotives which had been ordered by the Lancashire, Derbyshire & East Coast Railway in 1899. Being even more "financially challenged" than the H&BR ever were, the LD&ECR found themselves unable to pay for the completed engines, and consequently asked the builders to dispose of the engines themselves. Fortunately for all concerned, the H&BR readily consented to accept the locomotives: Kitsons lost very little financially, and the H&BR gained five new engines virtually overnight at a bargain price. Although outside the mainstream of H&BR locomotive development, the Kitson 0-6-2's (Classified F1 in 1908), introduced one feature which was to become almost a standard for future practice on H&BR engines: namely the use of balanced, Richardson-type slide-valves above the cylinders, driven by Allan Straight - Link valve-gear, via rocking levers. The only new locomotive design to appear after 1907 which did not have this feature were the Class F3 0-6-2 tanks of 1913 - 14, since these were essentially enlargements of Class F2, the design of which was under way at the time of F1's were acquired.

The five Class F1 locomotives put in many years of hard toil at both ends of the H&BR's system and even saw something of life elsewhere, under London & North Eastern Railway ownership. The last engine was finally withdrawn as LNER Class N11 in 1946, having also outlived its relatives which had actually gone earlier to the LD&ECR, by some eight years, and to which the LNER designated class N6.

An illustration of one of the three later engines used for Kitson's works photograph - hence, this engine could be No.46, 47 or 48. Fellow H&BR enthusiast Ron Prattley, with his wide experience of photography, has pointed out that Kitson's photographer used a wide-angle lens, which allowed considerably more of the cab front to be seen, and caused the chimney top to appear somewhat distorted. Attention is drawn to the wooden block dumb buffers below and between the normal sprung ones. The additional buffers were provided especially for shunting the scores of 'timber bogies' around Alexandra Dock. The curved corners to the side-plate lining should also be noted - it was the exact opposite of normal H&BR practice! *Laurie Ward.*

CLASS K 0-4-0 WELL TANKS.
(Kitson & Co. 1886-89.)

In comparison with the wealth of documentation existing for the more celebrated locomotives of the better-known companies, the H&BR's locomotives can justifiably be described as obscure. That being the case, then the following six locomotives could be likened to Churchill's view of Russia: "A riddle wrapped in a mystery inside an enigma."* The reasons for this are fairly straightforward to uncover however, for they all performed their duties entirely on the Alexandra Dock estate, largely out of sight of public gaze. Just occasionally they would make fleeting appearances around Hull to and from Springhead Works, in connection with repairs. To further complicate matters, due to the H&BR's parlous financial state for the first few years of its existence they were delivered piecemeal over three years, with two varieties appearing.

Kitson's 0-4-0 well-tank shunting engine design appeared in 1879, along with their patent valve-gear. According to Matthew Stirling, this was actually a German patent adopted by Kitson and used initially on tram-engines, although the truth of the matter may have been that he was thinking of Heusinger von Waldegg's modifications to the original Belgian Walschaerts gear; essentially the Kitson Patent Valve Gear was a rearrangement of Walschaerts.

As early as 13th August 1885, Matthew Stirling was asked to specify his requirements for shunting on Alexandra Dock, to gather manufacturers' drawings and specifications. Ahrons stated that the need for small shunting locomotives was felt soon after the appearance of the Kirtley G1 tanks, the 15ft rigid wheelbases of which caused both track and locomotive to suffer unduly on the sharpest curves. The fact that such curves were mainly from the quays and jetties and were for the most part set into cobbled surfaces tramway-fashion, may possibly have influenced Stirling

*The reference to Russia is entirely appropriate here, since the Baltic trade has traditionally been of great importance to Hull. These six little engines must have shifted millions of tons of cargo for and from Russia in the course of their working lives!

and the Board to choose a locomotive with such close affinity to a tram engine. Whatever the reasons, the 6ft 4ins wheelbase plus weight in working order of only 21½tons meant that the K Class engines could cope with the tightest curves on the lightest tracks.

These were the most likely factors which governed the decision by Lucas & Aird, the H&BR's contractors, to purchase one themselves. It appears quite prominently in a photograph taken at Weedley Springs in 1883, which is included in albums of views of the line under construction, and now kept variously in the Hull Central Library and Hull Museums' collections.

This particular engine had a rudimentary cab with neither upper side sheets nor back plate; a drumlike sandbox adorned the boiler top, which caused the steam dome to be sited further back than usual. Mechanical differences from later engines centred around the cylinders, which prominently displayed the shape of the valve chest cover, and the forward slope of the valve face. The union link, running forward from the crosshead, was considerably shorter than on later engines as was the single slide-bar. Since the attachment point of the slide bar bracket at its rear end to the locomotive mainframe was in very close proximity to upper back quarter of the front wheel, Kitson's drawing office staff may well have considered this to be a design flaw, which they rectified quite simply by lengthening the slidebar, piston rod and union link.

According to articles and notes by the late Ken Hoole in the North Eastern Railway Association's *Express* magazines Nos.112 and 113 published in 1988, this locomotive was Kitson's No.2363 of 1881; in due course becoming Newport Ironworks No.6 before passing into Dorman Long's ownership, it remained at work into the 1960's. Whether first-hand experience of this locomotive on the H&BR played any part in influencing Stirling and the Board is open to speculation; in any case, Lucas & Aird seemed to prefer the products of Manning, Wardle & Co.

In the event, the H&BR's initial modest order for five locomotives was but the first of many more from the Leeds manufacturer. Kitsons themselves stated that the H&BR locomotives were similar to some built for the Buenos Ayres Great Southern Railway, but this must have been

One of life's mysteries revealed! Probably the same locomotive as featured in the previous photograph, but this time with the side-panelling removed to reveal the valve-gear. The tube with the lid like a biscuit-tin, fixed vertically in front of the valve-gear trunnion-block, is actually the well-tank filler. Care would obviously be needed in filling the tank, for water does not form the best lubricant for locomotive bearings....! *W.B.Yeadon collection.*

One of the three earlier engines, No.43, 44 or 45. Differences in the cylinders and valve-chests should be noted in comparison with the later engines; the cab sidesheets and upper backplate were added by the H&BR, probably as the result of experience with the later engines. This locomotive has the more normal incurved lining for the side-panel corners; the right-hand side valve-chest cover forms a suitable place for a wooden toolbox, there being no flat tank tops and no room in the cab either!

mostly of a visual nature. The Latin American engines had cylinders 14ins x 21ins and 3ft 2in diameter wheels, but at that point the similarity in leading dimensions ceased. Due to the broader gauge, of 5ft 6ins, the well-tank capacity was greater (450 gallons), and the extra width presumably allowed an increase in cab and bunker size: the latter accommodated 1 ton of coal compared to 15 cwts on the H&BR engines. The Argentinean engines had higher boiler pressures - 160lb sq. in - which gave them a fractionally higher nominal tractive effort, of 12,984 lb.

The actual ordering and construction of the H&BR locomotives gives rise to bewilderment, for it would appear that the first five engines were allocated Works Nos.2951-5, although only three were initially delivered in 1886 to become H&BR Nos.43 - 45. Kitsons recorded these engines as all being tested in steam in February 1886, on 4th., 6th. and 9th. of the month respectively. The other two engines had either been temporarily cancelled, or else Kitsons agreed to postpone their construction until the H&BR could pay for them. Either way, the works numbers were held for these two engines. Matthew Stirling bears out Kitson's delivery records by reporting that only three shunting engines were at work by 21st November 1887, but in due course the other two were put in hand, for Kitson's records show that H&BR No.46 was steam tested on 20th December 1888, and No.47 the day after. One appeared in the works photograph.

The final engine was probably something of an afterthought: since it carried Works No.3128 it had not been envisaged initially but must have been ordered at the same time as its two predecessors, since Kitsons record it as being steam tested on 10th January 1889. It assumed H&BR No.48, and was most probably identical to Nos.46 and 47, since it followed them by but a few days.

These final three engines differed from those delivered in 1886 in several details, notably the covers around the cylinders, position of the lubricators on the smokebox sides, and the cabs. The South American engines referred to earlier had somewhat rudimentary cabs, and by all accounts this type was used on the H&BR machines although Springhead Works brought them more visually into conformity by fitting them with new cab fronts with upper side-sheets and full-height backsheets, although differences in the cab handrails were a giveaway as was the slightly ramshackle appearance of the cab roof which had been subjected to piecemeal alterations and adjustments to accommodate the other changes to the cabs. Yet another difference could be found in the wheel castings, for the earliest locomotives had balance weights cast as full segments between the two spokes opposite the crankpins, whereas this feature had been altered to a crescent-shape on the six H&BR engines. A final difference lay in the costs for the two batches: £1,120 each for the first three, and a mere £5 apiece more for the 1888/89 deliveries.

As if the origins, style and work of the six little Kitsons were not mysterious enough, even their most obvious features were apt to mislead the interested observer, for the Kitson valve-gear was hidden away behind the sheet iron panels: which caused such confusion that they were even described at least once in contemporary writings of a quite technical nature as side-tank engines! In passing, it is interesting to note that two later engines of 6ft wheelbase were built for the Cardiff Railway in 1898/99 as saddletanks with 850 gallons capacity, the valve-gear being exposed beneath the tank bottom edges since side-sheets were not fitted, whereas a later engine built for Newport Ironworks (their No.14 of 1914), had both saddletank *AND* side plates! The Cardiff pair eventually became Great Western Railway property and one survived at work until September 1963, earning a retirement in preservation, initially at Bleadon & Uphill in Somerset, and latterly at Didcot. Most likely the change to saddletanks was a measure to increase water capacity, and the use of well tanks was then abandoned.

Since the H&BR locomotives only had room for the Company initials on the side-panels, and nowhere else to paint the locomotive number except the bufferbeams (or cab backsheet), it is not surprising that individual engines cannot be identified from the few photographs - inevitably taken broadside on. One print though, has "No.44" written on the back of it and as this depicts one of the earlier engines, it is probably correct. This same photograph shows the engine to have had its Kitson built-up chimney (of rather Stirling Great Northernish derivation), changed for a cast-iron one, this time of very obvious H&BR style, albeit emanating from another Stirling! This replacement chimney had a curious throwback in style to the earliest Stirling Great Northern practice, for it carried a lamp-iron bolted on the front of it. The origins of this chimney are lost in the mists of time: whether it was a replacement due to wear and tear, or the result of dockside cargo (mis)handling is open to question. (In this instance, having had some slight experience of the rough-and-tumble of dock work your author inclines to the latter view!)

More accepted wear and tear was minimal, due to the moderate boiler pressures: for example, Stirling reported on 20th October 1891 that after $4\frac{1}{2}$ years the valves had never needed facing up since being put in, having only worn between $\frac{1}{2}$ inch to $\frac{5}{8}$ inch; and furthermore, no H&BR locomotive cylinder had needed reboring in the seven years from 1885 to 1891.

Despite being kept busy up to 1914, the resulting fall-off in trade due to World War I caused a downturn in the fortunes of the six Kitson dock tanks. Mr. William Westoby, ex-H&BR footplateman, recalled that the "Bug Crushers" (as the K Class engines were nicknamed), were rarely used by that time, and then primarily by Hollis Bros. in connection with their substantial timber importing business. This involved the movement of white timber, such as Scandinavian pit-props, on small, four-wheeled timber bogies of seven tons capacity from the quaysides to the stacking areas and yards. He recalled that by 1919 only one had a steam brake, the rest relied on handbrakes only despite all being equipped with both when new.

Withdrawal came rapidly after the North Eastern/H&BR amalgamation in 1922; the North Eastern drafting several of their own small four-coupled shunters to Alexandra Dock Shed as replacements. But that was not quite the end of the story however, for No.48 survived (in part), for another twenty or so years due to the fact that part of the frames, cylinders and wheelsets were presented to Hull Municipal Technical College as a full-scale, valve-gear model for study by the senior pupils. The late Ken Hoole, who attended the College between September 1927 and July 1932 recalled seeing these remains in a yard normally out of bounds to junior scholars, but since there was no boiler and considerable sections of the frames along with the leading wheelset had been removed, he had great difficulty recognising it all as having once been a locomotive!

Even these pieces give another twist to the story and leave the researcher with a final mystery, for at some indeterminate period between 1939 and 1945 these last parts of No.48 simply disappeared! Most likely though, it was judged that it was more use being dropped on or fired at the country's enemies rather than continuing to train the country's engineers, so was consigned to a wartime scrap salvage drive. Whatever the truth, with the abbreviated No.48 there also vanished the last mortal remains of an almost unknown and largely undocumented class of locomotives, which contrived to retain their reticent and evasive nature to the very end.

No.44 outside Alexandra Dock shed, circa 1921. The engine looks to have been well-used, and turned out without lining. The top of the tank filler can be seen just below the safety-valves. This is set further back than on the later engines, being in just the right position to decant spillage straight into the rear axle bearing! *W.B.Y coll.*

Class K Dimensions.

Cylinders: 2, outside. 14" x 21". (inclined at 6½" in 6ft.)
Motion: Kitsons Patent, (outside).
Boiler: Domed.
Max. diameter outside: 3' 4⅞".
Barrel length: 7' 3¾".
Firebox length outside: 3' 7".
Pitch: 5' 10".
Heating surface:
  Firebox 43 sq.ft.
  Tubes 110 @ 1¾" dia. - 391 sq.ft.
  Total 434 sq.ft.
Grate area: 8.75 sq.ft.
Ratio of grate area to heating surface: 1 to 49.6.
Boiler pressure: 140 lb/sq.in., later 120 lb/sq.in.
Wheel diameter: 3' 2½".
Wheelbase: 6' 4".
Length over buffers: 21' 1".
Weights: L - 10tons 19cwt; D - 10tons 11cwt = 21tons 10cwt.
Height to top of chimney: 10' 8⅛".*
Tractive effort @ 85% of boiler pressure: 12,722 lb.
Ratio of blast nozzle to cylinder diameter: 1 to 3.86.
Tank water capacity: 390 gallons (Kitson); 290 gallons (H&BR).
Bunker coal capacity: 15 cwt.

* Kitson's Works Drawing shows 10' 8⅛" whilst the H&BR Diagram Book shows 10' 8⅜". The differences in heights may be due to the H&BR refitting the entire class with new cast-iron chimneys, ¼" taller than the originals.

Summary: Class K 0-4-0 Well Tank.

H&BR No.	Works No.	Delivered*	Withdrawn	*Notes*
43	2951	4th February 1886	15/8/1922	
44	2952	6th February 1886	15/8/1922	Probably given new cast-iron chimney.
45	2953	9th February 1886	15/8/1922	
46	2954	20th December 1888	15/8/1922	
47	2955	21st December 1888	15/8/1922	
48	3128	10th January 1889	15/8/1922	Parts existed until WW2.

Notes:
* Delivery dates given here are actually Kitson's steam-test dates. Actual delivery would be some days later.
First three had slight differences to last three.
All engines had steam and hand brakes when new.

CLASS F1 0-6-2 TANKS (LNER CLASS N11).
Kitson & Co. 1899.

If any engines ever had an inauspicious start in life, it was these five engines which formed H&BR Class F1. They owed nothing of their inspiration to H&BR influence, being of a standard Kitson type which had been built for various smaller railway companies; examples could have been found on the Dublin & South Eastern Rly, various South Wales companies (Rhondda & Swansea Bay Nos.25 to 28 were identical to the H&BR F1 Class), the Lambton Rly in County Durham and the Lancashire, Derbyshire & East Coast Railway - to which the engines in question should actually have gone.

That particular company, like the H&BR, had its origins in the coal export trade, albeit new dockyard facilities (at Sutton on Sea), and similarly also, its original fairly modest plans were "hi-jacked" by over-enthusiastic speculators who sought to build a western extension. However, whereas the H&BR's expansionist faction had limited themselves to horizons no further flung than Halifax, those with similar ambitions for the LD&ECR entertained grandiose schemes for extension westwards from Chesterfield, via a spectacular transit of the Peak District to Buxton, thence by way of Macclesfield to Warrington, on the Manchester Ship Canal: thus forming a Coast to Coast route (which incidentally, duplicated the Great Central Railway). Despite its plans, sufficient capital to fund the entire scheme was not forthcoming, so for its short, independent life the LD&ECR existed as a headless and tail-less trunk centred in the Dukeries; going nowhere near Lancashire and in due course only reaching the East Coast at Grimsby thanks to the indulgence of the Great Central in granting running powers from Lincoln to Grimsby. Following the path blazed by the H&BR, the LD&ECR similarly found difficulty in persuading sufficient customers that it offered significant advantages by changing from

well-established patterns of trading, and after eleven years it gave up the unequal struggle in 1907, when the Great Central made an offer for take-over, which the LD&ECR directors found hard to refuse.

Since money (or lack of it), was the root of all the LD&ECR's evils, not surprisingly this situation also bedevilled affairs in their Locomotive Department. Until 1904, and the appointment of the redoubtable R.A.Thom, LD&ECR motive power affairs varied from ludicrous to pitiful: symptomatic of a small, struggling company teetering perpetually on the verge of bankruptcy. From the start, locomotive engineers came and went with disconcerting frequency and the locomotives suffered accordingly; a state of affairs which only serves to highlight how fortunate the H&BR was to retain the loyal service of someone as able as Matthew Stirling.

LD&ECR locomotive matters reached arguably their lowest point with the embarrassing debacle which led to the five tank engines appearing on the H&BR's Stock-List.

Having taken delivery of 18 locomotives from Kitsons already, and being entirely satisfied with the eight 0-6-2 tanks included within the above total, the LD&ECR Board decided that a further 15 locomotives of that type were required. These were ordered in three groups of five apiece - the fateful order for the final five being placed with Kitson & Co. on 21st July 1899. That the LD&ECR was financially in 'Queer Street', may be deduced from the fact that the Board had stipulated that no locomotives were to be delivered until July to December 1900, when they were to be paid for - providing that the price was to remain at the agreed figure of £2,790 each. An extension of credit terms by Kitsons was successfully obtained in order to pay for the first ten engines upon delivery (with Kitsons charging

A delightful study of No.98, taken during a break in shunting at Cudworth in 1912. The engine is in original condition, with built-up chimney and vacuum brakes. Of the individuals on the photograph, only the shunter standing on the right with his foot on the rail has been identified - a Mr.Sanderson. *Ian Scotney.*

Class F1 No.99 at Springhead, displaying a Stirling chimney and rerailing jack, also the loss of its vacuum brake equipment. To the north, in the background above No.99's firebox can be seen the elevated coaling-stage, brought into use late in 1907; the topmost tank of the water softening plant can also be seen. *N.P.Fleetwood.*

interest annually at the rate of 4½%), but matters finally came to a head with the delivery of the first engine of the third group to Tuxford, resplendent in LD&ECR lined black, and numbered 29. Not daring to seek the indulgence of Kitsons any further, the Board ordered that the engine was to remain in the shed and was not to be steamed under any circumstances. In an attempt to extricate themselves from their cash-flow crisis, the LD&ECR Board sought financial assistance from their ally, the Great Eastern Railway, which had played the part of LD&ECR sugar-daddy, since it had gained access to new traffic sources thanks to running powers granted over LD&ECR metals in exchange. This time though the Great Eastern declined to pick up the tab for they had plenty of their own engines which they could draft in, and by making liberal use of their running powers over the LD&ECR could easily clear any backlog of traffic. Finding that their sugar-daddy's wallet was this time tightly shut, the hapless LD&ECR Directors went off cap in hand to Kitsons in order to put them in the picture and beg them to retain the five engines in default, in the hope of their builder finding another customer.

Truly, before the dawn comes the darkest hour, and a solution was readily apparent which would satisfy all concerned and find a home for the five unwanted locomotives very quickly.

By pure coincidence on 15th November 1900, the H&BR Board had authorised six shunting tank engines and fourteen heavy tank engines, going on to place the order for construction

of the latter with Kitsons. 22nd January 1901 saw a letter from Kitson read out at an H&BR Board meeting, offering the immediate delivery of five engines built for the LD&ECR in exchange for five of the fourteen heavy tank engines currently on order. Kitsons offered the engines at £2,760 each and promised immediate delivery of two engines, with three to follow in February 1901. The H&BR took up this offer with some alacrity, for a number of probable reasons.

Firstly, the H&BR had at least driven the wolf from the door by 1900 and was about to embark on a period which would see it become a prosperous concern due to increases in traffic so massive, they came perilously near to overwhelming it. (This arose due to the opening of several new coal mines within the H&B's catchment area, which in turn had been widened by the opening of the South Yorkshire Junction Rly in 1894 and the Alexandra Dock Extension in 1899). The prospect of five new engines materialising instantly was irresistible, in order to try and keep up with traffic requirements.

Secondly, the LD&ECR engines were of similar size to those of the same type already on order, and similar also in weight, power, and cylinder dimensions. Indeed there may well have been some interchangeability of fittings, particularly if Kitsons had been allowed some latitude in the detailed design-work of the H&BR-ordered engines subsequently delivered. Such similarities had their limits though, for with their built-up chimneys, square topped cabs, round-topped side tanks and domed boilers, the LD&ECR engines seemed to hark back for inspiration to William Kirtley, for they owed not one jot to Matthew Stirling!

No.101 at Springhead in original condition, save for the rerailing jack, which it retained well into LNER ownership. Note the vacuum ejector exhaust pipe along the boiler, plus the tall, narrow "hooter" alongside the Ramsbottom safety-valves. The deep note emitted by the hooters gave rise to the nickname "Trawlers", which was applied to the F1 Class engines. *Hull Museums collection.*

An F1 (HB) at Springhead under North Eastern ownership in 1922 - renumbered 3101, but still lettered "H&BR". Note Stirling's chimney and smokebox door, two extra coal-rails and grid-iron type guards over the cab rear spectacle windows; also the absence of vacuum brake gear. 3101 still retains its original boiler (at that time 22 years old), but in February 1924 it received a new one, based on North Eastern practices. Note the old North Eastern 4-4-0 in the right background, sent to Springhead to help fill the gap created by scrapping the remaining H and H1 2-4-0's. *Ron Copeman collection.*

Class N11 (although still referred to as "Class F1 (HB)" on its bufferbeam!), 2481 (ex-H&BR No.100), at Springhead. The engine is in ex-works condition, and thanks to Stirling's chimney it still looks like an H&BR engine, although the wheel-and-handle on the smokebox door show the North Eastern's influence. Two extra coal-rails have also been fitted at some stage. *Ron Copeman collection.*

2479 (ex-98), has acquired an ex-North Eastern Worsdell-style chimney, but is otherwise unchanged from the previous view. The lamp irons on the front sandboxes are a legacy of the engine's LD&ECR origins; the H&BR fitted those over the front bufferbeam. *Ron Copeman collection.*

A view for the modelmaker! 2478 (97) stands inside one of the roundhouses at Hull Dairycoates shed in 1931, displaying its rear end to the world. *Locofotos.*

Thirdly, although the H&BR ultimately became quite prosperous it never became exactly opulent, so plain, Yorkshire canniness may well have played a part! At £2,760 each, the LD&ECR rejects were cheaper by £75 apiece than the Stirling equivalents which Kitsons were currently preparing to build. The fact was that the H&BR was unable to resist a bargain when it saw one, and this may well have been the clincher!

The five Kitson engines introduced one mechanical novelty to the H&BR which was largely unobserved except by Springhead's mechanical fitters, valve-setters, and the crews when oiling round, but which became adopted as virtually a new H&BR standard. This particular feature was the use of balanced Richardson slide-valves above the cylinders, driven by Allan Straight Link Valve-Gear via rocking levers. With the exception of the Kitson Class K Dock Tanks, every existing H&BR engine had Stephenson Link Motion driving directly 'D' type slide-valves, positioned back-to-back in between the cylinders. Although Allan Straight-Link was dropping out of favour by 1900, it evidently gave such satisfaction on the new engines that Stirling adopted it wholeheartedly, for every new design after 1907 incorporated similar mechanical features to the Kitson F1's.

Little time was lost in dispatching the five engines to the H&B, where they assumed numbers 97 to 101. In passing, it is probably worthwhile noting that had they gone to the LD&ECR, they would have been Class A Nos.29-33; their vacant numbers were in due course taken up by the massive Class D 0-6-4 tanks delivered in 1904. These engines became LNER Class M1, and survived until 1947, being colloquially referred to as "Chinese Crackers".

The F1's also achieved the ultimate in acceptance, being dubbed "Trawlers" by the Springhead staff, due to their deep-toned 'hooters' (reminiscent of those fitted to Caledonian Railway engines), emitting a sound which instantly brought to mind that made by the members of Hull's fishing fleet.

Initially however, the workplace of the F1's was well away from Hull at the other end of the H&BR system, for they took over sole responsibility for working all traffic over the South Yorkshire Junction Railway from Denaby, northwards through Sprotborough and Pickburn to Wrangbrook Junction. Although only a short branch line of 11 miles in length, it featured some heavy gradients which loaded coal trains had to surmount. These eastbound trains from Denaby and Cadeby collieries faced an immediate climb for a couple of miles at 1 in 100 (including the short Cadeby Tunnel). Nearer to Wrangbrook came another similarly graded ascent, this time for three miles, before the H&BR main line was reached.

Passenger services on the SYJcR were exceptionally short-lived, being abandoned as early as September 1903. With only two trains each way on weekdays and none on Sundays, the loss of passenger receipts hardly made a great deal of difference to the H&BR, but the F1's vacuum brake equipment remained in use on passenger stock, which continued to traverse the SYJcR on workmen's trains run for the benefit of miners. The mining communities along the line were also served by the occasional special train which traversed the line, especially in connection with Hull Fair, held each October. (The last special train along the SYJcR was as recent as the mid-1960's, albeit this time in connection with an enthusiasts' railtour. Motive power this time was still steam, in the form of an LNER Class B1, for of course by that time, the F1's were long gone).

In due course, as the H&BR motive power situation eased (from critical to acute), allowing traffic workings to be

A final view of 2478 (97), whilst shunting at Springhead. By the time of this picture, its chimney has grown a windjabber and it also has sprouted LNER Group Standard buffers - otherwise it appears little changed from the earlier view opposite.

rearranged, the F1's were mainly used as banking engines, with occasional turns to Cudworth and short goods workings through to Springhead to add variety. About the time of the introduction of the big Stirling Class A 0-8-0's, the vacuum brake equipment was removed from the F1's, and they were re-allocated to marshalling work: No.100 being based at Cudworth and the rest at Springhead, although the Hull engines ran transfer trip workings around the city to Alexandra Dock. No.100 (as 3100), was to be seen shunting at Bullcroft on the Hull & Barnsley & Great Central Joint Railway at the time of the North Eastern interregnum in 1922; this was a temporary transfer to Bullcroft Shed, No.3100 was standing in for F2 No. 3105, whilst the latter was away for heavy repairs.

As Class N11 No.2481, 3100 was back at Cudworth in August 1937, when No.2482 (H&BR No.101), joined it there. In the meantime No.2479 (98), had gone further afield, being transferred to West Hartlepool in November 1930. It remained in County Durham until December 1936, having spent its time shunting in the timber yards - a similar sort of job which it had left in 1930, and to which it returned upon its homecoming. Those engines which had remained in Hull had variously played the time-honoured game of 'musical sheds', being transferred between Springhead and the old North Eastern shed at Dairycoates as needs arose, between 1927 and June 1939. After that date, Nos.2478, 2479 and 2480 (97, 98 and 99), had more settled lives, working solely from Springhead. The other two returned to their spiritual home in late March, 1943, and all the survivors remained there until withdrawal, which occurred between January 1943 and May 1946.

Considering that the N11's had working lives of over forty years each, it is not surprising that they underwent several changes in appearance over the years. Since these have been meticulously detailed in *Locomotives of the LNER* published by the RCTS there is little point in re-iterating them here, although a brief resume of the main features may be in order.

The H&BR replaced chimneys and smokebox doors as and when necessary by new items of Stirling pattern, and also removed the wing plates from the smokebox fronts; but most changes took place after Grouping. The biggest alteration was not noticeable with this class, for although reboilering took place

from 1923, because the original boilers had been domed the change was not as evident as on the Stirling engines. After reboilering (although not necessarily at the same time as), all five engines received North Eastern style chimneys and smokebox doors. Being LNER North Eastern Area locomotives as opposed to LNER South Area machines, the N11's at least avoided the horrific Gresley 'flowerpot' chimneys which later disfigured many ex-Great Central engines, including some of the ex-LD&ECR N6 engines. Minor detail alterations concerned the smokebox door fastenings, addition of steps to smokebox fronts, numbers of bunker coal rails (the H&BR having fitted an extra two rails each to Nos.100 and 101). Darlington Works in due course fitted backing plates to the coal rails, and exchanged the "Trawler" hooters for two whistles of North Eastern pattern. Some items survived the entire lives of the locomotives without change: no engine had the steel bufferbeams or steam sanding altered, and Nos.97 and 98 managed to retain their LD&ECR style lamp irons on the front sandboxes in addition to acquiring lamp brackets of more usual style in the normal positions.

Darlington's reboilering programme involved new design work, using the drawings for the ex-North Eastern Class D17 4-4-0 as a basis, for although the H&BR had evidently renewed tubeplates and possibly inner fireboxes (a fact deduced from two different sets of figures for the F1's), the original boiler shells were still in use after 23 years' hard work. The new D17 derived boilers (given Boiler Diagram No.66 in 1928), were unique to the N11's, being shallower in the grate than equivalent types on the Stirling 0-6-2's. Since no spare boilers were built, the future careers of the N11's would be limited by the longevity of their new boilers, which as we have already seen, was 20 to 25 years. Proportions of the Diagram 66 boilers were somewhat different to those originally fitted. A final flourish to announce the new order was the fitting of Ross "Pop" safety-valves, in exchange for the old, open Ramsbottom type.

It may be wondered why the LD&ECR survivors and the H&BR engines were not classified identically by the LNER, since they had similar origins. However, whilst the H&BR engines had been almost frozen in time, the LD&ECR engines had been quite drastically altered. Due to the fitting of new boilers with Belpaire-type fireboxes, the cab spectacle-plates had been widened, and it seems that opportunity was also taken to widen the bunker and cab slightly, which gave a marginal increase in coal capacity. As the H&BR-purchased engines had acquired a North Eastern look, so the LD&ECR engines had taken on a Great Central appearance (albeit much earlier).

Perhaps we should, at this point, bear in mind that railways are 90% people and 10% machinery, and conclude this Part by consideration of the human angle. Years after the last F1 had wearily departed for the scrapyard at Darlington North Road, Mr. William Westoby recalled fondly that No.101 had been one of his favourite engines: "She was a grand 'un for steam." In his time with 101 and its regular driver, Harry Clark, he found that it steamed well on a thin fire, and would continue to make steam in abundance after an injector had been put on. He recalled those injectors (of the Gresham & Craven backhead type), as being rather tricky to start, particularly that on the left hand side, until Driver George Carson (a person we shall meet again within these pages), showed him the knack of persuading them to pick up. The fact that Mr. Westoby recalled the F1's as being in the 'Old Man's Link' graphically illustrated the localised nature of their work by the early 1920's. He also pointed out that the shallow grate was apt to give firemen problems in building up a good depth of fire. Some enginemen tackled this by removing the flame-scoop (baffle plate), from inside the fire hole door, the advantage of this being that they could swing the shovel blade higher into the firebox, thus pitching the coal off higher and throwing it further, in order to cover the front of the grate. (Leaving any part of the grate bare on a locomotive is a sure way of ending up in the condition once graphically described as "100 lb. of smoke and no steam!")

Finally, long after the F1's had gone to the Great Roundhouse In The Sky, the author recalls an exchange of repartee at Grosmont shed, on the North Yorkshire Moors Railway, which may cast some light on the prowess of these 'Kitsons'. This took place between the fans of Lambton Railway No.29, (a Kitson 0-6-2), and supporters of Lambton No.5, a Stephenson-built engine of comparable size to No.29. The merry badinage passing between both groups got more and more derogatory towards the 'opposition', whilst bravado regarding the prowess of their particular favourite grew in inverse proportion. Finally, the Stephenson supporters declared that

No. 29 was past it/useless/feeble/clapped out and wouldn't run down a pitshaft, whereas No.5 could pull anything and everything in Grosmont Yard up the 1 in 49 to Goathland, including the engine-shed. "Only the SHED?" echoed No.29's champion. "Ask it nicely, and 29'll pull GROSMONT to Goathland!!"

Class F1 Dimensions.

Cylinders: 2, inside. 18" x 26".
Motion: Allan straight-link via rocking levers.
Boiler: Domed.
Max. diameter outside: 4' 6" (1922); 4' 4" (Dgm.66)
Barrel length: 11' 6".
Firebox length outside: 6' 6" (1922); 6' 9" (Dgm.66)
Pitch: 7' 6".
Heating surface:
   Firebox 107 sq.ft. (1922); 99sq.ft (Dgm.66)
   Tubes 210 originally - 1,142 sq.ft
      208 @ 1¾" dia. by 1922 - 1,132 sq.ft.
      196 @ 1¾" dia., Dgm.66* - 1,062 sq.ft.
   Total 1,239 sq.ft. (1922); 1,161 sq.ft (Dgm.66)*
Grate area: 21 sq.ft. (1922); 19.5 sq.ft (Dgm.66)
Ratio of grate area to heating surface:
   1 to 59 (1922).
   1 to 59.53 (Dgm.66)
Boiler pressure: 160 lb/sq.in.; 175 lb/sq.in (Dgm.66)
Wheel diameter: coupled 4' 9"; radial axle 3' 9".
Wheelbase: 7' 10" + 7' 2" + 7' 6" = 22' 6".
Length over buffers: 36' 6½".
Weights: L - 14tons 1cwt. D - 15tons 11cwt. T - 16tons 2cwt. truck 12tons 10cwt = 58tons 4cwt.
Height to top of chimney: 12' 11".
Tractive effort @ 85% of boiler pressure: 20,099 lb. (1922); 21,976 lb. (Dgm.66)
Ratio of blast nozzle to cylinder diameter: 1 to 3.69.
Tank water capacity: 1,825 gallons.
Bunker coal capacity: 2½ tons.

* After 1932, the use of stay tubes was discontinued, so these figures became 200 tubes and 1,182 sq.ft.

Summary: Class F1 0-6-2 Radial Side Tank. LNER Class N11.

H&BR No.	Works No.	Delivered	NER No.	LNER No.	Reboilered	Withdrawn
97	3964	January 1901	3097	2478	September 1923	January 1943
98	3965	January 1901	3098	2479	September 1924	December 1944
99	3966	February 1901	3099	2480	September 1923	May 1946
100	3967	February 1901	3100	2481	November 1924	December 1945
101	3968	February 1901	3101	2482	February 1924	August 1944

Notes:
Each engine cost £2,760 when new.
LD&ECR Nos.29-33 had been reserved for these engines.
LNER Nos.9085-9088 were reserved for Nos.98-101 under the 1943 renumbering scheme, but none of them survived long enough to actually carry them.
Only 2478 (97) received Group Standard buffers and drawgear, in January 1939, plus NER chimney with 'windjabber', the only N11 so fitted.

N11 No.2482 (101), shunting on the eastern docks in Hull, in 1931. The vehicles behind 2482 are of interest, being 20-ton convertible covered vans/ bulk grain hopper wagons built to Great Western Railway drawings. They were always worked from King George V Dock, Hull, and consequently were lettered "Return to Silo, Hull". (King George Dock was built jointly by the NER and H&BR, and opened on the eve of World War I). *Locofotos.*

Ex-works at Darlington, 2481 (100) displays a change of chimney and smokebox door fastenings, in comparison to the ex-works photograph of the same engine at Springhead, some seventeen years earlier. The LD&ECR sandbox lamp irons have been removed at some stage, and the steam-pipes for the front sanders are draped around like a dowager's necklace. The boiler handrail is no longer continuous; grilles protect the cab rear spectacles. Gresley V2 No.4810, in the background, was built in October 1938, and at the time of the photograph is still in green although obviously not newly repainted. It appears to have a steel sheet in the front cabside window which was a wartime precaution in case of air-raids - and in which case this photograph can be dated as being around 1940 - 1941. (It is to be hoped that someone applied the handbrake on 2481 before shunting it round to Darlington shed en route for Hull, and thus avoided the risk of "modifying" the workshop doors in a manner both unauthorised and unwelcome!). *Ron Copeman collection.*

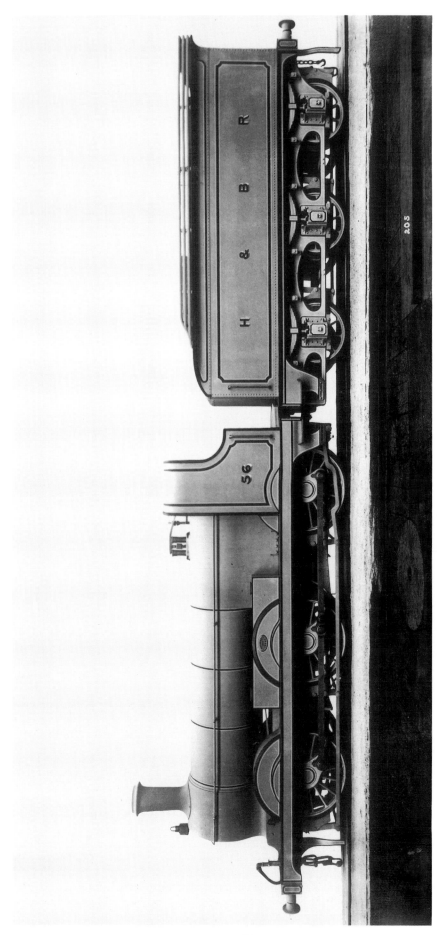

Kitson's works photograph was of No. 56, last of the 1889 order. Note that the engine has been equipped from new with vacuum brakes, and the tender has only two coal-rails (a third being fitted later - *see photo. of No.50*). The lining under the flared tender top was not just an embellishment for the works photograph, it can often be made out on engines in service also. Other details include lining on the guard-irons (probably for photographic purposes), and absence of flat brass beading on the small, quadrant-shaped splasher in front of the cab. Kitsons also favoured bent-pipe handrails on cab and tender. No. 56 was reboilered in September 1907.

Part 3. EARLY STIRLING CLASSES, 1889 - 1907.

If Hull & Barnsley Railway locomotives meant Matthew Stirling, then Stirling meant domeless boilers, so we are now finally getting to grips with 'proper' Hull & Barnsley locomotives. This section will deal with Classes B, C, F2, G2 and G3, but in order of construction. The first two classes listed were six-coupled tender engines, the last two being six-coupled tank engines and the F2 being a six-coupled, radial-truck, tank engine design. All could trace their ancestry back to Class C, and are dealt with in chronological order, if one regards Class B as a direct development of Class C. (Taking that yardstick as a basis should have brought Class F3 into this group also, for there was less difference between an F2 and an F3 than existed between Classes C and B, for example. However, despite much heartsearching your author has decided to leave the F3's until the very end of this volume, at the expense of making the layout of the book rather 'bitty'; after all the F3's represented the last vestiges of H&BR motive power, so it has been thought only fitting to let them also have the last word!)

Stirling's Class C (designated as such in 1908), appeared in 1889 with a 4ft 3ins diameter boiler, but like Topsy, "just gro'd" into a type with 5ft boiler by 1900. That type, given Class B designation in 1908, swelled in numbers as earlier Class C engines were reboilered to match: consequently Class C passed the way of the dinosaur and the dodo, in 1916 with the last reboilering; Class B mustered 55 engines within its ranks at the time of the North Eastern Amalgamation in 1922. (A variant of Class B had appeared in 1898 with a 4ft 9ins boiler; the six engines included in this small sub-species became extinct in 1921 when the last duly acquired its 5ft boiler).

Class G2 of 1892 was Stirling's second locomotive design, and his first attempt at a tank engine. They were unique in being the H&BR's numerically smallest class (with only three members), and in being the only locomotives built for the H&BR

by Robert Stephenson & Company, and unusual amongst shunting tank locomotives in having coupled wheels as much as 5ft in diameter. This demonstrates their direct descent from Class C, albeit with a slightly smaller boiler. Being such a small class, the three G2's did well to survive as long under LNER ownership as 1931.

1901 saw Stirling's second and final 0-6-0 side tank design take to the rails, in the form of Class G3. These, thanks to a six-inch reduction in wheel diameter working wonders with the nominal tractive effort, were considerably more powerful than the G2 class, and compared well with the most powerful such engines on the North Eastern Railway. Yorkshire Engine Company built the first six, which were joined by ten more from Kitsons in 1908, the last of which survived to become British Railways property, working far off the H&BR's system from Walton Shed, Liverpool, until withdrawal in January 1949.

Appearing virtually simultaneously with the G2's in 1901 were the nine members of Class F2. These were part of an order for fourteen such engines from Kitsons, the balance of which had been made up for by the purchase of the five Class F1's. The F2's may be regarded equally as lengthened G3's or as smaller-wheeled Class C's with tanks and radial trucks: they had the same 4ft 6ins diameter coupled wheels as Class G3, a figure upon which Matthew Stirling had settled for all further tank engine construction by the turn of the century. The F2's became quite widely-travelled engines under the LNER, and several even spent time working off their owner's system, albeit still within Yorkshire! One achieved notoriety due to suffering a disastrous collapse of the inner firebox in the H&BR's worst locomotive accident, another well outlived its brethren to survive long enough to become Nationalised; along with the single G3 plus all ten of Class F3, it represented one of the three classes of H&BR locomotive to be handed over to British Railways.

The mixed traffic capabilities of the Class C engines is well illustrated by this view of No.70 at Leeds (Wellington St.), having worked in with an excursion. No.70 was the first of many H&BR engines ordered from the Yorkshire Engine Co., Sheffield, arriving at Springhead in September 1897, and rebuilt in August 1912. These engines had different tube and firebox proportions and higher boiler pressures in comparison to the earlier Kitson and Vulcan engines; consequently they were rated as being more powerful than their predecessors.

STIRLING CLASS C. Introduced 1889.

The years 1886 - 1889 saw traffic through the H&BR's Alexandra Dock increase (as a percentage of the total traffic passing through the Port of Hull), from 18.9% to 25½%, and it is fair to assume that a considerable amount of this passed along the railway itself. Consequently by 1889 it was necessary to augment the stock of main-line locomotives.

Initially, Matthew Stirling had perforce to spend the first year or so of his H&BR service concerning himself with providing more wagons (the Company had opened for business in 1885 with only a total of 530 vehicles of all types for working goods traffic; all were of Kirtley origins). 1886-87 saw another 715 wagons of six different types ordered, only one of which was a re-order to one of Kirtley's designs.

Another problem for Stirling was the provision of a suitable water supply: Hull's water, being very hard, had a deleterious effect upon the locomotive boilers and availability of motive-power was to assume increasing importance as time went on.

As if that was not enough, the Company had initially no effective maintenance facility. At the time of opening Springhead Depot consisted of a running shed providing cover for 36 engines, a water tank on a timber trestle base plus some water cranes and a couple of wooden coaling stages, all in a 'green field site.' Repair facilities were rudimentary; those for heavy repairs being none existent, for the Company initially considered that heavy repairs could be carried out by contracts with the private locomotive builders. The bills for the first few such overhauls soon revealed this as a most expensive option, and it was quickly agreed in principle to establish proper 'in house' repair facilities. (History has a way of repeating itself, for several present-day, preserved railways have found themselves in precisely the same predicament and chosen exactly the same course of action!). Matthew Stirling had been fully aware of the likely course of events, for as early as September 1885 he had

presented his plans for the development of Springhead Works to the Board and found them fully receptive to his ideas; however due to financial constraints (ie: bankruptcy from 1884 to 1892), all expansion was subject to close scrutiny before authorisation.

With such piecemeal funding for vital developments at Springhead throughout the 1880's and 1890's it is perhaps a wonder that Matthew Stirling's first eight engines appeared when they actually did, especially when it is borne in mind that the H&BR Board had spent the previous two years hawking their Company round, in turn, the London & North Western, the Midland, and even the North Eastern Railway companies in the hope of either a working alliance or a merger, as they considered self-extinction as a way out of the H&BR's miserable existence. Still, despite Boardroom wranglings, behind-the-scenes intrigues and shareholders' meetings held in an atmosphere of turbulence, recrimination and rancour, the fact remains that Matthew Stirling was given the opportunity to cut his teeth as a locomotive designer at the relatively youthful age of 32 years.

The normal course of action taken by any locomotive engineer seeking to improve his company's locomotive stock was to produce quantities of locomotives latterly described as "mixed traffic". By the 1930's this meant 4-6-0's, but fifty years earlier six-wheeled tender locomotives (usually with all wheels coupled), with said wheels around 5ft in diameter came as close as anything to fulfilling the role of mixed traffic engines. With someone as pragmatic as Matthew Stirling in charge of H&BR locomotive affairs, it would be a safe bet that his first design would be for a six-coupled tender engine, with wheels of sufficient diameter to maintain a good turn of speed.

Given his Great Northern background plus his position as heir to well-established family locomotive traditions which were second to none, then it would have been quite easy to visualise the appearance of Matthew Stirling's first essay in locomotive

The last of the four engines from Vulcan Foundry, No.66 was delivered in July 1892 and reboilered in April 1909. This view shows the cab front lining, brass beading plus lining on the small splasher in front of the cab, different shapes to the ends of the tender flare lining and absence of lining on the guard-irons. Note also the lining along the firebox cleating-band - normal on H&BR painting, but omitted by Kitsons in their view of No. 56. The tender has three coal-rails, and the cab handrails are in stanchions; a practice favoured by Yorkshire Engine also, but not by Kitsons.

design, and it was naturally inevitable that he would at least attempt to provide locomotives with increased capacity as compared with the Kirtley 0-6-0's.

Amongst the Archives in Hull City Museums' railway collection is an outline drawing of an 0-6-0 of uncompromisingly Great Northern aspect, complete with built-up chimney and brass case around the safety-valves. On the reverse, written in Stirling's own hand are the only dimensions, which refer to the cylinders being of 18 ins diameter and 26 ins stroke. Measuring off the drawing gives a wheel diameter of 5ft and wheelbase of 7ft 3ins + 8ft 3ins - all being dimensions which correspond with Matthew Stirling's Class C locomotives rather than any of Patrick Stirling's Great Northern Railway types. (The sectioned drawing in question is in Matthew Stirling's style, and at 1inch to 1ft scale is clear enough to show how the locomotive should be constructed. Possibly copies of it were circulated to various interested manufacturers in order for them to base tendering quotations on: Kirtley may well have used LC&DR locomotive drawings in a similar way. The absence of dimensions from Stirling's drawing may well have been to allow each manufacturer some leeway in incorporating their own standard dimensions).

Stirling's locomotives as produced bore several noticeable differences from his initial drawing; it would appear that he moved more towards the styling refinements of his uncle's South Eastern Railway locomotives rather than following his father's lead in such matters. For example, James Stirling was credited with being the first engineer to use a 26 inch stroke on inside cylinder engines, a figure which his elder brother Patrick later took up with 160 six-coupled Great Northern goods engines built from 1873 - 1896. By using a similar figure Matthew was in keeping with the best of company! However, he followed his uncle again in the use of open, Ramsbottom safety-valves albeit in the more orthodox position over the firebox, instead of banishing them to a position on the back ring of the boiler as on his uncle's engines.

Liveries were also similar: James Stirling favouring lined black for his South Eastern engines and Matthew having introduced Invisible Green (nearly black), on the H&BR, but at this point similarities with South Eastern Railway engines ended. James Stirling's earlier engines were graced (for want of a better word), with tenders having outside frames with springs above footplate level, perforce leading to provision of a narrow tender body, along the upper sides of which ran a long horizontal handrail which completed their antediluvian appearance. Matthew drew on his Great Northern experience to produce a tender design directly derived from his father's later Great Northern practices. He also followed his father's footsteps in the arrangements of locomotive sandboxes - both the 5ft 2in coupled Great Northern goods engines and the new H&BR design had the sandboxes above the running plates, surrounding the driving wheel splasher on each side. Writing only a year or two after the time of the Class C's entry into service, the writer of *Locomotives and Railways* had remarked upon, "...the very striking resemblance they bear to their neighbours on the G.N.R." However, he considered that, "Of the two the H&BR engines are the neater in general appearance, especially as regards the finishing of the cab. These engines were constructed by Messrs. Kitson and Co., of Leeds and numbered 49 - 56, builders' numbers were 3138 - 3145.

"In 1892, the same firm built six more, they were numbered 57 - 62, makers' numbers 3504 - 3509.

"In the same year the Vulcan Foundry Company, Newton-le-Willows, built four of the same type, engine numbers 63 - 66, builders' numbers 1351 - 1354."

Added to these in 1897 were nine from the Yorkshire Engine Company (the first of many orders from this manufacturer), which duly became numbers 70 - 78; builders' numbers 547 - 552, and 560 - 562. All these groups of locomotives had 4ft 3ins diameter boilers and grate areas of 16¼ sq.ft, but the Meadow Hall engines had higher boiler pressure: numbers of tubes and heating surface totals also differed, even between the two batches of engines.

The H&BR's new Stirling engines represented an immediate and substantial increase in size and power over their Kirtley predecessors, and in order to show this as clearly and simply as possible, they are outlined in tabular form:

Table 3: **Comparisons between Kirtley and Stirling 0-6-0's.**

	Kirtley 0-6-0	Stirling 0-6-0	Approximate % increase
Cylinders, diameter x stroke	17" x 24"	18" x 26"	5.5% x 7.7%
Boiler:			
Pressure	140lb/sq.in	150lb/sq.in	6.7%
Diameters	4ft 3ins	4ft 3ins	nil
Barrel lengths	10ft 0ins	10ft 0ins	nil
Number of tubes	199 @ 1¾"	198 @ 1¾"	-0.51%
Tube lengths	10ft 4½ins	10ft 5ins	nil (effectively)
Tube heating surfaces	936½ sq.ft	950 sq.ft	1.5%
Firebox heating surfaces	101 sq.ft	100 sq.ft	nil
Total heating surfaces	1,037½ sq.ft	1,050 sq.ft	1.2%
Grate areas	16.25 sq.ft	16.25 sq.ft	nil
Ratio of grate area to heating surface	1 to 63.8	1 to 64.6	-4.4%
Ratio of blast nozzle dia. to cylinder dia..	1 to 3.57	1 to 3.78	nil (effectively)
Nominal tractive effort @ 85% B.P.	13,756 lb	17,901 lb	13.2%
Maximum Load limits	25 wagons	28 wagons	10.8%
Weights in working order (engine + tender)	64 tons 2 cwt	72 tons 15 cwt	11.9%

Yorkshire Engine chose No.74 to pose at Meadowhall. Points of difference with the Kitson and Vulcan engines are the treatment of engine and tender footplate drop-angles at the cab steps; absence of beading and lining from the rear quadrant splasher; different treatment of the tender flare lining and axle-ends on the locomotive. No.74 was reboilered in October 1911.

Table 3 has only given sizes of the main components to be altered. Needless to say, other items (apt to be overlooked), also came in for attention, as is graphically illustrated by a note in Stirling's own hand: "Kirtley's loco. ash pan door 3ft x 10ins. Spaces 23 between firebars ½in wide by 4ft 3½in long = 592¼ sq.ins. Mine - 3ft x 12in. Spaces 29 between firebars ³⁄₈in x 3ft 6in long = 456¾ sq.in." The importance of this is explained further by Stirling: "The total amount of air required by theory for the combustion of 1lb of bituminous coal is 150 cubic feet and as a goods locomotive burns from 40 to 45 lb per mile it would require from 6,000 to 6,750 cubic feet per mile by theory, but owing to various imperfections it is usual to provide half as much again of air, therefore from 9,000 to 10,125 cubic feet are required per mile and an engine of this type travels at the rate of 1 mile in three minutes. (Or 20mph - author). "Therefore from 3,000 to 3,400 cubic feet of air are required per minute to support combustion and avoid smoke."

Examination of *Table 3* shows that Matthew Stirling had gained marginal increases in very few areas of boiler design; most power gains being worked in below footplate level. The one big improvement in boiler design, ie: higher pressure, would have been made full use of by the larger cylinders. Having a longer stroke would have helped to make more use of the expansive properties of steam, which should have gone towards more economical working. The very slightly decreased blast nozzle to cylinder diameter ratio allowed for release of the extra steam with very little increased back-pressure; whereas this would draw up the fire more fiercely when working hard, if carried to extremes it could also in consequence throw increasing amounts of it out of the chimney, with detrimental effects upon property along the lineside!

The extra weight of Matthew Stirling's new engines was largely made up by heavier tenders of increased capacity; taking locomotive weights alone, the percentage increase was only 0.6% - a few more tons weight for adhesion purposes would not have come amiss.

Maximum load figures were those in force between Sandholme and Little Weighton for loaded mineral trains; (a full list of Load Limit Tables can be found in *Appendix 1* in vol.2). It may also be pointed out that the later Yorkshire Engine Company locomotives, Nos.70 to 78 had a slightly higher Load Class, and that Stirling's rebuilding of Kirtley's 0-6-0's to Class D put them in the same Load Class as his first engines.

It may well be wondered how Matthew's first essay in locomotive design measured up in comparison with similar types of the period, especially with those of Patrick and James Stirling, and with this in mind *Table 4* has been produced opposite.

Having perused *Table 4*, it can be seen that Matthew Stirling's first attempt was no mean effort, and compared favourably with the other two, particularly when it is borne in mind that they were the result of years of development. Still, it should also be remembered that Matthew was entirely familiar with his father's locomotives, having repaired and built them as part of his Doncaster apprenticeship, and then kept them in service as Shed Foreman at Colwick and later New England.

In service, the new 0-6-0's soon proved themselves to be worthy additions to the stock, but despite the enhanced power one was in trouble within a few weeks of entering service with broken eccentrics due to excessive slipping. The driver was suitably reprimanded, and possibly reminded that he now had an engine fitted with Gresham's steam sanding gear at his disposal!

At first glance, it might be thought that an apparent absence of balance weights had exacerbated the slipping, but Stirling had allowed for this by utilising the crank webs on the driving axle. In his view this was a perfectly satisfactory arrangement for wheels up to 5ft diameter, but beyond that size extra weights were needed at the appropriate places on the rims. The amount of crank axle balancing provided by Stirling was certainly sufficient for the Class C's to be used on excursion workings - one being photographed at Leeds (*see page 43*) whilst so engaged.

Table 4: **Comparisons between H&BR Class C, Great Northern Class J & South Eastern Class O six-wheeled coupled locomotives.**

	M.Stirling H&BR Class C	**P.Stirling** GNR Class J	**J.Stirling** SER Class O
Cylinders, diameter x stroke	18" x 26"	17½" x 26"	18" x 26"
Boiler:			
Pressure	150lb/sq.in	160lb/sq.in	140lb/sq.in
Diameters	4ft 3ins	4ft 2½ ins	4ft 4ins
Barrel lengths	10ft 0ins	10ft 2ins	10ft 3½ ins
Number of tubes	199 @ 1¾"	174 @ 1¾"	191 @ 1¾"
Tube lengths	10ft 4½ ins	10ft 6ins	Not known
Tube heating surfaces	950 sq.ft	830 sq.ft	858.25 sq.ft
Firebox heating surfaces	100 sq.ft	92.4 sq.ft	90.25 sq.ft
Total heating surfaces	1,050 sq.ft	922.4 sq.ft	948.5 sq.ft
Grate areas	16.25 sq.ft	16.25 sq.ft	15.75 sq.ft
Ratio of grate area to heating surface	1 to 64.6	1 to 56.7	1 to 60.2
Driving wheel diameters	5ft 0ins	5ft 2ins	5ft 2ins
Locomotive weight	36 tons 16 cwt	40 tons 5 cwt	35 tons 15 cwt
Tender weight	35 tons 19 cwt	38 tons 10 cwt	28 tons 5 cwt
Nominal tractive effort @ 85% B.P.	17,901 lb	17,466 lb	16,168 lb

There is little more to relate regarding the small-boiled Stirling 0-6-0's. 1905 saw them classified as 'B', (their original class designation being unknown). By that time Kirtley's 0-6-0's with 5ft boilers had become Class C, Class D being used to designate those with 4ft 3in boilers. Class A was used to show a development of the Stirling 0-6-0's with a 5ft diameter boiler, introduced in 1900. 1905 also saw a start made on rebuilding the 4ft 3in boilered Stirling engines with 5ft boilers, and engines thus rebuilt became members of Class A, also. By 1908 thirteen engines still remained to be dealt with, but the introduction of the big Class A 0-8-0 heavy mineral engines caused the 5ft boilered Stirling engines to be redesignated as Class B, displacing in turn the original 4ft 3in engines to Class C. The Kirtleys in turn ended up as Classes D and E respectively. The Stirling engine reboilering programme continued until 1914 whereupon Class C became virtually extinct, although No.76 was, according to the North Eastern's survey in 1922, not reboilered until October 1916. Reboilering and rebuilding dates for individual engines can be found in the Summary at the end of this section but annual totals may be found in *Table 5*. Further details of locomotive histories are to be found in the next section, *Stirling Class B 0-6-0's*, since all the engines just described ultimately joined that Class.

We should perhaps acknowledge that at average prices of around £2,600 each per locomotive, with average working lives of around forty years each the H&BR and its successors got their money's worth out of the Stirling engines, even when the costs of reboilering and crank axle replacements are taken into account; but perhaps we should leave the last word on the subject to Matthew Stirling. Taking the figure of £2,300 (the price of each of the eight Kitson engines of 1889), Stirling produced some figures which not only put the costs of locomotives into sharp perspective, but also cast some light on his rather puckish sense of humour: "Goods Engines. Weights and Prices of Locomotives.

	Loaded	**Unloaded**
6-coupled goods engine	37 tons	34 tons
3,000 gallon tender	30 tons 12 cwt	17 tons
	67 tons 12 cwt	51 tons

Price £2,300 = £45 per. ton or 45/- per cwt, or 4¾d per pound. "Thus locomotives in the wholesale market are a great deal cheaper - pound per pound - than horse-flesh. It is hardly to be expected however that we shall see at any of the locomotive works in this country a notice put up after the style that might be common in our Market Buildings:-
Locomotives are cheap today. Prices from 4¾d per pound and upwards!"

The second of Stirling's engines to appear was No.50, seen here on 19th September 1904, on the east end of Springhead shed yard. This engine was one of those from Kitson & Co., delivered in March 1889; reboilering came in August 1906. *Hull Museums collection.*

Table 5: **Yearly Reboilering totals, Class C 0-6-0's.**

1905	May: **49**
1906	May: **54**. August: **50**. September: **51**. November: **55**.
1907	February: **52**. June: **53**. September: **56**. December: **61, 64**.
1908	February: **59**. June: **65**. July: **60**. October: **58**. November: **63**.
1909	February: **62**. April: **66**.
1910	June: **57**.
1911	October: **74**.
1912	February: **71**. March: **73**. August: **70**.
1913	August: **72**.
1914	April: **75**. October: **77, 78**.
1916	October: **76**.
Total	27 engines.

Summary: Class C 0-6-0 Tender Locomotives.

H&BR No.	Works No.	Delivered	Reboilered to Class B	Withdrawn	*Notes*
49	3138	March 1889	May 1905	February 1926	(1)
50	3139	March 1889	August 1906	April 1925	(1)
51	3140	March 1889	September 1906	February 1926	(1)
52	3141	March 1889	February 1907	September 1928	(1)
53	3142	March 1889	June 1907	April 1925	(1)
54	3143	April 1889	May 1906	January 1929	(1)
55	3144	April 1889	November 1906	September 1928	(1)
56	3145	April 1889	September 1907	September 1926	(1)
57	3504	August 1892	June 1910	June 1933	(2)
58	3505	August 1892	October 1908	December 1933	(2)
59	3506	August 1892	February 1908	June 1933	(2)
60	3507	September 1892	July 1908	May 1937	(2)
61	3508	September 1892	December 1907	August 1926	(2)
62	3509	September 1892	February 1909	August 1926	(2)
63	1351	June 1892	November 1908	June 1936	(3)
64	1352	June 1892	December 1907	January 1935	(3)
65	1353	July 1892	June 1908	March 1934	(3)
66	1354	July 1892	April 1909	January 1934	(3)
70	547	September 1897	August 1912	July 1933	(4)
71	548	September 1897	February 1912	May 1937	(4)
72	549	October 1897	August 1913	January 1936	(4)
73	550	November 1897	March 1912	July 1937	(4)
74	551	November 1897	October 1911	August 1935	(4)
75	552	December 1897	April 1914	July 1937	(4)
76	560	December 1898	October 1916	May 1937	(5)
77	561	December 1898	October 1914	November 1935	(5)
78	562	December 1898	October 1914	September 1933	(5)

Notes:

(1) Built Kitson & Co., Leeds. Cost £2,300 each.
(2) Built Kitson & Co., Leeds. Cost £2,320 each.
(3) Built Vulcan Foundry, Newton-le-Willows. Cost £2,310 each.
(4) Built Yorkshire Engine Co. Meadowhall, Sheffield. Cost £2,550 each.
(5) Built Yorkshire Engine Co. Meadowhall, Sheffield. Cost £2,635 each.
NB: North Eastern and LNER numbers are included with details of the further histories of these engines as Class B in the tables at the end of the next section.

Class C Dimensions.

Cylinders: 2, inside. 18" x 26".
Motion: Stephenson Link; slide valves between cylinders.
Boiler: Domeless.
Max. diameter outside: 4' 3".
Barrel length: 10' 0".
Firebox length outside: 5' 6".
Pitch: 7' 2".
Heating surface:
  Firebox 100 sq.ft.*; 95 sq.ft.**
  Tubes: 199 @ $1^3/_4$" dia. - 950 sq.ft.*.
          190 @ $1^3/_4$" dia. - 900 sq.ft.**.
  Total 1,050 sq.ft.*; 995 sq.ft.**.
Grate area: 16.25 sq.ft.
Ratio of grate area to heating surface: 1 to 64.6*; 1 to 61.23**.
Boiler pressure: 150 lb/sq.in.*; 160 lb/sq.in.**.
Wheel diameter: engine 5' 0"; tender 3' 9".
Wheelbase: engine 7' 3" + 8' 3" = 15' 6".
            tender 6' 0" + 6' 0" = 12' 0"
Length over buffers: 48' $8^1/_8$".
Weights:
  Engine 36tons 16cwt.
  Tender 35tons 18cwt.
  Total 72tons 14cwt.
Height to top of chimney: 12' $10^5/_8$".
Tractive effort @ 85% of boiler pressure: 17,901 lb*; 19,094 lb.**
Ratio of blast nozzle to cylinder diameter: 1 to 3.78.
Tender water capacity: 3,000 gallons.
Tender coal capacity: 6tons 0cwt.

(* dimensions applicable to Kitson-built engines, 49-62, and possibly Vulcan Foundry locomotives 63-66; ** dimensions for Yorkshire Engine Co. locomotives 70-78.)

Note: Weights given above are for engines in full working order. Maximum axle loading was some 14 tons; empty weights around 34 tons 2 cwt 1qtr (engine), and 18 tons 12 cwt for an empty tender.

Under the Loading Classification scheme, first used in the Working Timetable from around the midsummer 1908, the enhanced tractive effort of the Yorkshire Engines Company - built locomotives 70-78 put them in Load Group C. This was abolished in 1914, when only No.76 remained to be reboilered: this would most likely have been done in 1914 also, except for the intervention of World War I. With the abolition of Load Class C, the subsequent load classes were simply moved up by one letter.

Since engines 57, 62, 63 and 66 remained to be rebuilt after the Summer of 1908, they were included in Load Class D, along with Kirtley 0-6-0's reboilered to Class D with 5ft 0ins diameter boilers. Effectively, Load Class D limited these engines to 24 x 12 ton wagons, or 28 x 10 ton wagons over the hardest part of the main line, the climb to Drewton Summit. Engines reboilered to Class B were put into Load Class B, which was calculated as being equal to 26 x 12 ton wagons, or 30 x 10 ton wagons. (Presumably Load Class C fell somewhere between Load Classes B and D).

(below) **No.78 was the last Class C built and dating from December 1898. It is seen at the west end of Springhead shed yard, blowing off gently and with the injector requiring slight adjustment to stop it dribbling. The engine shows signs of hard usage, but remains presentably clean. No. 78 lost its small boiler - and rakish good looks - in October 1914.**

No.81, as depicted here, is one of the 1898 delivery from Kitson & Co., of six locomotives with 4ft 9in diameter boilers. Nos.79 and 82 were loaned to the South Eastern & Chatham Railway in more or less this condition during World War I; all six were rebuilt with 5ft 0in diameter boilers by the H&BR, No.81 being first, in September 1913. Others were reboilered as follows:- No.84 August 1916; 80 March 1917; 83 September 1918; 82 September 1920 and 79 March 1921.

Class B No.86 was the second engine with 5ft 0in diameter boiler to be delivered from Kitson & Co in March 1900, and is seen at the west end of Springhead shed. Although obviously worked hard for a living, No.86 still looks very presentable. Reboilering came in April 1921.

CLASS B 0-6-0. (LNER CLASS J23). Introduced 1898.

Whilst the H&BR's Locomotive Department staff waited through the Autumn of 1898 with daily anticipation for the delivery of Nos.73 to 78 from the Yorkshire Engine Company, they were probably agreeably surprised to be able to accept Nos.79 to 82, from Kitson & Co.

Apart from their prompt delivery, these engines were (along with Nos.83 and 84 which turned up a month of so later), notable as representing the first step the H&BR took along the road towards bigger boilers, since they carried boilers of 4ft 9ins diameter - an increase of 6 inches upon their predecessors. Not only had the boiler barrel diameter been increased, but in consequence an extra leaf was added to each spring to cope with the extra weight, and the cabs were increased in width by some five inches to allow for more room around the wider firebox backheads. This increased width also did away with the need for coupling rod splashers alongside the cabs.

However, Stirling had already tied himself to a boiler barrel length of 10ft 0ins and firebox outside length of 5ft 6ins, so no increases could be made there without considerable alterations to frame stretcher spacings, frame lengths and even wheelbases - a task which would have entailed building virtually new engines. (Such boiler dimensions had probably been more or less forced upon Stirling by the necessity of providing boilers which were also compatible with the Kirtley 0-6-0's when the time came for renewal of their original boilers, thus sacrificing to some degree enhanced power in the interests of standardisation).

Fifteen months after the delivery of No. 84 (the last 4ft 9ins boilered 0-6-0), there appeared a further development - this time with a 5ft 0ins diameter boiler. At the time they were introduced (March 1900), these engines were carrying the largest diameter boilers in the British Isles. Stirling kept to this diameter for all reboilering and new construction of tender engines, with the exception of Class A 0-8-0's which carried 5ft 6ins diameter boilers. Until the introduction of these latter engines however, both larger boilered varieties of the 0-6-0 were classified as 'A' by 1905, only receiving Class letter 'B' in 1907 upon the introduction of the bigger engines.

The 0-6-0's introduced in 1900 saw yet another increase in cab width - this time to 7ft 0ins; again, there was no need for coupling rod splashers at the back wheels. Deliveries of 0-6-0 tender locomotives throughout 1900 totalled twelve, six apiece being built by Kitson & Co. and the Yorkshire Engine Co., but the final order for ten delivered in 1908 went entirely to Kitson's. Meanwhile of course, the ranks of 5ft 0ins diameter boilered Class B's were being swelled from 1905 by reboilerings of the earlier engines as their 4ft 3ins boilers became due for renewal. (At this point, it may be best to point out that for our purposes it will be best to avoid confusion by keeping to the 1908 H&BR Classification system, referring to bigger boilered locomotives as B and those with smaller diameter boilers as C, rather than complicate matters by further references to the 1905 scheme).

Ultimately, by the end of its independent existence the H&BR handed over fifty-five Class B engines, all with 5ft boilers acquired either from new or as a result of reboilering, but needless to say there were a number of detail differences between the various engines. These arose mainly due to the retention of the narrower cabs on reboilered engines, but also due to three manufacturers being involved in their production. For example Kitson & Co. used cab and tender handrails of bent pipe form, whilst the Vulcan Foundry and Yorkshire Engine Co. both favoured handrails fitted into stanchions. Depths of cabside cut-outs also differed: the early engines had the shallowest cabsides whereas the 1898 and 1900 Kitson engines had cut-outs of intermediate depth. The last ten, from Kitson & Co. (Nos 132 - 141 of 1908), had the highest cabsides to match the larger capacity tenders built with these engines, which held 3,300 gallons of water.

Other odd differences which crept in during the period of H&BR ownership included the shape of cab front spectacle windows; the acquisition (or otherwise), of chimney top 'wind jabbers' (to use the North Eastern's term for such fittings, rather than resorting to 'capucheon' - a Great Westernite import!). Most, if not all engines acquired two or three dog-clamps around the smokebox door lower part, and a number of them also had the tender coal rails cut down from across the tender back end, to finish in downward curves just aft of the bunker. Modifications which were of more significance to the crews of the Class B's were the fitting of Ross "Pop" safety-valves to No. 85 in 1920, in place of the usual open Ramsbottom valves; the fitting of No.60 with a Lytton superheater in 1912, and Phoenix superheating equipment to No.133 in May 1914. For details of the latter equipment, recourse to the Appendices may be undertaken, but sadly, no details of the Lytton type have come to light, save for the fact that it was of the smoketube/element type. This form of superheater had been perfected by 1900 on the Prussian State Railways by Professor Schmidt, and although the element-in-smoketube arrangement could not be patented, his method of using packed glands for sealing the element ends into the superheater header was. In consequence, locomotive engineers on other railways sought to evade this patent (and avoid Royalty payments), by devising their own methods of securing the all-important joints between elements and header. J.G.Robinson, on the Great Central Railway, devised a method of expanding each element's plain tube-ends into the header using a tapered mandrel and rollers (of similar form to the somewhat larger items used for expanding boiler tubes), but perforce worked through 90 degrees by bevel gears, manipulated through removable access covers on the header front. Extraction of the elements without cracking the cast header was a less simple proposition however: so much so in fact that one exasperated locomotive engineer was driven to remark that, "They advertise the Robinson Superheater as, 'A Sound-running Job', but it isn't! It's a Main Works' job!"

An easier method of fitting and removing elements was devised by Robert Urie with his "Eastleigh" superheater used on the London & South Western Railway, which involved a form of tapered plug and draw-up bolt for securing. Despite quite widespread use of both Robinson and Urie types, they were ultimately superseded by the "Melesco" ball and socket type of joint clamped in place by studs and nuts, or 'T' bolts and nuts.

So far as can be determined H&BR No.60 was the only locomotive to be fitted with the Lytton superheater, and as the accompanying photograph shows, the equipment involved a header arrangement as evinced by the access panel behind the chimney on top of the smokebox, which had been lengthened by some 8 inches. The form of element and header joints may well have led Robinson into conflict with Lytton, for G.G.Kennewell writing in "The Dalesman's Yorkshire Annual" in 1978 referred to, "....a slight controversy when the patent rights were questioned. However, this was soon settled when the two engineers involved got together and compared notes." Since all other H&BR locomotives were fitted with either Phoenix or Schmidt superheaters, the "controversy" must have involved Lytton's equipment: Robinson's invention dated back to at least 1911 whereas the "Eastleigh" superheater appeared only in 1914.

No.60 retained its unique fittings until October 1925, whereas No.133's Phoenix apparatus was removed in July 1919 although its extended smokebox did not necessarily disappear at the same time. (Before moving away from the subject of superheating-albeit only temporarily- it should perhaps be stated that F.H.Lytton was Matthew Stirling's Assistant, appointed in September 1908 at an annual salary of £250. He had left the H&BR by 1919, probably due to military service).

1908 marked a change in the use of the Class B's due to the delivery of the fifteen big Class A 0-8-0's the year before. It was found more expeditious to move export mineral traffic eastwards as far as Sandholme, up to the maximum loads permitted behind the Class B's over that section (38 ten-ton wagons or 33 twelve-ton wagons from Cudworth). Since they were allowed to continue from Sandholme eastwards over the Wolds to Springhead with reduced loads of 30 ten-tonners or 26 twelve-tonners, it became the practice to drop off the extra wagons at Sandholme and continue onwards with the lightened trains: as sufficient wagons accumulated at Sandholme, these were formed into longer trains to be worked forward to Springhead by the big Class A's. These 'out and home' workings from Springhead became known in due course as "Sandholme Bankers". Quite extensive sidings, a turntable and an independent Down goods relief road between Ings Wood and Sandholme had been decided upon in 1905 and were put speedily into use by 1907, such was the pressing nature of the problem. Trials with banking engines between Newport and Little Weighton in attempts to increase maximum loads over that section had been tried in August 1905, but were apparently unsuccessful - probably due to the difficulties in finding paths for the returning light engines between empty mineral workings and train-loads of Scandinavian timber for pit props.

The outbreak of war in 1914 virtually knocked the bottom out of the coal export trade almost overnight, at least as far as the East Coast ports were concerned. In consequence, the amount of work available was insufficient to keep all 55 Class B's gainfully employed. Meanwhile whereas traffic to the Continent from the East Coast ports diminished, some railway companies in other areas found that unaccustomed volumes of goods and minerals traffic were stretching their resources up to and even beyond the limits of their available resources.

1915 saw the nation slowly realise that it had a long, hard struggle ahead and that it had better gear itself up fully and take a more practical approach to fighting the war. Meanwhile various expediencies had to be resorted to in order to meet the more pressing and immediate needs. That year saw the Railway Executive Committee (in modern terminology, a 'Quango' set up especially for running the railway systems on a war footing), approach the H&BR on behalf of the Midland & South Western

Junction Railway to ask for the loan of an engine and crew. Similar requests for the loan of H&BR locomotives for the Highland Railway were also made, for that company was struggling to deliver the mountains of coal required at Scapa Flow to satisfy the voracious appetites of the Home Fleet's vessels. Both these requests were turned down, but the reason for this seemingly unhelpful attitude on the part of the H&BR was not too hard to find: they had already lent fourteen Class B's to the South Eastern & Chatham Railway.

The first intimation of this came on 5th March 1915 with a letter from the Railway Executive Committee, which realised that the war had caused a diminution of traffic across the North Sea but had the opposite effect on Cross-Channel traffic: even a "Contemptible Little Army" (to use the Kaiser's phrase), consumed enormous amounts of munitions and these amounts would increase throughout the war. Due to the insubstantial nature of the SECR's far-from-permanent way, a larger number of lighter goods engines would be more use than a few heavy goods engines. In consequence, since Stirling was due to visit London on 9th March it was convenient to arrange for him to visit R.E.L.Maunsell, the SECR's Locomotive Engineer, who had requested the loan of 14 or 15 six-coupled goods engines on 28th February. The two engineers duly agreed on a figure of fifteen engines, but two days later the H&BR Board temporarily acquired the characteristics of other boards inasmuch as they exhibited the tendency to become a bit wooden, for they proposed that some other company in direct contact with the SECR should make the loan, such as the Midland, Great Central or Great Northern and the H&BR should make up their motive power shortfall in turn. This bright idea appealed to nobody else so Maunsell was again in contact with the H&BR Board on 27th March; consequently the Board got its act together and agreed to hire out fifteen Class B's at a rate of £22/10/- per month.

Ultimately Nos.71, 73, 75, 77, 82, 87, 88, 92 and 93 left Springhead on 9th April 1915 to make their way south, crossing London via Acton Wells and Clapham Junction to reach their new home at Battersea. Following them on 12th April were Nos.91, 94 and 95, with 74 and 79 bringing up the rear the day after. (This made a total of 14 engines: an additional one had been turned down by the SECR from the list sent to them). The above numbers appear in the H&BR's records, and are reproduced in both Volume 2 of *The Hull & Barnsley Railway* and by D.L.Bradley in *The Locomotive History of the South Eastern & Chatham Railway*. Oddly enough, the RCTS (publishers of Bradley's work), list Nos.71, 73, 74, 75, 77, 79, 82, 83, 85, 86, 87, 92, 93, 94 and 95 (a total of fifteen engines), in Part 5 of their monumental *Locomotives of the LNER*.

Nos. 71, 73, 74, 75 and 77 were rebuilds from Class C engines built with 4ft 3ins diameter boilers; 79 and 82 still carried their 4ft 9ins boilers from 1898. Boiler ages therefore varied from 16½ years (Nos.79 and 82), to barely six months (No.77). Three however were destined to have but a brief sojourn in the South of England - the fireboxes on Nos.88, 91 and 95 were condemned in July 1915, the engines concerned being laid aside at Ashford Works until 6th August 1915 when they were returned to the H&BR. No.77 received light repairs at Ashford in April 1915, and the following year saw Nos.71, 73, 74, 75, 79, 82, 87, 92, 93 and 94 similarly dealt with. In due course all were given general repairs, emerging in unlined plain black but retaining their own numbers and the initials "H & B R" on the tenders. All returned north after their war service in October 1919 save

The right side of No.87 to compare with No.86, both being of the same group. No.87 is shown standing at the east end of Springhead shed; the buildings in the left background formed part of the works.

Here is Kitson's works photograph of No.90, the last of the 1900 series they built. This photograph was taken inside their workshops building - the round manhole cover to the left of centre foreground features in several of their photographs. The background was formed from white sheets pinned on a wooden framework, which hid the end wall, girders, overhead crane and other odd items of equipment - and part-finished engines - from view. The use of a wide-angle lens should also be noted.

Originally a Class C, No.65 stands in the sunshine at the north side of Springhead yard, soon after rebuilding to Class B in June 1908. No.65 was one of the four Vulcan Foundry engines delivered in 1892. The rebuilds retained their narrow cabs with coupling rod splashers alongside, as delineated by the upward curve in the lining at the bottom of the cab side.

for Nos.71, 73, 74 and 93 which remained until January 1920, leaving No.75 in exile "Down South", for it had been under repair at Ashford. Upon its return to traffic on 6th March 1920, it too was sent homewards to rejoin its comrades. (Whilst in Ashford Works in October 1919, No.75 had rubbed buffers with some very cosmopolitan company, for the Works were simultaneously dealing with three Robinson R.O.D. 2-8-0's on hire from the Government, Belgian State Railways' 0-6-0 No.2888 and Kent & East Sussex Railway No.6, as well as the more mundane representatives of SECR motive power!).

The H&BR hirelings were not as exotic an export to the SECR as may have been expected, for that Company was still operating some 43 domeless 0-6-0's of James Stirling's Class O design. The two types were readily distinguishable, for the O's had lost their black paint some years earlier in place of Brunswick Green, still panelled and lined elaborately in black, light green, red and yellow, at least on some engines which had been longer away from Ashford than others. Oval brass numberplates with red backgrounds appeared on the cabsides and tender backplates: compared with such a riotous magnificence of colour the H&BR engines can only be regarded as providing a model of restrained, sober good taste in the field of locomotive artwork!

Even the colourblind enthusiast could differentiate between the two types, for the SECR Stirlings had much smaller diameter boilers with safety valves half-way along the barrel plus the prominent smokebox wingplates, beloved more on the Scottish systems than South of the Border. Absence of sandboxes from around the driving wheel splashers also marked out the South Eastern's Stirlings from their Northern relatives. Tenders were vastly different also: James Stirling had tenaciously clung to the ancient, outside-framed variety, with springs prominently mounted above footplate level, and everything else mounted inaccessibly behind the frame plates. The position of the springs allowed for only a narrow tank, with capacity for a miserable 1,950 gallons of water and three tons of coal. One very up-to-date item carried by the SECR engines was steam reversing gear - how the "Chatham" crews took to winding the screw reversers on the H&BR engines has gone unrecorded.

What has passed down to us from posterity is the fact that the Class B's were not the most dynamic of machines; on their own system, despite their popularity they were regarded as apt to be rather shy steamers and the SECR crews also found them liable to prime (i.e. draw water over from the top of the boiler into the cylinders). Initially, all were shedded at Battersea and used on main line goods trains over the old London, Chatham & Dover section of the SECR, working turn about with the SECR - produced Class C 0-6-0's, which incidentally were a direct derivative of William Kirtley's final such design, the B2 Class. Their Kirtley ancestry is plain for all to see, as Class C No. 592 displays to this day in preservation.

In due course after a few months' experience with the Class B's, the SECR authorities redeployed them: Nos. 71, 73, 82 and 93 went to Tonbridge in August 1915; Redhill later received Nos.75 and 79, whilst Ramsgate welcomed 87, 92 and 94. By early 1918 Nos.71, 77 and 93 were working the straggling, heavily-graded branch from Redhill to Reading and the Great Western, hauling passenger and goods traffic alike. (This branch acquired considerable strategic value in wartime, transferring traffic from the north and west over the GWR directly to the Channel ports. Once the war ended, the Reading branch lapsed into its usual state of bucolic somnolence).

Meanwhile, Nos.75, 87 and 94 were engaged in pilot work around the War Department's port facilities at Richborough, near Sandwich. Whilst there they doubtless reminded a young engineer from the Great Northern Railway, one O.V.S.Bulleid, of his peacetime employment at Doncaster Works dealing with the remaining GNR domeless Stirling engines and most likely seeing Class B's in their native surroundings but a mile or two north of Doncaster. (At Richborough, Bulleid was pioneering the use of welding on barges: ironically a later war would again see him back in the South of England pioneering the use of welding, albeit this time on the locomotive fireboxes of his own Southern Railway Pacifics. The intervening years had seen him working as Gresley's Assistant, so he would nominally have had some responsibility for the Class B's in their declining years).

Since three engines had returned early from the south and a fifteenth had never gone, the H&BR again had a few spare locomotives. Five Class B's (numbers unrecorded), were lent to the North Eastern Railway to go some way towards making up the shortfall in their motive power left by the loan of all fifty relatively modern Class T1 0-8-0's to the War Department for service in France. This time however, the H&B's engines only moved a couple of miles south from Springhead, remaining within sight of the H&BR Neptune Street Branch - for they were all allocated to Dairycoates Shed! They were joined for some time by a number of the big Class A 0-8-0's, which were observed on goods workings north of York on the East Coast Main Line, so it is quite likely that the Class B's also found their way up there occasionally - a portent of things to come.

The interim period between the end of World War I and the Amalgamation with the North Eastern in 1922 saw inroads made into the arrears of maintenance which had built up. New boilers, ordered from contractors, were fitted (the last 4ft 9ins boiler was removed from No.79 in March 1921 for example), and further materials were ordered to expedite heavy repair work, much of which was ultimately to continue at Darlington.

Working practices were also changed - the "Sandholme Bankers" were abolished in favour of sending out the various H&BR 0-6-0 classes to hunt in pairs: either a couple of B's, or a B and an L/L1/LS, or any combination of two from the latter

No.77 stands at Stewart's Lane shed, Battersea. The photograph has been misleadingly dated as 16th October 1920, for No.77 had returned to the H&BR in October 1919. The H&BR engines had been working for some time as SECR. stock before interested observers realised that they were not odd engines which had somehow strayed down south. In 1916 a class B was observed by J.M.Robbins double-heading with an SECR 4-4-0 on a goods train at Wormwood Scrubs en route to the Great Western; a later observation at Mill Hill by G.H.Cannon was of one on a Midland Railway goods train. *H.C.Casserley.*

family group. This practice continued into LNER ownership, which not only saw the Class B's redesignated as Class J23 but also troubles arising by 1924 due to the importation of alien North Eastern Railway practices. By the end of that year, J.H.Smeddle, the Locomotive Running Superintendent based at York, wrote to A.C.Stamer, the Chief Assistant Mechanical Engineer, at Darlington Works to report, ".....having several cases of the intermediate screw couplings between engine and tender breaking, on the engines stationed at Springhead, Hull." He went on to say, "No doubt a number of these cases are due to the extra strain put upon the couplings by the double-headed trains," and asked Stamer, to, ".....go into this matter, with a view to having stronger couplings put on these engines, and thus avoid the detentions which are at present taking place: also having in mind the serious accident which occurred on the L.M.& S. Railway." Smeddle's enclosed list of afflicted engines reproduced here, underlines the serious nature of the problem:

"List of Engines, Springhead, Intermediate Screw Couplings Broken. 6 months, July to November 1924, inclusive.

Date	Class	LNER No.	(H&BR No.)
24th July	B	2441	(60)
24th July	L1	2408	(16)
13th August	B	2521	(140)
16th August	B	2441	(60)
27th September	A	2501	(120)
31st October	B	2431	(50)
3rd November	B	2455	(74)
5th November	LS	2418	(26)
13th November	A	2507	(126)
20th November	B	2517	(136)
24th November	L	2538	(157)
1st December	L1	2408	(16)
1st December	L	2541	(160)

As can be seen, breakages also involved the Class A 0-8-0's, which should hardly have needed double-heading, and the replacement link on 2408 (No.16) only lasted for some four months before it failed - that fitted to 2441 (No.60) didn't even last that long. It is also worth remarking that although the LNER's classification scheme had come into use, the class designations were those established by the H&BR in 1908 and still being used (perversely), by Darlington!

On 7th January 1925 F.A.Mackay, writing to Smeddle from the Locomotive Department, Springhead, was able to report that, "In the majority of cases the type of coupling breaking has been square thread when screw broken." Further enquiries, undertaken in Darlington works by R.J.Robson the Chief Draughtsman, revealed that, ".....the North Eastern Section type of square thread coupling, as used on passenger engines, was being worked in for the H.&.B. Section engines." Furthermore, ".....H.B. types of couplings have been considerably strengthened within recent years."

By 28th January 1925 a cure had been decided upon as R.A.Copperthwaite, the Locomotive Workshops' Manager of Darlington, was able to read in a letter from Robson which instructed him to revert to the original knuckle thread form as used by the H&BR, but to increase the thread root diameter from $2\frac{1}{2}$ in to $2\frac{3}{4}$ in , ".....in accordance with the enclosed Drawing, No.11179."

Just to underline the urgency with which replacements needed to be undertaken, Class A No. 2511 (130) chose 27th February 1925 to break its coupling link whilst shunting at Springhead, but with a programme of promptly replacing all square thread - form couplings and then the remaining original, more slender H&BR varieties, the problem seemed to be under control by the end of 1925.

But alas! The drawgear gremlins had one last trick to play,

for on 4th December they struck at the 1.25 p.m. mineral train from Cudworth to Hessle Haven.* We again find Smeddle writing to A.C.Stamer to tell him that Class A No.2508 (127), had "....failed between South Kirkby and South Elmsall owing to the engine intermediate coupling link breaking. On examination it was found that one trunnion of the coupling had broken, the material being flawed." This time, T.Robson of the Materials Inspection & Testing Department at Darlington became involved: he soon found that, "The fact that the trunnion had been turned to a square corner in the shoulder is quite sufficient to account for the accident." Thus an erroneous turner not only caused the incident, but probably indirectly caused much grovelling around under locomotives on the pit roads in Springhead Shed as fitters peered up into the grimy recesses between engines and tenders, trying to ascertain if any more couplings had similarly finished trunnions. However, on 26th January 1926, Ralph Robson was able to inform the Chief Assistant Mechanical Engineer that No.2508 (127) "....was last in the Works for repair in December 1923, therefore up to the present it has not been fitted with the new couplings."

Potentially far more spectacular opportunities for locomotive failures lurked within the boilers, due to their condition. Materials had been gathered for carrying out widespread repairs and renewals, but with the run-down of Springhead Works much of this along with heavy machinery and skilled personnel were transferred to Darlington in 1924. Odd items of hardware remained, as itemised in a list sent from Springhead dated 28th February 1926. This included numbers of flanged copper half-tubeplates, along with the comment, "It is not the N.E. practice to put half tube plates in." Being more accustomed to entertaining Lady Poverty than Lady Bountiful had led the H&BR into adopting such dubious practices, but the NER were not inclined to be niggardly when tackling their legacy of worn-out H&BR boilers.

The expediency of reboilering No.3055 (55) with the boiler off Kirtley 0-6-0 No.28A has already been referred to; this was done in May 1923. This boiler apparently had 205 tubes (fewer than the usual numbers of tubes in Class B boilers), and in consequence the inner firebox crownsheet was lower, as evinced

---

*The reference to Hessle Haven in Smeddle's letter is most curious: a glance at a rail atlas for the period shows that to reach Hessle Haven from Cudworth via. the H&BR was an operating improbability, if not an impossibility. Possibly Smeddle, as a "Running Man", rather than a "Traffic Man", could not bring to mind the relevant yard on the H&B Section, so simply put down the name of the first Hull yard to spring to mind!

---

externally by the noticeably lower position of the washout plugs. No.28A's boiler had commenced its working life in July 1904, and lasted for just over 20 years, seeing No.3055 through to September 1924 and yet another renumbering, this time as LNER No.2436.

Such stopgap measures would not do much towards really tackling the problem however, so it should come as no surprise to find that the NER's 1922 boiler programme provided for more replacement boilers for H&BR engines than for the North Eastern's own! Fifteen domeless boilers were quickly built at Darlington making use of the materials ordered by the H&BR, and by modifying the design of boiler fitted on the NER Class D (LNER Class H1) express passenger 4-4-4 tanks, a new design of boiler suitable for use on the H&BR Class B was speedily got up.

This new design was domed, superheated and 4ft 9ins diameter. Twenty were built from 1922 to 1925, and were initially a disappointment for engines fitted with them left much to be desired regarding their main function in life, to whit: making water boil.

On 29th March 1926, having only just overcome the problems of disintegrating drawgear, the Assistant Chief Mechanical Engineer's attention was again drawn to Springhead's wayward engines: "I am having strong complaints in regard to the steaming of the above class of engine with the superheated boilers," wrote J.H. Smeddle. (No doubt the "strong complaints" had been moderated somewhat from the forms in which they had been expressed by Springhead's footplate crews by the time they reached Smeddle's ears; but in view of the fact that it took nearly three years before action was taken, the same crews had probably worked up a better head of steam than their locomotives!) Smeddle's letter went on to say that, "Engine 2513 (132) which was fitted with a new superheated boiler came out of the shops with a 5 inch blast pipe, and the engine would not steam. The blast pipe has been reduced to 4¾" and there is a distinct improvement in the steaming qualities of the engine, but it is not yet altogether satisfactory.

"These boilers, I understand, have a reduced heating surface as compared with the saturated boiler, and is 294 sq.ft. less than the evaporating heating surface of the saturated engine, and 144 tubes as against 241.

"I shall be glad if you will kindly look into this matter and afterwards write me.

"J.H.Smeddle."

The reply came from R.J.Robson, Chief Draughtsman, Darlington Works on 27th April 1926, and is worth quoting in full because of its interest:

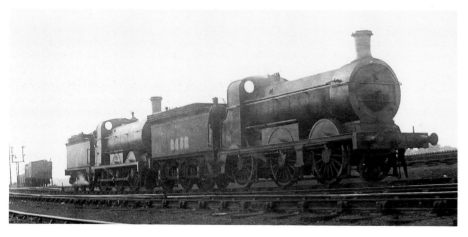

No.2452 (ex-H&BR 71), and an unidentified classmate back at Locomotive Junction after a day's shift. Note that both engines are rebuilt Class C engines; that the tender coal-rails are different and that 2452's LNER number has been patch-painted on the tender. It was the practice of double-heading on mineral trains which led to the outbreak of fractured drawbars in 1924, as detailed in the text. *Ron Copeman collection.*

3053 appearing as a North Eastern engine at Cudworth shed in 1923. Note the flat-topped number "3" - a Springhead works trait. *Hull Museums collection.*

"I have gone into the question you raise of the superheated boiler having a smaller heating surface than the original saturated boiler, and find that, in spite of a decrease of 137sq.ft. of heating surface (not 294 sq.ft. as per your letter), and a reduction from 17,184 lbs of steam per hour, to 15,482 lbs of steam per hour, (a saving of 1,702 lbs of steam per hour), the superheated boiler is rated at 745 H.P. as against 635 H.P. for the saturated type, an increase of 110 H.P. or 17.3%.

"With regard to the steaming, I find on reference to the drawings, the diameter of the blast pipe should be 4⁷⁄₈", and this has been reduced to 4³⁄₄" by your Shed Staff. This showed a distinct improvement, but is not yet satisfactory, and would suggest the other engines be altered in the same way. I will alter the drawings accordingly.

"The jet at present fitted to these engines uses 65% of the steam generated. Further economy could be effected by reducing the size of the holes in the jet, at present ⁷⁄₃₂" dia. to ¹⁄₁₆" diameter, which would reduce the steam used to 5.4%.

"In addition, to shorten the petticoat.....and have Engine No. 2513(132) altered, and report on working of same, before making the alteration general."

There matters rested until the end of the following month, when a further flurry of correspondence took place between York, Darlington and Springhead regarding performance of No. 2513, as altered.

24th May 1927 saw J.H.Smeddle writing from York, to A.C.Stamer that,".....I have had the undermentioned engines altered in the way indicated in your letter, and my Springhead Shed Superintendent now informs me that all these engines steam very much better, and I would therefore suggest that the whole of the engines of this class be similarly altered.

"It has been difficult to give you a definite opinion earlier, as we were using foreign coal to such a degree that it was difficult to come to a fair conclusion. Engine Nos.2433 (52), 2445 (64), 2446 (65), 2447 (66), 2455 (74), 2458 (77), 2470 (89), 2471 (90), 2472 (91), 2473 (92), 2474 (93), 2477 (96), 2513 (132), 2514 (133), 2518 (137)."

Three days later Stamer noted, ".....that the engines you have altered steam very much better and agree with you that all the superheated engines of this class should be similarly altered. Out of a total of 20 superheated H.& B. Class 'B' engines, I see you have altered 15, and perhaps you will instruct your Shed people to deal with the remaining five, viz., Nos.2438 (57), 2440 (59), 2441 (60), 2476 (95) and 2521 (140)."

Not wishing to be left out of the game of tinkering with H&B engines, R.J.Robson sent an internal memo. to R.A.Copperthwaite, the Locomotive Works' Manager at Darlington, enclosing drawings showing the blast pipe top to be 4³⁄₄ in diameter, the petticoat pipe shortened and a new blast

pipe and blower ring. He told Copperthwaite to, ".....note that there are 15 engines altered, and probably the remaining 5 will be dealt with by the Shed people, but in the event of any of these engines coming into your works, unaltered, perhaps you will alter them accordingly."

Before departing from the subject of superheated boilers it is worth noting that popular wisdom, handed down from the time of Professor Schmidt, would have everyone believe that unbalanced slide valves could not be used satisfactorily with superheated steam due to anticipated problems with lubrication at the higher steam temperatures involved: indeed the good Professor regarded piston valves as a sine qua non in the application of superheating. The LNER got round this problem simply by fitting mechanical lubricators to the locomotives concerned, and also probably trusting to the fact that as the boilers concerned only had 18 elements each, the degree of superheat would not be excessively high; all that can be added is that they appear to have been vindicated.

The superheater elements themselves were protected from possible burning out by the provision of a Darlington-type steam circulating valve. This valve and its associated handwheel control appeared on the left side of the smokebox; although the last of these boilers remained in use until November 1938, not one lost its steam valve in exchange for the familiar Gresley-style 'snifting' valve, prominently mounted behind the chimney on so many LNER engines.

The reboilering of 20 engines and scrapping of seven of the earlier Class B's in 1925 and '26 provided a breathing space, and gave the Darlington authorities another chance to come up with a satisfactory boiler design.

This time, advantage was taken of the fact that Stirling's Class J express passenger 4-4-0's and his last six wheeled-coupled designs of the L/L1/LS family were due for reboilering. All these engines and the Class B's had finished their H&BR careers with 5ft diameter boilers, and Darlington decided to retain this size. However, since the North Eastern had never built boilers of that diameter, new flanging blocks were produced which expedited the provision of endplates common to all H&BR tender engines (with the exception of the Class A 0-8-0's).

The new design for the Class B's came to be designated Type 64C upon introduction in 1928, and advantage was taken simultaneously of the opportunity to classify the B's (by now referred to as Class J23, at Doncaster, if not actually on the locomotives themselves or Darlington's paperwork) into three

No.3055 at Cudworth in 1924, carrying the boiler off Kirtley No.28A. This boiler was put on No.28 when it was rebuilt to Class D in 1904. 3055 is of further interest inasmuch as it is representing the "L.& N.E.R." *Ron Copeman collection.*

3096, seen at Cudworth as an "L.N.E.R." engine. Modelmakers should note how the tender guard-irons are bolted through the wooden sandwich-type bufferbeam.

Class B (HB) 3051D (note the letter suffix denoting a North Eastern area engine), seen at Cudworth. It has acquired the final form of lettering - "LNER", but still awaits its LNER number. *Ron Copeman collection.*

No.2513 (132), as rebuilt in February 1924 to Class J23/2. As related in the text, in this form the engines gave rise to complaints of poor steaming. Apart from alterations within the smokebox, it eventually received an extended cab roof and tall vacuum standpipe.

Class J23/2 No.2440 (H&B No.59), as rebuilt with superheated boiler in June 1926 standing in Hull Dairycoates shed. The tender guard-iron has obviously lost its argument with the rail-mounted stop-block....! *H.C.Casserley.*

parts. With three types of boiler in use it was quite obvious as to the way the class should be divided. Those engines still graced with H&BR domeless boilers of 5ft diameter became J23/1, their boilers being henceforth referred to as type 64A. J23/2 covered those engines fitted with the 4ft 9ins domed superheated boilers, which in turn became type 64B. Members of the final sub-species were the J23/3 locomotives, carrying the type 64C 5ft domed, saturated boilers.

Although fourteen 64C boilers were constructed, only a dozen J23's were to carry them: the unlucky thirteenth rebuild, No.2460 (79) being given a second-hand boiler off No.2439 (58) upon the latter's withdrawal in 1933. (This boiler had seen service on No.2439 for some 4 years 4 months). The two extra boilers built to Diagram 64C type and which remained unfitted to locomotives were put to stationary use - a fate which befell all too many of the replacement boilers built by the LNER, due to the engines for which they were built being withdrawn somewhat earlier than may reasonably have been expected. (Details of various boiler dimensions, numbers and exchanges may be found in the relevant tables in the *Appendix, vol. 2*).

One item which had affected somewhat the appearance of some H&BR engines including representatives of Class B, was the introduction of extended smokeboxes from August 1922 onwards. These were 8½ inches longer, the extended base being flat in order to clear the hinged 'piano lid' which allowed top side access to the cylinder and valve chest covers. The object of this particular exercise was to allow the chimney to be moved forward by 6½ inches, thus allowing far better access around the back of the chimney petticoat pipe to get at the regulator body and valve: as with all domeless engines this vital control had a rather out-of-sight, out-of-mind existence in the sulphurous, "infernal regions," of the upper smokebox. No.3138 (soon to become LNER 2519) was the pioneer, and others altered included LNER Nos.2454 (H&B No.73), 2456 (75), 2457 (76), 2459 (78), 2461 (80), 2464 (83), 2465 (84), 2515 (134), 2516

(135), 2520 (139) and 2522 (141). No.2457 (76) only received its longer smokebox in July 1935 from No.2454 (73) after a 64C boiler was put on the latter. Nos.2515 (134) and 2516 (135) were fitted in June 1923 and December 1922 with longer smokeboxes, but lost them upon rebuilding with Diagram 64C boilers in March 1928.

Not all differences and alterations were confined to the front ends of the locomotives, though. After 1925 cabs also came in for their share of attention as most engines received rearward extensions to the roofs. These were neatly done in the style adopted by Stirling for his later tender engines and were in no way a blemish as regards the tidy appearance of the class. No.2519 (138) was the first, (ex-Works 28th September 1925), but ten earlier engines departed this world retaining their original Stirling short cabs to the end: (Nos.2430, 2431, 2432, 2433, 2434, 2436, 2437, 2442, 2443, 2463 - H&B Nos.49, 50, 51, 52, 53, 55, 56, 61, 63, 82). The fitting of long roofs was completed by 17th September 1929 with 2447 (66).

Spectacle windows were also a mixture - both round and profiled types being an assortment unconfined to any particular batch, although all engines built new after 1900 with 5ft boilers appear to have had round cab spectacles. An odd episode occurred in 1928, when R.J.Robson pointed out to the Darlington Works Manager that Engine No.2522 (141) had been fitted with larger diameter cab spectacle windows of North Eastern pattern in February 1925 and that this was about to create a problem, for: "...this engine is being reboilered, and the clothing carried through to the backplate, the present N.E. type of window is too large, and it will be necessary to revert to the original H.& B. window. For this purpose, I herewith sent you the following drawing:-

"Dg.No.12638D. Cab Window. Classes B, G3. F3. J. L1.

"Will you please arrange for two of these windows to be made, as soon as possible, as Engine No.2522 is almost ready to leave the shops."

Such episodes as this (plus others that had doubtless occurred but escaped unrecorded), would surely have reinforced the prejudices of the old H&BR staff, that what was sauce for the North Eastern goose was not necessarily so easily digestible when served up on the H&BR gander, but on occasion Springhead's records left something to be desired.

To return briefly to the grimy recesses stuffed with spilt coals which can be found under the floorboards of most tender engines, we find Ralph J. Robson again writing to R.A.Copperthwaite on 28th January 1925:

"CLASS B(HB) DRAG BEAM.

"I am in receipt of your letter of the 26th. instant, and note that you are asking for a drawing showing a Steel Plate Drag Beam. Several of these engines were originally built thus, but were found to be too light, and the latter builds were fitted with a cast iron drag beam, to Dg. No.11194. A pattern for this is, I understand, available at Springhead, and I shall be glad if you will work to this drawing."

Copperthwaite's plaintive reply, dated 9th February, carried a hint of desperation at being faced with yet another trivial problem seemingly about to be blown up out of all proportion by cruel fate, ".....for your information I give you below copy of letter received from the Springhead Shed Master respecting the pattern in question, viz:-

'Your letter of the 31st ulto. I cannot find trace of pattern for above drag beam. The drawings are away from here, and the Patternmaker deceased recently.

'I am of the opinion that this particular engine, namely 2437 (56), fitted with a special drag box casting at the time the larger boiler was fitted.'"

Two days later, Robson again wrote from Stooperdale to bring some cheer to Copperthwaite:

"CLASS B(HB) DRAG BEAM.

"In reply to your letter of the 9th. instant. About half of this class of engine were originally built with a built up steel plate drag. On rebuilding with a larger boiler, the majority were fitted with a cast iron drag beam, but a few engines are still running with the original steel plate drag.

"On account of the increased weight required for adhesive purposes, it would be advisable to fit the cast iron drag in preference to the steel plate one, and I would therefore recommend that you make a new pattern to Dg. No.11194, already in the shops."

Finally, a cryptic comment handwritten below in pencil suggests that an age-old dodge available for use in any sizeable organisation was about to be resorted to by Robson: in short, one way out of a problem is to try and dump it on someone else's desk:

"Perhaps you would prefer taking this up with Mr.Stamer." (One is also left with the sneaking suspicion that someone from Darlington had paid a hurried visit to Matthew Stirling in retirement, and asked him if he could recall when and which engines got cast iron dragboxes).

With as many as fifty-five engines it was inevitable that numerous minor detail differences appeared within the class. These are summarised in detail in the admirable RCTS series on LNER locomotives, (Part 5), or may be looked up in the various tables at the end of this section, but a brief outline may be appropriate here.

Perhaps the most readily noticeable differences concerned chimneys: most of the class had acquired wind-jabbers by Grouping, and odd, shorter chimneys appeared on

Nos.2438(57), 2460(79), 2472(91) and 2477(96) as the result of expediency in Darlington Works when being rebuilt with domed boilers.

North Eastern style twin whistles appeared on domed rebuilds, but domeless engines retained single whistles, albeit occasionally changed from bell to organ-pipe varieties.

Vacuum brake standpipes, initially of the short H&BR type, began to disappear altogether as the North Eastern's favoured method of below-bufferbeam connections was introduced. Then came a complete change of mind at Darlington from December 1928, which caused tall standpipes to be fitted instead, although no domeless engines appear to have been so equipped.

Stirling's dished smokebox doors with lamp irons thereon were gradually replaced by a stouter NER type, with flanged rim seating firmly on a reinforcing ring around the smokebox opening, the lamp irons being placed over the door on the front plate. No.2454 (73) was the last to retain its Stirling door, until reboilering with a 64C boiler in July 1935. Some domed engines had wheel and handle smokebox door fastenings, others were locked by the customary two handles, as were the Stirling doors under the H&BR. Latterly at any rate, the H&B had added two, then three dog-clips around the lower part of the doors to guard against distortion of those parts, exacerbated by accumulations of burning cinders in the smokebox bottoms.

Tenders had also come in for their share of attention: after the end of World War I, the H&BR had cut the coal rails off the back ends of some sixteen tenders and curved the truncated side portions down to meet the flared-out topsides just behind the coal bunker space. This style had been introduced with the Class J 4-4-0's in 1910 and subsequently appeared on the twenty engines of the L/L1/LS family. From July 1923 the LNER fitted backing plates behind the coal rails within the section along the coal bunker only, on all the tenders. From H&B times up to 1932, other additions concerned the equipping of some 23 engines with steam heating apparatus. Sometimes this was only fitted to the tenders, but in other instances the necessary connections were put under the bufferbeam at the locomotive's front end.

Such equipment became of more importance in the work performed after 1929 by the Class B's (or as we should now more properly refer to them, Class J23), for having started life as mineral engines they ended up as secondary passenger locomotives: a situation which arose due to two main reasons.

Firstly, the Hull coal export trade having been greatly dislocated due to the First World War, never really recovered from the effects of the General Strike in May 1926 and the Miners' Strike which dragged on for a further six months subsequently. This caused many J23's to become redundant and to be put into store for months on end at Springhead, but since twenty carried new superheated boilers and a further eight carried relatively new domeless boilers, work was sought for them off their parent system. In consequence, October 1927 saw seven of them transferred to York Shed.

Secondly, the LNER had purchased large numbers of ex-War Department R.O.D. 2-8-0's constructed to J.G.Robinson's Great Central Railway design - sufficient numbers being acquired in fact, that together with the 41 Gresley Class O2's, they filled the LNER's requirements for heavy goods engines throughout its existence. In 1929 the decision was taken to transfer a number of these to Springhead and Cudworth sheds to allow them to put their not inconsiderable strength into dragging coal over Drewton Summit. In the words of the late Bob Sedman, one-

No.2441 (60) lost its boiler with Lytton superheater in October 1924, as shown here at Springhead, receiving a new 4ft 9in boiler with Schmidt superheater instead. Note the steam circulating valve on the smokebox just below the handrail, plus the North Eastern chimney. *Ron Copeman collection.*

Another one for the modelmakers! The right-hand (driver's), side of 2441 (60), clearly showing the mechanical lubricator between the leading driving wheels plus the atomiser for cylinder lubrication on top of the leading splasher. The front vacuum hose is neatly hidden away under the bufferbeam in North Eastern fashion. 2441 is seen in store inside Springhead works in April 1934, both works and engine being grossly under-utilised.

An early variation on the theme of J23/2, No.2446 (65), is shown at Springhead as rebuilt in March 1925; it also has an NER-style chimney, wheel-and-handle on the smokebox door and below - bufferbeam vacuum pipe, but is unusual in retaining its H&BR jack and short cab roof.

2452 (71), at Springhead showing its LNER number patch-painted on the tender, brake ejector exhaust pipe alongside the boiler plus NER-style front vacuum pipe alteration. This engine had been involved in a minor collision on 16th March 1899 at Barchard's Bridge, Hull. It had been left standing on the Up line, then overlooked by the signalman who accepted another train into the section already occupied by No.71. *Ron Copeman collection.*

time H&BR footplateman, "We only really sorted the job out when we got the R.O.D.'s," which was about as good a testimony that any 'foreign' engine could get from any railwayman whose allegiances lay with another company.

Their immediate success removed any possibility of the J23's returning to the coal trains so December 1929 saw six more leave Springhead, being transferred in pairs to Shildon, Stockton and Darlington sheds, displacing the indigenous ex-North Eastern Class C's (LNER Class J21 0-6-0's), to the scrapyard. 1930 saw more J23's leave Springhead, this time being sent to seek their fortunes at Scarborough and Whitby on summer excursion traffic. No.2514(133), broke new ground, spending some six months working the Middleton-in-Teesdale branch. Of the 43 Class J23's still extant in 1932, only 21 remained on the H&B Section - and 13 of them were at Cudworth. Other allocations numbered 5 at Malton, 4 apiece at York and Whitby, 3 at Darlington, 2 at Heaton and one each at Pickering, Scarborough, Shildon and West Hartlepool sheds. In due course Middlesbrough received 3, and one was to grace the environs of Normanton shed throughout 1936-'37. Temporary transfers to cope with summer traffic swelled the ranks at Malton and Whitby, and seasonal excursions took the Hull-based engines along the Coast and across the Yorkshire Moors to Whitby. Nearer home they hauled special trains to Beverley races and were no strangers either on the branch lines which radiated eastwards from Hull, to Hornsea and Withernsea. A familiar sight at Hull Paragon Station throughout the early '30's was a train of elderly, non-corridor carriages with a well-warmed up J23 at the head: none too clean, but gamely sporting a headboard proclaiming, "Hornsea Express" or "Withernsea Express" as the case may be.

1935 saw the withdrawal of Nos.2519 and 2520 (138 and 139) from Springhead, and with them ended the long association of the class with their parent system. These two had been retained at Springhead especially for working the daily pick-up goods to South Howden; although these two were the last to remain on the H&B Section, J23's were still a familiar sight around Hull

for several were still at Dairycoates shed. Naturally, whilst allocated to ex-NER sheds some J23's saw action only on high days and holidays, for human nature being what it is, footplate crews preferred their "own" ex-NER engines or newer locomotives such as the North Eastern - inspired Gresley J39 0-6-0's. The H&B engines, not always well-received in ex-NER sheds, spent lengthy periods in store - until sheer necessity forced shed staff into lighting them up.

1937 marked the end of the line for most surviving H&BR locomotives. The year opened with sixteen J23's still in service, but fourteen of them failed to see the year out. Meanwhile some had seen a little more of the LNER system, for Nos.2460 (79), 2469 (88), 2476 (95) and 2518 (137) were transferred to Doncaster for six to eight months before being returned to the North Eastern area for scrapping. The record for most southerly meanderings of J23's under the LNER went to No.2441 (60), which was shedded at March from November 1936 to February 1937, during which time it was borrowed by Cambridge shed for a week.

The last two J23's, Nos.2460 and 2476 (79 and 95, of types J23/3 and J23/2 respectively), were withdrawn from Whitby shed on 5th November 1938, having seen out their last summer season on the lovely branch lines in the area. It was a tribute to Matthew Stirling's work that they should have been versatile enough to be usefully employed on work unimagined by him as he first schemed out his design in the late 1880's; but probably the most notable engine to be withdrawn in the last months of the Class J23's was No.2469 (88).

F.A.S.Brown, enthusiastic chronicler of Great Northern engines and the Stirling family, recalled seeing it bowling along north of Doncaster in the summer of 1937, but never recorded its true significance: for 2469 represented not only the last domeless H&B engine but also the last surviving Stirling-family, domeless locomotive in service: surely there have been few candidates more deserving of preservation?

MODIFICATIONS AND DETAIL ALTERATIONS TO CLASS B/LNER J23 LOCOMOTIVES

In view of the fact that Class B/J23 engines were so common on the H&BR (some 29½% of the Company's locomotive stock), and especially because they saw such a variety of use over such widespread areas throughout their lives, the following summary has been compiled with the railway modelmaker especially in mind. On any 1930's period, LNER branchline model set in what was the NER's old Southern or Central divisions, it is virtually essential to have at least one representative of Class J23 (in whichever of its three forms), if not as the "branch engine", then working through on an excursion!

It follows that in order to construct an accurate model of a particular locomotive at a set period in its life, detailed information about that locomotive is vital and many constructors may well have been put off by the lack of sufficiently detailed information. The following table has been drawn up from photographs of particular engines - where details are given they are correct for that engine at that particular period in its life, but not necessarily throughout its entire life. Only verifiable details are given, and for ease of reference are listed for each locomotive in numerical order, in table form opposite and overleaf.

2457 (76), was unique in gradually re-assuming an earlier appearance. Although seen here at Middlesbrough on 4th August 1936, it has been reboilered with another domeless type; albeit the smokebox is of the extended type, it has an H&BR chimney and smokebox door. The tall LNER-type vacuum brake standpipe is also not dissimilar to the original H&BR style. *Ron Copeman collection.*

In store in Springhead on 3rd February 1934, No. 2464 (83), is in substantially late H&BR condition, but the addition of the step between the front coupled wheels should be noted.

MODIFICATIONS AND DETAIL ALTERATIONS TO H&BR CLASS 'B', LNER CLASS J23.

(A)	(B)	(C)	(D)	(E)	(F)	(G)	(H)	(I)	(J)	(K)	(L)	(M)	(N)
49	HBR	D/L	HBRS	HBR	2H	HBR	S/R	R	HBR	?	?	5/05 to ?	-
50	?	?	?	?	?	?	S/R	?	?	from 1924	?	-	-
(51) 3051D	LNER(2)	D/L	HBRS	HBR	2H+3C	HBR	S/R	R	HBR	-	3L	3/22-10/24	-
52	LNER(3)	D/L	HBRS	?	?	HBR+W	S/R	R	HBR	-	3L	6/24-3/25	-
(53) 3053	NER	D/L	HBRL	HBR	?	HBR	S/R	S	HBR	-	3L	?/23	-
54	?	?	?	?	?	?	?	?	?	?	?	?	-
(55) 3055	LNER(1)	D/L ex28A	HBRS	HBR	2H+3C	HBR+W	S/R	S	HBR	?	?	5/23-9/24	Boiler off Kirtley 0-6-0
(56) 2437	LNER(2)	D/L	HBRS	HBR	?	HBR+W	S/R	S	NER	nil	3L	9/24-9/26	Tender coal rails cut back
(57) 2438	LNER(3)	D/SH 64B	LNERL	LNER	2H	NERS+W	L/R	R	NER	after 1932 E+T	3L s/w 1932*	1929-6/33	2 whistles
58	HBR	D/L	HBRS	HBR	2H+3C	HBR	S/R	S	HBR	-	3L	c1921	-
(59) 2440	LNER(2)	D/SH 64B	LNERL	?	?	NER+W	L/R	R	LNER	after 1924 E+T	3L	6/26 to ?	-
60	HBR	D/L/SH	HBRL	HBR	2H+3C	HBR+W	S/R	R	HBR	-	3L	1912-1922	Lytton superheater
3060	LNER(1)	D/L/SH	HBRL	HBR	?	HBR+W	S/R	R	HBR	-	3L	1923-6/24	Lytton superheater
2441	LNER(3)	D/SH 64B	LNERL	LNER	2H	NER+W	L/R	R	NER	after 1924 E+T	3L	10/29-5/37	2 whistles
61	?	?	?	?	?	?	S/R	?	?	after 1924 E+T	?	?	-
(62) 3062	HBR	D/L	HBRS	HBR	2H+?C	HBR+W	S/R	R	HBR	-	3L	4/22 to ?	LNER no. in 10/1924
(63) 2444	LNER(3)	D/sat 64C	LNERS	LNER	2H	NER+W	L/R	R	NER	-	3L	? to 6/36	2 whistles
(64) 3064	LNER(1)	D/SH 64B	LNERL	LNER	W+H	NER+W	S/R	R	NER	-	3L	7/23-6/24	2 whistles
2445	LNER(2)	D/SH 64B	LNERL	LNER	W+H	NER+W	S/R	R	NER	after 1924 T only	3L	6/24 to ?	2 whistles
2445	LNER(3)	D/SH 64B	LNERL	LNER	W+H	NER+W	S/R	R	NER	after 1924 T only	3L	? to 1/35	-
(65) 2446	LNER(2)	D/SH 64B	LNERL	LNER	W+H	NER+W	S/R	R	NER	-	3L	3/25 to ?	-
2446	LNER(2)	D/SH 64B	LNERL	LNER	W+H	NER+W	L/R	R	NER	-	3L	?	-
(66) 2447	LNER(2)	D/SH 64B	LNERL	LNER	W+H	NER+W	S/R*	R	NER	-	3L	4/25 to ?	2 whistles
70	?	?	?	?	?	?	?	?	?	1930-32 E+T	3L to screw	?	-
(71) 2452	LNER(2)	D/L	HBRS	HBR	2H+3C	HBR	S/R	R	NER	-	3L	7/24 to ?	-
(72) 2453	LNER(2)	D/L	HBRS	HBR	2H+?C	HBR+W	L/R	R	NER	-	3L	5/24-9/28	Tender coal rails cut back *
2453	LNER(3)	D/sat 64C	LNERS	LNER	2H	NER+W	L/R	R	LNER	?	screw	9/28-1/36	-
(73) 2454	LNER(3)	D/L	HBRL	HBR	W+H+3C	NER+W	L/R	R	NER	-	3L	? to 7/35	Tender coal rails cut back
(74) 2455	LNER(3)	D/SH 64B	LNERL	LNER	2H	NER+W	L/R	R	NER	-	3L	? to 8/35	Tender coal rails cut back *
(75) 2456	LNER(3)	D/L	HBRL	LNER	2H	HBR+W	L/R	R	NER	-	3L	? to 7/37	Tender coal rails cut back
(76) 2457	LNER(3)	D/L	HBRS	LNER	2H	HBR+W	L/R	S	NER	-	3L	? to 7/35	Boiler off 2454 fitted 7/35
2457	LNER(3)	D/L	HBRL	HBR	2H+3C	HBR+W	L/R	S	HBR	-	3L	7/35-8/37	-
77	HBR	D/L	HBRS	HBR	2H+2C	HBR+W	S/R	R	HBR	-	3L	1920	On S.E.C.Rly.
3077	HBR	D/L	HBRS	HBR	2H+2C	HBR+W	S/R	R	HBR	-	3L	1923	Tender coal rails cut back **
2458	LNER(2)	D/SH 64B	LNERL	LNER	W+H	NER+W	L/R	R	NER	-	3L	1/24 to ?	Tender coal rails cut back
2458	LNER(3)	D/SH 64B	LNERL	LNER	2H	NER+W	L/R	R	NER	?	?	? to 11/35	Tender coal rails cut back
(78) 2459	LNER(3)	D/sat 64C	LNERS	LNER	W+H	NER+W	L/R	R	NER	by 1924 E+T	3L	8/29-9/33	Tender coal rails cut back
(79) 2460	LNER(2)	D/L	HBRS	HBR	2H+2C	HBR	L/R	S	NER	-	3L	1931	-
2460	LNER(3)	D/sat 64C	LNERS	LNER	W+H	NERS+W	L/R	S	LNER	-	3L	2/35-11/38	-
(80) 2461	LNER(3)	D/L	HBRL	HBR	2H+3C	HBR+W	L/R	S	NER	-	3L	?/31-12/33	Tender coal rails cut back
(81) 2462	LNER(3)	D/sat 64C	LNERS	LNER	2H	NER+W	L/R	R	LNER	-	Screw	?/34 to ?	2 whistles
(82) 3082	NER	D/L	HBRS	HBR	2H+2C	HBR+W	S/R	S	HBR	E+T	3L	1923	-
(83) 2464	LNER(2)	D/L	HBRL	HBR	2H+3C	HBR+W	S/R	S	NER	-	3L	2/24 to ?	Tender coal rails cut back
2464	LNER(3)	D/L	HBRL	LNER	2H	HBR+W	L/R	S	NER	-	3L	?/34-7/37	Tender coal rails cut back
(84) 2465	LNER(3)	D/L	HBRL	LNER	2H	HBR	L/R	S	NER	-	3L	? to 3/34	-
(85) 3085	NER	D/L	HBRS	HBR	2H+2C	HBR	S/R	R	HBR	E+T	?	?/23-9/24	Coal rails cut back. Ross pop.
86	HBR	D/L	HBRS	HBR	2H	HBR	S/R	R	HBR	-	3L	?/1900	As new
2467	LNER(3)	D/L	HBRS	LNER	2H	HBR+W	L/R	R	NER	-	3L	? to 2/34	-
(87) 2468	LNER(2)	D/L	HBRS	HBR	2H+2C	HBR+W	L/R	R	NER	-	3L	?	Tender coal rails cut back
(88) 2469	LNER(3)	D/L	HBRS	HBR	2H	HBR+W	L/R	R	NER	-	3L	?/35-10/37	Ejector pipe along boiler
(89) 2470	?	?	?	?	?	?	?	?	?	?	?	?	?
(90) 2471	LNER(2)	D/SH 64B	LNERL	LNER	W+H	NER+W	S/R	R	NER	-	3L	5/24 to ?	-
(91) 2472	LNER(2)	D/SH 64B	LNERL	LNER	2H	NERS+W	L/R	R	NER	?	?	?/192?	-
2472	LNER(3)	D/SH 64B	LNERL	LNER	2H	NERS+W	L/R	R	LNER	E+T 1930-32	Screw	8/32-1/36	-
(92) 2473	LNER(2)	D/SH 64B	LNERL	LNER	W+H	NER	L/R	R	NER	-	3L	?/192?	Tender coal rails cut back
2473	LNER(2)	D/SH 64B	LNERL	LNER	W+H	NER	L/R	R	NER	-	3L	5/33	$
(93) 2474	LNER(3)	D/SH 64B	LNERL	LNER	W+H	NER+W	L/R	R	NER	-	3L	?	Tender coal rails cut back
2474	LNER(3)	D/SH 64B	LNERL	LNER	2H	NER+W	L/R	R	NER*	-	3L	1930's	Tender coal rails cut back
94	HBR?	D/L	HBRS	HBR	2H+2C	HBR+W	S/R	R	HBR	-	3L	1922-23	Tender coal rails cut back
2475	LNER(3)	D/sat 64C	LNERS	LNER	2H	NER+W	L/R	R	LNER	-	3L	6/29-5/37	Tender coal rails cut back
95	HBR	D/L	HBRS	HBR	2H+?	HBR	S/R	R	HBR	-	3L	7/1900	Ex-works
2476	LNER(2)	D/SH 64B	LNERL	LNER	W+H	NER+W	S/R	R	NER	-	3L	6/24 to ?	-
2476	LNER(3)	D/SH 64B	LNERL	LNER	2H	NER+W	L/R	R	LNER	-	3L	? to 11/38	-
96	HBR	D/L	HBRS	HBR	2H+2C	HBR	S/R	R	HBR	-	3L	1907	-
3096	LNER(2)	D/L	HBRS	HBR	?	HBR	S/R	R	HBR	-	3L	?/24-11/25	Tender coal rails cut down
2477	LNER(3)	D/SH 64B	LNERL	LNER	2H	NERS	L/R	R	NER	-	3L	8/31-5/37	Chimney windjabber c34

continued/

(A)	(B)	(C)	(D)	(E)	(F)	(G)	(H)	(I)	(J)	(K)	(L)	(M)	(N)
(132) 2513	LNER(2)	D/SH 64B	LNERL	LNER	W+H	NERS+W	S/R	R	NER	-	3L	2/24 to ?	HBR buffers
2513	LNER(3)	D/SH 64B	LNERL	LNER	W+H	NERS+W	L/R	R	LNER	L+T 1930-32	Screw 1930-2	? to 5/37	Group Standard buffers
(133) 2514	LNER(2)	D/SH 64B	LNERL	LNER	W+H	NER+W	L/R	R	NER	-	3L	2/24 to ?	HBR buffers
2514	LNER(3)	D/SH 64B	LNERL	LNER	2H	NER+W	L/R	R	LNER	L+T	Screw	? to 5/37	Group Standard buffers
(134) 2515	LNER(2)	D/sat 64C	LNERS	LNER	2H	NER+C	L/R	R	NER	-	3L	3/28 to ?	HBR buffers
2515	LNER(3)	D/sat 64C	LNERS	LNER	2H	NER+C	L/R	R	LNER	?	Screw	? to 7/35	Group Standard buffers
(135) 3135	NER	D/L	HBRL	HBR	2H+2C	HBR	S/R	R	HBR	-	3L	? to ?/24	Plain tender axleboxes
2516	LNER(2)	D/sat 64C	LNERS	LNER	2H	NER+W	L/R	R	NER	L+T 1930-32	Screw 1930-2	3/28 to ?	HBR buffers
(136) 2517	LNER(2)	D/L	HBR	LNER	2H-W+H	HBR+W	L/R	R	NER	-	3L	?	Iracier tender a/box. HBR bfs
137	HBR*	D/L	HBR	HBR	2H+2C	HBR	S/R	R	HBR	-	3L	1914-22	Plain tender axleboxes
2518	LNER(2)	D/SH 64B	LNERL	LNER	W+H	NER+W	L/R	R	NER	-	3L	8/1933	Iracier tender axleboxes
2518	LNER(3)	D/SH 64B	LNERL	LNER	2H	NER+W	L/R	R	LNER	-	3L	6/36-11/37	Group Standard buffers
(138) 3138	HBR	D/L	HBRL	HBR	2H+3C	HBR+W	S/R	R	HBR	-	3L	1922	Iracier tender axleboxes
2519	LNER(2)	D/L	HBRL	HBR	2H+3C	HBR+W	L/R*	R	NER	-	3L	6/1933	Iracier tender axleboxes
139	HBR	D/L	HBRS	HBR	2H+2C	HBR	S/R	R	HBR	-	3L	pre 1914?	Plain tender axleboxes
2520	LNER(3)	D/L	HBRL	HBR	2H+3C	HBR+W	L/R	R	NER	-	3L	5/33-2/35	Iracier tender axleboxes
(140) 2521	LNER(3)	D/SH 64B	LNERL	LNER	2H	NER+W	L/R	R	LNER	?	Screw	5/35-7/36	Iracier a/box. GS buffers
141	HBR	D/L	HBRS	HBR	2H+?C?	HBR	S/R	R	HBR	-	3L	3/1908	Ex-works. Plain T.a/boxes
2522	LNER(2)	D/L	HBRL	HBR	2H+3C	NER+W	S/R	R	NER	-	3L	5/1927	Plain tender axleboxes
2522	LNER(3)	D/sat 64C	LNERS	LNER	2H	NER+W	L/R	R	LNER	L+T from ?	Screw	6/35-5/37	Iracier a/boxes. GS buffers

Key:

(**A**) Engine number. (**B**) Livery. (* possibly unlined).
(**C**) Boiler. (**D**) Smokebox. L - Long; S - Short.
(**E**) Smokebox door. (**F**) Door fastenings.
(**G**) Chimney. (**H**) Cab. (* from 28/9/25)
(**I**) Cab spectacles. (**J**) Brake standpipes. (*NER - Loco, LNER - Tender)
(**K**) Steam Heat. (**L**) Couplings. (3L - 3-link)
(**M**) Date, if known. (**N**) Additional notes. (* 2 Bell whistles; ** HBR livery, NER number; $ Tender exchanged for Kitson type. Full coal rails and 'pipe' handrails.

2469 (88), seen with Sentinel railcar "Ebor" at Whitby shed on 19th April 1935, remained more-or-less as depicted here until withdrawn in October 1937, when it represented the last domeless Stirling-family locomotive in main-line service. It seems a great pity that Sir Nigel Gresley apparently overlooked its significance and did nothing to get it set aside for preservation, for he had long admired Patrick Stirling's work, and Matthew Stirling had co-sponsored his application for membership of the Association of Railway Locomotive Engineers. *Ron Copeman collection.*

NOTES.

Note B - **Livery**:

In some cases, the North Eastern simply applied their numbers in the 3000 series to cabsides and bufferbeams without undertaking a full repaint: hence, such a number followed by the entry 'HBR' in the livery column. An NER number followed by the entry 'NER' in the livery column indicates a full repaint.

'LNER (1)' indicates the initials 'L & N E R' (sometimes with stops), on the tender side, with the number given painted below. For details of application of LNER numbers to individual engines, refer to the Class Summary at the end of this section.

'LNER (2)' indicates the initials 'L N E R' (without stops), and with number below, applied to tender sides.

'LNER (3)' shows a locomotive carrying the 1928 LNER livery, i.e. company initials on the tender side but locomotive number on the cabside. Needless to say this took some time to work its way through surviving locomotives, in fact those withdrawn up to 1930 or 1931 may well have gone directly to the scrapyard without acquiring this particular style. (Fuller details of H&BR livery styles are given in the relevant Appendix in vol. 2).

Note C - **Boilers**:

'D/L' refers to the H&BR domeless 5ft diameter design, eventually classified as Diagram 64A by the LNER.

'D/SH 64B' refers to the LNER 4ft 9ins diameter, superheated-domed type, to Diagram 64B.

'D/SAT, 64C' refers to the LNER 5ft diameter, saturated-domed type, to Diagram 64C.

Note D - **Smokebox**:

'HBR' refers to the ordinary, 'short' type of H&BR smokebox, with 'waisted' lower sides, being flared out at the base to form a seat on the top of the cylinder casting.

'HBR Long' refers to a development of the above, similar but for an extension of some $8Z \backslash x$ inches forwards. This forward extension was given a flat base which extends out above the hinged cover over the cylinder front ends. It could be that this type was built to the same drawings as were made for No. 60 when fitted with its Lytton superheater in 1912, but it was left to the North Eastern to actually fit them, from August 1922 onwards.

The reason for this would be to allow chimneys to be moved forward, giving better access to the regulator valve.

'LNER Long' refers to the type fitted exclusively to those engines fitted simultaneously with Dgm.64B superheated boilers. Although superficially similar to the HBR Long-type, they were without the waisted lower sections.

'LNER Short' refers to the type fitted exclusively to those engines fitted simultaneously with Dgm. 64C domed, saturated boilers. Again, they were without the lower side waisting, but their fronts were in line with the leading ends of the cylinder casting.

Note E - **Smokebox Doors**:

'HBR' refers to the dished, Stirling type.

'LNER' refers to the stouter, rimmed LNER types. It should be noted that earlier LNER doors were of a smaller diameter than those fitted later. Photographic evidence would tend to indicate that all reboilerings to 64B emerged with smaller doors; by the time 64C reboilerings were being carried out the bigger diameter doors were introduced, and fitted in consequence. Locomotives with H&BR smokeboxes needing new doors before 1927-28 or so would have been given one of smaller diameter; after that time the larger doors were applied. No attempt has been made in the Table to indicate door sizes, since from many angles it is difficult to decide just which door is fitted: handrails and camera angle are apt to obscure the door outlines.

Note F - **Door Fastening**:

'2H' refers to two handles, as under the H&BR and the later LNER period.

'W&H' refers to the North Eastern style of wheel and handle.

'+?C' refers to the fitting of dog clamps by the H&BR from around 1907 onwards: initially two clamps were fitted, but by about 1918 or even earlier this had given way to three. It would appear that all the HBR Long-type smokeboxes had doors with three clamps. Question marks indicate that in some cases clamps can be seen on a photograph but the number is indiscernible, or it cannot be made out if in fact they are fitted at all. No LNER door was given any dog-clamps.

2457 (76), standing by the south side of Springhead's boiler wash-out plant, shows on its bufferbeam that it is still a "Class B (HB)" on 21st June 1931. *H.C.Casserley.*

Note G - **Chimneys**:

'HBR' refers to the plain, cast-iron Stirling chimney.

'NER' refers to one of the various types of chimney fitted by the LNER. These were of NER style; none of the J23's had any of the LNER designs inflicted upon them - especially that example of an aesthetic disaster nicknamed the 'flowerpot' type!

'+W' refers to the fitting of a windjabber, or capucheon.

It should also be noted that domed rebuilds Nos. 2438(57), 2460(79), 2472(91) and 2477(96) were given a shorter type of chimney when given LNER boilers purely as a matter of expediency in Darlington Works. (Photographic evidence would tend to show that No.2513 (132) was also similarly fitted).

Note H - **Cab**:

This section refers solely to the addition of extensions to the cab roofs: 'S/R' referring to the original H&BR Stirling short roof; 'L/R' refers to the extended roof, introduced from September 1925 - No. 2519(138), to September 1929 - No. 2447(66), on all except ten engines.

Note I - **Spectacles**:

This refers to the shape of the two windows (spectacle glasses), in the cab front sheet or spectacle plate (a term which dates back to the 1840's before locomotives were given cabs). 'R' therefore refers to round spectacles, 'S' refers to shaped spectacles, which appear to have been gradually introduced on to the Class B engines from 1914: possibly as a result of the introduction of similarly shaped spectacles on the Class L/LS 0-6-0's. Fitting of such items to the Class B's appeared to be on a random basis, and doubtless the effects of World War I exacerbated that process.

Note J - **Brake Standpipes**:

'HBR' refers to the original brake pipe of medium height, standing above the footplate level on all the Class B engines.

'NER' refers to the North Eastern's favoured system, whereby vacuum pipes were tucked neatly out of the way below the bufferbeams: the snag here being that other pre-Grouping companies used tall standpipes on their locomotives and carriages.....(Although rubberised, vacuum brake hoses are not renowned for their qualities of stretchability, so the art of coupling up a North Eastern engine to a carriage with tall standpipe involved a struggle reminiscent of the unfortunate Laocoon and the serpents...!)

'LNER' refers to the fact that by the 1930's (Darlington having lost much of its autonomy upon the retirement of A.C.Stamer), the North Eastern Section fell into line with the rest of the system, but engines gradually lost their NER type fittings in favour of tall LNER standpipes from December 1928, under the "Unification of Brakes Programme." It is not clear however that H&BR-type fittings which may have survived were directly replaced by the taller pipes: also, the very few photographs of tender rear ends seem to indicate that tenders may have retained standpipes throughout their lives, the NER connections being confined to the locomotives only.

Note K - **Steam Heat**:

A 'dash' in this column indicates that fittings cannot be discerned in the photograph, or that the locomotive concerned was not at that time so fitted. By the end of 1924, the following locomotives are recorded as being fitted with steam heat pipes at both ends: Nos. 2431(50), 2440(59), 2441(60), 2442(61), 2459(78), 2466(85). In addition, Nos.2445(64), 2463(82), 2470(89), 2474(93) and 2476(95) had been fitted with connections at the tender end only. 1930 - 1932 saw Nos. 2438(57), 2451(70), 2471(90), 2472(91), 2513(132), 2516(135) and 2522(141) equipped at both ends, their three link coupling being simultaneously exchanged for screw couplings.

Nos.2471(90) on 13th July 1932, 2472(91) on 15th July 1932 and 2521(140) on 12th August 1932, were equipped with Vincent Raven's mechanical fog-signalling apparatus in 1931, as a result of their considerable usage on the East Coast Main Line. (This equipment had a short life on the locomotives concerned: due to the advent of colour light signals on the main line, the apparatus was abandoned on 30th October 1933).

Note L - **Couplings:** All Class B engines originally had three link couplings since they were primarily intended as goods engines. This did not preclude their use on passenger work, since obviously the carriage screw couplings could be used when undertaking any passenger work. As a result of their increasing use on such work though, various locomotives acquired screw couplings as detailed previously, and eleven received screw couplings and steam-heat connections at both ends - 2438(57) being the first, from July 1929 and 2521(140) being the last, on 22nd August 1932.

Note M - **Dates**:

Where a reference photograph is dated, the single date given represents that engine in a particular condition at that specific time, although naturally that same condition could be representative of a considerably longer period in the life of that engine. Where two dates are given, they represent the earliest and latest dates for an engine's existence in that particular condition.

Note N - **Additional Notes**:

It may be taken that all domed, rebuilt engines had the brake ejector exhaust pipes running along the boiler barrel on the right hand side; a few domeless engines may have acquired this feature also: No.2469(88) being one and 2452(71) being another, at some stage in their later existence. Note that domeless engines (with the exception of No.3085 at Grouping), retained their Ramsbottom safety valves but all domed boilers carried Ross 'Pop' safety valves. These were of the same type on both superheated (64B) and saturated (64C) boilers but appeared to be of different heights, for those on the 64B boilers were bolted onto a pad which the seat casing covered whereas those on the 64C type were mounted directly atop of the firebox shell plate; consequently the fitted cover partly concealed the safety valves in this instance.

The Kitson 1908-built engines all retained round cab spectacles and full coal rails, but it is evident that there was a programme of fitting new 'Iracier' axleboxes to some of these engines even under the H&BR, and at least half acquired Group Standard buffers at some stage, easily identified by the stepped stock and square flange.

Whistles under the H&BR were fitted singly to each locomotive, but the NER twin whistle arrangement appeared on the domed rebuilds. The domeless engines kept a single whistle, but in some instances the H&BR bell-type whistle was exchanged for an NER organ-pipe variety.

The steps between the leading and driving wheels were fitted to engines as they passed through Darlington Works from July 1923 onwards, with No.3064(2445) being the first. Nos.2430/1/2/4/42(49,50/1/3/61) never received these steps. Although Springhead gave general repairs to Nos.3051D(2432) dated 30th Nov. 1923, 2464(83) 29th Feb.1924, 3052(2433) March 1924, 2455 and 2456(74/5) in April 1924, they did not fit steps. Consequently, these engines had to wait until their first Darlington repair, although the only attention they gave No.2432 was to scrap it - hence the lack of steps on this engine.

J23/2 No. 2472 (91), at York on 28th August 1932. The addition of screw couplings and Group Standard buffers should be noted.

J23/3 No.2453 (72), as rebuilt in September 1928 with 5ft 0in diameter saturated boiler, is seen here approaching Levisham on the Whitby-Pickering line; now better known as the North Yorkshire Moors Railway. *Ron Copeman collection.*

An example of a tender exchange: 2473 (92), was a Yorkshire Engine Co. locomotive built in 1900, hence it has cab handrails fitted in stanchions, whereas its tender can be seen to have bent pipe handrails, as used by Kitson & Co. This photograph was taken on 20th May 1933 near Cottingham South signal-box, on the outskirts of Hull. 2473 was working the York-Hull pick-up, although still (nominally at any rate), shedded at Springhead.

Summary: Class B 0-6-0 Tender Locomotives. LNER Class J23.

HBR No.	Works No.	Delivered	To Class B	NER No.	LNER No.	Reboilered	Withdrawn	Notes
49	3138	3/1889	5/1905	3049	2430	-	2/1926	
50	3139	3/1889	8/1906	3050	2431	-	4/1925	
51	3140	3/1889	9/1906	3051	2432	-	2/1926	
52	3141	3/1889	2/1907	3052	2433	To J23/2 - 3/1925	9/1928	
53	3142	3/1889	6/1907	3053	2434		4/1925	
54	3143	4/1889	5/1906	3054	2435	-	1/1929	
55	3144	4/1889	11/1906	3055	2436	-	9/1928	
56	3145	4/1889	9/1907	3056	2437	-	9/1926	
57	3504	8/1892	6/1910	3057	2438	To J23/2 - 9/1926	6/1933	
58	3505	8/1892	10/1908	3058	2439	To J23/3 - 8/1929	12/1933	
59	3506	8/1892	2/1908	3059	2440	To J23/2 - 6/1926	6/1933	
60	3507	9/1892	7/1908	3060	2441	To J23/2 - 10/1925	5/1937	
61	3508	9/1892	12/1907	3061	2442	-	8/1926	
62	3509	9/1892	2/1909	3062	2443	-	8/1926	
63	1351	6/1892	11/1908	3063	2444	To J23/3 - 3/1928	6/1936	
64	1352	6/1892	12/1907	3064	2445	To J23/2 - 7/1923	1/1935	
65	1353	7/1892	6/1908	3065	2446	To J23/2 - 3/1925	3/1934	
66	1354	7/1892	4/1909	3066	2447	To J23/2 - 4/1925	1/1934	
70	547	9/1897	8/1912	3070	2451	To J23/3 - 8/1929	7/1933	
71*	548	9/1897	2/1912	3071	2452	To J23/3 - 12/1931	5/1937	
72	549	10/1897	8/1913	3072	2453	To J23/3 - 9/1928	1/1936	
73*	550	11/1897	3/1912	3073	2454	To J23/3 - 7/1935	7/1937	
74*	551	11/1897	10/1911	3074	2455	To J23/2 - 4/1924	8/1935	
75*	552	12/1897	4/1914	3075	2456	-	7/1937	
76	560	12/1898	10/1916	3076	2457	-	5/1937	
77*	561	12/1898	10/1914	3077	2458	To J23/2 - 1/1924	11/1935	
78	562	12/1898	10/1914	3078	2459	To J23/3 - 8/1929	9/1933	
79*	3786	10/1898	New	3079	2460	To J23/3 - 2/1935	11/1938	(1)
80	3787	10/1898	New	3080	2461	-	12/1933	(1)
81	3788	10/1898	New	3081	2462	To J23/3 - 3/1932	7/1937	(1)
82*	3789	10/1898	New	3082	2463	-	3/1928	(1)
83	3790	11/1898	New	3083	2464	-	5/1937	(1)
84	3791	12/1898	New	3084	2465	-	3/1934	(1)
85	3912	3/1900	New	3085	2466	-	11/1932	(2)
86	3913	3/1900	New	3086	2467	-	2/1934	(2)
87*	3914	4/1900	New	3087	2468	-	12/1933	(2)
88*	3915	4/1900	New	3088	2469	-	10/1937	(2)
89	3916	4/1900	New	3089	2470	To J23/2 - 7/1923	2/1934	(2)
90	3917	4/1900	New	3090	2471	To J23/2 - 7/1923	6/1934	(2)
91*	604	5/1900	New	3091	2472	To J23/2 - 3/1924	1/1936	(3)
92*	605	6/1900	New	3092	2473	To J23/2 - 2/1925	2/1933	(3)
93*	606	6/1900	New	3093	2474	To J23/2 - 7/1923	7/1937	(3)
94*	607	6/1900	New	3094	2475	To J23/3 - 6/1929	5/1937	(3)
95*	608	7/1900	New	3095	2476	To J23/2 - 10/1923	11/1938	(3)
96	609	8/1900	New	3096	2477	To J23/2 - 12/1925	5/1937	(3)
132	4555	2/1908	New	3132	2513	To J23/2 - 2/1924	5/1937	(4)
133	4556	3/1908	New	3133	2514	To J23/2 - 10/1923	5/1937	(4)
134	4557	3/1908	New	3134	2515	To J23/3 - 3/1928	7/1935	(4)
135	4558	3/1908	New	3135	2516	To J23/3 - 3/1928	7/1935	(4)
136	4559	3/1908	New	3136	2517	-	7/1937	(4)
137	4560	3/1908	New	3137	2518	To J23/2 - 10/1924	11/1937	(4)
138	4561	3/1908	New	3138	2519	-	6/1935	(4)
139	4562	3/1908	New	3139	2520	-	2/1935	(4)
140	4563	3/1908	New	3140	2521	To J23/2 - 11/1925	7/1936	(4)
141	4564	3/1908	New	3141	2522	To J23/3 - 3/1928	5/1937	(4)

Notes:

* Loaned to SE&CR during WWI. (1) Built Kitson & Co. at £2,697 each. Boilers 4' 9" diameter.
(2) Built Kitson & Co. at £3,020 each. (3) Built Yorkshire Engine Co. at £2,995 each. (4) Built Kitson & Co. at £3,220 each.

An unusual view of J23/2 No.2477 (96), in Darlington works' yard on 15th August 1931. It has just been newly outshopped after repairs (its domed boiler was fitted in December 1925), and Darlington's painters, working alfresco to put the finishing touches to it, take advantage of the summer sun. Notice that the front bufferbeam indicates it is a "Class J23 (HB)" - a sign of the declining influence of Darlington in LNER locomotive affairs. *W.B.Yeadon collection.*

2477 and friends in Whitby shed yard on 6th August 1934. All three engines are ex-H&B stock - 2477 is a J23/2; 2469 (85) and 2460 (79) remain as J23 engines, being domeless. *J.Hooper collection.*

Class B Dimensions.

Cylinders: 2, inside. 18" x 26".
Motion: Stephenson Link; slide valves between cylinders.
Boiler: Domeless.
Max. diameter outside: 5' 0".
Barrel length: 10' 0".
Firebox length outside: 5' 6".
Pitch: 7' 8".
Heating surface:
  Firebox 107 sq.ft.
  Tubes 241 @ 1³/₄" dia. - 1,139 sq.ft.*
      246 @ 1³/₄" dia. - 1,163 sq.ft.**
  Total 1,246 sq.ft.* 1.270 sq.ft.**
Grate area: 16.25 sq.ft. initially 15.9 sq.ft.*
Ratio of grate area to heating surface: 1 to 78.36*. 1 to 79.87**
Boiler pressure: 175 lb/sq.in. (*&**)
Wheel diameter: 5' 0" engine. 3' 9" tender.
Wheelbase:
  Engine 7' 3" + 8' 3" = 15' 6".
  Tender 6' 0" + 6' 0" = 12' 0".
Length over buffers: 48' 8¹/₈".
Weights:
  Engine 42tons 8cwt.
  Tender 35tons 19cwt.
  Total 78tons 7cwt (Tender for Nos. 132-141 = 38tons 18cwt).
Height to top of chimney: 13' 2".
Tractive effort @ 85% of boiler pressure: 20,877 lb. (*&**).
Ratio of blast nozzle to cylinder diameter: 1 to 3.78.
Tender water capacity: 3,000 gallons. (3,300 gallons on Nos. 132-141 only).
Tender coal capacity: 6tons.
(* dimensions applicable at December 1922; ** dimensions applicable by 1933, to domeless Diagram 64A boilers, by which time the use of five tubes for 'staying' purposes had been discontinued).

Boilers for Nos.79-84, built Kitsons, 1898.
Boiler: Domeless.
Max. outside diameter: 4' 9".
Pitch: not known but probably 7' 6¹/₂".
Heating surface:
  Firebox 100 sq.ft.
  Tubes ? @ 1³/₄" dia. - 900 sq.ft.
  Total 1,000 sq.ft.
Grate area: 16.25 sq.ft.
Boiler pressure: 150 lb/sq.in.
Tractive effort @ 85% boiler pressure: 17,901 lb.

Boilers for Nos.85-90, built Kitsons, 1900.
Boiler: Domeless.
Max. outside diameter: 5' 0"
Pitch: 7' 8".
Heating surface:
  Firebox 100 sq.ft.
  Tubes 207 @ 1³/₄" dia. - 988.5 sq.ft.
  Total 1,088.5 sq.ft.
Grate area: 16.25 sq.ft.
Boiler pressure: 170 lb/sq.in.
Tractive effort @ 85% boiler pressure: 20,288 lb.
Weight in full working order: 42 tons 6 cwt (engine only).
The Yorkshire Engine Co. give the following figures for

Nos.91-96. built in 1900.
Heating surface:
  Firebox 95 sq.ft.
  Tubes 209 @ 1³/₄" dia. - 989 sq.ft.
  Total 1,084 sq.ft.

Boilers introduced 1905 (most likely for rebuilding Class C engines).
Boiler: Domeless.
Max. outside diameter: 5' 0".
Pitch: 7' 8".
Heating surface:
  Firebox 108 sq.ft.
  Tubes 245 @ 1³/₄" dia. - 1,160 sq.ft.
  Total 1,268 sq.ft.
Grate area: 16.25 sq.ft.
Boiler pressure: 170 lb/sq.in.

Boilers to Diagram 64B introduced 1923.
Boiler: Domed, superheated.
Max. outside diameter: 4' 9".
Pitch: 7' 6¹/₂"
Heating surface:
  Firebox 105 sq.ft.
  Tubes: 126 @ 1³/₄" dia.*- 596.9 sq.ft.
      131 @ 1³/₄" dia.**- 619.5 sq.ft**.
  Flues 18 @ 5¹/₄" dia.- 255.8 sq.ft.
  Boiler H.S. total 956.7 sq.ft.*; 976.1 sq.ft**.
  Elements 18 @ 1³/₃₂" dia.- 173.6 sq.ft.
  Total 1,131.3 sq.ft*; 1,147.8 sq.ft**.
Grate area: 15.37 sq.ft.
(* dimensions applicable at December 1923; ** dimensions applicable by 1933, following discontinuance of the use of boiler stay-tubes.)

Boilers to Diagram 64C, introduced 1928.
Boiler: Domed, saturated.
Max. diameter outside: 5' 0".
Pitch: 7' 6¹/₂".
Heating surface:
  Firebox 108 sq.ft.
  Tubes: 227 @ 1³/₄" dia.* - 1,075.75 sq.ft.*.
      234 @ 1³/₄" dia.** - 1,109 sq.ft.**.
  Total 1,183.75 sq.ft.*; 1,217 sq.ft**.
Grate area: 16 sq.ft.
(* dimensions applicable at December 1928; ** dimensions applicable by 1933, following discontinuance of the use of boiler stay-tubes.)

(opposite) **The usefulness of the H&BR 0-6-0's is underlined by this photograph of Hornsea town station in the 1930's, for all three engines visible were once the property of the H&BR. That on the left may be of the L/LS family (LNER Class J28); the one on the turntable was originally a Class B of the Kitson 1908 delivery. The engine on the headshunt is J23/3 2475 (94), and had been rebuilt in June 1929.** *T.E.Rounthwaite.*

One of the Kitson 1908-built engines as rebuilt to Class J23/2, No.2514 (133), stands at Springhead. Despite the cab roof extension, its crew have rigged up a wagon-sheet to provide even more protection. *Laurie Ward*.

(centre) Another engine to retain its H&BR appearance relatively intact was 2520 (139), seen at Springhead on 6th May 1933 with its driver (presumably), attending to the coupling-rod bearing. Note the bike-clips at the leg-bottoms of his overall trousers; not just an odd quirk or sartorial oversight, but a characteristic feature of Hull's footplatemen during the steam-age. They prevented coal-dust working its way up the legs and making them filthy - an important consideration in those days when many homes had no bath, or even hot water on tap.

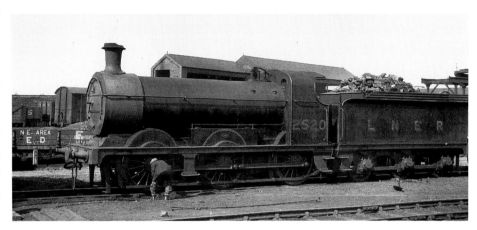

2518 (137) ambles along the H&BR main line near Barmby Moor on 27th June 1936 with a train of mostly empty mineral wagons. On this level stretch, the fireman can be seen taking things easy and admiring the scenery. *A.G.Ellis.*

The last Class B built was No.141, seen here as J23/3 No.2522 - although its bufferbeam still proclaims it to be a "Class B (HB)". *Ron Copeman collection.*

CLASS G2 0-6-0 SIDE TANKS. (LNER CLASS J80). Introduced 1892.

Three years after the introduction of Matthew Stirling's first design (which as we have already seen, was destined to become the largest H&BR class), came his second design - this time though, the initial delivery of the three engines 67, 68 and 69 would be fated to remain the smallest class on the H&BR.

This was not the only claim to individuality by these engines: they were the only locomotives constructed for the H&BR by Robert Stephenson & Company, of Forth Street, Newcastle upon Tyne - the oldest firm of locomotive builders in the World, established 1823, as their advertising liked to point out. (Robert Stephenson & Co. later moved to a more spacious site at Darlington, with considerably better equipment than the six blacksmith's forges and a shear-legs, which was virtually all that George and Robert Stephenson, Edward Pease and Michael Longridge had started with. Despite the move to Darlington the firm never forgot its roots, for its telegraphic address of, "Rocket, Darlington", reminded potential customers throughout its final years of its origins back in the heady, pioneering days of steam locomotion).

The G2 Class (as they were by 1908, any earlier and differing designation having disappeared into the mists of time), were unusual for 0-6-0 tank engines in having wheels of five feet in diameter. Normally such engines had wheel diameters ranging from around 4ft 1ins to 4ft 7ins; the LNER acquired no other 5ft coupled tank engines apart from a handful of geriatric ex-Great Central Sacré locomotives and two Wheatley North British Railway engines of similar vintage. Both these groups, incidentally, were saddle tanks; Matthew Stirling's trio were further distinguished by having side tanks.

This feature was possibly slightly unexpected in view of the fact that all his father's shunting locomotives with which Matthew Stirling had dealt with were invariably saddle tanks. By not making use of this feature Matthew was following the example set by his Uncle James, for the latter had introduced eight Class R side tanks on the South Eastern Rly between June 1888 and April 1889. These engines by a curious coincidence also had large coupled wheels of 5ft 2ins diameter, which dimension they had in common with his earlier Class O tender engines. The two South Eastern classes also had much more in common - boilers, cylinders, valve-gear and wheelbase for example - and since the O's had appeared in 1878, the R's could be

regarded as a development of that type. It is evident that James Stirling had produced his new shunting engine with the minimum of extra design work, and herein may lay the reasoning behind Matthew Stirling's Class G2 engines.

At the Hull, Barnsley & West Riding Junction Railway & Dock Company's Annual General Meeting of 1892, Company Chairman Lieutenant Colonel Gerard Smith was able to report that they had enjoyed a very satisfactory year's trading. From the tone of his report one feels that this was as unexpected as it was welcome; Colonel Smith could report that as a result of this windfall, they had been able to add ten six-coupled tender engines and three tank engines to stock (although four of the tender engines had been ordered from Vulcan Foundry the year before). Thus after having met the usual fixed charges and working expenses, and even declaring a small dividend, the balance was distributed amongst the railway's various departments. The rolling stock and workshops department probably got the lion's share, since 1892 saw plans drawn up for the provision of a wagon works, running shed extension, additional locomotive workshops and offices. Much of this work was deferred for some years, but the boiler and engine houses were built. (One wonders how the heavy machinery installed at Springhead the year before was powered in the meantime - doubtless various contrivances decidedly Heath Robinsonian in nature were rigged up!)

Matthew Stirling may well have been allocated a larger sum than he anticipated for spending on more locomotives, the types ordered being left to him to decide; but as with many such allocations of funds the catch may have been that the sum in question had to be spent by the end of the financial year, hence a deadline being imposed on the time available for design work and tendering processes.

More H&B 0-6-0 goods engines were easily taken care of on a "repeat prescription" basis, but few late Victorian locomotive engineers with any modicum of self-respect would condescend to re-order any design originated by a predecessor! Thus it followed that Matthew Stirling would probably have been mortified by any suggestion that he should add further engines to William Kirtley's G1 design no matter how excellent they may have been, (although the Rhondda & Swansea Bay Railway were

G2 0-6-0T No.68 at Springhead. Essentially a tank engine version of Class C, having wheel diameters, cylinders, valve-gear, boiler and fittings in common. The mainframes also had more in common with Class C than the later G3 class. The deep footplating angle-iron should be noted, also the safety-chains on the bufferbeams in addition to three-link couplings. The tank tops followed Kirtley's G1 Class engines in style, having rounded outer top edges and the filler half-way along. H&BSF.

No.69 in pristine condition at Springhead. Further points to note are the buffers with parallel stocks - most if not all of Matthew Stirling's engines had tapered stocks. The safety-chains have either been hung up out of the way or removed. *Hull Museums collection.*

glad enough to order five virtually identical engines from Beyer Peacock in 1885. These were R&SBRly Nos.1, 3, 5 - 7, which in due course became Great Western Railway Nos.799, 801, 805 and 806.)

So having foresworn the easy way out, Stirling was probably left with the necessity of working up a new design in double - quick time, hence the desirability of introducing as few modifications as possible from the existing 0-6-0 tender engine drawings. It therefore followed that the G2's had wheelbases, wheel diameters, boilers, cylinders and valve gear in common with their Class C predecessors; original design work being confined to extension of the frames for some five feet behind the rear axle to accommodate a bunker, plus cab and side tanks. Indeed, for the latter he may well have used Kirtley's - or rather Beyer, Peacock's - drawings, since the G1's and G2's tanks carried the same 850 gallons of water and featured round tops to their outer edges!

In short therefore, although nominally a tiny, non-standard class of only three engines, the G2's incorporated a mass of parts which could be regarded as standard - and that could account for their lengthy existence under the LNER. (The vexed question of non-standard locomotives incorporating many standard parts as opposed to standard types which, through development came

to incorporate many redesigned items which were not interchangeable with those on earlier engines, was never really resolved on Britain's railways. One locomotive engineer aptly expressed the down-side of "standardisation" when referring to the splendid LMS "Black Five" 4-6-0's: "A standard class of 842 individual locomotives!").

If Matthew Stirling had indeed followed his uncle's lead in deriving a tank engine from a tender engine, his H&BR design presented a considerably different appearance from its South Eastern forebears. The latter had their safety valves in James Stirling's preferred position on the boiler back ring rather than over the firebox, and also sported the wide, smokebox wing-plates more usually associated with engines of the Scottish companies. James Stirling had also fitted wide, flared-out copings around the tops of tanks and bunkers; Patrick Stirling had fitted flat-topped tanks with beaded upper edges on the outsides for the Great Northern 0-4-4 tanks built to his designs, but as we have already noted Matthew Stirling eschewed both these influences.

One item in which his father's latest GNR practices may have influenced Stirling Junior was, paradoxically, in the provision of a decent cab, for the Autumn of 1891 saw Patrick Stirling equip his latest saddle tank engines with full cabs rather than continuing with the half-cab style he had used from 1878. Those same GN half-cabs also sported flared-out bunker tops not unlike those on the South Eastern tanks, but in contrast to the adequate cover provided by Patrick Stirling's half-cabs (at least when going forwards!), the SER engines were provided with a canopy so flimsy that it resembled a parasol rather than anything solid enough to be worthy of bolting to a steam locomotive! In due course though, James Stirling replaced these adornments with "proper" cabs which bore considerable resemblance to those of his nephew "Up North", for after all, even the "Sunny South" has its off-days.

No.68 seen as "L.& N.E.R." Class J80 No.2449 after rebuilding at Springhead with the old North Eastern Railway "901" Class boiler in May 1923; the H&BR taper-stock buffers should also be noted. This photograph was taken at Alexandra Dock circa 1926. *Laurie Ward.*

Some fourteen years earlier in early February 1909, No.68 had the breakdown crew busy near Locomotive Junction. One of the more playful habits of Stirling-type push-pull regulators was a tendency to ease themselves open after having been closed; apt to be slightly disconcerting when coming to a halt at a station, and occasionally very painful if they blew open suddenly! The G2 had been left in Springhead shed while raising steam, but nobody noticed that it had been left in forward gear. Consequently, with the rise in steam pressure the regulator forced itself open and the engine ran away of its own accord. However, 68's attempt to reallocate itself to Cudworth inevitably ended at the Lodge Lane overbridge. New brickwork put in after Class B No.95 had tumbled down the embankment three years earlier, after over-shooting signals, can be seen to have suffered in its turn; various items such as the smokebox door, ashpan, chimney and coupling-rods have been removed to make it easier to recover the engine. A watchman's hut has been set up, in case of further removal of parts by souvenir-hunters or itinerant scrap-metal collectors. The engine can be seen to retain its safety-chains, but may have lost its vacuum brake equipment. Springhead works can be made out in the right distance - hidden behind the workshops buildings was Matthew Stirling's office, where the hapless individuals implicated in No.68's escapade were given a roasting by "The Boss" soon after....! *J.M.Proud.*

In common with the Kirtleys and earlier batches of Class C and B 0-6-0's (as well as the GN and SER locomotives), Matthew Stirling's G2's had plain, unfluted coupling rods, and like all those engines (except for the earliest batches of GNR saddle tanks), they were also fitted with vacuum brake equipment.

This feature enabled them to work passenger trains and thanks to their large wheels, to be able to do so at a good turn of speed. Consequently, although initially put to work on coal traffic along the branches from Monckton and Monk Bretton collieries, they played a part in working light passenger trains and excursions, being invariably called upon each October to haul

special trains to Hull Fair. In view of this addition to the normal repertoire of tank engines, it seems that the H&B missed an opportunity of not trying to utilise at least one G2 at the east end of the line on what could be termed "outer suburban" work; even if possible demand was limited, an attempt to stimulate it may have brought in some welcome passenger receipts.

By 1922 the chance to do this had been lost for all three had been converted to steam brakes only, so upon taking over the North Eastern found all three on their familiar job of shunting coal-wagons, albeit at the east end of the H&BR in the yards at Springhead and on Alexandra Dock.

The North Eastern also found that these three engines were very well-worn. Their survey revealed that all three apparently still retained their original crank axles, although new cylinders had been fitted to No. 67 in April 1913 and No. 69 in June 1912. Boilers had been retubed in March 1920 (67), November 1916 (68) and January 1922 (69); the latter engine receiving a new firebox at the same time. (The other two had also been given new inner fireboxes but so far back in the dim and distant past that the NER's inspectors didn't bother to make a note!). Suffice to say that the boiler barrels were the original ones, and thirty years old! Only those on the Kirtley G1's and the six little Class K shunters were older, and the NER lost no time in disposing of those classes; consequently reboilering the three G2's was a matter of considerable urgency.

As a stop-gap measure in May 1923 No. 3068 (as it was by then), was fitted at Springhead with a second-hand boiler, six years old, from an old Fletcher North Eastern Railway "901" Class 2-4-0 express engine. This boiler not surprisingly was domed, and had a barrel three inches longer than the original H&BR type together with a smaller grate area. (Clearances between inside big-ends on back centres and firebox throat-plates were apt to be somewhat minimal at times, so at least the "901" boiler offered a substantial improvement in that area at least!). The boiler barrel was evidently a much closer fit at the front end, for 3068 retained its original smokebox and chimney. Backhead injectors had to be changed though, since the clack valves on "901" boilers were fitted to the sides of the boiler barrel, thus entailing an amount of additional replumbing also. This boiler carried a pressure of 160 lb/sq.inch, an increase of 10 lb over the originals, thus providing an increase in nominal tractive effort also. The old "901" boiler served 3068 until withdrawal from Springhead in July 1931 as LNER No.2449, but survived as spare for another three years before being fitted to N12 No.2487 (ex-H&BR Class F2 No.106), for another four years' service, going for scrap along with that engine.

Meanwhile, Darlington Works had been busily drawing up a new domed boiler design to the same overall dimensions as the originals, albeit with alterations to the heating surfaces and a slight reduction in grate area. These boilers were fitted to the two other G2's (by now classified as LNER J80), in 1924; the boilers themselves were classified as Diagram 71B in 1928.

These boilers were also interchangeable with classes J75, N12 and N13 (H&BR classes G3, F2 and F3), and in demonstration of this fact the boiler off No. 2450 (69) was re-used on two J75's after its withdrawal. That from No.2448 (67) went on to serve in a stationary capacity in the LNER's Southern Area until April 1947, for 2448 had bade farewell to Hull in November 1925, having been transferred to Immingham until withdrawal in September 1930.

The last of the trio, 2450 (69), was withdrawn from Springhead shed in August 1931, having served the LNER for 8½ years.

Even though the class was only three strong, detail differences had appeared, especially under the LNER. These involved the removal of re-railing jacks in 1924, although 2449 (68) kept its jack until its visit to Darlington Works in April 1927. That visit saw it acquire an LNER smokebox door, and its "901" Class boiler (classified as Diagram 69 by the LNER in 1928), was graced with a North Eastern-style, brass trumpet-shaped cover around the previously open Ramsbottom safety-valves, and two NER whistles replaced its single H&BR type. Under the H&BR, No.68 lost its original buffers with parallel stocks in exchange for the more usual Stirling-type with taper stocks and slightly smaller heads. The H&BR also plated behind the three bunker coal rails.

Alterations to the whistles, removal of jacks and fitting of LNER smokebox doors took place in 1924 on No. 2448 (67) and 2450 (69), both of which acquired Ross "Pop" safety-valves with their new Diagram 71B boilers. All three retained their Stirling H&BR chimneys until withdrawal.

The three engines worked faithfully for a total of 105 years and 11 months, and must have paid for themselves many times over. The H&BR's outlay of £5,700 for all three was certainly money well spent.

Summary: Class G2 0-6-0 Side Tank. LNER Class J80.

H&BR No.	Works No.	Delivered	NER No.	LNER No.	Reboilered	Withdrawn
67	2781	August 1892	3067	2448	Dgm.71B/May 1924	September 1930
68	2782	August 1892	3068	2449	Dgm.69/May 1923	July 1931
69	2783	September 1892	3069	2450	Dgm.71B/May 1924	August 1931

Note: When new each engine had cost £1,900.

Class G2 Dimensions.

Cylinders: 2, inside. 18" x 26".
Motion: Stephenson Link; slide valves between cylinders.
Boiler: Domeless.
Max. diameter outside: 4' 3".
Barrel length: 10' 0".
Firebox length outside: 5' 6".
Pitch: 7' 2".
Heating surface:
  Firebox 100 sq.ft.
  Tubes 198 @ 1¾" dia. - 950 sq.ft.
  Total 1,050 sq.ft.
Grate area: 16.25 sq.ft.
Ratio of grate area to heating surface: 1 to 64.61.
Boiler pressure: 150 lb/sq.in.
Wheel diameter: 5' 0".
Wheelbase: 7' 3" + 8' 3" = 15' 6".
Length over buffers: 31' 7".
Weights:
13tons 4cwt + 15tons 5cwt + 17tons 6cwt = 45tons 15cwt.
Height to top of chimney: 12' 10⅝".
Tractive effort @ 85% of boiler pressure: 17,901 lb.
Ratio of blast nozzle to cylinder diameter: 1 to 3.789.
Tank water capacity: 850 gallons.
Bunker coal capacity: 2tons (LNER Diagrams give bunker capacity of 3¼ tons, although this figure seems too high).

The above dimensions apply to Class G2 at December 1922, when fitted with Diagram 71A type, domeless H&BR boilers. When new, figures were:-

Heating surface:
  Firebox 96 sq.ft.
  Tubes (number unknown) - 957 sq.ft.
  Total 1,053 sq.ft.
Grate area: 16 sq.ft.

Dimensions for No.3068 with Class "901" boiler (Diagram 69).
Boiler: Domed.
Max. outside diameter: 4' 3"
Barrel length: 10' 3".
Firebox length outside: 5' 6".
Heating surface:
  Firebox 98 sq.ft.
  Tubes 205 @ 1¾" - 995 sq.ft.
  Total 1,093 sq.ft.
Grate area: 15.16 sq.ft.
Ratio of grate area to heating surface: 1 to 72.09.
Boiler pressure: 160 lb/sq.in.
Tractive effort @ 85% boiler pressure: 19,094 lb.
(This boiler had been built in December 1916 and had only worked on NER. No.352 from February 1917 to June 1922)

Dimensions for Nos.2448 and 2450 with Diagram 71B Boilers.
Boiler: Domed.
Heating surface:
  Firebox 99 sq.ft.
  Tubes 205 @ 1¾" dia. - 972 sq.ft.
  Total 1,071 sq.ft.
Grate area: 15.5 sq.ft.
Ratio of grate area to heating surface: 1 to 69.09.
Boiler pressure: 175 lb/sq.in.
Tractive effort @ 85% of boiler pressure: 20,877 lb.

A pleasing study of 2450 (69) standing in the early afternoon sunlight at the south-east corner of Springhead shed. Additional guard-rails can be seen fitted over the cab rear spectacles and the hole in the bufferbeam marks where the safety-chains were fitted. The big 5ft 0in wheels can be seen to have necessitated a flat coupling-rod splasher at the back-end of the tank, and the wheel splasher protruding half-way across the cab doorway forms a stumbling-block for the unwary. *Ron Copeman coll.*

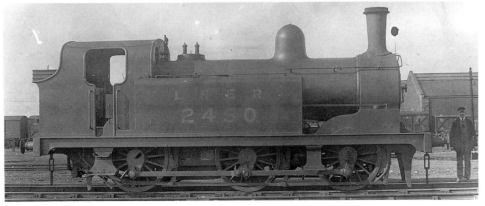

Luckily for intending modelmakers, the other side of 2450 (69) was also photographed! The North Eastern twin-whistles can be made out, and all three J80's retained their H&BR chimneys throughout their lives. Springhead's six-road wagon repair shops can be seen in the right background. *Ron Copeman collection.*

Posing in front of Springhead's water-softening plant, in 1931, 2491 (110) still retains its vacuum brake equipment, although the ejector exhaust-pipe along the boiler, train-pipe below the footplate angle and NER-type below-bufferbeam hose show that it has been completely re-plumbed since being acquired by the LNER. Note also the cab roof ventilator. *Locofotos.*

CLASS F2 0-6-2 RADIAL TANKS. (LNER CLASS N12).
Introduced 1901.

By 1900, the H&BR had achieved a position of stability and was looking forward to further steady growth from that hard-won basis. Coal traffic was increasing due to the widening of the H&B's catchment area with the opening of the Denaby Branch, and more collieries were being sunk within range of the H&B. Furthermore, the Wath-on-Dearne Branch was due to open in 1902, so the provision of further suitable motive power would be essential.

In the midsummer of 1901 the H&BR had 101 locomotives in its stock lists; 65 of these were six-coupled goods and mineral engines. Ten further engines were the Kirtley 2-4-0's, suitable only for passenger and express goods workings such as fish and perishables; the remaining twenty-six locomotives were all tank engines. Of these, six were Alexandra Dock's dinky little shunters, and twelve more were the effective, albeit moderately - sized Kirtley G1's (and furthermore getting rather long in the tooth by 1901). The three Stirling G2's were fully occupied around the Barnsley area, likewise the new F1 0-6-2's were similarly giving their full and undivided attention to the Denaby Branch, so clearly there was no spare locomotive capacity on the H&BR particularly when it is borne in mind that a proportion of the locomotive roster was out of service under repair at any one time.

Construction of the Wath Branch had commenced in late July 1899, construction to take two years: the need for future additional locomotives being established, Stirling therefore had a reasonable amount of time in which to work up the outline for a new design.

The Wath Branch, although only 8¾ miles long, was heavily graded. Climbing out of Wath at around 1 in 115 for two miles through Hickleton and Thurnscoe, it then descended to Moorhouse and South Elmsall at 1 in 120, with a final two mile climb at 1 in 132 and 1 in 300 to Wrangbrook Junction and a meeting with the Denaby Branch and the H&BR main line, whence trains would continue their eastward progression behind tender locomotives.

Since the Wath Branch engines would be working for a full shift some seven or eight miles out along the main line from their shed at Cudworth, then a more plentiful coal supply than the meagre two tons capacity of the G2's was required. This in turn meant a longer back-end, necessitating a pair of carrying wheels under the

rear footplate. The main decision here was whether to employ a radial-arm type pony truck, or use a radial axle arrangement instead. Stirling opted for the latter course, which was to give every satisfaction in service.

Probably hindsight caused him to move away from the 5ft diameter wheels of the G2's in favour of 4ft 6in wheels as on the Kirtley G1 engines. (This latter figure appearing on the F2's may have owed something to the constraints of standardisation and the ordering and storing of spare tyres: this figure was henceforth standardised by Stirling for all future tank locomotive construction). The use of smaller diameter wheels meant an amount of redesigning, although the use of as many of the well-proven, six-coupled drawings as possible is evident, for the F2's had valve-gear, cylinders, coupled wheelbase and boilers in common with classes C and G2.

That there would be a need for additional shunting engines also was recognised, for on 15th November 1900 the H&BR Board authorised Stirling to proceed with the ordering of six "ordinary shunting tank engines" and fourteen "heavier tank engines," Kitson & Co. of Leeds being successful in being awarded the contract for the "heavier tank engines" whilst Yorkshire Engine Company won that appertaining to the six shunters - *(see Class G3)*.

With Class F1 we have already seen that two months after the new tank engines were authorised, Kitson's had contacted the H&B Board regarding the availability of these surplus LD&ECR engines; as a consequence of their acquisition the order for the new F2 tank engines was reduced to nine. (One is tempted to reflect that since Matthew Stirling must have had the last word as to the suitability of the F1's, his strong spirit of self-sufficient independence was overcome by his canny Scottish nature when presented with a bargain: by purchasing the F1's the H&BR saved £375 in total, each F1 being priced at £2,760 as compared with the F2's at £2,835 each).

To what extent Kitson & Co. were allowed to work in their own "standard" components is difficult to determine for the F2's

Driver Harry Chester photographed in the middle of attending to the lubrication of 109 at Kirk Smeaton station in 1905. The smaller splashers resulting from the use of 4ft 6in diameter wheels are clearly seen, in comparison to the G2 0-6-0 tanks; the fluted coupling-rods, safety-chains and vacuum gear should be noted also. Furthermore, the width over cab and tanks was the same; on all other H&BR six-coupled tank engines the tanks were wider than the cab. *Derek Vine/Hull & Barnsley Stock Fund.*

The LNER took drastic measures with 3104, fitting it with a "901" Class boiler in June 1923. The actual rebuilding work was done at Springhead, as may be evident by their use of the flat-topped number "3". *Ron Copeman collection.*

radius at the centre of the box of 6ft 3⅛ ins, matching in turn the similarly finished faces of the hornblocks through which it slid. The cannon box was not allowed simply to flap around unrestricted, however: two horizontal coil springs set parallel with the axle constrained its movements sideways, being set to deflect 4½ inches under a side loading of 17cwts, thus steadying the back end of the locomotive around curves. Springing for suspension purposes was taken care of by two leaf-springs above the radial axle, their centres bearing down in cast cupped pads which in turn rested on top of the cannon box, one at each end. (Leaf-type bearing springs on the three coupled axles were below each axlebox). Inevitably, with the need to ensure adequate rigidity around the 'set' in the frames and the radial axle, the back-end frames below the cab and bunker were well stayed both vertically and horizontally.

A vacuum brake cylinder was suspended from two trunnions on a horizontal plate stay, which lay about twelve inches below cab floorboard level: this was a much stouter arrangement than on F.W.Webb's London & North Western Railway "Coal Tank" 0-6-2's, in which the brake cylinder was directly bolted under and to the cab floor. Application of the brake having an equal and opposite reaction on the top of the cylinder had the effect of giving the crew the distinct feeling of going up in the world, as the cab floor flexed under the imposed stresses!

Above the footplate level, a commodious bunker 6ft 3½ ins long by 7ft 10ins wide held 3 tons of coal and a tank of 798 gallons capacity. This end tank had its own filler and was linked additionally to each side tank via balance pipes below the cab doors. The side tanks held 380 gallons of water apiece; thus the total water capacity amounted to some 1,558 gallons. The side tanks had rounded tops to the outer edges, this by now being as much an established Matthew Stirling feature as it was of William Kirtley, Beyer, Peacock or Kitson & Co.

Inside, the cab measured some 3ft 11ins from the firebox backhead fittings to the bunker at waist level, due to the bunker intruding into the back of the cab by about eighteen inches. This intrusion formed a shelf of adequate width for a grown man to stretch out along; with the aid of a greatcoat and a sack, stuffed palliasse-fashion with clean rags, it was quite feasible to take forty winks in reasonable comfort during a night-shift, providing the foreman wasn't around and assuming that things were slack - not that there were many opportunities for catching up with missed sleep during the first few years in the lives of the F2's, however.

All nine were delivered in November and December 1901, (Kitson's Works Numbers 4070 - 4078), and took up their work from Cudworth Shed as H&BR Nos.102 - 110. They were allocated to the task of working the Wath Branch from its opening in 1902, but also found their way down the Denaby

bore little resemblance to their predecessors, and not only in appearance. It may be recalled that the F1's had balanced slide-valves above the cylinders, driven via rocking levers by Allan Straight - Link valve - gear; but the F2 engines had "D" type slide valves in an upright position between the cylinders, being driven directly by Stephenson Link Motion. Naturally, the absence of steam domes on the F2's marked them out as having emanated from a different design tradition to the F1's.

The Class F2 engines were typical of the Stirling family in appearance, although they and their close relatives the F3's were destined to be the only 0-6-2 tank engines to emerge at the hands of the three Stirlings, for neither Patrick nor James perceived the need for any on their railways. Consequently, in view of their unusual nature your author considers it worthwhile to give a fairly complete description of the F2's.

As indicated earlier, they were basically similar to Stirling's C and G2 classes from the cabs forward, the main difference being driving wheels of six inches lesser in diameter. This set the boiler pitch or centre-line, at 6ft 11ins - three inches lower than on the two preceding Stirling classes.

In comparison with Class F1, the F2 fireboxes were considerably deeper and had a far gentler slope forwards on the grate; the ashpans had front damper doors only.

The usual Stirling push-pull regulator handle was fitted, the valve itself being of the grid-iron pattern mounted horizontally in the smokebox; it was operated directly from the handle by a rod running the full length of the boiler, inside the main steam pipe. That other essential control, namely the reverser, took the form of a lever, as on all the H&BR's tank engines.

The main novelties of the Class F2's lay aft of the cab doorways and below footplate level, as a result of the radial axle arrangements. The rear wheels (of the inevitable H&BR 'standard' 3ft 9ins diameter), had a total sideplay of six inches, which with a radial axle system entailed the mainframes being set closer together. The mainframes, stoutly constructed from 1⅛ inches thick steel plate, were set parallel at 4ft 1½ ins apart from the front bufferbeam back to a point in line with back of the beading up the rear edge of the cab doorway. From there, they tapered inwards to the rear over a distance of about 3ft 6ins, to finish up being set 3ft 6ins apart for the final 4ft or so to the rear bufferbeam.

The radial axle itself ran in a form of cannonbox, the vertical latitudinal faces of which were machined to match a

Branch and after its opening in 1916, along the Hull & Barnsley & Great Central Joint Railway. Wherever they were, the work was all the same: haulage of short-distance goods trains, marshalling mineral trains in colliery sidings, plus an occasional passenger turn along the branches. These would seem to be reasonable tasks for such rugged engines as the F2's, save for one factor: the H&BR experienced such an increase in traffic as to come very close to overwhelming it.

Export coal tonnages alone transported over the H&BR in 1901 amounted to 1 million tons; a mere five years later this had risen to 3 million tons, and in the meantime the only additions to the locomotive stock were the six Class G3 shunting engines ordered from the Yorkshire Engine Company at around the same time as the F2's were ordered, but delivered early in 1902. Consequently by 1905 the shortage of non-passenger motive power was becoming critical, hence Matthew Stirling's request for the Board to permit him to order six more large 0-6-0's, (presumably of Class B). The Board felt unable to grant Stirling's request, probably in view of the fact that they had already authorised £6,100 to be spent at Springhead: additional machine tools had been purchased earlier, but the improvements in hand from 1905 to 1907 involved virtually doubling the size of Springhead Shed, accommodation for 40 locomotives being increased to 72. Provision of a new, elevated covered coal-stage, more locomotive sidings and an additional turntable (at 55ft diameter, a portent of things to come!), were all measures designed to increase locomotive availability both on a day-to-day running basis and also with regard to maintenance. (Mileages between running repairs for H&BR locomotives was 40,000 miles, a figure extended to 60,000 miles in World War I - years later the unfortunate LMS Garratts, bedevilled by archaic Midland Railway design practices, could only knock up a miserable 20 - 25,000 miles between shoppings, whereas a group of "Black 5" 4-6-0's built in 1948 averaged an exceptional 150,000 miles or so apiece before their first intermediate repairs. The latter figures were quite extraordinary; those for the H&BR's engines under wartime conditions can be regarded as a fair average).

Having been turned down for his six additional engines in 1905, the following year saw Matthew Stirling have some success, permission being granted for him to seek tenders for ten large tender locomotives (the Class A 0-8-0's), but June 1906 saw him reporting that this total was still five engines short of the number needed to fulfil all the traffic requirements.

By August 1907, delivery of the ten Class A's initially ordered was complete, so it would appear that the motive power crisis was over (or at least eased), but sadly, matters were in fact rapidly coming to a head. The same month saw Stirling reporting to the Board that he urgently needed ten each of additional goods and tank engines, and he produced a very good case to support this contention - worth quoting reasonably fully. He stated that there were daily diagrams for 13 passengers engines, 61 goods and 50 tank locomotives to cover, but he could only deploy 8 passenger locomotives, 59 goods and 38 tank engines. (These figures would tend to indicate that at any one time, Springhead Works had two Kirtley 2-4-0's under repair and that five goods engines were perforce employed on passenger work. Furthermore, although six 0-6-0's were similarly in the Works and out of commission at any one time, no provision was made for overhaul of tank engines! The implications of this will become clear in due course).

Stirling went on to explain further that out of the 105 engines at hand each day, 15 were stopped for at least 12 hours in the day for running repairs and boiler washouts; consequently the shortfall was being made up by running other locomotives on double trips each day, thus shortening the time between general repairs becoming necessary. (There are two sides to the argument regarding locomotive utilisation - smaller numbers of engines worked hard will wear out faster and absorb more money and time whilst under repair; on the other hand a larger number of locomotives enjoying easier lives will not require shopping as often nor necessarily as thoroughly. They will, however, be less productive per unit and also represent a bigger proportion of capital investment tied up: the latter side of the coin may well please the company's locomotive engineers, but not necessarily the company's accountants!)

As a result of Stirling's representations that August, a further five Class A 0-8-0's were immediately ordered, but too late! Breaking point for the H&BR Locomotive Department's rapidly-fraying shoestring was reached the following month.

Around three after midnight on 25th September 1907, the mining community of Wath was abruptly blasted into wakefulness when Class F2 No.109 blew up with an awesome bang. It had been about to haul a mineral train northwards to Wrangbrook; the fireman was making his way back through thick fog, having gone forward on foot to the signal box to collect the train staff for the journey along the single line. Meanwhile, Cudworth shed's Driver John Edward Brook was attending to the fire, building it up for the climb ahead to Hickleton, when the inner firebox collapsed. The resulting explosion was of great violence: No.109, weighing some 58 tons, was lifted bodily several feet into the air to land with its back end off the rails, its wheels settling down into the ballast. The ashpan and grate were blown off and a large section of the inner firebox was blasted outwards, to land in Wath Main Colliery yard, some 130 feet away. The unfortunate Driver Brook took much of the force of the explosion directly through the open firehole door, being blown out of the cab of 109 to be found badly scalded and bruised some 400 yards away, in the Great Central Railway's sidings. He was taken to the Beckett Hospital, Barnsley, where he died of his injuries some four hours later.

Under a Statutory Order of 1895 No.109's explosion was duly reported to the Board of Trade, which sent Mr. Thomas Carlton, its Marine Department boiler specialist, to investigate on behalf of Lt.Colonel von Donop. Carlton's meticulous investigation was to reveal the sorry state of affairs which were existing on the H&BR as a result of its paucity of motive power.

He found that a group of about 30 stays near the bottom of the firebox left-hand side had given way. These stays, of $7/8$ inch diameter copper, lay within the area subjected to direct action of the fire; their domed, riveted heads had burned away until finally they had become too short, the ends being *BELOW* the outer surface of the copper inner firebox plate. Cudworth Shed's boilersmiths had hammered away at these stays, caulking them so frequently in vain attempts to keep them steamtight that the screw threads on both plates and stays had become damaged, and distorted to such a degree that the plate was insufficiently supported. Finally a small number of adjacent stays failed first, causing the copper plate to pull off the remaining stays, ultimately tearing away from the tube plate and backplate simultaneously through the stay-holes; rather like tearing through the perforations on a sheet of postage stamps. The copper sheet, representing the entire left side of the inner firebox, was thus blasted away from the outer shell, down onto then through the grate before being forced below the foundation ring, finally peeling completely off the latter to dislodge the ashpan before commencing its flight into Wath Colliery: an awesome and salutory demonstration of the powers of steam.

No.109 had arrived on the H&BR in December 1901 and had its first general repair in 1905 at Springhead Works, after which it returned to Cudworth where all further maintenance was undertaken. The shed foreman there realised that by March 1907 No.109's stays were becoming suspect, but rather than renew them he had the boiler pressure lowered from the normal 170 lb/sq.inch by 10lb. (Renewal of stays, although a reasonably straightforward task, involves considerable stripping down if the outer firebox is to be properly exposed. As No.109 was a side tank engine, this would entail removal of one tank and part of the boiler cladding at least; but since the stays in question were at the bottom of the firebox, clothing would need removing and the boiler lifted from the frames to allow access to the stay heads. Removal of the boiler in turn meant releasing the firebox side bearers, removal of the main steam pipes between regulator and valve chest, and the fitted bolts holding the smokebox to the cylinder block and mainframes. These bolts in turn were behind the leading splasher - sandbox assemblies. Some piping and auxiliary controls, such as the damper handle, may well

have needed disconnecting also: all in all, not a job to be lightly embarked upon at a running shed, even one with a set of shearlegs!).

Not long before the accident, the shed foreman was warned by a boilersmith that it was high time No.109 was sent to Springhead for repairs, and on the day preceding the accident Driver Parker had reported that 109's boiler was priming and that tubes, roofbolts and side stays were leaking. However, since No.106 was due back from repair at Springhead the Cudworth foreman decided to hang on and await its return before sending No.109 away: an unfortunate decision in view of the consequences, for which the shed foreman was held entirely responsible by Carlton.

At the Inquest on Driver Brook, it was averred that he had repeatedly said that nothing would be done to remedy No.109's poor condition until someone had been killed; nevertheless, the jury returned a verdict of "Accidental Death", albeit adding that the company's officials committed an error of judgement in not having the engine overhauled before it exploded. It seems unlikely that Stirling was totally unaware of the parlous state of some of his engines, but representations by his hard - pressed foremen wouldn't necessarily mean that he could conjure up more engines, as we have already seen. If anything, the H&BR Board were the real villains of the piece having cut things just a little too fine, thereby putting their officers and staff at risk in the performance of their every day duties; but as if to make amends, they allowed Stirling to order 20 new engines for delivery in 1908. (These turned out to be the last ten of Class B, plus ten more G3 tank engines). Recognising that Stirling had been hard-pressed throughout the period 1901 - 1908 they granted him an assistant, Francis Henry Lytton, from 29th September 1908 at an annual salary of £250, and finally voted their long-suffering Locomotive Engineer a salary of £1,000 per annum from May 1908.

If any crumb of comfort could be gained from the distressing affair at Wath, it was that Stirling's boiler designs and Kitson's workmanship were both sound enough to prevent total disintegration of 109's boiler; indeed, it was repaired and continued in use until December 1923 - a total of 22 years.

Once the upheavals caused by the Wath explosion had died away, life returned to humdrum normality for the F2's. Grouping found all except No.3104 at Cudworth, and that engine returned westwards from Springhead early in 1924. In November 1924 the LNER reallocated No.2486 (105) and 2489 (108) to Cudworth's sub-sheds at Bullcroft and Denaby respectively. Following the General Strike and the following six month - long Coal Strike of 1926, the F2's (by now LNER Class N12), were finding work in short supply (a total change-round from the situation twenty years earlier). May 1927 saw No.2491 (110) transferred to Springhead for about six months, then in November it was hired out to the Derwent Valley Light Railway at York until February 1928. It returned to the Derwent Valley in October 1928, probably just in time to partake in operating the "Blackberry Pickers' Specials" for which the DVLR was renowned. At the end of the year though, the DVLR sold its two old, ex-North Eastern Railway four-wheeled carriages, as a result of which the need for a vacuum brake fitted engine on that line disappeared; so January 1929 saw 2491 (110) exchanged for No.2485 (104), which had lost its vacuum equipment in June 1923 in exchange for a steam brake only. 2485 was destined to lead a bucolic existence ambling along the Derwent Valley line for the next $7\frac{1}{2}$ years. throughout this period it normally resided

2485 (104) in York shed on 7th May 1935. At this time, 2485 was working the Derwent Valley Light Railway, and had probably been brought round to the LNER shed for a boiler wash-out and additional odd jobs beyond the capabilities of the DVLR's modest facilities. Monday morning would see 2485 steam off around York along the Foss Islands goods branch, to take up its DVLR duties from Layerthorpe again. It may be noted that the engine carries "Class N12" on the bufferbeam.

in the DVLR's small shed at Layerthorpe, York, but every other weekend saw it trundle round that city over the Foss Island goods branch to the LNER mainline shed at York North for washing-out and odd maintenance beyond the capabilities of the DVLR's staff. The DVLR did provide their own stores and footplate crew throughout the hire period. Whilst the other eight N12's were employed on the inevitable shunting and hauling coal trains, 2485 (104) was hauling tanks of motor spirit to the Russian Oil Products' depot at Murton, wagonloads of stable manure, vans of livestock, the prolific potato crop of 1929, hay, straw and domestic coal over the DVLR for the farming communities along the valley of the River Derwent. (Lists of the DVLR Annual Mileage and Tonnage Rates are to be found in the Appendix).

In July 1936 2485 (104) returned to Cudworth and 2490 (109) took its place, remaining on the Derwent Valley Light Rly until October: doubtless its turn of duty on that line proved considerably less stressful than its early years on the Wath Branch. No.2483 (102) replaced 2490, becoming the DVLR's engine until July 1938 when No.2488 (107) became the final N12 to be used on the Derwent Valley. The line had an axle load limit of seventeen tons so the N12's with a maximum axle loading of 16¾ tons were ideally suited. Although off the LNER's metals, when at the southern end of the DVLR (at Cliff Common, some 15½ miles away from Layerthorpe), the hired N12's were just about within whistle-sound of their fellows on the H&BR main line, some five miles south at Asselby - but some N12's were to venture much further away from their old system than that!

Late May 1927 saw Cudworth Shed relinquish Nos.2488 (107) and 2489 (108) to Dairycoates, but there was still insufficient work in Hull. Consequently November that year saw them both travel northwards, 2489 going to East Hartlepool Shed for five months to help in shifting timber before returning south to Cudworth to eke out its remaining days. Meanwhile, 2488 was sent to West Hartlepool Shed, where it is hoped it received a more favourable reception than the unfortunate albeit possibly apocryphal monkey! Whatever its reception on Teeside, its sojourn there was for a mere five weeks before travelling north - westwards across County Durham to Ferryhill, and the extensive marshalling yards which were once provided there. Here, although in unfamiliar surroundings, No.2488 (107) was on familiar duties - shunting coal trains. So ideally suited was it for this task that it remained at Ferryhill for over seven years. June 1935 saw it returned to familiar surroundings at Cudworth for a flying visit before being sent to Dairycoates within the month, but Cudworth reclaimed it in October 1936. Another move came in August 1937, this time to Springhead, but after exactly a year it was sent off to the Derwent Valley line for the last three months of its life.

Other N12's found themselves in even more exotic locations for the LNER's Southern Area suddenly became aware of the usefulness of the class from early 1935, for Woodford (Great Central) claimed 2484 (103) as its own for a month before returning it to Cudworth. The wandering life evidently got to 2484, since it departed its native heath in January 1936 for

2486 (105) during its time on the old Lancashire, Derbyshire & East Coast Railway from November 1938 to 1942, and seen here at Tuxford shed. Note the extra additions to 2486's bunker, rendering rearward vision through the spectacles down to zero, and also the small tablet on the front buffer-beam, showing its LNER Southern area freight load "2" - a relic of its days at Ardsley. The artless simplicity of the shelter may be remarked upon, run up from old rail and corrugated iron. *N.E.Stead collection.*

Ardsley to spend the last eleven months of its life, never to return to the H&B system. February 1937 saw its replacement there arrive in the form of No.2486 (105) from Springhead. It was to remain at Ardsley until November 1938, by which time it had outlived all its fellows. At this point the LNER developed a strange reluctance to scrap her, allocating her instead to Tuxford on the erstwhile LD&EC system: the wheel had turned full circle at last, one H&BR engine transferred there had partly made up for the five engines lost by the LD&ECR to the H&BR some forty years earlier! 2486 (105) became Tuxford's wagon works pilot engine until 1942, but under the LNER the engine led a charmed life, for it was then sent to Springhead as wagon works pilot for the remainder of the LNER's existence. British Railways however took a less respectful view of their odd acquisition, withdrawing it in August 1948. A final insult was to allocate it a new number 69089 - but as nobody actually got around to painting it on the sides of the old engine, she went off to Darlington scrapyard still proclaiming herself as an "NE" engine, albeit sporting No.9089 (a number it acquired as a result of the LNER's massive renumbering scheme of 1946).

Another N12 which had found a home at Ardsley was 2487 (106), from January 1936. It was to spend the last 2½ years of its life there, until withdrawal in September 1938. All the three Ardsley N12's were working over the old East & West Yorkshire Union Railways, especially the Newmarket Colliery Branch; being designed to shift slow, heavy trains over stiff gradients they were ideal on these duties.

One N12 latterly had odd moments of glory: No. 2491 (110), during its nine years at Springhead found itself appearing on the odd passenger working. As a vacuum braked engine (all the others except No.2490 were steam braked by 1925), No.2491 had gone rather too late to the Derwent Valley Light Railway to be much use on their passenger services, which had been withdrawn in 1926 - hence its exchange in 1929 for No.2485 (104) from Hull, an engine with steam brake only. No.2491's continuous brake proved much more useful around the Hull area, for most passenger services along the H&BR line were by then being operated by Sentinel steam railcars, which at times left something to be desired in the matter of reliability. So occasionally 2491 had its fling on the North Cave passenger services, going to the rescue of or standing in for failed Sentinels. Sometimes it was a Botanic Gardens' ex-Great Northern Ivatt Class C12 4-4-2 tank which threw a tantrum and preferred to remain sulking on shed, thus giving 2491 the chance of being its understudy. However, there was one role which 2491 made its own: every October the mining community of Hickleton had an excursion to Hull on the occasion of the Saturday opening of the week-long Fair, and the old N12 was the inevitable choice of motive power. As the RCTS *Locomotives of the LNER* volume points out, "there....were few opportunities indeed, as late as 1936, to ride in a passenger train for 47½ miles hauled by an engine with a straight-back boiler."

The same publication also details reboilerings and detail alterations, and the reader is referred to the relevant volume

2483 (102), somewhere in ex-North Eastern territory (probably the old NER's Central Division area, judging from the short, wooden signal finials). The engine looks rather woebegone - someone has run off with the front left-hand buffer, and taken down the back right-hand coupled wheel spring; one brake-block and the brake pull-rods can also be seen to have been removed. Note also the extra coal-rail. *Ron Copeman collection.*

2491 trundling along with a freight over the H&BR embankment around Hull, between Perth Street West and Spring Bank West, on 18th February 1933. The bufferbeam lettering proclaims it as being of "Class HB N12" - Darlington would get it right one day....! *Laurie Ward.*

for these. Also, a full table of boiler exchanges and renewals under the LNER may be found in the relevant appendix in vol .2, but a summary of the main alterations is worth noting here.

Five boilers were built to Stirling's designs at Darlington, from materials gathered at Springhead in the early 1920's. One was fitted to a J75, the other four appeared on N12's Nos.3109 and 3110 (LNER Nos.2490 and 2491), and 2486 and 2489 (H&B Nos.105 and 108). Darlington fitted all the boilers save No.2489's, which was fitted at Springhead and additionally acquired the H&BR's final type of extended, flat-bottom smokebox similar to the type already dealt with under Class B. This boiler was transferred to No.2484 (103) in October 1934, serving with that engine until its withdrawal in December 1936; the other boilers served with their respective engines until their withdrawal. This boiler change made 2484 a unique locomotive inasmuch as it lost a domed, replacement boiler for a Stirling domeless type! One of these domeless boilers was sold into industrial use at J.H.Ashton Ltd., of Salford in April 1939; the other four were scrapped after ceasing work in 1937.

Prior to the construction of these boilers, as a stopgap measure Darlington had sent a 1917-built domed boiler (from "901" Class 2-4-0 No.156, which had been withdrawn in August 1922), to Springhead Works where it was fitted to 3104 in June 1923. As noted under Class G2, these ex-NER boilers were three inches longer in the barrel and had a shorter firebox and smaller grate. No. 3104, as LNER 2485, was to retain this boiler throughout its remaining life, including its lengthy service on the Derwent Valley line. Initially, this boiler had open

Ramsbottom safety valves but in June 1933 a typical NER brass "trumpet" casing was fitted around them. October 1934 saw 2487 (106) acquire the same type of boiler, complete with Ramsbottom valves in brass casing. All the Darlington-built domeless boilers were equipped from new with Ross "Pop" safety valves.

Mid-1924 saw design work completed on a domed version of the H&BR 4ft 3ins diameter boiler to the same external dimensions but with altered internal arrangements. These carried fifteen more tubes but had a slightly smaller grate area plus a marginal increase in boiler pressure of a mere 5 lb/sq.in. This new type (designated Diagram 71B from 1928), found its way on to the remaining four N12's between 1924 and 1925, and in due course also appeared on the N13 0-6-2's (H&BR Class F3), two of the J80's and various J75's: in fact the first use of the type was on J75 No.2494 in July 1924. As just noted of course, two N12's lost these boilers in favour of domeless Diagram 71A and "901" Diagram 69 types respectively. The "901" Class boiler fitted to 2487 (106) in October 1934 had been removed from Class J80 No.2449 (68) in July 1931 and been spare for nearly 3¼ years.

No. 2486 (105) which survived alone for so long until 1948, received Diagram 71B boilers from Class N13 engines in 1942 and 1945 having lost its domeless boiler in 1934; these later boilers were to a revised design done in 1930.

Regarding that characteristic locomotive fitting, the chimney, it may be said generally that Darlington replaced H&BR chimneys with their own style whereas Springhead retained the "native" type. Initially though 3110 (LNER 2491) and 2488(107)

2484 (103), inside Springhead shed, with added front step, but retaining only three coal-rails and a domeless boiler actually assembled by Darlington in 1923 from parts gathered together at Springhead for the purpose. The boiler seen here was fitted to 2484 in October 1934, as a replacement for an LNER domed type fitted in January 1925. It is worth mentioning that these Darlington-built boilers are readily identifiable by their use of Ross "Pop" safety-valves, and that this particular boiler, after its service on 2484, was sold off for further use in industry. *Ron Copeman collection.*

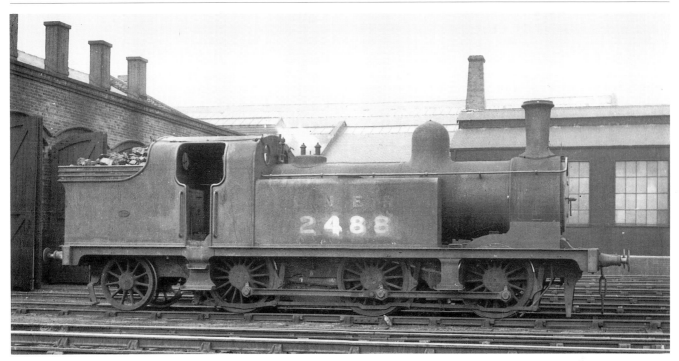

2488 (107), outside Springhead shed, retains its Stirling chimney although it has acquired a domed boiler, LNER smokebox door, front step and plated-in coal-rails. This engine, like most of the N12 0-6-2's, served its time on the DVLR, albeit only from August to October 1938. *Ron Copeman collection.*

slipped through Darlington unchanged, although 2491 was caught up with eventually. Nos.2485 (104) and 2489 (108) kept their H&BR chimneys to the end although 2485 latterly acquired a touch of distinction by acquiring a "windjabber", as did 2491 (110) on its North Eastern type.

Springhead left the single, bell-type whistle alone on each of its two rebuilds although both received a single NER organ-pipe in exchange in the 1930's. Darlington fitted its customary twin whistles to its seven rebuilds, although 2483(102) and 2486 (105) lost their organ pipe whistles in November 1934 and January 1945 respectively, to retain their single bell-shaped type only.

Smokebox doors were the usual Stirling dished type, retained on the two Springhead rebuilds albeit with the addition of two dog-clips round the lower edge. Unlike the Class B, F2 engines never had lamp irons on the smokebox doors. No.2489 (108) may well have gone to the scrapyard with its H&BR door, whereas 2485 (104) received an NER smokebox door in June 1933. As usual, twin handles kept the doors shut but the North Eastern wheel and handle type appeared in the 1920's, although the next decade saw 2484 (103), 2486 (105), 2487 (106) and 2488 (107) revert to twin handles.

From 1923 continuous handrails around the smokebox were altered on the domed engines in connection with altered blower jet controls, although 3104 (LNER 2485) retained its original handrail and was given an independent blower control rod in addition upon its June 1923 reboilering. This was on the right-hand side, whereas the later rod - within - handrail type of control running above the level of the tank tops, was fitted on the left side.

Bunker coal rails, originally three in number, were eventually plated behind by the LNER which also fitted an additional rail to 2483 (102), 2485 (104), 2487 (106), 2489 (108) and 2491 (110). Finally around 1937 Ardsley fitted (rather

untidily), another two coal rails at wider spacings thus greatly increasing bunker capacity: this modification affected 2486 (105) and 2487 (106), and 2484 (103) also in 1936.

A unique fitting on 2491 (110) which possibly dated from late H&BR days was a cab roof ventilator, which took the form of a steel plate supported on four short columns over an opening cut in the cab roof.

Starting with 3110D (ex-Works 30th November 1923), Darlington added a footstep just ahead of the tank on each side. All except 2485 (104) were so fitted, and despite two further general repairs at Darlington, lack of them passed unnoticed.

The two engines retaining vacuum braking underwent the inevitable changes from short H&BR bufferbeam standards, through the NER below - bufferbeam connections to the tall LNER standpipes on 2491 (110) only, in November 1932.

After all the changes made to these engines, it seems remarkable that buffer stocks somehow escaped attention, although some larger-diameter heads appeared on odd engines. All retained the original H&BR buffers with tapered stocks until the bitter end - even 2486 (105) in its long - drawn - out, twilight existence as the sole representative of Matthew Stirling's first essay into the design of 0-6-2 tanks. It had also become the longest-lived H&BR engine, amassing a respectable 47 years of hard work.

That the F2's were useful and popular engines seems pretty well beyond doubt in view of their widespread service, goodly lifespan and the incontrovertible fact that N12's served the Derwent Valley Light Railway longer than other locomotive type (at least in the steam era). The mandatory use of 2491 on the Hickleton to Hull Fair specials is also testimony to the versatility of the class - thankfully the H&BR's old four wheeled carriages had long since gone out of service, otherwise even the more boisterous fairground rides may well have remained something of an anti-climax in comparison to the return journey!

Evidently that black sheep of the F2 family, No.109, retained an obdurate nature for many years after the Wath incident, as if to pay everyone back for its sad neglect at that time. William Westoby recalled that Driver George Carson was uneasy when around engines blowing off at the safety valves: he had apparently been in the vicinity when 109 had exploded, and never quite trusted it after that.

Mr. Westoby also recalled an episode when he and Driver Burrows were given 109 one day instead of their usual F3, No.156. It seems that 109 needed its slide valves refacing and careful attention paid to their setting, for although it would produce steam in abundance when standing still it was a different matter as soon as the regulator was opened! They duly protested bitterly about having to take 109 but to no avail, for it being a Sunday there was nothing else available. But Driver Burrows was not to be beaten. Muttering, "Owld on, Billy," to his fireman, he disappeared into the gloom of Springhead shed for a few minutes before returning to the engine whereupon he climbed on the front of 109 and opened its smokebox door, there to quietly set about perpetrating some misdeed or other out of view of "Young Billy". Suffice to say that for the remainder of that day's shift, No.109 steamed like the proverbial pig in a rainstorm, but upon returning to Springhead for disposal the secret of its uncharacteristic co-operation in the matter of producing steam was soon revealed! Upon opening the smokebox door William Westoby found that Driver Burrows had fitted a "jemmy" to the blastpipe top! This was a fitting placed over the blastpipe nozzle to cut down its area, thus increasing back-pressure but

sharpening the exhaust and drawing up the fire. Such illegal modifications were taken a dim view of by "Authority", which made rigorous if arguably misguided attempts to discourage their use. However, Driver Burrows had not resorted to some beautifully contrived artefact crafted by a sympathetic blacksmith in Springhead Works: instead 109's recalcitrant nature had been overcome by nothing more than "scroungings" from around the shed, to whit: an old firebar and odd three-link couplings. The bar had been laid across the blastpipe top and held in place by the couplings, one link on each being slipped over the firebar and the remaining links being dangled around the blastpipe to keep the bar in place. Rather like the steam locomotive itself, it could only be described as crude but effective!

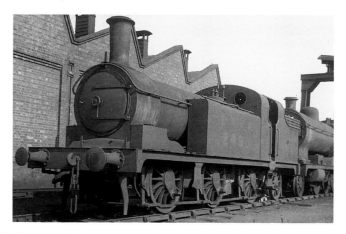

Summary: Class F2 0-6-2 Radial Tank. LNER Class N12.

HBR No.	Works No.	Delivered	NER No.	LNER No.	Reboilering	Withdrawn
102	4070	November 1901	3102	2483*	Dgm.71B/September 1924	July 1938
103	4071	December 1901	3103	2484	Dgm.71B/January 1925	December 1936
					Dgm.71A/October 1934	
104	4072	December 1901	3104	2485*	Dgm.69/June 1923	March 1937
105	4073	December 1901	3105	2486	Dgm.71A/April 1924	August 1948**
					Dgm.71B/August 1934	
106	4074	December 1901	3106	2487	Dgm.71B/September 1924	September 1938
					Dgm.69/October 1934	
107	4075	December 1901	3107	2488*	Dgm.71B/October 1924	October 1938
108	4076	December 1901	3108	2489	Dgm.71A/February 1924	February 1937
109	4077	December 1901	3109	2490*	Dgm.71A/December 1923	December 1936 $
110	4078	December 1901	3110	2491*	Dgm.71A/November 1923	October 1936

Notes:

* Locomotives hired to Derwent Valley Light Railway (see text for dates).

** Withdrawn as BR No.(6)9089.

$ Blew up at Wath 25/9/1907.

Kitsons price per loco. £2,835.

Boilers: LNER Diagram 69 = ex-NER "901" domed boiler. LNER Diagram 71A = ex-HBR domeless boiler. LNER Diagram 71B = LNER domed type introduced in 1924, derived from HBR domeless type.

Vacuum brake equipment removed fron Nos.102-108, (2483-2489), at the same time as reboilering was carried out, and steam brakes only substituted.

Under BR, (6)9089 was included in the Route Availability Scheme as R.A.4, and given power Class 4F, (i.e: Class 4, Freight only). However, whilst allocated to Ardsley, 2486 was given a 'general' repair at Doncaster works in August 1938, where it received a small, cast plate showing a raised figure 2, denoting its Southern Area Freight Loading Classification. It retained the plate on its front bufferbeam until withdrawn ten years later. Neither 2484 or 2487 went from Ardsley for repair at Doncaster; 2487 went there for one in September 1938 but was cut up instead.

Class F2 Dimensions.

Cylinders: 2, inside. 18" x 26".
Motion: Stephenson Link; slide valves between cylinders.
Boiler: Domeless.
Max. diameter outside: 4' 3".
Barrel length: 10' 0".
Firebox length outside: 5' 6".
Pitch: 6' 11".
Heating surface:
  Firebox 104 sq.ft.
  Tubes 194 @ 1³/₄" dia. - 951 sq.ft.
  Total 1,055 sq.ft.
Grate area: 16.25 sq.ft.
Ratio of grate area to heating surface: 1 to 64.92.
Boiler pressure: 160 lb/sq.in.
Wheel diameter:
  Coupled 4' 6".
  Radial axle 3' 9"
Wheelbase: 7' 3" + 8' 3" + 7' 6" = 23' 0".
Length over buffers: 35' 10½".
Weights:
12tons 17cwt + 16tons 11cwt + 16tons 15cwt + 11tons 17cwt
= 58tons 0cwt.
Height to top of chimney: 12' 10⁵/₈".
Tractive effort @ 85% of boiler pressure: 21,216 lb.
Ratio of blast nozzle to cylinder diameter: 1 to 3.789.
Tank water capacity: 1,559 gallons.
Bunker coal capacity: 3tons.
The above dimensions apply to Class F2 at December 1922, when fitted with Diagram 71A type, domeless H&BR boilers.

Boiler to Diagram 71A built at Darlington in 1923.
Boiler: Domed.
Max. outside diameter: 4' 3".
Heating surface:
  Firebox 102 sq.ft.* 104 sq.ft.**
  Tubes 190 @ 1³/₄" dia* - 899 sq.ft.*
  Tubes 191 @ 1³/₄" dia** - 904 sq.ft.**
  Total 1,001 sq.ft.* 1,008 sq.ft.**
Boiler pressure: 170 lb/sq.in* 160 lb/sq.in***.

*   Figures correct for boilers as built, 1923.*
**   Figures from 1928.*
*** Boiler pressure shown as 160 lb/sq.in from 1932.*

Boilers to Diagram 71B, built at Darlington from 1924.
Boiler: Domed.
Heating surface:
  Firebox 99 sq.ft.
  Tubes 205 @ 1³/₄" - 972 sq.ft.
  Total 1,071 sq.ft.
Grate area: 15.48 sq.ft.
Ratio of grate area to heating surface: 1 to 69.09.
Boiler pressure: 175 lb/sq.in.
Tractive effort @ 85% boiler pressure: 23,197 lb.

Boilers to Diagram 69 (ex- "901" class), fitted to Nos.3104 (LNER 2485), and 2487 (106)
Boiler: Domed.
Barrel length: 10' 3".
Firebox length outside: 5' 6".
Heating surface:
  Firebox 98 sq.ft.
  Tubes 206 @ 1³/₄" dia. - 999 sq.ft.*
  Total 1,097 sq.ft.*
Grate area: 15.16 sq.ft.
Ratio of grate area to heating surface: 1 to 72.36.
Boiler pressure: 160 lb/sq.in.
Tractive effort @ 85% of boiler pressure: 21,216 lb.
* Note that these figures are not in agreement with those for the similar boilers fitted to Class G2 No.3068 (2449) and Class G3 No.3116 (2497), nor with those boilers still on the ten remaining Class "901" engines taken over by the LNER. These all had 205 tubes, 4 sq.ft less tube heating-surface and total heating surfaces of 1,093 sq.ft.

(opposite) **2490, at Cudworth, cannot be far from its final journey to Darlington in December 1936. It had probably just returned from the DVLR, having served there from July to October 1936.**

(below) **The end came for 2491 at North Road in November 1936. It was a pity the DVLR had not decided to buy their own locomotive - an N12 - the ideal choice!**

116, last of the Yorkshire Engine Company's batch of six G3 engines built during 1901 - 1902, used for the works photograph. Note the shape of the mainframes, being shallower between the rear wheels than on the later Kitson engines; the rounded shape of the front sandboxes and heavy brass beading around the front splasher make further distinguishing features.

CLASS G3 0-6-0 SIDE TANKS. (LNER CLASS J75). Introduced 1901.

With the early 20th. century increases in mineral traffic leading to further anticipated requirements for shunting locomotives, Stirling busied himself with producing a new type. He doubtless based his designs on the existing Class G2, but decided to sacrifice their capacity to run quickly enough for passenger work in exchange for enhanced power when shunting - an effect of using 4ft 6ins diameter wheels. However, since he was drawing up specifications for the F2 0-6-2 radial tanks at virtually the same time, Matthew Stirling probably utilised as many items as possible on both classes. In which case the G3's could be regarded as being sawn-off F2's just as much as being but small-wheeled G2's!

It may well be that Stirling had been able to devote more time and thought to producing a shunting engine than he had when the G2's were produced; consequently he was able to carry out the necessary redesigning of the frames in order to accommodate the smaller diameter wheels (unless much of that work had already been done in connection with the F2 engines).

Since the H&BR Board had granted him permission to order twenty tank engines, and fourteen of those were the 0-6-2 tanks of Classes F1 and F2, Matthew Stirling was only able to order six G3's initially. These by way of a change, were turned out by the Yorkshire Engine Company and proved to be the only tank engines built by them for the H&BR.

Delivery of them took place contemporaneously with the F2's throughout December, then into January and February 1901 -'02; they took up running numbers following on immediately after them, thus becoming H&BR Nos.111 to 116 (Yorkshire Engine's Works Nos. 655 - 660).

Similarities with the F2's were the boiler pitch (at 6' 11", this was three inches less than on the G2's), and the fluted coupling rods, which had been left plain in section on the G2 class.

After the Wath boiler explosion in 1907 the H&BR Board began to appreciate that when their Locomotive Superintendent said he had insufficient engines he actually meant it, so they allowed him to order ten more G3's in 1908. This time the order went to Kitson & Company, the locomotives being delivered (oddly enough), before the last ten Class B 0-6-0 tender engines - which were also being built by Kitsons. The Class B's took Nos.132 - 141 despite being delivered later; the G3's took up Nos.142 - 151. Possibly

Kitsons had been requested to turn out the G3's before commencing the Class B engines in view of the pressing need for more shunting engines. (Since the orders for these thirty engines must have been placed late in 1907, the Board cannot have wasted much time after the Wath incident at the end of September and neither did Kitsons, since they delivered the first three G3's before the end of January 1908).

Not surprisingly, with two builders responsible for the sixteen G3's there were detail differences between the two batches. These included trifling differences in the profile of the lower edge of the mainframes, but the frames on both groups nevertheless had more in common with the F2's than with the G2's - frames on the latter engines were clearly derived directly from the Class C 0-6-0's. More evident points of difference regarding the respective G3's were the use of rounded edge sandboxes, splashers delineated by prominent brass beading at the edge and tank top handrails bent downwards at the ends on the Yorkshire locomotives. Those from Kitson & Co. had longer, angular sandboxes with small, round access plates on the sides; plain splashers and handrail stanchions to support the tank top handrails. Another point of difference lay in the two parallel rows of bolt heads retaining the cab upper section, being prominent on the Kitson locomotives.

Prices differed between the two batches also: Yorkshire Engine had charged £2,460 per locomotive for Nos.111 - 116; the mild inflation of Edwardian England meant that six years later Kitson had to charge £160 more for each locomotive.

Upon delivery the first six were set to work on the Wath and Braithwell colliery branches, whereas the later engines were distributed more evenly, being put to shunting duties at both Cudworth and Hull. They were powerful machines, their 19,890 lb nominal tractive effort being exceeded on the North Eastern only by the ten Class L (LNER J73) 0-6-0 tanks.

The LNER saw them initially employed mostly in the Hull area, especially at Alexandra Dock and on transfer trips for short distances over H&B Section tracks - not necessarily a life of ease,

113 at Springhead on 19th September 1904: note the different treatment given to the lining of the sandbox/splasher and the cab/bunker sub-assemblies when compared with the version in the works photograph. *Hull Museums collection.*

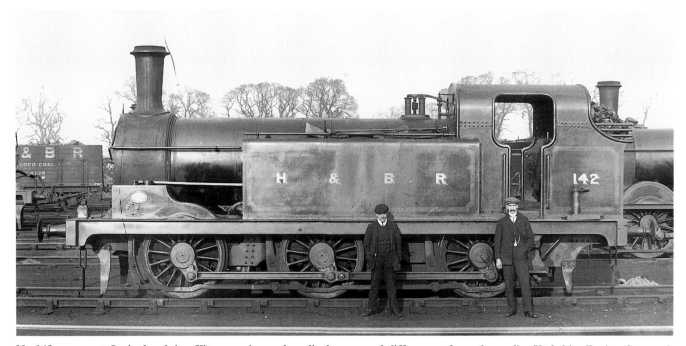

No.142 as seen at Springhead, is a Kitson engine and so displays several differences from the earlier Yorkshire Engine Co. products. The deeper rear mainframes, brake pull-rods bent to clear the coupling-rod bearings, angular front splasher with access cover and no beading, small coupling-rod splasher behind the tank and alongside the cab, tank handrails in stanchions and two rows of parallel bolt-heads on the cab sides are the visible points of difference. One of the H&BR's big Locomotive Coal wagons, No. 4138, may be seen on the left.

as we shall see in due course. One engine was usually seconded to the wagon works at Springhead, No.2530 (149) being photographed there soon after reboilering in May 1927. On the occasion of its being favoured for portraiture it was coupled to the H&BR breakdown train, which would tend to suggest that Springhead's Carriage & Wagon Pilot also doubled up as breakdown train engine.

As ever though, the LNER took over the inevitable problem of life-expired boilers: understandably the older half-dozen Yorkshire engines presented the more urgent problem.

February 1923 saw 3116 (LNER 2497) given a North Eastern Railway boiler built in December 1916 from an old "901" Class 2-4-0; the G3 kept its new acquisition until October 1936. Although carried out under the auspices of the LNER, they had not then had sufficiently lengthy an existence to work out a "corporate image"; hence 3116 appeared strictly as a North Eastern engine!

The next rebuilding took place in July 1924 when 2494 (113) was fitted with the LNER's domed, redesigned version of the H&BR boiler. This new type (classified as Diagram 71B in due course), eventually found its way on to all the G3's (also reclassified as J75), except for Nos.2495 (114) and 2526 (145). These two managed to retain domeless boilers to the end. Even No.2497 (116) was brought into line for the last seven months of its life, but the replacement of its twenty-years old "901" Class boiler for such a short time could hardly have been justified economically.

Of the two domeless engines, No.2495 (114) received a boiler of that type built new at Darlington from parts sent up from Springhead; No. 2526 (145) was given one second-hand from N13 No.2405 (H&BR Class F3 No.13). Coincidentally, both engines received these boilers in December 1927, and both were condemned in May 1937.

The entire class lost their Stirling chimneys in exchange for North Eastern types, although Nos.2494 (113), 2496 (115) and 2528 (147) still sported their H&BR chimneys for some time after acquiring domed boilers. No.2527 (146) achieved a touch of individuality by sporting an NER chimney complete with windjabber, from a Darlington Works visit in December 1934.

Safety valves were invariably of the Ross "Pop" type on the LNER domed boilers, and domeless No.2495 (114) also acquired them. The other domeless engine, No.2526 (145), retained H&BR Ramsbottom safety valves throughout its life. The other odd man out, No. 2497 (116), during its existence with the "901" boiler also retained the North Eastern's rather stouter version of Mr. Ramsbottom's invention, albeit modestly hidden from view within the customary brass "trumpet".

The H&BR's single bell-shaped whistle bolted to the cab front was exchanged on fourteen engines to the NER's favoured twin-whistle arrangement, usually when they visited Darlington for reboilering. Domeless No.2526 (145) retained a single whistle, albeit changed to an organ-pipe example, and No.2497 (116) was similarly dealt with. Although Darlington Works had seen fit to grace it with an ex-North Eastern boiler, they were too modest to go the whole hog and give it their customary twin whistles in addition! They also did the same to No.2529 (148) upon its visit to Darlington Works in December 1924; at least it emerged with its domeless boiler intact. However, when sent there again in February 1928 to receive a domed boiler, the twin-whistle fitters caught up with it at last.

H&BR smokebox doors - without lamp irons, as with other Stirling tank locomotives - were quickly replaced by the NER type, and their larger diameter necessitated the raising of the handrails over the doors of the two domeless engines to allow them to open. The other engines had the handrails raised to

3116 with the ex-"901" Class boiler, fitted in February 1923. The roof of Alexandra Dock shed can be seen to be equally deserving of emergency treatment, also.

3142 in Alexandra Dock shed yard, after attention at Darlington Works - hence the NER chimney, smokebox door and fittings. In the distance can be seen the coal hoists for tipping wagon loads of coal into ships holds; export coal was the raison d'etre of Alexandra Dock.

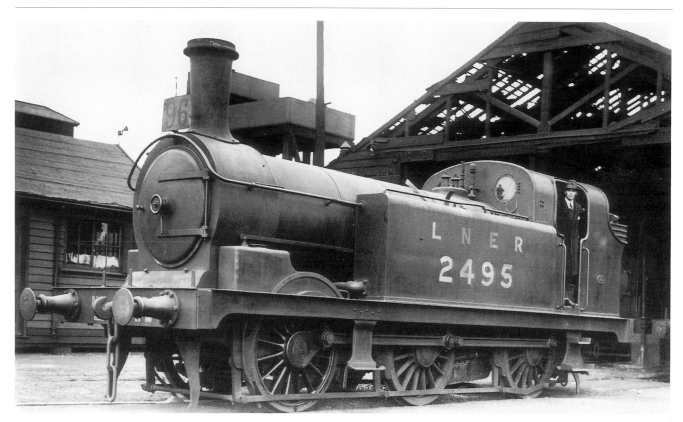

2495 (114) with a Darlington-built domeless boiler and Stirling chimney, outside Alexandra Dock shed. Its bufferbeam can be seen to proclaim it as a "Class G3 (HB)". *Laurie Ward.*

2526 (145) at Springhead on 16th May 1936, still retains its H&BR Ramsbottom safety-valves.

2532 after its last shopping at Darlington in February 1945. The paintwork has only been cleaned down, for the LNER's contracted initials and the number can be seen to have been re-applied on patch-painted panels, although the bufferbeams have new red paint on them. *Ron Copeman collection.*

the level of those on the side tanks, since new blower valves were fitted on the sides of the smokeboxes in line with the handrails, down the centre of which ran the new valve control - rod.

Bunker coal rails were plated in as each engine visited Darlington, a task completed by May 1927 with No.2531 (150).

Rerailing jacks were removed from all engines after Grouping, although No.2523 (142) contrived to retain its jack until October 1932 - by which time it was working at Immingham. Nos.2494, 2529 and 2531 (113 and 148/50), kept theirs after being so renumbered.

Buffers were unchanged save for two examples: 2528 (147) acquired the NER parallel variety by the early 1930's. This type had hollow parallel rams with internal coil springs, and were of stouter construction than the H&BR type. Also, by the time of its withdrawal in 1949 No.8365 (ex - 2532, H&BR No.151), had acquired LNER Group Standard buffers, with their characteristic stepped stocks.

The first four engines repaired at Darlington were Nos.3148 (on 20th December 1922), 3145 (11th January 1923), 3142 (12th January 1923) and 3116 (15th February 1923). All emerged with "NER" on the tank sides, the North Eastern's 24 inches-wide brass numberplates on the bunkers and front footsteps added on both sides. No.3150 (repaired at Springhead on 11th June 1923), emerged with "L&NER", plus 9 inch standard number plates, but without front steps. 3112 (ex-Springhead 27th June 1923), was treated similarly, as was "LNER" 3147, (24th August 1923), and "LNER" 3111D and 3149D in November 1923; all these five had to wait until their first Darlington visits to receive footsteps. No.2528 (147), was the last of the class to get the additional steps, leaving Darlington on 23rd January 1928.

As well as changing the appearance of the J75's the LNER also changed their workplaces, sending 2523 (142) to Immingham in September 1926, where it was to remain for the rest of its life. No.2529 (148) also became a Southern Area engine, as did 2528 (147) and 2532 (151).

In the case of 2529 (148), after serving initially at Immingham it ended its days appropriately enough at New England shed, where it demonstrated to all and sundry how well Matthew Stirling, former shedmaster had done since he had joined the H&BR over forty years before.

No.2528 (147) saw other parts of the LNER's Southern Area, spending several years at Boston interspersed with a period at Peterborough East just across the way from 2529 (148) from June to October 1937; but the palm for Most Travelled J75 goes to 2532 (151).

After serving for ten years at Immingham, October 1936 saw 2532 transferred to Doncaster. Being well enough supplied with home-grown 0-6-0 tanks of Patrick Stirling, Ivatt and Gresley origin, 2532 not surprisingly spent considerable periods in store, but the advent of World War II changed matters for naturally the LNER could not allow perfectly good engines to stand around unused. November 1940 saw the need for a powerful shunting engine arise at Huskisson Dock, Liverpool, so 2532 was duly sent across the Pennines to a new home at Walton-on-the-Hill shed. There it was to remain until withdrawal under British Railways' ownership, although ostensibly still the property of the LNER since nobody had got round to giving the war - weary old engine a lick of paint since May 1946, when someone had at least got round to applying its 1946 number, 8365, plus the letters "NE". January 1949 found BR deciding they could finally dispense with 8365's services, so ten years after its fellows

Immingham shed on 17th June 1934 had 2529 (148) on its books. Note the tapered-stock buffers at the front, and parallel ones at the rear!

it finally followed them to the Darlington scrapyard, although they duly entered it as being "G.C.Section Book Stock."

Perhaps we may best conclude with recording something of the reminiscences of those who had to work with the G3's, and one stirring episode in particular. William Westoby recalled one particular night shift, working from Alexandra Dock Shed. Fireman Westoby and his driver took a G3 (more properly by then, a J75), round to the oil terminal at Saltend, just east of King George V Dock (and like the latter built and operated jointly by the H&BR and the North Eastern before World War I). There they found 141 tank wagons, full of petrol, all marshalled up into one enormous train and awaiting transfer to the sidings on King George Dock prior to forwarding by main line engines. A week or two earlier on a similar working another crew had shifted 136 wagons in one train with their J75, so our heroes decided that they could do better and would try and take the lot in one go! A terrific battle ensued, with displays of fireworks from the chimney top and frantic slipping as the grossly overloaded little engine fought for adhesion. The contents of the sandboxes were soon used, so recourse was had to throwing

shovelsful of ash ballast under the wheels, but then a more alarming crisis made itself glaringly obvious: the pyrotechnics from the chimney had set the sedge - grasses alongside the line on fire - and 141 wagons held rather a lot of petrol! Nothing daunted, both footplatemen used the firing shovels as firebeaters, leaving their noble steed to make its way in the world as best it could, for there was no chance of it gaining enough speed to leave them behind! Finally, the entire parade drew up in the sidings at "King", before uncoupling and heading nonchalantly off to the next job, leaving groups of astounded dockers and impressed railwaymen gazing after them - and most likely recounting the number of wagons in the train! Even allowing for the fact that these were of different types and capacities (so much so that any attempt to work out a tonnage is pointless), it was still an extraordinary achievement and speaks volumes for Matthew Stirling's design work and the workmanship of its builders. Sadly, we cannot give the plaudits to either Kitson & Co. or the Yorkshire Engine Company, for today William Westoby has but one regret about that evening's escapade: try as he might, he was unable to recall the number of the J75 which had served over and above the call of duty on that evening so very long ago.

2532 (151) clearly showing the cab to be narrower than the tanks, also the small coupling-rod splashers alongside the cab. *Jim Stork collection.*

Summary: Class G3 0-6-0 Side Tanks. LNER Class J75.

HBR No.	Works No.	Delivered	NER No.	LNER No.	Reboilering	Withdrawn	Notes
111	655	December 1901	3111	2492	Dgm.71B/December 1926	September 1937	(1)
112	656	December 1901	3112	2493	Dgm.71B/August 1926	June 1937	(1)
113	657	December 1901	3113	2494	Dgm.71B/July 1924	May 1937	(1)
114	658	January 1902	3114	2495	Dgm,.71A/December 1927	May 1937	(1)
115	659	February 1902	3115	2496	Dgm.71B/June 1926	September 1937	(1)
116	660	February 1902	3116	2497	Dgm.69/February 1923 Dgm.71B/October 1936	May 1937	(1)
142	4545	January 1908	3142	2523	Dgm.71B/August 1927	June 1938	(2)
143	4546	January 1908	3143	2524	Dgm.71B/October 1927	May 1937	(2)
144	4547	January 1908	3144	2525	Dgm.71B/February 1928	June 1937	(2)
145	4548	February 1908	3145	2526	Dgm.71A/December 1927	May 1937	(2)
146	4549	February 1908	3146	2527	Dgm.71B/September 1924	September 1937	(2)
147	4550	February 1908	3147	2528	Dgm.71B/January 1928	March 1939	(2)
148	4551	February 1908	3148	2529	Dgm.71B/February 1928	July 1937	(2)
149	4552	February 1908	3149	2530	Dgm.71B/May 1927	May 1937	(2)
150	4553	February 1908	3150	2531	Dgm.71B/May 1927	June 1937	(2)
151	4554	March 1908	3151	2532	Dgm.71B/October 1927	January 1949*	(2)

Notes:

(1) Built by Yorkshire Engine Co. cost £2,460 each.

(2) Built by Kitson & Co. cost £2,620 each.

* Withdrawn as BR (6)8365. Under BR (6)8365 was included in the Route Availability Scheme as R.A.5, and given Power Class 3F, (i.e: Class 3, Freight only). After scrapping at Darlington, (6)8365's boiler was salvaged, to serve on an N13 class 0-6-2T for a further 3½ years.

Boilers: LNER Diagram 69 = ex-NER "901" domed boiler. LNER Diagram 71A = ex-HBR domeless boiler.

LNER Diagram 71B = LNER domed type, introduced in 1924, derived from HBR domeless type.

2528 (147) after reboilering in January 1928; "Class J75" plus new buffers appear at the front of the engine, and a fourth coal-rail has been fitted at the back end. *Jim Stork collection.*

Class G3 Dimensions.

Cylinders: 2, inside. 18" x 26".
Motion: Stephenson Link; slide valves between cylinders.
Boiler: Domeless.
Max. diameter outside: 4' 3".
Barrel length: 10' 0".
Firebox length outside: 5' 6".
Pitch: 6' 11".
Heating surface:
  Firebox 104 sq.ft.
  Tubes 194 @ 1³/₄" dia. - 951 sq.ft.
  Total 1,055 sq.ft.
Grate area: 16.25 sq.ft.
Ratio of grate area to heating surface: 1 to 64.92.
Boiler pressure: 150 lb/sq.in.
Wheel diameter: 4' 6".
Wheelbase: 7' 3" + 8' 3" = 15' 6".
Length over buffers: 32' 2½".
Weights:
13tons 3cwt + 16tons 8cwt + 17tons 16cwt = 47tons 7cwt.
Height to top of chimney: 12' 10⁵/₈".
Tractive effort @ 85% of boiler pressure: 19,890 lb.
Ratio of blast nozzle to cylinder diameter: 1 to 3.789.
Tank water capacity: 850 gallons.
Bunker coal capacity: 3tons (given as 2tons on final HBR Diagram).

The above dimensions apply to Class G3 at December 1922, when fitted with Diagram 71A type, domeless H&BR boilers.

Boiler to Diagram 69 (ex- "901" class), as fitted to No.3116 (LNER 2497), February 1923.
Boiler: Domed.
Max. outside diameter: 4' 3".
Barrel length: 10' 3".
Firebox length outside: 5' 6".
Heating surface:
  Firebox 98 sq.ft.
  Tubes 205 @ 1³/₄" - 995 sq.ft.
  Total 1,093 sq.ft.
Grate area: 15.16 sq.ft.
Ratio of grate area to heating surface: 1 to 72.09.
Boiler pressure: 160 lb/sq.in.
Tractive effort @ 85% boiler pressure: 21,216 lb.

Dimensions for Class J75 locomotives fitted with LNER domed boilers to Diagram 71B.

Boiler: Domed.
Max. outside diameter: 4' 3"
Barrel length: 10' 0".
Firebox length outside: 5' 6".
Heating surface:
  Firebox 99 sq.ft.
  Tubes 205 @ 1³/₄" - 972 sq.ft.
  Total 1,071 sq.ft.
Grate area: 15.5 sq.ft.
Ratio of grate area to heating surface: 1 to 69.09.
Boiler pressure: 175 lb/sq.in.
Tractive effort @ 85% boiler pressure: 23,197 lb.

2495 (114), 2530 (149) and 2596 (115) gathered together pending withdrawal by the LNER in 1937.

Another wandering G3 - 2523 (142) at Immingham shed, ex-GCR territory.

23rd January 1949 saw 2532 back at Darlington. Although renumbered 8365, it would never receive its BR number 68365, being scrapped instead just a few days after this photograph was taken. *Ron Copeman collection.*

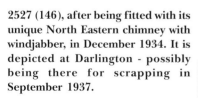

2527 (146), after being fitted with its unique North Eastern chimney with windjabber, in December 1934. It is depicted at Darlington - possibly being there for scrapping in September 1937.

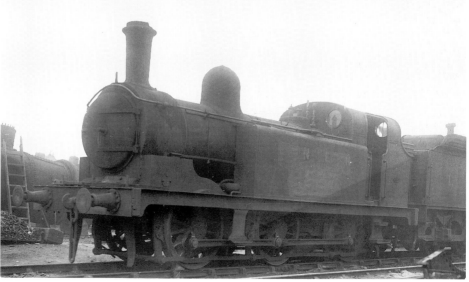

Stirling super-power! Anyone who dismisses the Stirlings - on the grounds of Patrick Stirling's singles and James Stirling's earlier 4-4-0's - as being simply the designers of rather delicate-looking express locomotives should study this view of the first "Tiny" very carefully! No.117 has clearly seen some service, but is in "as built" condition. Visible under the boiler between the two middle splashers is the manhole, which allowed full access to the boiler barrel after removal of the tubes. This was a feature often omitted from domed boilers, for the dome fulfilled the dual purposes of housing the regulator valve and allowing access.

Part 4 - LATER STIRLING CLASSES, 1907 - 1915.

Matthew Stirling had, in 1907, reached the mature age of 51 years and been in charge of H&BR locomotive affairs for some 22 years by the time he embarked on his final designs. These covered six classes of but four types, only one class of which was developed directly from a pre - 1907 design: to whit, the F3 radial 0-6-2 tanks, which were in essence a more beefy version of the F2 class of 1901.

The number of locomotives produced in this second and final Stirling phase totalled a mere fifty; five less than the ultimate number of Class B's alone, but if quantity was lacking quality was certainly there: indeed, some types could arguably be regarded as excellent!

The new Stirling era opened in the most spectacular way with the appearance of the massive Class A 0-8-0's. When introduced, they would have raised the eyebrows of the staff in any railway company's locomotive department but originating as they did from a company as relatively insignificant as the H&BR, they were nothing less than sensational! The Class A's firmly established an arrangement of valves and valve gear which effectively became a new H&BR standard: open-backed, balanced slide valves above the cylinders, driven by Allan straight-link valve gear via rocking levers. This arrangement as we have already seen, was introduced to the H&BR with the five F1 Class radial tanks from Kitson's in 1901.

If the year 1907 opened a new era for the H&BR, 1910 saw the end of a greater one, for it marked the appearance of the last Stirling family express locomotives. These, the H&BR's Class J, were the only purely passenger locomotives instigated by Matthew Stirling and the only 4-4-0's on the Hull & Barnsley. As 4-4-0's, they may be compared more fairly with James Stirling's designs for the Glasgow & South Western, and South Eastern Railway rather than anything which actually appeared on the Great Northern under Patrick Stirling. Sadly, the Class J's never really had the opportunities to gain similar renown to their predecessors from the other members of the Stirling family, on other metals.

The final truly original H&BR engines were twenty which formed a "family group" consisting of Classes L, L1 and LS (and which the LNER lumped together as Class J28). These were a very successful combination of the Class A machinery under the Class J boiler, mounted on a frame with six wheels, coupled. Five members of Class L1 were optimistically encumbered with "Phoenix" smokebox steam-drying equipment (one hesitates to refer to it as "superheating"), and five more were saturated, as were all five of Class L. Class LS benefited from Schmidt smoketube/element superheaters, and were among the best engines on the H&BR. It can only be regretted that one of these boilers was never tried out on a Class J; but as it was, the five LS engines formed a worthy finale to the story of H&BR locomotive development.

However, since your author considers (rightly or wrongly), that Class LS of 1915 was but a development of Class L1 of 1911, then the last H&BR design has to be Class F3 introduced in 1913. These were a heavier version of Class F2, having increased tank capacity, no vacuum brakes and for some odd reason a boiler pitched a few inches higher, which entailed a slightly shorter chimney.

An indication that the initial phase of H&BR locomotive affairs was drawing to a close lay in the fact that exactly half of the post-1907 designated engines were regarded as replacements for the Kirtley engines. Twenty-five of the original engines were displaced to the duplicate lists by fifteen of the L/L1/LS family, five of the F3's and all five Class J 4-4-0's.

The withdrawal (in most cases years before the end of their economic working lives), of the majority of the post-1907 engines was an indication of the state of affairs brought about by the Depression and the world financial situation in general, and its effect on the LNER in particular. The big Class A engines which had entered service amidst such high expectations, were (with the exception of the three odd G2 Class engines), the first of Matthew Stirling's designs to disappear completely; this regrettable state of affairs being achieved by November 1931.

They were followed a few years later by the Class J's, meanwhile the first of the L/L1/LS group had gone; although the last survived until 1939, it only outlived the last two engines of Class B by a year.

Thus out of all the locomotives dealt with hereon only the ten Class F3 engines became British Railways' property, and furthermore became the only H&BR class to enter Nationalisation in their entirety. The last survived until 1956, but sadly official inertia, indifference and lack of imagination allowed it to go for scrap - an unworthy end for the last vestige of H&BR motive power and which has been a matter of some regret ever since, not least of all on the part of your author.

Class J No.38 in classic pose at Springhead; note the H&BR's useful habit of painting cylinder sizes on the front bufferbeam - "19½ x 26" (inches), in the case of this class.

CLASS A 0-8-0 MINERAL ENGINES. (LNER CLASS Q10). Introduced 1907.

It must have seemed to the interested observer that the year 1907 represented the zenith of mankind's mastery of the natural world, through the applied skills of its engineers. Land, sea and sky were demonstrably seen to have been overcome, for although British engineers were not necessarily the leaders of transport technology in all three areas, they were certainly among the front runners. September 1907 saw the British Army (not exactly renowned for its innovative nature), launch its first airship. Taking off from Farnborough the 120-foot long craft made a 3½ hour flight, circling London. (Although the Wright Brothers had demonstrated heavier-than-air flight four years earlier, it was to be 1908 before such a wonder was displayed in British airspace).

Another maiden voyage took place simultaneously with that of the airship: the Cunard liner "Lusitania", the World's largest vessel, had moved its 710-foot length (representing a bulk of 31,500 tons), across the Atlantic Ocean at a record average speed of 23 knots; consuming a mountainous 1,000 tons of coal per day in order to do so.

Not to be outdone by the Merchant Navy, the Royal Navy launched the World's largest cruiser, HMS "Indomitable", on the Clyde and just to make sure that they kept numbers of ships well ahead of any upstart Continentals, launched another Dreadnought-class battleship, HMS "Bellerophon", at Portsmouth.

Meanwhile back on terra firma, the year 1907 opened with the first long-distance car rally, from Peking to Paris; then it saw the first Isle of Man motor cycle TT race and culminated with the opening of the World's first motor racing track at Brooklands, near Weybridge.

Rail transport also saw its new marvels: Union Station Washington was opened, modelled after (of all things), the Baths of Diocletian; whilst at home the London & South Western Railway proudly announced that the new facade of Waterloo Station was finished (although the station rebuilding was not to be completed until 1922).

Achievements of locomotive engineers also managed to reach the pages of *Engineering* in 1907, despite being overshadowed by the extensive photographic supplement devoted entirely to the "Lusitania". Outstanding amongst the contributions from the world of railway locomotive engineering were the new, four-cylinder compound express 4-6-0's for the Prussian State Railways, notable for the application of Professor Schmidt's new method of superheating. Compounding was also a feature of the new eight-wheels coupled, heavy goods locomotives introduced by Mr. Hughes on the Lancashire & Yorkshire Railway. Even the Hull & Barnsley Railway made its contribution to 1907's cornucopia of technological marvels, with description and illustrations of their new heavy mineral engines occupying four pages of *Engineering* for 15th November 1907.

The accompanying text gave a plain, straightforward description of the work and construction of the new engines, but not surprisingly we have to look elsewhere for their origins and subsequent history. Although by far the biggest engines on the Hull & Barnsley Railway they had one thing in common with the smallest, the Class K dock tanks, inasmuch as both acquired a somewhat enigmatic history. In the case of the big engines this is more difficult to explain, since they started life amidst such a "high profile" fanfare of hopes and expectations.

Engineering stated that the new heavy mineral engines "....were giving every satisfaction...." Dr. Parkes described them as being "....of outstanding design....", sentiments echoed by David Smith, writing in the *Railway World* in 1960; yet a short time after their introduction extra bonus payments were having to be made to entice footplate staff to work them! Even at the end of their lives, footplatemen at the ex-North Eastern shed at Selby created such a furore at having been given them that a fruitless search for other suitable work elsewhere was undertaken, immediately prior to their withdrawal.

To try and find the reasons behind the apparent fall from grace of the H&BR's big goods engines, we may as well start (as Matthew Stirling probably did), with consideration of the needs for a new design of engine considerably bigger than Class B. Stirling's assessment of the H&BR's motive power situation around the mid-1900's has already been discussed at some length under Class F2, but it is worthwhile reminding the reader that from 1 million tons in 1901, the H&B's export coal traffic alone had risen to 3 millions by 1906.

A different viewpoint for the photograph of No. 117. This picture was used by the group of artists working under the F.Moore banner to produce a coloured postcard in the 1900's, although they picked out more of the area in shadow under the footplating and obliterated the two sets of metals in the foreground with "grass" - a portent of what was to happen sixty years later.... *J.B.Stork.*

A rare view of an H&BR train - 120 hustles empty mineral wagons along the main line in East Yorkshire, between South and North Cave stations. *Memory Lane, Hull.*

Furthermore, annual freight-train mileage over the H&BR in 1905 stood at 1,203,850 miles: two years later by the time the big engines appeared, that figure had risen to 1,577,331 miles - a 23.6% increase!

It may be one thing to establish the desperate need for more locomotives on the H&BR, but quite another to establish responsibility for the design of the new engines. It has been averred that the H&BR had engaged in litigation against the Yorkshire Engine Company in an attempt to secure compensation for the unsuitability of the new engines, yet the facts do not support this. Firstly, the favourable report in *Engineering* appeared after the first of the new engines had been in service for some nine months - surely enough time for them to have established their worth. Secondly there are no records of actions brought either by the H&BR or the Yorkshire Engine Company in the Law Reports from 1901 to 1910, although the H&B may just possibly have threatened it, as we shall eventually see. Moreover, if the H&BR had any doubts whatsoever regarding the products of the Yorkshire Engine Co., they would surely not have placed further orders with them when there were so many other manufacturers trading at the time; yet the five engines of Class L were built at Meadowhall. Finally, if the H&BR engines had been so abysmal, the LNER would surely have scrapped them as soon as possible rather than go to the trouble and expense of providing new boilers for them all.

Yet another legend which had circulated around Springhead was that the design of the big engines was largely the work and responsibility of Lytton, Stirling's assistant. It was averred that Stirling was never in favour of the big 0-8-0's at all and that there were differences of opinion between the two; but as we have already seen, Lytton was appointed on 29th September 1908 - after the whole class had seen at least ten months' work! Although he may well have disagreed with "the Boss" as to the later deployment of the engines, Lytton clearly had no influence whatsoever on their design.

By some accident of history a copy of the *Specification of Eight-Wheels Coupled Goods Engines and Tenders* has survived, and this may well give us the truth of this matter. This document, including the "Form of Tender" ("Tender" meaning "Submission of offers to construct" in this instance!), is in the form of a printed booklet running to some thirty-two pages, dated 1906 and bearing the name "M.Stirling, Loco.Eng.", at the end of the text. In it, Matthew Stirling details dimensions, methods of construction, quality and types of materials, fittings and test procedures. The H&BR Company Secretary, George Scaum, also took up three pages of the Specifications booklet, laying down the General Conditions, obligations, responsibilities and liabilities in law by which any prospective locomotive builder had to agree to be bound. One particular sentence written by Scaum is worthy of quoting in full: "The Engines must be finished in every respect in the most complete manner and to the entire satisfaction of the Company's Locomotive Engineer, who shall at any and at all times be at liberty to inspect the same, either personally or by deputy, and to reject any which he or his Deputy may consider deficient or defective, either as regards material or workmanship." This, together with the fact that the dimensions listed in the Specifications booklet correspond in almost every case with the completed engines, would seem to be irrefutable evidence that the H&B got exactly what they had asked for!

The Specifications Booklet also refers to accompanying drawings, so it can be assumed that Matthew Stirling drew up the design outline and specifications largely single-handed, before any involvement with the Yorkshire Engine Co. He must have started work on the big goods project early in 1905 since the Specifications booklet is dated 1906; and furthermore the YEC's agreement with the H&BR regarding acceptance of the contract dated from 30th May 1906.

They undertook to build ten engines, the first two to be delivered a mere five months after contract date then two per month to be delivered afterwards. The H&BR had stipulated penalties of, ".....twenty pounds(£20) per week for each engine in arrear, as and for agreed liquidated damages", so not surprisingly Yorkshire Engine had no time to lose. A mere two days after finalising the contract they made a start on the preparation of sets of working drawings. Despite starting on this order, (No.E158), with such alacrity, the Sheffield manufacturers failed to meet their promised delivery deadlines by some four months - the first engine being delivered in February 1907 (by coincidence the anticipated original delivery date for the last two!). Each engine had cost £3,560: thus the entire contract was worth £35,600 - but the Yorkshire Engine Co. saw their profit margin on this totally wiped out as deliveries of the remaining engines were likewise delayed and the H&BR doubtless invoked their penalty clauses in the contract! The effect of this upon the unfortunate Yorkshire Engine Co. was reported at their Annual General Meeting in Sheffield, the summary of which, published in *Engineering* on 28th February 1908 is worth quoting: "Mr.G.B.Walker, presiding at the Yorkshire Engine Company Annual General Meeting on 19th February, was very frank in his recital of the gloomy events of the past year's working of the firm. He said that a year ago they were crowded with satisfactory orders, and now they had to come forward with a balance-sheet showing a loss of nearly £12,000, with certain sums remaining unsettled in relation to contract penalties. Explaining the unsatisfactory nature of some of the firm's contracts, Mr.Walker said that on a substantial contract for engines to a railway company they had lost, taking into consideration all dues and charges, £500 per engine. The very fullness of their order-books, he said, had resulted in extra losses, because they had to work at great pressure and overtime. They were working against penalties, with higher costs than they would ordinarily have had. The manufacture of motor chassis, too, which was a new department, had not turned out satisfactorily. The meeting lasted two hours, and some pertinent questions were put by a few shareholders."

Assuming that the H&BR order was indeed the "substantial contract", then the Yorkshire Engine Company lost a total of £5,000 on the ten engines, or around ⅕th. of the total value of the contract. (Basically, if worked out on a price per ton basis, the H&BR had paid for nine engines and eight tenders: the hapless builders in effect provided one engine and two tenders free of charge! Another way of looking at it could be to estimate that Yorkshire Engine Company's workforce numbered probably around 800 men in 1907. Assuming their weekly wage to be about £2 - 5 - 0d., then the loss on the H&BR contract would represent the entire workshop's staff payroll for over a fortnight!! Little wonder that, ".....some pertinent questions were asked by shareholders." Also, possible reluctance or tardiness in complying with the penalty clauses in the contract may have led the H&BR to threaten legal action and thereby given rise to the legend of litigation).

The new engines took up H&BR Numbers 117 to 126; curiously, delivery of No.121 was in August 1907, some two months after the delivery of Nos.125 and 126; (presumably No.121 had not been, ".....finished in every respect in the most complete manner and to the entire satisfaction of the Company's Locomotive Engineer.....!").

Despite the fact that George Scaum had reserved the right for, "The said Locomotive Engineer..... to have full power, at any time, to rescind this contract, if at any time, in his opinion, sufficient speed has not been shown or made in the execution of this contract.....", Stirling and the H&BR Board were happy enough to award a further contract to the Yorkshire Engine Company on 13th March 1907 for a further five locomotives. Delivery was to commence in September 1907 - and despite even more onerous penalties for late delivery, the Sheffield builders were happy enough to accept the order. This time, the first of the five engines was delivered on time and the last reached the H&BR in November 1907. Understandably, Yorkshire Engine Company's price for this order (No.E166), had gone up appreciably to £4,250 each, although the only differences between the two orders lay in the larger front sandboxes fitted to this later batch.

The second order took H&BR numbers 127 to 131, following on directly behind their predecessors; all became Class A under the 1908 scheme - the first letter of the alphabet for the first rank of H&BR motive-power! The first ten occupied Yorkshire Engine Works numbers 899 to 908; the additional five

had Works numbers 942 to 946, but this should not be taken as implying that the Yorkshire Engine Company had built thirty-four locomotives in the meantime, for they honoured anything they built with a Works number, be it colliery winding engine or replacement ship's boiler! (YE Co. Works' numbers 715 to 722, to Order C122 were given to eight boilers dispatched to the H&BR around 1901, for example).

Having unravelled the tangle of controversies surrounding the origins of Class A, we should now try and cast a little light on their gloomy reputations to see if we can discern the reasons for their apparent failure to gain universal acceptance. Perhaps the ideal way of doing this would be to inspect one of the full-sized engines, an option which is only open to us now in our imagination unfortunately; but let us try and think ourselves back on that bright, crisp day in February 1907, about to have a very close look at No.117 as it stands on an engine-pit in Springhead shed, newly-delivered from Sheffield.

Our first sight of No.117 is through the brick arch of the shed doorway, and the first impression we get is of its sheer size: the massive smokebox, some 6ft 3in diameter and centred at 8ft 2in above rail level, seems to fill the entire doorway. We note the big cylinders, 19 x 26 inches, for their dimensions are obligingly painted on the front bufferbeam.

Walking around the engine, we notice the smallish wheels - 4ft 6inches in diameter - and the small splashers over them complete with well-polished, heavy brass beading around the edge of each one. The mainframe top edge runs level with the tops of the splashers and about a foot below the bottom of the boiler; thus from the normal trackside viewing angle a fair amount of daylight is visible below the boiler barrel (anticipating in a more modest way by 50 years the British Railways Standard 9F Class 2-10-0's, nicknamed "Spaceships" for a similar reason).

No.117 also shared another characteristic feature with the 9F's inasmuch as both had Belpaire fireboxes. That on No.117 was no slab-sided affair as on the Midland and early LMS six or eight-coupled locomotives; instead, Matthew Stirling had stipulated that the lower lagging sheets should follow the firebox plates fairly closely and that the upper firebox edges should be generously curved. (The use of the Belpaire firebox on Class A was a unique feature amongst all Stirling family locomotives, although consideration was given to so fitting the next H&BR type - the Class J 4-4-0's of 1910).

Accompanying Matthew Stirling's unique firebox is a positively immense boiler of no less than 5ft 6in diameter and four feet longer than those of the Class B 0-6-0's, being 14 feet long in the barrel. A quick peep in the smokebox reveals that the shed labourers are to be kept busy with the flue brushes on "shed days", for this massive boiler carries 229 copper tubes, arranged in a horizontal diamond pattern.

Moving further along the locomotive we note the cab, unusual in being without side windows or even a cut-out at the back end, but at least with a roof extending well back over the tender fall-plate.

Continuing our walk back alongside No.117, we note that the tender is similar to those behind the Class B 0-6-0's, but due to a wider tank it holds 3,300 gallons of water (an increase of 300 gallons capacity). Oddly enough though, its nominal coal capacity has been decreased by one ton, down to four: thus it would seem unlikely that the Hull & Barnsley management intend No.117 to venture far off its native system, unlike the Class B's with their not-infrequent forays on excursions over "foreign" metals.

No. 123 leaves no doubts as to its power in this impressive view taken at Springhead, where extensions to the shed appear to be under way. *Hull Museums collection.*

(centre) 125 raises the echoes as it starts out of Springhead yard with a train of empty minerals and pit-props for West Riding collieries. Note the extra sand-box found necessary, fitted in front of the driving-wheel splasher.

(bottom) Several points worthy of note present themselves in this view of No. 129. Firstly, the engine has been fitted with the additional sandboxes, and being one of the five engines from the second order, has the bigger front sandboxes with the filler set into the footplating. The cab roof has a ventilator, and the style of cab lining should be noted. Usually, the sides were lined in a panel-shape, although the Yorkshire Engine Company's photograph as reproduced in *Engineering* shows the lining executed as seen here. The cabside shows the alleged "Porthole", although some have averred that this is actually a mark on the photographic negative, it should be borne in mind that several H&BR enginemen were adamant as to its existence and the reason for it. Finally, the engine would appear to be at Sandholme rather than Springhead, possibly on a "Sandholme Banker" working. *J.B. Stork collection.*

2509 (128) in NER goods livery but carrying its LNER number, depicted in front of the bike shed at Springhead. Being in an area of flat, low-lying land, cycling to work was the norm for Hull's citizens, and railwaymen's bicycles were often taken on engines and brake-vans so as to avoid picking them up from the far side of the city before going home in case a working finished up some miles away from the parent depot or shed. Between 2509's tender and the smokebox of the engine behind it may be glimpsed Springhead wagon shops. *Ron Copeman collection.*

Returning to the front end of 117, let us now climb down the steps into the pit underneath the engine, having of course first ensured that nobody is going to move it in the meantime!

Taking care not to bang our heads on the front coupling's lower link and keeping an eye open in order to dodge the whisps of steam and drops of very hot water which invariably issue from any engine in steam, we pass under the cylinder block; the eight underhung leaf springs for the driving axleboxes are prominent in two rows, receding away into the gloom under the back-end of the locomotive.

Looking upwards from near the front axle, we may feel that Mr. Stirling could have made the cylinders even bigger in diameter, but that could have meant smaller bearings for the axles - as it is, they are a generous eight inches diameter by nine inches long. (No.117's bearings were larger than those on the LMS 0-8-0's and their Beyer-Garratt articulated engines, both types appearing some twenty years later and both being bedevilled with inadequate bearings and poor mechanical design, which led to their withdrawal in the 1950's just as soon as more satisfactory motive power became available in sufficient quantities. Ironically, the LMS eight coupled engines went to the scrapyards before most of the engines they were meant to replace: the London & North Western Rly's G2 Class 0-8-0's).

But of more interest than No.117's axleboxes is its valve-gear, which is what we have really come underneath to have a look at! We spot the obvious features immediately - that the valves are driven by Allan Straight-link valve gear, via rocking levers. This is a new arrangement on a Stirling locomotive, but we have already met with it on the Kitson Class F1 radial tanks of 1900. Being reasonably astute observers, we notice that the eccentric rods are quite short (3ft 3in between centres), and that the valves are above the cylinders in steam chests of a good depth - a fact confirmed by a glance at the general arrangement drawing, which also reveals that the valves are of the open-backed, balanced type; again a broadly similar arrangement to the F1's. (Allan Straight-link valve gear and balanced slide valves have certain advantages over the more usual back-to-back valves with Stephenson link motion, but for a fuller discussion as to the

merits - and demerits - of the various arrangements employed on the H&BR, please refer to the relevant sections in the appendices in vol.2).

Whilst underneath No.117 we notice that the plate steel mainframes, $1\frac{1}{8}$ inches thick, are securely braced by the cast-steel motion plate and two transverse stays: one between the second and third axles, the other immediately in front of the firebox casing; in addition the cast iron drag-box, cylinder block and bufferbeam also act as very substantial bracings.

Moving further back under the engine we notice the ashpan, some two feet deep at the front end but humped over the rear axle to leave a depth below the grate of only around nine inches from that point to the back. Although there is sufficient room to have deepened the ashpan behind the axle and also fitted a damper door, the opportunity to have done so has not been taken. Still, many other engines have a front damper only and shallow ashpans and steam perfectly well (provided the ashpan is properly emptied), so we may reserve judgement on this arrangement!

Under the dragbox we note a steam brake cylinder operating via a substantial cross-shaft; a flexible metallic tube forms a steam connection with a similar cylinder under the leading end of the tender. This arrangement is easier to keep in good order than that fitted to the North Eastern's eight-coupled engines, which utilised a mechanical linkage to apply the tender brakes. Failure of the link was apt to leave the locomotive short of sufficient brake-power; fortunately such failures were mercifully rare, but tended, when they did occur, to be spectacular.

A quick look underneath 117's tender reveals its similarity "below decks" to the earlier varieties behind the Class B's, save for one big difference - all the earlier Stirling tenders (and indeed all those built after the Class A's), have vacuum brakes; thus the Class A tenders are the only ones by Matthew Stirling not to have continuous brakes.

Having finished our inspection underneath No.117, we may as well pass right under the tender and scramble out of the pit at the back of the tender. (Pits for steam locomotives are

2510 (129) seen here at Springhead, remains substantially as built, save for additional sandboxes, cab roof ventilator, three dog-clips on the smokebox door and "Iracier" tender axleboxes. *Ron Copeman collection.*

normally far shallower than those provided years later for diesel traction, and also kept much cleaner in 1907 than they became at the time of transition to diesels, with the accompanying run-down of steam).

Whilst on our imaginary viewing of the new engine we have not yet come across any aspect deserving particular criticism, but there remains just one place left which we have not yet examined: the footplate. This is of greater importance than may be imagined (even by locomotive engineers and designers!), for it is where the crews spend most of their working lives and its layout affects how they perform their tasks, their comfort and even their safety. (One thinks at this point of the pre-Grouping Great Western Railway tender locomotives, their drivers having to lean uncomfortably across the reversing screw in order to look ahead; or of the North Eastern firemen with bruised and bandaged knuckles, having come into forceful contact when swinging the shovel with the famous - or perhaps infamous - "fish fryer" screens above the firehole door; but probably the most notorious example of bad practice appeared on the London, Tilbury & Southend Railway. Many of their drivers lost finger-ends due to illicit tinkering with the steam-reversing gear, fitted in the cab - nobody bothered to fit cover-plates to discourage such meddling. The otherwise - exemplary London & North Western Railway's G2 Class can also be added to the list of uncomfortable locomotives, possessing perch-like seats the size of a church misericord and having a joint in the cab roof guaranteed to channel rainwater into a gentle trickle down the back of the driver's neck; at least No.117's cab looks as though it will turn the weather pretty well).

So without further ado let us climb aboard the locomotive for a look at the footplate arrangements. As we climb on, we find that we are about a foot higher than is apparent from outside

the engine, since wooden floorboards have been built up to around that height above the external footplate level. Having climbed into the cab and taken that instinctive look at the gauge glasses to check the water-level in No.117's boiler, there are several things that strike us. Firstly, the inside of the cab is painted in Indian Red - hardly the most restful of colours and a distinct contrast to the dark paintwork on the outside of the engine. Secondly, the sheer size of 117's huge boiler becomes almost overwhelmingly apparent as we gaze up at the pressure gauge, away in the gloom above the top of the firebox over seven feet above footplate level! We also note with surprise that the red line on the gauge shows the engine's working pressure to be 200 lb.per square inch - a remarkably high pressure for 1907.

The regulator handle of the usual Stirling push-pull type, dominates the firebox backhead as it stretches horizontally right across it from one side to the other. Centred at well over five feet above footplate level, it is at rather too high a position for a short driver to reach comfortably. Although well supplied with windows in the cab front, two of these are above the firebox (and therefore at the same level as the pressure gauge), and so high as to be virtually useless. Luckily, raised floorboards built up on either side of the cab, platform-fashion, raise one's vantage point by some fifteen inches, but that for the driver is a mixed blessing. Extending across the cab floor by some two feet three inches it is too wide to lean across comfortably, and rather too narrow to stand on and feel completely at ease since the reversing lever and its base take up much of the platform's width. Also, a driver six feet or more in height standing on the raised floorboards would, whilst obtaining a good view out, find his head in rather too close a proximity to the cab roof. A shorter driver would at least be able to see out of the lower part of the right-hand front window.

The use of lever reverse on No.117 is rather curious for the Specifications booklet required the fitting of screw reverse; in fact we may well feel that on such a big engine a steam-powered reverser wouldn't come amiss, either. (Matthew Stirling's uncle, James, had considered it a worthwhile fitting on far smaller locomotives than No.117, after all).

Another feature unlikely to endear itself to drivers is the absence of somewhere to sit; at least the fireman has a locker with a hinged wooden lid upon which to sit, but it is at such a low level that it is impossible to keep any sort of a proper lookout on the road ahead.

(Considering that mineral engines are likely to spend much of their time waiting in goods loops and sidings for their more fleet-footed brethren to hurtle by on workings with a higher level of prestige, the lack of proper seats seems to be an inexplicable oversight, although the H&BR is largely free from both conflicting junctions and traffic of higher priority).

Our imaginary inspection of the H&BR's splendid new locomotive has only been possible thanks to having taken liberties with Time and Space, but we may as well stretch credibility to the extent of imagining that we are now invited to drive No.117 out of the shed westwards down the locomotive yard, then set back to the coal stage.

A look through the fire-door flap reveals a good depth of hot fire, well burnt through after the delivery run over the Midland Railway from Meadowhall and the forty-six miles along the H&BR from Cudworth, but a couple of shovelsful under the door won't come amiss.

No.117's fireman attends to this, using the flap in the firehole door rather than opening up the door itself - those H&BR footplate staff who had followed Matthew Stirling from the Great Northern Railway are quite used to this type of door, it being another example of GNR practice employed on the H&BR.

Although there is room for a good depth of fire under the door on 117 since the back end of the grate is set 1ft 9in below the bottom of the door-ring, we don't overdo things and smoke out the entire shed. Instinct makes us check that the cylinder drain taps are still open (confirmed by a glance at the position of the operating lever by the right-hand cab side and nearly as prominent as the reversing lever), so without further ado we move to put 117 into forward gear.

Standing on the tender fall-plate behind the driver's wooden platform we find the lever at a convenient height, but as we move it forward it becomes too much of a stretch, since in full fore-gear, the top of the lever comes within three inches of the cab front! So we try again, now standing on the platform. This time, the lever is rather too low for convenient operation, and we cannot bring full strength to bear on it as we could if standing behind it. Still, it goes into fore gear readily enough despite a little stiffness due to its newness, thanks to the self-balancing feature of Allan link motion and the open backed slide valves not being much harder than piston valves to move across.

With the tender handbrake off, a stretch on tiptoe brings the lever for the whistle into reach (one can imagine all manner of chains or bits of twine being rigged up in order to make it less of a stretch!), and with a gentle "pop" on the whistle to warn anyone in the vicinity that we are about to move the engine, we make the reach upwards to grasp the regulator handle. We pull it firmly but gently open, closing it again as soon as we feel No.117 start to move; then giving the big engine a little more steam we

roll out into the wintry daylight. Thankfully, we note that the regulator operates surprisingly easily - for a start, the gland packing is new, not having had long enough to bake itself into a mass of hard, dry fibres (unless it gets changed before reaching that unhappy state!), and secondly, the regulator valve itself is something of a novelty. Instead of a flat valve subject to full boiler steam-pressure sliding horizontally over the valve port-face, we have two vertical sets of ports facing each other longitudinally at the end of the main steam pipe. The valve itself is of the relieved type which "..... consists of two gun-metal valves..... one being bored out to receive the turned portion of the other, and..... fitted with gun-metal rings for the purpose of preventing the passage of steam to the back of the valves, thus relieving the regulator of excessive steam-pressure," according to the description in *Engineering*.

Having moved about an engine-length we shut the cylinder drains, and ceasing to proceed through hissing clouds of steam we can see where we are going and give 117 sufficient steam to trundle steadily along at a brisk walking-pace at which point in the proceedings we become aware of an odd phenomenon of the engine. The exhaust, instead of having a deep gruffness which we might have expected, gives a distinct whistling noise with each beat: a sort of mid-pitched, "Chiff-chiff! Chiff-chiff!" sound, which seems a rather whimsical noise for such a massively-purposeful, no-frills piece of machinery such as No.117 to make. (Such a sound was not unique to the H&BR Class A's - years later, the Maunsell Southern Railway 4-6-0's of the S15 and N15 "King Arthur" classes also exhibited similar musical aspirations; they and the Class A's had similar exhaust - pipe and blast arrangements, consisting of an iron casting in the form of an inverted "Y". As the steam ways and passages lost their original shape due to the build-up of hard, carbonised oil, the engines gradually lost their ability to whistle - unless during the course of overhaul someone took the trouble to burn out or chip away the accretions of carbon, thus putting the engines quite literally back "on song").

As 117 proceeds merrily along in the general direction of Locomotive Junction we find that due to track curvature our view ahead is rather restricted. As there is no side window, we shut the regulator and trusting that it will not blow itself back open again (a disconcerting fault to which push-pull regulator handles are prone if the glands are left on the slack side for ease of operation), we retreat on to the fall-plate and lean out over the cab doors to look out around the side of the cab. At least the cab doors are at a good height, 3ft 3in above the cab footplate level, so we can rest our hands on them and lean quite comfortably and safely over them with just the movements of engine and tender rising and falling independently over the rail-joints to make us slightly uneasy.

Having come far enough down the shed lines to clear the points for the coal-stage, we have to dodge back into the cab to apply the steam-brake, for the handle is just out of reach when looking out around the cab side-sheet. Again comes another stretch as we heave the reversing lever over into back-gear; the yard points having been changed, we can set back towards the old wooden coal stage (soon to be replaced by a splendid new ediface being built in brick, just to the north). At least now we are running in reverse we get a clear view out over the tender, particularly as it is somewhat down on coal. As we draw up alongside the coaling platform we bring the engine to a halt, then applying the handbrake, setting the engine in mid-gear and leaving the drain taps open, we climb off. As Springhead's

Table 7: COMPARISONS BETWEEN IVATT GNR AND STIRLING H&BR 0-8-0'S

	Ivatt 0-8-0	**Stirling 0-8-0**
Class	K1, introduced 1901. (LNER class Q1)	A, introduced 1907. (LNER class Q10)
Cyls, dia. x stroke	20" x 26"	19" x 26"
Valve gear	Stephenson link, slide valves on top of cylinders, driven via. rocking levers	Allan straight-link, balanced slide valves on top of cylinders, driven via rocking levers.
Boilers	Domed, round-top	Domeless, Belpaire
Pressures	175 lb/sq.in	200 lb/sq.in
Diameters	4ft 8ins	5ft 6ins
Barrel lengths	14ft 8⅝ ins, over front extension ring: actually 12ft 8⅝ ins	14ft 0ins
No. of tubes	191 @ 2" dia.	229 @ 2" dia
Tube heating surfaces	1,302 sq.ft	1,728 sq.ft
Firebox heating surfaces	137 sq.ft	131 sq.ft
Total heating surfaces	1,439 sq.ft	1,859 sq.ft
Grate areas	24.5 sq.ft	22 sq.ft
Ratio of G.A. to total H.S.	1 to 58.73	1 to 84.5
Firebox length outside	8ft 0ins	7ft 6ins
Boiler pitch	8ft 4¼ ins	8ft 2ins
Wheel diameter	4ft 8ins	4ft 6ins
Total wheelbase: engine	17ft 8ins	16ft 6ins
T.W: engine and tender	41ft 4ins	40ft 0⅜ins
Tender wheel diameter	4ft 2ins	3ft 9ins
Tender wheelbase	13ft 0ins	12ft 0ins
Tender water capacity	3,670 gallons	3,300 gallons
Tender coal capacity	5 tons	4 tons
Total weights in W.O.	95 tons 10 cwt	100 tons 19 cwt
Length over buffers	54ft 7ins	53ft 9⅜ ins
T. E. @ 85% of B.P.	27,650 lb	29,548 lb

"black gang" set to work, we retreat to avoid getting covered in coal-dust, and this gives us a chance to stand back and take an overall view of No.117.

One thing which strikes us immediately is the similarity between the H&BR's new engine and the "Long Tom" 0-8-0's introduced on the Great Northern Railway in 1901 by H.A.Ivatt - Patrick Stirling's successor. No.117 could almost be regarded as a slightly larger version of the GNR engines - certainly it is far from being a basic enlargement of the Class B 0-6-0's as the late Ken Hoole tends to imply in the two-part standard history (*The Hull & Barnsley Railway, Vol.2*).

The GN engines have domed boilers, and a cab cut-out just big enough to lean on and look ahead whilst still remaining within reach of the brake handle at least; an attribute of considerable help when shunting, for example. (Further comparisons between both railway Companies' respective 0-8-0's are to be found in *Table 7*).

At this point in the narrative though, it is high time we thanked all those responsible at Springhead for so indulging us, bid them farewell and return to our own times!

Having returned to the present, we can, with the benefit of hindsight assess the Class A's in service in a more orthodox fashion!

After a relatively short time in service, as with any new design there were odd teething troubles to overcome. Lack of ability to produce steam was not one of these problems, however; at least not after the footplate staff had become accustomed to them. William Westoby recalled them as being excellent steamers, in fact he recalled No.126 as being a "lovely engine", and his particular favourite when it came to producing steam. Only one aspect of the design came in for almost immediate alteration, for it was soon found that the capacity of the leading

sandboxes was inadequate in bad weather, the contents being used up too soon. Another odd occurrence was that the same sandbox filler lids, protruding from below the footplate drop-angle, cut some of the clearances on various shed roads at Springhead just a little too fine: in fact William Westoby stated that on one shed road, more sharply curved than the others, the sandbox lids would invariably be flipped off as they came into sharp contact with the brickwork around the shed door! Not surprisingly the last five engines were modified before construction, being given deeper sandboxes with the filler lids set flush into the footplating. Since the first ten were never altered (although Springhead Shed obviously had been!), this difference provided a ready means of distinguishing between the two groups.

Despite the increased capacity of the sandboxes on the last five, sand for forward running was still apt to be inadequate so a further supply was provided by means of additional boxes fitted up immediately in front of the splashers over the second wheelset. This supply was gravity fed as opposed to steam operation for the original apparatus. The additional sandboxes were quickly fitted to all fifteen engines by the H&BR, but the additional supply was converted under the LNER to steam operation on all engines, probably at the time they were reboilered.

Enough sand was essential when it came to providing sufficient grip for the Class A's, despite the 61 tons 11 cwts of the locomotive alone in working order. (Including the tender, the H&BR Diagram Book gave Class A engines a weight of 100 tons 19 cwts - thus they were the only locomotives from the Stirling family to tip the scales at over 100 tons!). Along with the 19 tons 3 cwts increase in weight over the Class B's, tractive effort also increased by some 41% to 29,548 lb, which in operating

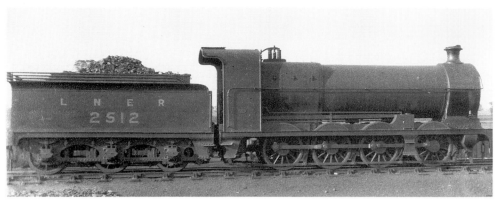

2512 (131) was the last Class A to be delivered, in November 1907. It is shown here largely in unaltered condition, in direct contrast to the next view. *Ron Copeman collection.*

terms meant that they could work 45 loaded ten-ton wagons on mineral trains over the Wolds from Sandholme to Hull. The Class B's were limited to 30 ten-ton wagons over the same section of line. The increased haulage capacity was obtained at a price however - a footnote to the H&BR's "Loads for Goods Engines" tables dated 29th March 1920, stated that, "Class A engines must not work on the Denaby Branch, or to Neptune Street, Cannon Street or Sculcoates. 20-ton Brake Vans to be worked as far as possible with Class A engines." The write-up in *Engineering* was less specific, stating that, "These engines are engaged in working the heavy mineral traffic from the South Yorkshire coal-fields to the Alexandra Dock, Hull, in which service they are giving every satisfaction, being more powerful than the engines previously used for this traffic."

At the time the *Engineering* account was written, the Class A's may well have been "...giving every satisfaction....", but by the time those words appeared in print (November 1907), events had moved on apace.

It will be recalled from the previous chapters that in late September 1907 Class F2 No.109 had blown up at Wath, killing Driver Brook and also exposing the lamentable state of some of the H&B's boilers. To cap it all, the footplatemen were now expected to work engines carrying steam pressed at an exceptional 200 lb/sq. inch!

It should perhaps be added that boiler pressures had risen by the turn of the century to a general average of 180 lb/sq.inch, from the 50 lb pressure the Stephensons had used in the

"Rocket" in 1829. By around 1906 the Great Western Railway had standardised a pressure of 225 lb.sq. inch for their largest engines, and the Midland Railway were using 220 lb/sq. inch on a few compounds. 200 lb/sq. inch pressure was also to be found on various North Eastern Railway express passenger locomotives of 4-4-0, 4-6-0 and 4-4-2 wheel arrangements, but at the end of that company's independent existence Darlington's last prestige design, namely the five Raven Pacifics, still retained that pressure whilst their new three-cylinder 4-6-0's and 0-8-0's made their way in the world with boilers carrying 180 lb/sq. inch. In 1926 the LMS produced the excellent Hughes' "Crab" 2-6-0's with boilers also pressed at 180 lb/sq. inch, and moreover two further years were to pass before Nigel Gresley finally moved from 180 lb/sq. inch to 220 lb/sq.inch for his Pacifics. Thus it may be reasonably argued that with the Class A's, Matthew Stirling was some twenty years ahead of many engineers on other railways.

Understandably, once the initial "honeymoon" period with the Class A's had worn off, the footplatemen found the weak points of the new engines. The unhandy layout of the cab and controls have been elaborated upon already, but no self-respecting Edwardian British enginemen were going to be seen as letting the side down by complaining that any type of locomotive was uncomfortable. Attempts by successive locomotive engineers to do their enginemen a good turn by providing them with commodious cabs in line with American practice usually met with an undeservedly churlish response from the Masters of the Footplate.

Ironically, the first recording of an engineer having kindness thrown back in his face was Matthew Stirling's father, Patrick, on the Glasgow & South Western Railway in the late 1850's. Having produced an 0-4-2 tender engine type (which was good enough to merit successive enlargements in further construction not only on the G&SWR but also later on the Great Northern Railway, as well as being copied by James Stirling in the 1870's and by Campbell on the Maryport & Carlisle Railway), Patrick Stirling was quite downcast by the reception his enginemen had given to the cabs fitted to this early type. This first cab was oblong in side elevation and had a round "porthole" in each side in addition to the usual spectacles in front. Stirling family legend has it that the despondent Patrick Stirling unburdened his troubles on his eldest sister, Jane, who was acting

(left) **2512 again, but after rebuilding with a domed boiler based on the ex-North Eastern J27 Class 0-6-0. The new J27-type chimney should be noted, also the new cab spectacle-plate, with considerably bigger spectacle windows. The engine was photographed in ex-North Eastern territory near Cottingham, with a goods train from York to Hull.** *Laurie Ward.*

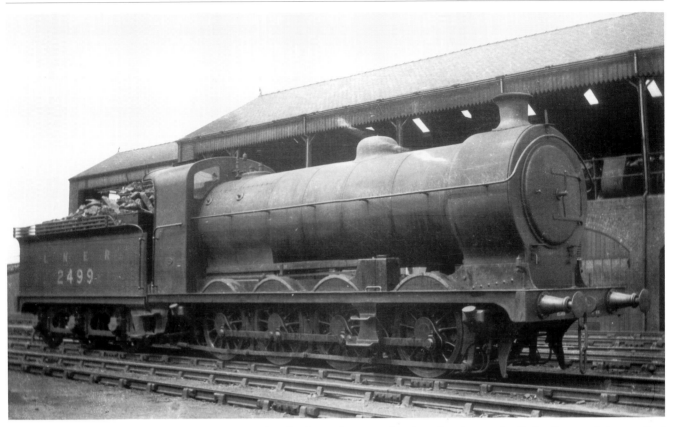

2499 (118) at Springhead after reboilering. Note that the front plate covering the valve-chest and cylinder front-ends is a vertical replacement for the originals, which followed the curve outlined by the upper frames. The bufferbeam still proclaims 2499 to be a "Class A (HB)". *Ron Copeman collection.*

as housekeeper for him at Kilmarnock. The redoubtable Miss Stirling took up a sheet of pasteboard and her dressmaking scissors and cut out a new shape: which proved acceptable not only to her brother but ultimately the G&SWR locomotivemen (and of course, many others on quite a number of other railways!).

Soon after Stirling fell foul of recalcitrant railwaymen, we find Bouch on the Stockton & Darlington Rly similarly coming a cropper in 1860. The crews of the locomotives concerned (the 4-4-0's "Brougham" and "Lowther"), took great exception to being closed in by the American-style cabs fitted to them, even though their work took them over the Pennines at Stainmore between Barnard Castle and Kirkby Stephen - an area not exactly noted for the balminess of its winter climate. Consequently, Bouch reacted by providing a roofless, chin-height weatherboard on the next engines, the "Saltburn" Class 4-4-0's of 1862.

Forty years later saw G.J.Churchward on the GWR put a side window cab on one of his engines, but again this caused so much grumbling that the offending edifice was soon removed, and "Footplate Amenities" were placed at the foot of the GWR's programme of matters deserving of improvement.

It is the writer's considered opinion that in most (if not actually all), industrial disputes the reasons specified as grievances are not in fact the real ones and furthermore, alleged grievances are all too often dropped and left unresolved when offers of pay increases are made: and events on the H&BR followed the inevitable, unsatisfactory course.

Not wishing to be left open to ridicule and accusations of "going soft", particularly from the North Eastern men next door

(who paradoxically had enjoyed the best locomotive cabs in the country for some twenty years), the H&BR crews centred their grievances around the unusually high boiler pressure of the Class A's, although in view of the Wath explosion it has to be conceded that they had a very fair point. Consequently some difficulties were in due course found in getting men to work the Class A's, until the H&BR management dangled the inevitable carrot of financial incentives in front of the men. Top-rate drivers' pay on the H&BR in 1907 was 7s.6d. per day, and for firemen 4s.9d. - but the rates of pay were raised to 8s.0d. for the drivers and 5s.3d. for firemen on the big engines.

Furthermore, the engines were placed in a special "link" incorporating attractive turns of duty, so from then on there was to be no shortage of crews for the Class A's. So although they never became really popular with their own men, the big engines settled down to do good work and even gained the ultimate accolade in the form of a nickname. Using the same form of inverted logic later displayed by Great Central enginemen when faced with Robinson's big 2-8-0's, the H&B footplatemen were unoriginal enough to dub Mr. Stirling's masterpieces as "Tinies". Henceforth that nickname was in use on the H&BR as much (if not more so), than their official designation.

The "Tiny Link" turns were by and large on the "Sandholme Banker" workings introduced in November 1907 (when all 15 "Tinies" had been delivered). Out - and - home workings within a shift had formed the rationale behind all main-line goods workings, although in the crisis year of 1907 this led to excessive hours being worked by enginemen and guards - to

"Good God! What on earth's *THAT*? What have they done to my engine?" exclaimed driver Tommy Saddington as he set eyes upon 2504 (123) with its exhaust steam injector, standing outside Springhead shed. The offending object was tucked away under the cab behind the step so is lost in the shadows, but the elbow from the blastpipe can be seen beside the smokebox, then the grease separator and its drip trap is prominent between the two rear wheels, with the last length of piping for the exhaust steam running back towards, then under the rear sandbox. The front sanders can be seen to be steam-operated, as revealed by the small-bore steam piping. *Ron Copeman collection.*

the extent that many were having to contravene Board of Trade regulations regarding twelve-hour working days.

Initially, Stirling and R.Y.Vickers, Superintendent of the Line, arranged for increasing numbers of Cudworth - based engines to drop off their trains at Sandholme and return westwards from there with empties or loads of pit-props. Meanwhile, the detached loaded mineral trains were taken directly to Alexandra Dock for export or to the various Hull depots in the case of land-sale coal, by Hull based engines. Block trains of coal for the nearby gasworks and the Hull Corporation's Electricity Generating Station were taken to Sculcoates Goods Yard directly (latterly the Corporation's power station fuel was transported in their own wagons, a fleet some sixty strong by the 1920's).

Since the "Tinies" were of course barred from the coal yards at Cannon Street, Sculcoates and Neptune Street, the operational headaches entailed in providing suitable engines for the various trains may best be imagined! Relief was soon at hand, however, in the form of extra sidings brought into use at Springhead by 1908; from that time onwards virtually all coal trains started or terminated there, with the exception of the aforementioned block trains.

With the opening of a Down Goods Relief Line (west of Sandholme, since the H&BR's "Down" line led in the Hull direction), plus provision of a turntable and compact marshalling yard from November 1907 also at Sandholme, not only Cudworth crews benefited. It then became the normal working practice for Hull crews working coal trains eastwards to

halt at Sandholme and drop off excess wagons before proceeding on their way over the Wolds. As the extra wagons accumulated at Sandholme they were marshalled up into full trainloads for forwarding. It was on these Sandholme to Springhead mineral workings, the "Sandholme Bankers", that the powerful "Tinies" came into their own, although their crews were possibly to find that the most trying part of their day's work was shunting the yard at Sandholme! Still, on the basis of swings and roundabouts, crews of the smaller engines benefited, because the pause at Sandholme gave them a chance to sort the fire out prior to the gruelling climb over Drewton summit.

To give some perspective to just what was involved in shifting the amount of traffic offering, it may be noted that every 24 hours the eastern end of the line saw 80 to 90 trains each way per day, approximately half of these being coal trains. Coal exports were at their peak between August and November, so naturally considerably more than 40 or 45 coal trains would be called for at those times. Frequently the Traffic Department organised special coal trains at very short notice: in one instance they instructed the Locomotive Department that they should prepare engines for an additional 40 special coal trains - for the next day! (At that time the H&BR had 166 locomotives, so the appearance of 40 extra ones in traffic at such short notice was a considerable achievement, reflecting great credit upon the organisational skills and dedication of Matthew Stirling and his staff. One should also acknowledge the achievement of the Traffic Department's staff in Hull at the H&B's George Street offices, for there must have been considerable juggling with trainloads when Springhead dug out everything able to turn its wheels: old Kirtley Class D's rated at 25 ten-ton wagons, through Stirling Class B's able to take five more, to the Class A's and their ability to deal with 45 wagons! The H&BR may have been insignificant in size when compared with systems such as the London & North Western, the Midland, or the North Eastern, but one has to take cognisance of the fact that many bigger and more famous companies would have been in severe difficulties if called upon to conjure up an increase in locomotive availability of 24% at 24 hours' notice).

To return to the "Tinies" themselves, though. The additions and alterations to sanding gear have already been dealt with, but one addition appeared for a time on No.129. This was a porthole - style window (reminiscent of those in the sides of the original cabs which had got Patrick Stirling into trouble some fifty years or so earlier), but in No.129's right-hand cab sidesheet only. The late Bob Sedman recalled that this was to cast more light on the displacement lubricator. These usually have glass tubes or glazed apertures in order to check on and regulate the rate of delivery of the oil droplets to the cylinders as necessary. This of course would account for the fact that only one cabside was so dealt with, but by the time of LNER ownership the porthole had been removed and the hole plated in. Either the experiment was not as successful as hoped or the lubricator was changed for a different type, rendering the window useless. (Whether the fitting of it in the first place had been prompted by the fitting of a different pattern of displacement lubricator is not known, for all the engines had displacement lubricators when new. Possibly the extra window was a half-hearted experiment to try and alleviate one source of grumblings from the crews, with No.129 just happening to be the engine selected for alteration).

An alteration which did appear on all engines of the class was a ventilator at the back of the cab roof. Not shown on the first General Arrangement drawing, these items were probably added by Springhead Works and initially took the form of a low, fixed cover with small holes at the sides. Later, a taller variety with a adjustable cover was fitted, most likely due to the original type being inadequate. (Such ventilators were not provided to let fresh air into a cab, but to ensure the escape of hot and combustible gases which would accumulate in the cab roofs).

There matters rested, at least until the outbreak of War in 1914. Maintenance difficulties at that time probably led to the decision to lower boiler pressures to 175lb/sq. inch in common with the six-coupled tender engines and although a retrograde step as far as power output was concerned, it still left the Class A's with a respectable tractive effort of 25,860 lb., and besides, mineral traffic was no longer offering in such quantities due to dislocation of Hull's export coal traffic by the war. This was evident from the fact that the H&BR was able to lease the 14 Class B engines to the South Eastern & Chatham Railway, and further underlined by the loan of ten old 12-ton brake vans of Kirtley vintage, also to the SECR. Moreover by 1919 several Class A's were themselves on loan, this time to the North Eastern Railway. The NER had lent fifty relatively new, eight-wheels coupled engines of Class T1 - the entire class in fact - to the War Department for the duration. These engines, although broadly similar to the "Tinies" in size, weight and power, had outside cylinders and plain, vertical slide valves. They were also rather older, the first having been built in 1902. The departure of these engines to France naturally left quite a sizeable gap in the ranks of North Eastern heavy mineral engines, so a few Class A's were

doubtless welcomed with open arms by the NER's Operating Departure if not by the footplate staff themselves. By 1919 Nos.117, 120 and 125 were noted as being on loan to the North Eastern and shedded at Hull Dairycoates, although the late S.H.("Percy") Jackson, from Springhead's Carriage & Wagon Department recalled quite emphatically that a total of five engines of Class A had been loaned. He also remembered his brother, one of Dairycoates shed footplate staff, considering the "Tinies" to be quite dismal engines. However, Percy took the opportunity upon being back at work, of asking the H&B men how to get the best out of the big engines and duly conveyed the accumulated wisdom back to his brother, who glumly intimated that he was so desperate to get the confounded things to do a decent day's work that he'd try anything. The following day saw Percy ask the inevitable question as to how he had fared this time, but the smiles and enthusiastic, "My, they don't half steam!", were answer enough. (Family ties clearly transcended Corporate loyalty in Hull - at least for some of the time! Even Edward Watkin, the H&BR's very able General Manager, was apt to refer to the North Eastern as, "Our friends across the road"!).

With several "Tinies" working far and wide from Dairycoates by 1919, the North Eastern with its usual efficiency soon took official cognisance of the fact by including them in the form of an amendment in their Loadings Book; it rated them as being equal to the Class T engines (the slightly older, piston valve version of Class T1). With their 28,100 lb. tractive effort - slightly more than the Class A's with their reduced pressure - it is hardly surprising that once officialdom woke up to this fact, they had to react by amending the amendment; thus the Class A's became limited in the NER's Loading Book to hauling 90% of a Class T load.

Whilst on the NER the "Tinies" were noted as sometimes working north of York along the East Coast Main Line. Ironically, after Grouping Class T/T1 engines (by then LNER Class Q5), were shedded at Springhead and were seen at work on the H&B Section until 1927.

By the time of the merger with the North Eastern in 1922, all the Class A's were back at Springhead and generally run-down and war-weary. Springhead Works made a start on bringing them up to scratch, and the process continued under the North Eastern interregnum, with Nos.3123 and 3118 being dealt with at Springhead in July and August 1922 respectively; meanwhile Nos.3121 and 3131 visited Darlington in June; they also added the NER's 3000 to the existing H&BR numbers. No.3128 went there in July to be followed by 3122 and 3126 in November 1922. From August 1924 of course, all heavy repairs ceased at Springhead due to the run-down and closure of the works, although lavish facilities still existed there for light and intermediate repairs.

Naturally, Darlington features began to appear on the engines. No.131 (as LNER no.2512), received an organ-pipe whistle in November 1924, as did 2510 (previously HBR No.129), in April 1925. Most engines lost their rerailing jacks on the first Darlington visit, but 3126 still retained its jack after being lettered "L.& N.E.R.". Approximately half the class received the "Iracier" type tender axleboxes, fitting apparently commencing under the H&BR possibly with No.121, although that engine's tender had the plain-type axleboxes with worsted pad lubrication after April 1926. Since similar changes occurred on other engines, and of course as the "Iracier" axleboxes were only suitable for fitting on outside bearings, it would tend to indicate that an amount of tender-swapping took place within the class. (Details

The right-hand side of 2504 shows nothing remarkable except for the well-polished brass beadings on the splashers. Perhaps this was driver Saddington's way of showing that 2504 was still "his" engine, no matter what those Philistines up at Darlington had done to it! The odd trestle-like affair on the roof of Springhead shed at its west end was actually to carry the telegraph wires. The H&BR main lines ran alongside the shed south wall, leaving insufficient space between the rails and wall to allow for the usual telegraph posts. (This of course begs the question as to whether it might not have been simpler to have sited posts on the *other* side of the main line at that point....!). *Laurie Ward.*

of Class A tenders and dates concerning fitting or otherwise of "Iracier" axleboxes may be found amongst the tables at the end of this Section). It is evident that fitting of the "Iracier" axleboxes continued well into LNER ownership. (Details of the "Iracier" axleboxes may be found in the Appendix in vol.2).

Windjabbers appeared on the chimneys of Nos.2508(127), 2509(128) and 2510(129) at the time they carried their original boilers.

The debacle of Darlington's disintegrating drawbars also affected some of the "Tinies", Nos.2501(120), 2507(126), 2508(127) and 2511(130) being noted as having been variously afflicted with drawgear that was not up to the required standards of ruggedness. (The ailments of H&BR tender drawbars have been dealt with more completely under "Class B").

The LNER, as a matter of course, redesignated the "Tinies" as Class Q10 - North Eastern 0-8-0's took up Classes Q5, Q6 and Q7; Q8 and Q9 being left blank (presumably in case any development of the native NER classes should be undertaken in the future). Darlington, as noted earlier, didn't give a hoot of their organ-pipe whistles for all the tidy-minded schemes emanating from that alien manufactory down the East Coast Main Line at Doncaster; as far as they were concerned a T was still a T, likewise Classes T1, T2, and T3 had never changed - and since Matthew Stirling had decreed that his big engines should be Class A, who were they to argue? Thus they continued to apply the original pre-Grouping Class - letters to the front bufferbeams of the respective mineral engines in time-honoured fashion; none survived long enough to acquire "Class Q10", remaining as "Class A(HB)" for the rest of their lives.

At the time of Grouping, the Q10 boilers were coming up for renewal having served for seventeen years (four of them being under wartime conditions). Although the need to reboiler the Q10's was not desperate, the Darlington authorities preferred to keep ahead of the situation rather than keep life-expired boilers in service longer than they ought to by relying unduly on borrowed time and hopefulness. Initially they considered the possibilities of fitting similar boilers as on Class Q6 engines (a bigger, superheated development of Class T, and along with the Robinson "ROD" 2-8-0's widely considered to be one of the best British heavy mineral locomotives). The Q6 (NER Class T2), boiler, although of the same diameter as the Stirling boilers on the "Tinies" were (at 8ft 0 in), longer by 6 inches outside the firebox and 1ft 7½ in longer in the barrel than the 14ft 0 in of the "Tiny" boilers. An amount of alteration work to the frames and cross-stays would have been entailed in fitting the Q6 boilers, and then the backheads may well have protruded rather too far into the cabs. Nothing daunted however, Darlington then decided to design a new boiler based on the North Eastern P3 (LNER J27) 0-6-0 type, this work being done by February 1924.

The new boilers, of similar external dimensions to the originals were domed, although much more noteworthy was the disappearance of the Belpaire fireboxes in favour of the round-top type. Essentially the new boilers were a stretched version of the type fitted to the J27's, having the same 5ft 6in diameter, the same number (254 at 2 inches diameter) of boiler tubes and the same 180lb/sq.ins pressure. The Q10's tractive effort altered yet again, this time increasing to a marginally higher 26,593lb, although oddly enough weight in working order apparently decreased by as much as 4¼ tons on the locomotive alone, to 57 tons 6cwt. (Empty weights were originally given as 51 tons 16 cwt, and after reboiling as 51 tons 1 cwt. The Belpaire fireboxes could hardly have held an extra 3½ tons of water, since the entire boiler contents would have weighed around 6 tons. Perhaps Matthew Stirling had displayed a rare touch of vanity: by deliberately giving out the weight of his new engines a few tons heavier than they actually were, he would have joined that small, select band of early 20th. century British locomotive engineers who had produced "big engines" weighing in at over that magical figure of 100 tons. In that respect of course, he had put his illustrious father and only slightly - less lustrous uncle well and truly in the shade!).

Along with the new round fireboxes, new cab spectacle plates had to be provided and the opportunity was taken to improve the lookout forward by incorporating one larger window at each side, doing away with the two little square windows situated almost uselessly above the firebox.

Boiler handrails were set higher on the reboilered engines, no longer matching the horizontal section alongside the cab; the new blower-valve rod ran down the centre of the left-hand side boiler handrail. The new boilers also had two washout plugs on each side of the firebox, the originals having had three per side. Ross "Pop" safety-valves, NER twin-whistles, new smokeboxes and doors to North Eastern pattern plus J27-type chimneys completed the new look for the "Tinies", which was first displayed to all and sundry at Springhead by No.2505(124) in October 1924. Before the month was out, 2507(126) also returned southwards with its new boiler, and November saw 2504(123) dealt with similarly. Darlington really went to town on 2504: it became (so far as is evident), the only Q10 - except for 2501(120) - to receive wheel-and-handle locking for its smokebox door, but furthermore it rolled up at Springhead graced (for want of a better word), with an exhaust steam injector; the associated plumbing being fitted somewhat prominently along the left-hand (fireman's), side of the locomotive. Darlington's fitters had doubtlessly stood back and admired their completed handiwork, but its reception at Springhead was vastly different! Most likely (such being the way of things), no advice was proffered by Darlington as to how best to operate the mysterious gadget, the H&B Section footplatemen simply being left to puzzle things out for themselves. William Westoby vividly recalled a small group of enginemen standing beside 2504, lost for words as they gazed at the latest indignity inflicted upon them. Driver Tommy Saddington however spoke for them all when he set eyes upon "his" 2504: "Good God! What on Earth's *THAT*? What have they done to my engine?" Similar sentiments (more or less strongly expressed), were possibly communicated to Darlington in due course, for no other H&BR engine received an exhaust steam injector and although it is not known for how long No.2504 retained its unique fitting, it may well have been removed some time before its withdrawal.

Another odd fitting appeared on 2498(117) from 9th January 1931 but this aroused no strong feelings, being only a windjabber atop the chimney; the only instance of such an item appearing on a Q10 in domed condition. (This was also the last occasion a "Tiny" visited Darlington Works for repairs).

Reboiling of the "Tinies" was completed in March 1928 with 2512(131) being attended to; thus the class became more or less uniform in appearance once again.

All were still on the H&B Section, albeit 2500(119) and 2508 had been re-allocated to Cudworth shed early in 1924 and January 1925 respectively, but the Fates had begun to turn against the Q10's the year after - even though reboiling was still in full swing.

1926 saw the General Strike and the coal strike which endured for six months; the year after the LNER bought yet another job-lot of one hundred ex-ROD Robinson 2-8-0's - bargains at a mere £340 each! The situation on the H&B Section was unfortunate, for the coal export trade in particular never really recovered after the coal strike, and 1929 saw two unconnected events which would ultimately seal the fate of the "Tinies".

Firstly, having got their new purchase in good order, the LNER found they had sufficient engines to spare to try some of the Robinson engines on the H&B Section, where they were so successful that by the year end they had taken over all the main duties at both Springhead and Cudworth sheds. Secondly, by the end of 1929 the Wall Street Crash heralded the trade slump, which began to have world-wide repercussions by 1930.

Autumn 1929 saw only three Q10's remaining on the H&B Section: Nos.2498(117), 2502(121) and 2503(122), all at Springhead; four others had been transferred to Hull Dairycoates, including 2500(119) from Cudworth. No.2501(120) was sent on trial to Tyne Dock shed, near South Shields, and 2507(126) similarly went to another Tyneside shed, namely Borough Gardens. Two months on saw 2507 sent to Selby (November 1929), where it was joined by 2499(118), 2504(123), 2505(124), 2506(125), 2509(128) and 2511(130) from Springhead and 2508(127) from Cudworth.

At Selby, the "Tinies" were set to trip-working between nearby collieries and the yards at Gascoigne Wood, (a task for which they should have been ideally suited), but the H&BR engines aroused great discontent amongst Selby's enginemen. All too often such complaints came to nothing: a few years on, Hull enginemen were most displeased when given ex-Great

2503 shunting at Beverley - or the driver prefers to see where he's been rather than look at where he's going. The engine is commendably clean, not having been long out of Darlington works. The cabside numbering and "Iracier" tender axleboxes should be noted. *Ron Copeman collection.*

2502 (121) on the GN section, probably at March shed. Sadly, the "Tinies" were not welcomed off their native system, being fated to do all their best work in the Hull area. *Ron Copeman collection.*

2505 (124) can be seen to have been fitted with "Iracier" axleboxes, otherwise is a fairly typical example of a Class Q10 - or "A (HB)" - with domed boiler. *Ron Copeman collection.*

Northern Ivatt - inspired 4-4-2 tank engines of Class C12 but were simply told to get the better of them and get on with the job, there being nothing else available. The outcry from the Selby men caused by having the "Tinies" inflicted on them was much more effective though - to the extent that four North Eastern Q6 0-8-0's were sent there in July 1930, as partial replacement. November 1930 saw further Q6 transfers, plus examples of the massively-powerful Q7 engines along with their close relatives the B16 4-6-0's appearing respectively at Springhead, Selby and Dairycoates, causing the "Tinies" to be put into store, for as the depression bit deeper the LNER had increasing numbers of heavy mineral engines surplus to requirements.

One last attempt was made to appease the Selby men - December 1930 saw No.2503(122) leave Dairycoates in exchange for Selby's 2511(130), since 2503 had been given "improved sanding arrangements." (This was an experimental reversion to gravity sanding for the driving wheels, done in July 1930. The effort involved may well have been better expended on rearranging the cab and controls in order to make conditions more congenial for the crews).

But the Selby men were not to be mollified by supposedly better sanding arrangements, so by January 1931 all the Q10's had departed from Selby unmourned and unsung. Still, the LNER could hardly allow the "Tinies" to stand idle for too long, especially in view of the fact that they all had comparatively new boilers. Since they were surplus in the North Eastern Area, it was decided they should try their luck in the Southern Area of the LNER.

So January 1931 saw ten transferred to Mexborough - but that shed already had insufficient work for its own "Tinies" - of Great Central origin - without trying to gainfully employ the newcomers. Evidently the LNER authorities realised this, for six of the Mexborough engines were sent on to March, from July to September. Three were there for only six weeks and none stayed there for more than fourteen, since March found exactly the same problem with their deployment as did Mexborough. Nos.2504(123) and 2507(126), were also allocated to Doncaster at the same time for a mere five days, but yet again the problem of insufficient work for heavy mineral engines told against their effective deployment. Indeed, the LNER Southern Area authorities had already embarked on withdrawing their own GNR Ivatt "Long Tom" 0-8-0's which, as may be recalled, bore considerable similarity to the "Tinies".

May 1931 had seen No.2500(119) withdrawn for scrapping, and in view of the circumstances just outlined it was not surprising to find the others all being returned to Selby and Dairycoates by September 1931, pending almost immediate withdrawal, the last in service being 2502(121) in November 1931. By coincidence that engine had been the one held back by the builders for some reason, so it was fitting that it should have been the last to work, making up in some small way for its late appearance at Springhead! Also by coincidence, the month before saw not only the biggest single withdrawal of the "Tinies", but additionally the death of their designer, Matthew Stirling, in his 74th. year. Thus the man and his most notable creations both departed this world more or less simultaneously.

The LNER hadn't quite finished with the "Tinies" however, even after reducing them to piles of broken metal, for none of their domed boilers had seen more than seven years' use, and in point of fact seven of them had yet to see four years' work. The result was that fourteen ex-North Eastern Railway Class Q5

0-8-0's were rebuilt, thus creating Class Q5/2. A fifteenth engine (No.771), was to have been reboilered, but it was decided to retain one Q10 boiler as a spare. Rebuilding took place between July 1932 and June 1934, and involved fitting new smokeboxes and shorter chimneys (of the type fitted to the North Eastern B16 4-6-0's by the LNER). New and bigger cabs were also provided with the side-windows set higher than on the originals, and finally the steam reversing gear was updated to the latest single-handle control type, from the old two-handle variety. Even the boilers themselves were reclassified: from Diagram 51 to Diagram 56A, despite the fact that they were not altered in any way. (The original H&BR domeless Belpaire boilers had not lasted sufficiently long enough to become included within the LNER Boiler Diagram Book, although from 1924 the engines in domeless condition were referred to as Class Q10/1, their rebuilt brethren being Class Q10/2. Both sub-divisions fell from usage after March 1928 upon the reboilering of the entire class being completed).

Class Q5 engines affected by reboilering included Nos.642, 644, 653, 657, 658, 659, 660, 661, 769, 939, 1054, 1062, 1320 and 2119. Only 2119 was a piston-valve engine, the others were all equipped with slide valves, so consequently were amongst those which had seen war service in France. Only Nos.644, 658 and 939 reverted to the original boiler type: 644 in 1945, the other two in 1943; the others all went for scrap along with their Q10 boilers from 1946 onwards. They received new LNER numbers under the great LNER renumbering scheme of 1946, in the 3200 - 3300 series; just one Q5/2 received its British Railways number 63322 in November 1948 before following its classmates into North Road scrapyard, Darlington, in February 1949. Class Q5 itself was swept from the face of the earth in its entirety by the end of October 1951. (Reboilering dates, numbers and renumberings etc., may be found in the various tables at the end of this section).

Not only the boilers themselves became spare with the extinction of the Q10 engines; they also left a convenient gap in the LNER number series from 2498 to 2512. All the numbers were duly resurrected, 2498 and 2499 appearing in due course on two Gresley K3 Class 2-6-0's; but Nos.2500 to 2508 came into much greater prominence on the Gresley A3 Pacifics (all names and numbers of those engines concerned being listed at the end of this section). However, the real glory was reserved for Nos.2509 to 2512, for these numbers were allocated to the immortal Gresley streamlined Pacifics of Class A4: "Silver Link", "Quicksilver", "Silver King" and "Silver Fox". Suffice to say within these pages that the A4's achieved what the H&BR "Tinies" never did - a widespread popular following amongst both railwaymen and enthusiasts. The exploits of the "Silver" A4's made it a matter of some regret that one of the four was not earmarked for preservation but in view of the fact that six other A4 engines have been, then your author inclines to the view that a Q10 would also have been a deserving candidate for preservation! It would be reading too much into things to suggest that Gresley's masterpieces were purposely given the numbers of old Matthew Stirling's most spectacular design, but it was a neat if unintentional form of compliment when it is recalled that Matthew Stirling had seconded Gresley's application to join the Association of Railway Locomotive Engineers many years earlier!

In their time the "Tinies" were as striking as the A4's were, some thirty years later. Even in our own times if any H&BR engine earns a reference in more general locomotive histories than this one, it invariably seems to be the Class A's which shuffle forward

into the limelight: Brian Reed acknowledges them in his *150 Years of British Steam Locomotives*, as does the late Professor W.A.Tuplin, in *British Steam Since 1900*.

The locomotives themselves made a lasting impression on those who saw them with an enthusiast's eye: the late Willie King (eventually to join the H&BR as lamp-man at Little Weighton), retained throughout his life the vivid memory of that February morning back in 1907 when No.117 made its first run through Little Weighton on its delivery from Meadowhall. He recalled Driver Wordsworth as being at the regulator, and very proud to be entrusted with the Company's first big mineral engine - and brand-new at that!

Years later W.B.Yeadon, as a young railway enthusiast whose earliest loyalties lay with the London & North Western Railway and then the London, Midland & Scottish Railway after 1922, came to settle in Hull. Being faced with either finding another interest or changing his allegiances to the LNER, he decided in due course that the latter course of action was the more palatable choice! Hence his interest in the Q10's was only transitory, for by the time in question most of them were standing on the scrap lines at Dairycoates awaiting their final journeys, but even so he recognised them as being something "......a bit different and rather special." (Quite an admission from someone used to the LNWR, which probably made the greatest use of inside cylinder, eight-coupled freight engines of any company in the Western hemisphere!)

Even photographs of the Class A's can make an impression on the beholder. The late 1950's saw a small boy, staying at his Grandmother's in Sheffield. Forsaking the delights of watching the trams, or the trains on the not-too-far distant Midland main line, one day he found a dog-eared copy of *The Wonder Book of Railways*, printed about 1917. His attention was drawn to the single contribution which the Hull & Barnsley Railway had made to the book in the form of a copy of a works photograph, broadside-on, of No.121. This immediately pointed to the facts that the Hull & Barnsley had at least a hundred and twenty-one engines and that some of them were very big indeed (far more impressive than the Midland Railway 4F Class goods engines for instance, a photograph of one of which appeared at the foot of the same page as that featuring 121). The picture of that latter engine was to set the boy off trying to find out more about the other H&BR engines - and ultimately led him (in more mature years!), to come across that same photograph in the pages of *Engineering* for 1907, in the course of writing this book.....!

Summary: Class A 0-8-0 Mineral Engines LNER Class Q10

HBR No.	Works No.	Delivered	NER No.	LNER No.	Reboilering to Q10/2	Withdrawn
117	899	February 1907	3117	2498	September 1926	October 1931
118	900	March 1907	3118	2499	March 1928	August 1931
119	901	March 1907	3119	2500	June 1927	May 1931
120	902	March 1907	3120	2501	March 1928	August 1931
121	903	August 1907	3121	2502	April 1926	November 1931
122	904	April 1907	3122	2503	November 1926	October 1931
123	905	May 1907	3123	2504	November 1924	October 1931
124	906	May 1907	3124	2505	October 1924	August 1931
125	907	June 1907	3125	2506	October 1927	August 1931
126	908	June 1907	3126	2507	October 1924	August 1931
127	942	September 1907	3127	2508	March 1927	October 1931
128	943	October 1907	3128	2509	February 1925	October 1931
129	944	October 1907	3129	2510	October 1927	August 1931
130	945	October 1907	3130	2511	January 1925	October 1931
131	946	November 1907	3131	2512	March 1928	October 1931

Notes:

Engines 117-126 were constructed to Yorkshire Engine Co's Order No.E158 and cost £3,560 each.

Engines 127-131 were constructed to Yorkshire Engine Co's Order No.E166 and cost £4,260 each.

Dimensions Class A 0-8-0 Mineral Engines.

Cylinders: 2, inside 19" x 26"
Motion: Allan Straight-Link, driving open backed balanced slide valves on top of the cylinders, via rocking levers.
Boiler: Domeless, Belpaire firebox
Max. diameter outside: 5' 6"
Barrel length: 14' 0"
Firebox length: 7' 6"
Pitch: 8' 2"
Heating Surface:
  Firebox: 131 sq.ft*, 133 sq.ft**, 138 sq.ft***
  Tubes: 229 @ 2" dia. = 1,728 sq.ft
  Total: 1,859 sq.ft*, 1,861 sq.ft**, 1,866 sq.ft***
Grate Area: 22 sq.ft
Ratio of Grate Area to Heating Surface:
  1 to 84.5*, 1 to 84.59**
Boiler Pressure:
  200 lb/sq.in (lowered to 175 lb/sq.in during WW I).
Wheel Diameters:
  4' 6" (engine); 3' 9" (tender)
Wheelbase:
  Engine = 6' 0" + 5' 3" + 5' 3" = 16' 6"
  Tender = 6' 0" + 6' 0" = 12' 0"
  Total = 39' 10³/₄ "*, 40' 0³/₈ "**
Length over Buffers:
  53' 7³/₄"*, 53' 9³/₈"**
Weights:
  engine 61T 11C;
  tender 39T 8C;
  total 100T 19C
Axle Loads:
  Engine L 14T 16C, D 16T 18C, I 16T 3C, R 13T 14C.
  Tender L 12T 16C, M 13T 12C, R 13T 0C.
(Weights given for engines in full working order).
Height to top of chimney: 13' 2"
Tractive Effort @ 85% of Boiler Pressure:
  29,548 lb @ 200 lb/sq.in
  25,860 lb @ 175 lb/sq.in
Ratio of blast nozzle to cylinder dia.: 1 to 3.454.
Tender water capacity: 3,300 gallons
Tender coal capacity: 4T 0C

* Dimensions as given in last H&BR Diagram Book. ** Dimensions as recorded in first LNER Diagram. Differences in total wheelbase and overall length arose due to differences in engine and tender coupling - whether this arose as a result of remeasurements of altered drawbar arrangements is uncertain. *** Dimensions as given in *Engineering*, November 1907.

Dimension for LNER Class Q10, Rebuilt with Diagram 51 Domed, Round-Firebox type boilers.

Boiler: Domed
Max.diameter outside: 5' 6"
Barrel length: 14' 0"
Firebox length outside: 7' 6"
Pitch: 8' 2"
Heating Surface:
  Firebox: 144 sq.ft
  Tubes 254 @ 2"dia. = 1,906 sq.ft
  Total: 2,050 sq.ft
Grate Area: 22 sq.ft
Ratio of Grate Area to Heating Surface: 1 to 93.181
Boiler Pressure: 180 lb/sq.in
Weights:
  Engine 57T 6C
  Tender 39T 8C
  Total 96T 14C
Axle Loads Engine:
L 14T 18C, D 15T 4C, I 14T 6C, R 13T 8C.
(Tender remained unchanged - already given).
Height to Top of Chimney: 13' 0"
(Shown on Section Diagram as fitted with windjabber).
Tractive Effort @ 85% of Boiler Pressure: 26,593 lb

(opposite) **The end was drawing near for 2511, seen taking on coal at Dairycoates "Cracker". Before long it would be stored nearby out of use, pending its final journey to Darlington along with its classmates.**

(below) **2511 (130) at Springhead, as first outshopped by Darlington with number and initials on the tender, which also has "Iracier" axleboxes.** *W.B.Yeadon collection.*

Disposals of Class Q10 Boilers and Numbers

	Boiler to Q5/2 Class				Number to Gresley LNER Class:-		
Q10 No.	No.	Date.	Wdn. as No./Date	Class	Name		Wdn. as No./Date
2498	657	August 1933	63322 February 1949	K3	-		61971 March 1961
2499	653	December 1933	3316 April 1949	K3	-		61972 September 1962
2500	642	June 1933	3320 March 1947	A3	WINDSOR LAD		60035 September 1961
2501	661	January 1933	3325 March 1947	A3	COLOMBO		60036 November 1964
2502	1062	February 1934	3306 December 1948	A3	HYPERION		60037 December 1963
2503	769	April 1934	769 December 1946	A3	FIRDAUSSI		60038 November 1963
2504	1054	April 1934	3305 May 1949	A3	SANDWICH		60039 March 1963
2505	659	September 1932	3324 October 1947	A3	CAMERONIAN		60040 July 1964
2506	644	May 1934	3310* June 1948	A3	SALMON TROUT		60041 December 1965
2507	2119	October 1932	3253 November 1948	A3	SINGAPORE		60042 July 1964
2508	1320	May 1934	3263 November 1948	A3	BROWN JACK		60043 May 1964
2509	939	May 1934	3302* September 1947	A4	SILVER LINK		60014 December 1962
2510	660	June 1934	3301 December 1948	A4	QUICKSILVER		60015 April 1963
2511	658	July 1935	3323* November 1948	A4	SILVER KING		60016 March 1965
2512	658	July 1932	3323* November 1948	A4	SILVER FOX		60017 October 1963

* Actually withdrawn as Class Q5/1. Engines concerned reverted to 4ft 9in. diameter boilers at the following dates: 644 - December 1945; 658 - October 1943; 939 - May 1943. Only 769 did not survive long enough to acquire its allocated 1946 number, 3329; and only 63322 acquired its BR number, although (6)3305 was the last survivor!

Fitting of "Iracier" axleboxes on Class A tenders.

HBR No./Condition		LNER No./Condition		Notes
	If fitted		*If fitted*	
117	-	2498	-	-
118	-	2499	Yes	After March 1928, if not earlier.
119	-	2500	-	-
120	-	2501	-	-
121	Yes	2502	?	Plain after April 1926, and in 1931.
122	-	2503	Yes	After August 1929, if not earlier.
123	-	2504	-	Plain after November 1924, if not earlier.
124	-	2505	Yes	After August 1929, if not earlier.
125	-	2506	-	-
126	?	2507	Yes	Fitted by June 1923, as 3126.
127	-	2508	Yes	Plain in 1924, and before March 1927.
128	?	2509	Yes	Before and after February 1925
129	?	2510	Yes	Fitted by 1925.
130	-	2511	Yes	After August 1929, if not earlier
131	-	2512	Yes	Before March 1928.

Notes: It would appear that the LNER fitted the "Iracier" axleboxes when the engines were at Darlington for reboilering. Only No.121 can be definitely identified as having been given the "Iracier" boxes by the H&BR and its loss of them may have been as the result of a tender exchange. This would have been within the class because only the Class A's were not fitted with continuous brakes; all other Stirling H&BR tender engines were. The above table would tend to indicate that ten sets were initially ordered.

3127 can be seen to have its NER number patch-painted on the bufferbeam. This photograph has been stated to have been taken on the North Eastern near York in 1924, but the signals reveal a location on the H&BR main line - probably around West Bank Hall, between Carlton station and Aire Junction.

2509 (128) looking as splendid as the later machine which later took up its number after scrapping - SILVER LINK. With polished splasher beading, lubricators, spectacle frames, whistles and safety-valves, plus burnished handrails and smokebox door fittings and hinges, a clean black engine can look very smart. *Ron Copeman collection.*

A classic study of No.41, standing at Springhead and showing to perfection the clean, uncluttered lines of the last Stirling-family express engines. *J.B.Stork collection.*

CLASS J 4-4-0 EXPRESS ENGINES. (LNER CLASS D24). Introduced 1910.

Ask any group of railway enthusiasts (with a reasonably broad knowledge of pre-Grouping locomotives), to name a Stirling express engine and inevitably they will come up with the Great Northern Railway 8 ft. bogie single-driver type, introduced by Patrick Stirling in 1870. More probing may cause James Stirling's various bogie four-coupled classes for the South Eastern Railway to be brought to mind. Further interrogation may bring mention of Patrick Stirling's 7ft 6in GNR six-wheel singles (the ultimate development of that much-copied early type generally referred to as a "Jenny Lind"). James Stirling's earlier 4-4-0's for the Glasgow & South Western Railway may also crop up, but even prompting with a double-barrelled shotgun may fail to elucidate the fact that the last Stirling express locomotives were those which Matthew produced for the Hull & Barnsley Railway.

Patrick Stirling's 8 foot singles earned their lasting fame due to the fortunate preservation in working order of the first - No.1, of 1870 - as much as for their many years of creditable service at the head of the GN's best express trains. Yet although the '8 footers' were Patrick Stirling's own favourites, he would readily admit in private conversation that the 7ft 6in 2-2-2's ran better, and in fact No.1 performed quite indifferently during its first years in service.

The reason for this was that No.1 as built left a good deal to be desired regarding steam-production due to its restricted grate area, but the solution was at hand. Also dated from 1870 was a General Arrangement Drawing signed by J.C.Park, then Patrick Stirling's Chief Draughtsman (so presumably working to his instructions), for a 4-4-0. This would have had front-end arrangements identical to No.1, but with coupled wheels of 7ft diameter and a firebox 6ft 2in long outside (compared with that on No.1 at only 5ft 6in long). Stirling senior's strong aversion to coupled locomotives on express workings is too well-known to warrant repeating here, but it seemed likely that he would just have to accept that situation, until either he or Park in a moment of inspired lateral-thinking hit upon the idea of

trying the boiler for the 4-4-0 on the second bogie single (perversely numbered 8, No.2 not appearing until 1871). The result was everything that could be hoped for - the new boiler henceforth became the standard for the bogie singles and the 4-4-0 proposal was shunted off forever, joining the ethereal ranks of "proposed" locomotives (probably as numerous as those schemes which were fully worked out and actually took to the rails). Patrick Stirling had held that the larger the driving wheel the greater the adhesion, despite the fact that a big-wheeled, single-driver would, of necessity possess limited driving axle-weight. In this he was proved correct, for his singles could (and did), equal any 2-4-0* in the haulage stakes - although his own engines of the latter type were always inferior in both boiler and cylinder power. With the ability to haul on occasion as many as 26 four-wheeled carriages from King's Cross to Peterborough at an average speed of 47 mph., the single wheelers held an unrivalled position on the GNR. Until the end of his life in 1895 whilst still in office, Patrick Stirling never felt the need to produce anything bigger than the bogie singles, although the last six brought out just before his death were considerably increased in both size and weight. They required a loading of 19¼ tons on the driving axle to produce the necessary adhesive weight, which was rather excessive for those days: some rails on the GN main line in 1894 may just possibly have dated from the 1860's!

With Patrick Stirling's unswerving loyalty to the single-driver express locomotive established, we therefore have to look to James Stirling for four-coupled bogie express types. Following soon after Patrick Stirling's ephemeral outside-cylindered 4-4-0 scheme came an arrangement, in 1871, which established

---

* Any normal 2-4-0 that is! The H&BR's Kirtley engines, as rebuilt to Class H1 by Matthew Stirling from 1900 were amongst the most powerful 2-4-0's in the country - but by 1900 his father's 4-2-2's were relegated to the Lincolnshire branch-lines.

No.33's driver has every reason to look out with an air of hauteur from his lofty perch on the footplate! Even though standing on one of the centre roads in Sheffield (Midland) station, these locomotives were in no way overshadowed by the Midland's little red engines - the Class J locomotives underlined the transformation in the H&BR's Sheffield services from their inauguration in 1905. *W.L.Good.*

No.35 when almost brand-new, shows the original style of reach-rod with the flamboyant curve over the driving splasher. The deep mainframing over the bogie wheels is also prominent in this view.

virtually a British standard type. Still of the bogie four-coupled type it was the positioning of the cylinders which marked it out, for they were placed between the frames over the bogie centre. Its originator was (rather surprisingly), Thomas Wheatley of the North British Railway, a company not normally renowned for its innovative prowess. (The first of the type, No.224, was to add notoriety to notability in 1879, taking an early bath when the first Tay Bridge went down. More fortunate than the other victims, No. 224 was fished off the bed of the Tay after four months, being repaired and putting in another 39 years of service before scrapping - testimony to the rugged durability of the steam locomotive).

James Stirling was next to take up the type, building 22 domeless engines between 1873 and 1877 for the Glasgow & South Western Railway, the first two being fitted with steam reverse gear. These engines ran the joint G&SWR/Midland Railway 'Scots' expresses between Carlisle and Glasgow - among the fastest trains in the country at that time.

The type then appeared south of the Border for the first time when S.W.Johnson turned out two for the Great Eastern Railway in 1874, although by the time they appeared he had moved to the Midland Railway, where he produced ten similar engines in 1876-77. By then the inside cylinder, four-coupled bogie express engine with inside frames had become a well-established type, forming the greater part of express locomotive construction until 4-4-2 and 4-6-0 types appeared in 1898-1900.

James Stirling took his 4-4-0 type with him to Ashford when he joined the South Eastern Railway in 1882. A firm believer in standardisation, he produced 394 locomotives for the South Eastern Railway of but six classes and just four wheel

arrangements. His 129 express locomotives were entirely 4-4-0's of only three classes, each rather larger than its predecessor; the last class simply having enlarged boilers, thus retaining the standardised frames and machinery. These last engines were turned out when something with more "muscle" was really called for, but like his elder brother on the Great Northern just a year or two earlier, James Stirling had become set in his ways and unwilling or unable to bring about the changes necessary. Still, they were sound enough in design and performance to be considered more worthy of retention under Southern Railway ownership than the remaining examples of William Stroudley's "Gladstone" 0-4-2 express engines from the old London, Brighton & South Coast Railway; one of the most outstanding examples of late Victorian express locomotive design.

Clearly therefore Matthew Stirling had two sound design examples from within his own family to follow if he so chose; but despite the fact that he may well have had great respect and affection for his father's bogie singles it was glaringly obvious that such engines could well be next to useless on the H&BR, a line which by its physical nature and the nature of its traffic required qualities of adhesion rather than the ability to run freely at speed.

There were of course other alternatives to a 4-4-0 which Matthew Stirling could have considered. As mentioned above, 4-4-2 and 4-6-0 types were in service by the turn of the century; something of that sort could well have been worked out using the Class A boiler. However, the various 4-6-0 types had by 1910 generally proved to be disappointing; only Churchward on the Great Western had really mastered the disciplines necessary in order to produce sound examples of the new type. By 1910

No.38 at Little Weighton on one of the mock accident/ambulance trains. Stationmaster Marriott is standing by 38's cab. The first carriage is a BRC&W Co. semi-corridor lavatory brake-third, one of three built in 1910 and one of which is preserved by the Hull & Barnsley Railway Stock Fund at Goathland, on the NYMR. *John Hague.*

various designers, unsatisfied with their 4-6-0's for express work at least, were even returning to 4-4-0 types, albeit larger than those built in the 1890's. Some engineers had found the 4-4-2 type to be the answer, but a non-driving axle at the back end of an engine was apt to cause insufficient adhesion at crucial moments - something best avoided on the H&BR! Furthermore, the Class A's were banned from the line down to Cannon Street so an express engine of comparable size may also have been similarly restricted, and Hull (Cannon Street) station was after all the Company's main passenger station! Besides, the H&BR passenger workings simply had no need for a big engine and Matthew Stirling was too pragmatic to build such machines purely for prestige reasons.

Another alternative was the 2-4-0. Kirtley's H&BR passenger engines had proved entirely satisfactory and Matthew Stirling had given them a new lease of life by judicious modifications and reboilering, but in point of fact the 2-4-0 was as obsolete a type as the single-driver by 1910. The North Staffordshire Railway had produced three in 1907: they had markedly short lives, being withdrawn in 1920, and represented the last of that wheel arrangement constructed for a railway in this country.*

Although the Sheffield express services were well established, Kirtley's 2-4-0's were getting rather long in the tooth, and the H&BR had achieved a sound enough financial position to devote some funds for further improvements to its passenger services. Thus the time was ripe for Matthew Stirling to consider future express motive power requirements around 1908.

We have already seen that nothing bigger than a 4-4-0 was required to fulfil the H&BR's passenger requirements: since the Company possessed but a dozen bogie carriages in 1908, the whole lot could have been worked as a single train by just one 4-4-0 of fair size and in reasonable order!

The planned new class could well have been based directly on James Stirling's practices, for as we have seen he was responsible for a total of 151 4-4-0's which served two companies and their successors for many years, but possibly Matthew Stirling may have looked much further afield for inspiration.

Initial consideration of the 4-4-0 project involved a Belpaire firebox - not surprisingly since work on the passenger engines must have been commenced shortly after the delivery of the Class A goods engines if not earlier, and of course these locomotives had Belpaire fireboxes. As a result, the front end elevation of the 4-4-0 in this initial phase bore some considerable

* At the risk of undue pedantry, the Isle of Man Railway 2-4-0 tank "Mannin" dates from 1926, but of course was built for a railway of 3ft gauge.

"Class J (HB)" 2425 (33) in Hull Botanic Gardens shed, with an elderly NER 4-4-0 for company. It still retains its jack and front vacuum brake standpipe but has lost its Kitson workplates. The windjabber dates from late H&BR days, or the time of the NER/H&BR amalgamation in 1922.

resemblance to the rebuilt 2P class locomotives of the Midland Railway, but this affinity ceases the moment that the side elevation is viewed. The Belpaire firebox and shape of the front mainframes above the footplating strongly resemble the Standard 4-4-0's for the Indian Railways. These engines mainly differed in appearance to Matthew Stirling's projected 4-4-0 due to their typically commodious Indian cabs, domed boilers and that front-end fitting known variously and confusingly as a "pilot" in the USA and a "cow-catcher" in Britain.

The Indian Standard 4-4-0's appeared in 1904 with boilers of 4ft 8¼in diameter initially, but by 1911 a batch with 5ft 1¼in boilers were turned out for the East Bengal Railway by Nasmyth, Wilson & Co. Ltd., of Patricroft, Manchester. This group were comprehensively described in *Engineering* in 1912, and after due comparison of the published leading dimensions of the Indian engines with those of the H&BR locomotives (both as initially schemed and as built), it is hard to escape the conclusion that to some extent Stirling's engines could be regarded as heavier, "pocket" versions of those on the sub-Continent.

These dimensions are set out for the purposes of ready comparison in *Table 8* below.

This possible influence from overseas practice upon British designs would be far from unique - one should bear in mind the strong American influences which led on the North Eastern to the Class V Atlantics; the big 5ft 6in diameter boilers appearing on the P2 and P3 0-6-0's: their 40-ton bogie coal wagons: batches of vertically-planked, flat-sided carriages and most obviously evident in its electric locomotives and rolling stock. The Great Western was not averse to copying the Americans either - the

Churchward 43XX Class 2-6-0's were introduced in 1911 as a result of GWR officers observing the good work which such engines performed across the States. Gresley's Pacifics borrowed heavily from their Pennsylvania Railroad counterparts and as for the LMS, E.S.Cox relates in *Locomotive Panorama* how the cylinders and valve-gear of the Horwich "Crab" 2-6-0's were schemed out "....following a most intensive study of recent American practice as described in certain currently available publications." (Cox was too modest to state that as a 24-year old junior draughtsman, he had worked up the design for those engines largely single-handed, so was in a position to know what had gone on).

Regarding fittings, we have already met with Walschaert's valve-gear, Belpaire fireboxes and Schmidt superheaters on the H&BR, but the net could well be cast wider to encompass Trick ports, Trofinoff valves, Kylchap exhausts, Giesl ejectors, Crosti boilers, Caprotti valve-gear, Cartazzi axles and of course that essential but often overlooked item, namely the feedwater injector, which was invented by Monsieur Henri Giffard! All these items and many more appeared on various British locomotives at some time or other.

Having therefore considered the point that Matthew Stirling may well have done a certain amount of reading through the contemporary railway and technical publications before putting pencil to paper, we should now turn to the Class J's as built.

Second thoughts regarding standardisation (or the loss of it), may well have led to the substitution of bogie wheels 3ft 9in diameter rather than introduction of an odd size of 3ft 3in

Comparisons between Indian and H&BR 4-4-0 engines.

	Indian Rlys. Standard 4-4-0	H&BR 4-4-0 Projected	H&BR Class J as built
Cylinders (2, inside)	18½" x 26"	18½" x 26"	18½" x 26"
Valve gear	Stephenson + rocking levers; flat slide valves on top.	Allan + rocking levers; balanced slide valves on top.	Allan + rocking levers; balanced slide valves on top.
Boiler	Domed, Belpaire.	Domeless, Belpaire.	Domeless, round-top.
Max. diameter outside	4' 8¼" / 5' 1¼"	5' 0"	5' 0"
Barrel length	11' 0"	11' 0"	11' 0"
Firebox length outside	7' 4½"	6' 6"	6' 6"
Pitch	8' 10½"	8' 7½"	8' 7½"
Heating surfaces:			
Firebox	150 sq.ft	132.6 sq.ft	126 sq.ft
Tubes	210 @ 2" dia. = 1,250 sq.ft	249 @ 1¾" dia. = 1,296 sq.ft	245 @ 1¾" dia. = 1,272 sq.ft
Total	1,400 sq.ft	1,428 sq.ft	1,398 sq.ft
Grate areas	27 sq.ft	19.65 sq.ft	19.4 sq.ft
Boiler pressure	180 lb/sq.in	170 lb/sq.in	170 lb/sq.in
Driving wheel diameter	6' 2"	6' 6"	6' 6"
Bogie wheel diameter	3' 7"	3' 3"	3' 9"
Wheelbase (loco only)	6' 0" + 7' 5" + 9' 6" = 22' 11"	6' 6" + 7' 7" + 9' 3" = 23' 4"	6' 6" + 7' 3" + 9' 3" = 23' 0"
Length over buffers (E+T)	54' 8⅝"	54' 1⅞"	54' 1"
Weight in full Working Order.	95 tons 12 cwt	93 tons 10 cwt	95 tons 12 cwt
Axle loads (maximum)	17 tons 10 cwt	-	18 tons
T.E. @ 85% of boiler pressure.	18,398 lb	16,485 lb	16,485 lb

Note: Existing "standard" designs of tenders used on the respective engines. The Indian engines were built for 5' 6" gauge, hence a greater width between the frames and across the firebox. Despite the fact that the Indian engines were bigger than the H&BR examples they both came in at the same weight, which reflects the fact that by the nature of things Indian permanent-way and infrastructure was apt to be less substantial than at home. The higher tractive effort (T.E.) of the Indian engines was achieved by the use of smaller driving wheels plus slightly higher boiler pressure.

2426 (35) shows the first version of LNER green, once things had settled down. Note the removal of Kitson's worksplate from the front framing, the cab roof ventilator and Darlington's removal of the front vacuum standpipe - although inexplicably, they never dealt with those on the tender in a similar manner. *Ron Copeman collection.*

diameter. (Presumably the 3ft 2½in wheels of the Class K tanks was overlooked; or else standardised tyres suitable for use in both applications were impossible to achieve for technical reasons). In the event, it was possible to arrange for sufficient depth of frame to allow the bigger wheels to be used.

Regarding main frame upper leading edge profiles, the usual styling treatment was to give them either a concave form (as on the North Eastern Class S and S1 4-6-0's and the V Atlantics), or simply take a straight line from below the smokebox downwards to the bufferbeam (as on the Midland's Class 2P 4-4-0's and Urie's 4-6-0's on the London & South Western Railway). Needless to say there were many variations on the theme of upper frame profiles, some engineers even cut down the upper frames to such an extent that they did not protrude above the footplating. This course of action was apt to lead to frame weakness over the leading bogie wheels - Churchward's Great Western engines of the 1900's with American-style bar frames in that area suffered from front-end frame weakness to such an extent that tie-rods were in due course fitted between the bufferbeams and smokebox saddles, again as per American practice. An alternative to hacking chunks of metal out of the front frames over the bogie wheels was to "set" the frames in over the bogie, then taper them inwards from the front of the cylinders to behind the bufferbeam - although this option was more normally resorted to in order to gain an extra inch or two diameter on outside cylinders (as on the NER S and S1 4-6-0's for example).

However, Matthew Stirling preferred to follow the example of the Indian Standard engines, which certainly left nothing to be desired in the matter of front frame strength. In fact Kitson's (builders of the Class J's), seemed to be so taken up with this front end design that it reappeared again on the massive Baltic tank engines which they built for the Furness Railway in 1920, and which bore a considerable likeness - forward of the tanks - to the Class J engines.

The substitution of round-topped fireboxes for the Belpaire type may have occurred due to Kitson & Co. It is just possible that they had no suitable flanging blocks for the manufacture of plates to make Belpaire fireboxes for 5ft diameter boilers, and

the cost of making such blocks would have been exorbitantly high if set off against only five engines. Kitsons had of course built plenty of engines for the H&BR with round-topped fireboxes and 5ft boilers (most recently as 1908), so had no difficulty in producing something similar for the Class J's. Besides, there was never an overwhelming case to be made that Belpaire fireboxes were better steam producers than round-top fireboxes (Gresley and his two successors certainly did not think so), but such fireboxes made it easier to fit the crownstays and provided useful extra storage space for steam. It was a pity nevertheless, that Stirling was unable to wait another couple of years when Kitson & Co. built twenty Robinson 2-8-0's for the Great Central, for these had 5ft boilers and Belpaire fireboxes. They also built further such engines to Ministry of Munitions orders in World War I, and re-used the boiler design in very similar form on the aforementioned Furness Railway Baltic tank engines. By suggesting several changes to the original boiler design in order to utilise the 2-8-0 boiler design and components as much as possible they expedited construction of the Furness engines, and possibly followed a precedent established with the H&BR Class J's if not earlier. Thus there is at least one recorded instance of contractors suggesting alterations to completed designs at some stage in the construction process.

So the last Stirling express locomotives took shape at Kitson's throughout the latter part of 1910, all being delivered that December. The five engines (Kitson's Order No.377V), cost a total of £15,250, took up the builder's numbers 4700-4704 and H&BR Nos.33, 35, 38, 41 and 42. It will be realised that these H&BR numbers were already carried by five Kirtley 2-4-0's - three with small boilers and two with the large 5ft diameter type. Although the H&BR could therefore regard these old engines as written off and replaced, it was not in a position to actually go ahead and scrap them. Consequently, the old engines were given the dubious honour of starting off a duplicate list - those concerned carried this mark of faded glory in the form of a letter "A" painted on their cabsides.

The delivery of the Class J 4-4-0's marked the completion of the five-year metamorphosis undergone by the H&BR's best passenger trains. October 1905 had seen the through Hull

(Cannon Street)-Sheffield (Midland) express services commence with six-wheel carriages on loan from the Midland Railway, but headed by a Kirtley 2-4-0. Then came the next phase of the operation when the Midland reclaimed its carriages, and due to the late delivery of new bogie carriages the H&BR had to use its old four-wheeled stock. Thus between April 1906 and February 1907 the H&BR fielded a late Victorian train - twenty years beyond its "sell-by date", so to speak! After February 1907 deliveries of the twelve new bogie carriages from R.Y.Pickering & Co. of Wishaw ushered in Phase Three; Phase Four lasted for twelve months from December 1909 to December 1910, being heralded by deliveries of the thirteen new bogie carriages built by the Birmingham Railway Carriage & Wagon Co. The Sheffield services finally reached their ultimate level of perfection from December 1910, with the delivery of the new express engines; thus the H&BR could justifiably take pride in the warm approval which its new trains aroused in the contemporary railway press and those travellers which knew them.

At the time of the introduction of the Sheffield services in 1905 the *Railway Magazine* had noted that, "....passengers who desire can still change at Cudworth to and from the Midland Railway....", but after 1907 this may have been with some regrets on the part of those who had to, for two years on the *Railway Gazette* described the Pickering carriages as, "....of the most modern and luxurious design...." and ....extremely comfortable." By 1910, the *Railway & Travel Monthly* wrote thus of the Birmingham carriages: "Some of the finest non-vestibuled corridor coaches now running are those belonging to the Hull & Barnsley Railway, which work in the through expresses between Hull and Sheffield (Midland)."

The new H&BR trains must have presented an eye-catching spectacle at Sheffield (Midland) with a Stirling "Straightback" 4-4-0 in very dark green picked out with red and blue lining, embellished with the Company's armorial device on the driving wheel splasher and set off with plenty of polished metalwork. It matched the varnished teak carriages with their gold and blue lettering and lining, and roofs finished in white lead. Again, a fair smattering of Company crests along the carriage sides left the beholder in no doubt as to who they belonged, and the polished door and grab-handles demonstrated to all how proud their owners were of their new stock. There could be no risk whatsoever of confusion with the Midland's own trains: engines and clerestory-roofed carriages alike were magnificently turned out in Crimson Lake. Despite the splendour of their own stock, the Midland staff must have looked admiringly upon the H&B's expresses, for setting aside the fact that the H&B Board had sanctioned the building of a shed at Springhead expressly for the purposes of painting and varnishing carriages (and also installed vacuum cleaning equipment there in 1912), the locomotives for the Sheffield trains also came in for lavish daily attention.

One task which Matthew Stirling took upon himself in the hectic years from 1905 to 1908 was the daily inspection of the Sheffield engine after Springhead's cleaners had finished with it. This was no mere cursory affair: "The Boss" strode across to the engine equipped with a pair of white cotton gloves and with these on, he felt behind all the nooks and crannies and especially along the backs of the spokes - and woe betide the cleaners if the gloves were dirtied! William Westoby recalled that cleaning the Class J's was a difficult job, for it was a long stretch upwards to clean that part of the wheels and spokes hidden behind the splashers. He recalled that the cleaners used paraffin "swabs" to shift dirt, but were not supposed to remove fresh oil from off the engine; hence craftier members of the cleaning gang would put a smear of clean oil back on! He also stated that by the time his career on the footplate commenced, Matthew Stirling had delegated the task of inspecting the express locomotives to his assistant, Leonard Hyde (son of the H&BR's Company Secretary, and who had replaced Lytton after he had left the H&BR). Such fastidiousness seems inconceivable today but at least the H&BR didn't go to such lengths as the Glasgow & South Western Railway, which cleaned its engines reserved for the Anglo-Scottish Pullman workings with Best Lucca olive oil!

Only one aspect of the presentation of the Sheffield sets may have left something to be desired - to whit, the appearance of the crews themselves, for the H&BR never issued its men with uniform overalls. They received peaked caps without insignia plus a dark, bottle-green overcoat, lined with a red blanket-like material. Bob Sedman once recalled the incredibly hard-wearing qualities of these overcoats. He wore his last one for years after the demise of the H&BR, but it succumbed in due course when it got caught up in the chain of his motorbike and ripped to shreds. Since the crews had to provide their own clothes, durability and economy were paramount. Consequently many of the men chose to wear corduroy trousers, frequently of a buff colour, but any old jacket or waistcoat sufficed to complete the motley garb of Stirling's men!

So much for the entry into service of the Class J's, but what of the engines themselves? As may be expected, originating with a Stirling they were neat but plain of outline and less endowed with curves than Patrick Stirling's 19th. century engines. Like the Class A's, the smokeboxes were not waisted-in immediately above the frames, and like all Matthew Stirling's earlier H&BR engines they were perfectly smooth and unblemished, being without external pipes and assembled with countersunk rivets. Prominent below the smokebox were two rows of hexagonal-headed bolts, turned and accurately fitted, which retained the smokebox and cylinder casting in place. Below footplate level, a third row was visible just above the bogie, securing the bogie stretcher casting in place immediately below the cylinder block.

The bogie itself was of the Adams type, with plate side-frames and equalising beams located between the frames and the back faces of the wheels. Suspension was provided by inverted leaf-springs, one within each equalising beam inside a large "pocket". Adams bogies had sprung side-control and this was the only occasion such a bogie was used on any Stirling locomotive. For his 8ft bogie singles Patrick Stirling had used a simple fixed pin with some side play, a perfectly adequate arrangement; but with nothing to prevent the bogie swivelling completely round, it could be lethal in the unfortunate event of a derailment. James Stirling used an odd arrangement of his own devising on his 4-4-0's, involving a triangular link connecting two pins. The leading pin took the thrust from the bogie framing and transmitted it via the triangular link to the main centre-pin, which had 1½ins total side-play. Although James Stirling claimed his arrangement gave steadier and safer riding than the Adams bogie, it is doubtful whether this was actually achieved in practice although any shortcomings in this matter may well have been due to the use of a bogie wheelbase of only 5ft 4in. Probably the most telling verdict on James Stirling's bogie was that no other locomotive engineer appears to have copied it - including his nephew!

Still below footplate level, the driving wheels of Matthew Stirling's 4-4-0 were unusual (for one of his engines), in having

Following the merger with the North Eastern in 1922, Springhead outshopped 3038 in the full splendour of NER Saxony green. Apart from lack of cast brass cabside numberplate and front upper mainframes painted black, their version was completely orthodox. Unlike more recent livery changes which have been far from beneficial to the recipients, the NER green in no way detracted from the appearance of these imposing locomotives, although doubtless this did little to mollify the H&BR's "other ranks". One is left to conclude therefore that the effects of 3038's repaint were mainly psychological than visual.

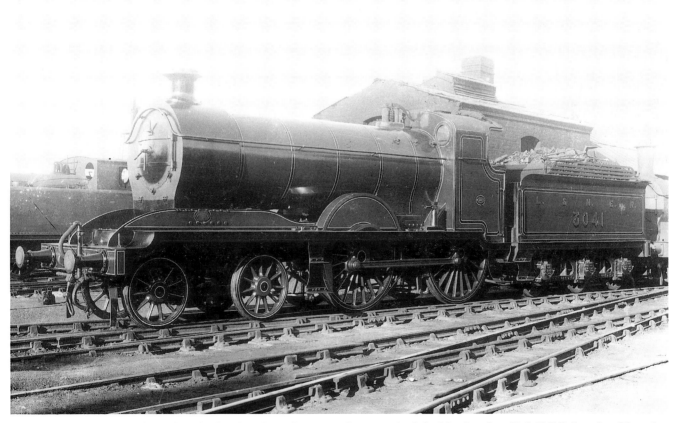

3041 was the next Class J through Springhead, and may be seen to have acquired the identity of an "L.& N.E.R." engine. Note also that Springhead adopted the NER practice of painting the upper front frames in green rather than black as per Doncaster's practice. *Ron Copeman collection.*

2426 on a Hull-Beverley local in 1932. *Laurie Ward.*

2427 at Selby South - probably engaged in station pilot duties rather than actually working a train. *Ron Copeman collection.*

2428 (41) retains its H&BR fittings - smokebox door and vacuum brake standpipe - but has no windjabber on its chimney. The tender has also lost the stops and ampersand previously carried. *Ron Copeman collection.*

balance-weights. It may be recalled that with diameters up to 5ft, wheels could be balanced satisfactorily by careful design of the inside crank-webs, but the Class J's had the biggest wheels on the H&BR, measuring 6ft 6in diameter.

Sandboxes were provided either side of the driving wheels and behind the rear coupled wheels also.

The footplating itself was unique in style on H&BR engines, being raised above the arcs described by the coupling rods, but dropped down at the front to meet the bufferbeam and at the cab to meet up neatly with the tender dragbeam. Raising its level thus got around the need for the long coupling-rod splashers as found on the Kirtley 2-4-0 engines and also on the proposed Belpaire version of Class J. It gave them a lighter, sleeker look, especially in comparison to those handsome heavyweights on the North Eastern, in the form of the Class R1 4-4-0's. Despite their 5ft 6in diameter boilers and 6ft 10in wheels, from most angles they looked to be all cab roof and splasher - an appearance largely given by their low, straight footplating and full-width splashers.

The H&BR engines followed established GNR and NER practices (as well as that of their own system, usually), of having heavy brass beading around the splashers - even the little driving wheel crank-pin splasher and the quadrant splasher immediately in front of the cab were thus finished!

The cab itself was strongly reminiscent of the typical Stirling cabs on the Class B's, but with the rearward roof extension of the Class A engines. Here at last was a characteristic Stirling cab which gave cover to the crews at least as adequately (if not better), than those of Kirtley's engines. Interestingly enough for his last design of 4-4-0, the South Eastern Railway Class B of 1898, James Stirling had provided cabs very much in the style of William Kirtley; only the domeless boilers readily proclaimed their ancestry.

The boilers for Matthew Stirling's new express engines were longer than the earlier types and distinguished by three washout plugs on each side of the firebox, just above crownsheet level. All earlier 5ft diameter boilers had two plugs per side, due to their shorter fireboxes. Although a non-standard type was thus introduced (on the face of it), to the H&BR, this undesirable situation was turned to advantage in 1911 with the introduction of the Class L1 0-6-0 engines which utilised the same boilers. Since these engines followed on consecutively from the Class J's, it would seem to be a foregone conclusion that design work on the two types was undertaken more or less simultaneously in order to make the maximum use of what was in effect a new, updated, standard boiler design for the H&BR. (It may well also illustrate just how costly new flange blocks were, since the total of fifteen boilers for the Class J and L1 engines may still have been considered insufficient by the H&BR to offset the cost of the putative flange blocks).

On the right-hand side of the engines, the reversing gear reach-rod swept up prominently in an enormous arc right over the driving wheel splasher, to some degree spoiling the neat outline of these engines. However they were altered within a very short time to run much more directly from the reversing screw link to the weighshaft, being tucked neatly behind the splasher. It would appear that the original arrangement was too delicate, being liable to flexing and thus causing erratic valve-events. Whether Springhead's blacksmiths did a remarkably skilled piece of recycling of the original reach-rods, made new ones or simply fitted replacements made by Kitson's is one of those fascinating details lost irretrievably in the mists of time.

The tenders displayed yet another re-arrangement of the tank and coal-space; the final version as it turned out of that development process commenced in 1907 with the Class A's and continued with the last batch of Class B's delivered in 1908. The Class J tender coal rails were swept aft of the bunker space to leave the rear tank top unfenced. At the front end, one large tool locker was situated well forward transversely across the right hand side; clearance for the brake handle was provided simply by not fitting another locker, thus allowing the front bulkhead for the coal bunker to be set further forward. Hence this type of tender held 5½ tons of coal, a worthwhile increase over those fitted to the "Tinies". Other lockers were fitted in the engine cab, providing adequate arrangements for sitting down.

Below footplate level there was little of note except for steam-heating being fitted from the start, and more noticeably the introduction of the "Iracier" axleboxes. A detailed description of this device is to be found in the Appendix in vol.2, but suffice to say here that it was an invention of the redoubtable Driver Carson of the H&BR, the mechanical details being worked out by one of the foreman fitters, a Mr. Wood. Basically it consisted of a flat disc plate affixed to the axle end, which flung oil up to the top of the bearing as the axle turned. They were readily identified from afar by their shield-shaped covers. So far as can be determined, their appearance on the Class J's was the first on a British locomotive.

All this innovation and attention to detail was wasted on some observers, however. As a small boy, the author's late father lived near the Midland main line in Sheffield and not infrequently saw the Class J engines trundling light up to the Midland's Millhouses shed for servicing, having dropped off their carriages at the Midland station. Reminiscing years later, he recalled them as "....funny-looking, blackish things!"

Their crews may well have called them harsher words than that, for in service they acquired a reputation for sluggishness. William Westoby describes them as being much slower than the old Kirtley 2-4-0's to get into their stride. Bob Sedman averred that it was due to the use of Allan straight-link valve gear, which in his view was not conducive to good results on fast passenger engines. On the other hand, G.G.Kennewell recalled in the 1978 *Daleman's Yorkshire Annual* that his father, an H&BR driver, "....always spoke highly of them." Allan straight-link had also been applied to the L&NWR 2-4-0's of the "Precedent" class from 1874, and those engines were no slouches in the matter of covering the ground, so possibly Matthew Stirling had applied the valve gear rather unhandily or maybe additional circumstances militated against the most effective use of steam by his 4-4-0's. (More complete considerations of H&BR valve gear applications may be found in the Appendix, vol.2).

Still, the Class J's were the tools provided by Matthew Stirling for his men to move trains with, so they just had to get on with things for better or worse. Although mainly used of course on the Sheffield services from Hull, the Class J's also hauled excursions which at times took them surprisingly far off their native system. Not infrequently they appeared in Leeds and Bradford, having used the connection at Hensall Junction to get on to the Lancashire & Yorkshire Railway's Goole-Knottingley line, proceeding thence via Methley. They used the L&YR to an even greater extent on the bi-annual staff excursions, turning up at Blackpool on a number of occasions; more rarely they appeared at Morecambe thanks to the Midland, and on a few runs they even saw Llandudno, having got there over the LNWR. They also headed excursions to Aintree and through

2429 (42) at Dairycoates, to the north side of the wheeldrop shed. Note the windjabber and also that the splasher top appears to be painted black, rather than the more normal green.

the Peak District - these being open to the public - and may possibly have taken in the Lakes as well, although on these latter workings it was the usual custom for the H&BR's stock to be taken on from Leeds behind a Midland or LNWR engine, the H&B's locomotive and crew spending a day in Leeds pending return of the excursion.

A reminder of the salad days of the Class J engines can be found on the H&BR's timetable covers for the period. These depicted in full, glorious colour no less, a Class J striding proudly along at the head of an immense train apparently made up of every bogie carriage the Company owned (plus a few more for good luck!), set in a fanciful sylvan landscape more strongly reminiscent of Baslow or Keswick than Barnsley or Kirk Smeaton! The foliage around the lineside together with the heather-clad hills, blue in the distance, seemed to suggest that the H&B had somehow got Claude Lorrain to try his hand at commercial instead of Baroque art! Still, at least the H&BR's multi-hued timetable cover gave passengers something to look at whilst their trains traversed the sheer-sided chalk cuttings around Little Weighton.

Sadly, this midsummer night's dream came abruptly to an end with the outbreak of hostilities in 1914. Although its impact was not as immediate as on the coal export business and little change was made to the frequency of the established passenger services, as the war became more serious and widespread it was inevitable that cut-backs would be made. Consequently the January 1917 timetable saw the end of the through Sheffield services along with the Night Mail train. Hull (Cannon Street) saw nine trains each way per day on weekdays, only two each of which ran through to Cudworth. Consideration was even given to closing the H&BR to passenger traffic on Sundays, but in the event it was decided to leave one through train each way. The Sheffield services and the Night Main were never to re-appear after World War I, due to the impending amalgamation. The H&BR's passenger stock came into its own briefly through 1919

with the repatriation of German prisoners-of-war, but 1921 (the last full year of passenger working), produced very poor results due to the emergence of competing local motor-'bus services.

With the H&BR joining the LNER Group in 1923, it was inevitable that its inconveniently-situated Cannon Street station would soon close, for there was plenty of room at the old North Eastern's Hull (Paragon) station.

Throughout 1923 and '24, work continued apace on a connection near Walton Street off Spring Bank West, between the H&BR Section and the ex-NER Hull-Beverley line. Sunday 13th July 1924 saw the last Cannon Street-Cudworth train depart behind No.41, (by then renumbered as LNER Class D24 No.2428). With its return at 5.55 p.m., the H&BR's unequal struggles to build up satisfactory levels of income from its passenger train services were well and truly over. Henceforth, it was up to the LNER to make whatever half-hearted initiatives it felt like.

Curiously enough, three different D24's were credited with the melancholy task of having worked the last Cannon Street train - another typical instance of confusion over H&BR locomotive history! This arose because the *Hull Daily Mail* and the *The LNER Magazine* both published a photograph purporting to be of 2427 (38) working the last train, which was actually the 5.40 p.m. departure of the day before. Then 2429 (42) was depicted in another Hull newspaper, *The Eastern Morning News*, but in reality this photograph was taken on the day following the closure, when 2429 was engaged in clearing the station of empty carriage stock. Obviously a Sunday off work took precedence over considerations of nostalgia, enthusiasm or the accurate recording of history as far as the respective journalists were concerned!

One other odd episode which allegedly took place between 1918 and the Amalgamation was the working of a Class J into Doncaster (York Road) station, via the newly-opened Hull & Barnsley and Great Central Joint Railway on the occasion of a special train to Doncaster Races. Invariably, surviving H&BR staff insist that it took place but are unable to provide information as to dates, train consist, engine number or names of the crew. Perhaps the safest verdict on this particular exploit would be delivered by a jury composed of Matthew Stirling's fellow-countrymen: "Not proven!" However, in view of the adamancy of the H&BR men it may also be held as, "Not disproven" either!

With the closure of Cannon Street and the transfer of services to Paragon, the five D24's were also reallocated to the ex-North Eastern shed at Botanic Gardens, which provided engines for the vast majority of Hull's passenger workings. Henceforth Springhead only reclaimed the D24's as its own when in for light repairs or towards the ends of their lives when they spent increasingly lengthy periods in store.

The D24's continued to handle Cudworth passenger workings, but Botanic frequently purloined them for other workings - consequently they appeared on occasion at Leeds and Doncaster, and more often on excursions at Scarborough. Another odd working on which a D24 sometimes put in an appearance was the daily fish train; leaving Neptune Street around lunchtime, it made an aromatic circuit around the city via the Walton Street connection to Hull (Paragon), for forwarding to its destination behind a Gresley K3 or an old NER 4-6-0 of Classes B13 or B14. The initial leg of the journey was apt to be behind anything with vacuum brakes and wheels capable of turning - hence the appearance of a medley of motive power between 1925 to 1933 particularly, which encompassed anything and everything from old NER N8 0-6-2 tanks to the D24's!

January 1932 saw passenger services on the H&BR cut back from Cudworth to South Howden, but ironically the last through train was headed by an old North Eastern J21 0-6-0, No.1516. Although Sentinel railcars had taken over some of the more local workings on the H&B Section, the D24's still appeared at times on Howden trains although they were probably not too welcome on such workings since one leg of the journey had to be done tender-first. Increasingly, the D24's saw usage off their own system on fast trains between Hull and Leeds, Doncaster or Scarborough around 1930 - 1932; they also gave good service on the cheap evening excursions to Bridlington, from Hull.

April 1931 saw 2425 (33) and 2427 loaned to Selby, and although more welcome at that shed than the Q10's had been, the two engines did little work there beyond pottering about the station on carriage pilot duties - a sad come-down for the last Stirling express design. Still, at least these two were actually being used; two years later they were all spending lengthy periods in store within the gaunt, echoing workshop buildings at Springhead - largely unused since the LNER had removed

the heavy machinery in 1924. No.2425 did not last out 1933, being withdrawn that August, and two more followed in December; 2427 only survived one more month, which left 2429 to work out its final months before following its classmates into oblivion in September 1934. Its appearance was by then so shabby and down-at-heel that scrapping it was almost merciful, but even under LNER ownership the D24's had not always looked so disreputable.

We have already considered their splendid appearance when new, but the H&BR did carry out a few minor modifications in addition to the change in the shape of the reach-rods.

Late in H&BR days a fourth tender coal-rail was fitted and a third dog-clamp fitted to the smokebox door at the six o'clock position, in addition to the original ones at approximately four and eight o'clock. Cab roof ventilators were fitted late on to Nos.35 and 41, and when given its domed boiler in November 1929, No.2429 also received one. The other two were never so fitted.

As a result of the dislocation due to World War I, the H&B like several other companies, experimented with oil firing. On 25th June 1921 an H&BR Board Minute noted that one 4-4-0, a 2-4-0 and an 0-6-0 had been converted, and furthermore one 0-8-0 and an 0-6-2 tank would be ready within a few days. Only the 4-4-0 was identified, being No.35, and was noted as "....regularly running the 1.05 p.m., 4.15 p.m. and 7.15 p.m. passenger trains, daily mileage 164." Furthermore, it was noted as consuming between 32 to 42lb per mile of fuel oil, compared with 52 lb of coal per mile. Sadly, respective costs were not quoted. Just how long the five engines concerned in the oil firing trials retained their equipment is not known.

Application of the North Eastern's lovely Saxony Green livery took place in full splendour only on 3038, in November 1922. The large brass oval numberplates customarily used on the NER were not fitted, recourse being made instead to the H&BR - style shaded characters on the cabside, thus producing a hybrid version of the NER passenger livery. The others retained H&BR livery but with their NER 3XXX series numbers applied in similar fashion to 3038. May 1923 saw 3041 outshopped from Springhead in LNER green with number and "L.& N.E.R." on the tender, the figure "3" being given a flat top.

2428 standing at Neville Hill shed, during a turnaround on workings to and from Hull. *Laurie Ward.*

Next to appear was 3035 in September 1923, displaying exactly the same style save for the tender lettering being altered to read "L.N.E.R.", a style which Darlington never used. Two months later 3033 appeared; the stops had been dropped in the meantime. February 1924 saw 3042 join its fellows in acquiring green livery; there matters rested for just two months until April 1924 when LNER numbers were applied at the following dates: 2425 and 2426 in May 1924; 2427 in April 1924; 2428 in June 1924 and 2429 in July 1924. No.2427 (still in North Eastern livery), remained an oddity carrying its LNER numbers on the cabsides in H&BR-style numerals and on the front bufferbeam in the North Eastern's larger style. It finally achieved uniformity with the others in October 1925. So often changes of livery have not always suited locomotives, but in the case of the D24's they still looked very smart in light green - of whatever shade!

Darlington had the usual field-day when it came to effecting minor modifications to the D24's. Initially, they contented themselves with plating behind the tender coal-rails and fitting wind-jabbers to the chimneys on 2425, 2426 and 2429 only, and additionally returning 2425 and 2429 to Springhead with organ-pipe whistles in exchange for their H&BR single-bell type.

Smokebox doors wore out on 2425 and 2427 before the engines were reboilered, to be replaced by the smaller-diameter type of NER smokebox doors fastened by a wheel and handle and with the lamp irons transposed from the doors to the top of the smokebox door ring.

Darlington could not resist the temptation of tinkering with the sanding gear either, as an exchange of notes between our old friends J.H.Smeddle, A.C.Stamer, R.J.Robson and R.A.Copperthwaite reveals. Evidently the workshops at Darlington had gone ahead of their own volition and fitted steam-sanding: with not wholly-satisfactory results. J.H.Smeddle, Running Superintendent at York, explained the problem which had arisen with his first note, dated 9th April 1925, addressed to A.C.Stamer, the Assistant Chief Mechanical Engineer:

"I have a complaint from my Hull Shed Superintendent that the H.& B. engines which have been to the Works have had their sand gear taken off, and our steam sands fitted.

"H.& B. engine No.2429 Class "J" is at present in the Works, and I shall be glad if you will arrange for the sand pipes of this engine to be carried underneath the brake cross stay instead of over the top, as the Hull Superintendent is having these to alter on account of the pipes being liable to break off as the engine brake blocks get worn."

R.A.Copperthwaite, Darlington Locomotive Works Manager gave the reason for the alteration on 4th June in answer to A.C.Stamer, who had obviously passed on Smeddle's complaint:

"....the sand pipes in question were placed over the brake bar in accordance with our usual practice so as to give the sand direct and greater fall. Sufficient allowance was made between the brake bar and the pipes for the clearance of the brake blocks.

"There are no drawings for these pipes."

Despite Copperthwaite's assertion at the end of the first paragraph, he dutifully arranged for 2429 to have the sandpipes led below the brake cross-bar and in view of his last sentence it comes as no surprise to find that R.J.Robson, Chief Draughtsman, became involved. The latter reported on 17th July that:

"A drawing is in hand showing these alterations, which will be forwarded to you in due course."

Thus by midsummer 1925 it only remained for the other engines at Springhead to be brought into line with the drawing - No.11595, "Arrangement of Steam Sanding. Class J(HB)" - and a copy was duly sent there, via J.H.Smeddle at York.

3rd July 1929 saw Smeddle again contacting A.C.Stamer, for he realised that the five D24's were under-utilised but incapable of giving total satisfaction on other duties unless they received some attention. His letter is of considerable interest, and worth quoting in full:

"H.& B. Section "D24"(J) Type Engines.

"We have five of the "D24" type engines (fitted with vacuum brake) in stock at Springhead Shed, and I am anxious that these engines should be utilised on the local Passenger workings in the Hull Area when the carriage sets are fitted with the vacuum brake. Before this can be done, however, the engines, in my opinion, require some alteration.

"We have carried out experiments with these engines on the Sheffield working, but unfortunately the engines lost time, mainly due to injector trouble.

"I am afraid that if we did put them into traffic we would still be faced with a great deal of trouble with the injectors. I understand that they have always given a certain amount of trouble even in the H.& B. days, but that the original injectors were better than the ones supplied since they were in the Works. The present injectors have a steam passage to attach to the steam sanding apparatus and this restricts to a certain extent the ordinary passage to the injector. It is not, of course, the injectors themselves that cause the trouble but the pipes between the tender, the injector and the position of the injector on the boiler. "The engines would be considerably improved if they were fitted with footstep injectors, and I should like to try one of these engines fitted in this manner, and suggest one be sent into the works to be fitted.

"The slide valves have given considerable trouble due to the fact that the top faces have been considerably reduced through wear and instead of the faces being renewed when the engines were in Darlington Works they have been simply planed down which have increased the distance between the top and bottom face to the extent that it is greater than the opening of the steam chest cover. The result is that it is not possible to fit valves in a satisfactory manner.

"I shall be glad to hear that you agree to one of these engines being sent into the Works to be fitted with the footstep injectors, and to have the valves attended to so that we may use it on the Sheffield or Doncaster turns.

"J.H.Smeddle."

Points of interest arising from this are that the LNER Brake Unification Programme was proceeding apace - the carriage sets referred to being of North Eastern origin and therefore having Westinghouse air brakes. Secondly, it was ironic in the extreme that the D24's couldn't run to Sheffield satisfactorily over a much easier route than that for which they were designed, but in view of the problems the balanced slide valves were giving it is evident that they had become quite well-worn despite the lengthy periods in store; a situation prevailing when Smeddle wrote.

Having passed the letter onwards, A.C.Stamer was informed on 23rd July 1929 by R.J.Robson that the five D24's were due for complete overhaul: new boilers fed by footstep type injectors were to be fitted, but he proposed to do nothing about the valves as he considered that to be "....a shop problem, and probably you will take the matter up with the Work's Manager."

The upshot was that Stamer immediately arranged for one of the engines to visit Darlington for reboilering and attention to the valves on 24th July. The engine concerned turned out to be 2425, and it duly reappeared in its new form in September 1929.

The result of Darlington's attentions was not fully satisfactory unfortunately, for in solving one set of problems they had created yet another! So 14th October saw J.H.Smeddle, doubtlessly somewhat exasperated by these antics, fire off another missive to his colleagues at Darlington:

"Engine No. 2425 - Class "J" Hull.
"The above engine was returned from Darlington Works during week ending September 28th. with the front (steam) heater pipe taken off. I shall be glad to know the reason of this, as it will cause considerable inconvenience as the engine works a train from Howden tender-first....."

".....send the necessary material to Hull for fitting the heater pipe on to the front of the engine, instead of sending the engine back to Darlington."

The reply came back on 28th October from Mr. F.W.Carr at Darlington Works, via A.C.Stamer:

"When engine No.2425 was at these Works it was fitted up to drawing No.13642.D. which bears a special note "Existing Steam Heating Gear on front of Engine not required", and the apparatus was therefore removed.

".....as certain alterations were made to the engine whilst it was in these Works, I am afraid that the old material cannot be replaced just as in the same manner as before. It would be advisable, therefore, for the engine to be returned to the Works to be fitted....."

Two days later Stamer received R.J.Robson's comments:

"It is standard practice on N.E.Tender Engines to fit steam heating on the tender only, a few exceptions being made to suit local requirements.

"In his letter of July 3rd. 1929, the Running Superintendent stated that he wished to use these engines on the Sheffield or Doncaster turns, presumably already worked by N.E.engines without front heating.

"As the existing arrangement of heater pipes on the Class "J" engines had to be entirely altered, due to the fitting of footstep injectors, and as the front end fittings were possibly not required, they were dispensed with."

The next memo. was a reply from A.C.Stamer to R.J.Robson, dated 5th November:

".....Mr.Smeddle points out that these engines occasionally have to run tender first to Howden, Hornsea or Withernsea in their ordinary booked working and that he is unable to turn these engines in time to take this working. Mr.Smeddle says it is very necessary that they should be fitted with steam heating at the front end, and I should be glad if you would let Mr.Carr have the necessary drawings for this to be done."

By the time the second D24 - No.2429 - reached Darlington in November 1929, matters had been sorted out; all engines were to be fitted with steam heat connections at the front end as they passed through Darlington Works, and it was arranged that 2425 would return there for the necessary plumbing work to be done.

The following year saw J.H.Smeddle writing to A.C.Stamer to remind him of ".....the necessity for fitting understep injectors to these engines if they do not get new boilers whilst they are in

2429 (42) fairly near home, being photographed at Dairycoates. The buildings in the left background are the fish market sheds, which once stood along the north side of the old Saint Andrew's Dock.

the Works, and I would remind you that you have undertaken to fit steam heating at the front end."

Four days later, on 11th April 1930, R.J.Robson replied on Stamer's behalf:

".....there are 5 engines of this type, 2 of which have been fitted with new boilers, one is now in the works being reboilered, and there are 2 boilers standing in the works for the last 2 engines.

"With regard to the footsteps and steam heating, these will be fitted when the engines come into the shops."

The new boilers were domed replacements to Type 58B; the domeless originals had lasted far enough into LNER ownership to be designated 58A. The domed boilers were pressed to 175 lb/sq.in, just 5 lb higher than the original type; consequently tractive effort increased somewhat to 16,790 lb - comparable with the North Eastern R1 (LNER D21) 4-4-0's, but nearly ten tons lighter in weight than the latter.

Along with reboiling came new chimneys of the same pattern as the North Easter Z (LNER C7) 4-4-2 engines save for the radius of the base; all these chimneys had windjabbers, which often became rather moth-eaten around the edges!

Ross "Pop" safety-valves appeared on the new boilers and the vacuum ejector exhaust pipes were led along the right-hand side of the engines, rather spoiling their clean lines. NER twin whistles appeared on them all, as did twin steps on the smokebox fronts.

2429 somehow retained its rerailing jack throughout its life; the others all lost theirs at an early date under LNER ownership.

The new look for the D24's was completed by a coat of black paint picked out with single red lining - a surprisingly smart livery when kept clean, and strongly reminiscent of the H&BR livery they first appeared in.

Smeddle's desire to use them from Hull on Leeds, Sheffield and Scarborough fast trains was largely realised throughout 1930-1932, but time and circumstances were moving against the D24's. From 1927 to 1930, thirty-six new, three-cylinder 4-4-0's of Class D49 (attributed to Gresley but largely designed at Darlington under Stamer and R.J.Robson's auspices), were turned out and

allocated to the North Eastern and Scottish Areas of the LNER. Small classes of odd North Eastern engines had been going to scrap since the late 1920's, so five engines having virtually nothing in common with other North Eastern 4-4-0's were obviously very vulnerable. Another twenty-eight D49's were delivered up to the end of September 1934; with each one delivered, the Grim Reaper (carrying a cutting torch rather than a scythe!), took one step nearer to the D24's.

2425 was the first to go in August 1933, but money was still being spent copiously on the others: October 1933 saw 2426 emerge from a heavy repair at Darlington Works. This must have been largely for nothing, for it was withdrawn at the end of December along with 2428. In January 1934, 2427 followed them to Darlington North Road scrapyard, leaving 2429 to eke out its solitary existence until its final summons to Darlington came in September.

The new domed boilers, the fitting of which had inadvertently brought such problems for Smeddle, had seen very little use: they averaged only 3 years 10 months on each D24, and lengthy periods in store had latterly taken up much - too much - of that time.

Not surprisingly the boilers were re-used: two at Springhead in a stationary capacity and two went to Stratford for similar use. That from 2428 reappeared on another Hull & Barnsley engine in the form of LNER Class J28 0-6-0 No.2416 (H&BR Class L1 No.24), in February 1934. It served with that engine until its withdrawal in October 1938, when it too was put to stationary use.

The Hull & Barnsley's 4-4-0's could be regarded as little more than a flamboyant gesture if judged against the minimal income generated by the passenger services. Still, locomotive engineers cannot be expected to allow for the consequences arising from a possible world war, which lay over four years in the future at the time the Class J's were designed. Had the war not happened it is likely that their seven years of service on the Sheffield trains could well have been at least doubled - which would be about as long as any class of express engine could reasonably expect to survive in top-link service. Some classes of engines on railway systems of far more renown than the H&BR couldn't even match the seven years' prominent service of the Class J's, and without even the excuse of a World War for being unable to live up to the expectations of their designers.

Summary: Class J 4-4-0 Express Engines. LNER Class D24.

HBR No.	Works No.	Delivered	NER No.	LNER No.	Reboilered with Dgm 58B type	Withdrawn
33	4700	December 1910	3033	2425	September 1929	August 1933
35	4701	December 1910	3035	2426	July 1930	December 1933
38	4702	December 1910	3038	2427	July 1930	January 1934
41	4703	December 1910	3041	2428	April 1930	December 1933
42	4704	December 1910	3042	2429	November 1929	September 1934

Notes: Kitson & Co. Order No.377V. Cost £3,050 each.

Class J Dimensions.

Cylinders: 2, inside - 18½" x 26"
Motion: Allan Straight-Link, driving open backed, balanced slide valves on top of the cylinders via rocking levers.
Boiler: Domeless
Max .diameter outside: 5' 0"
Barrel length: 11' 0"
Firebox length outside: 6' 0"
Pitch: 8' 7½"
Heating Surface:
  Firebox - 132 sq.ft*; 126 sq.ft**
  Tubes - 245 @ 1¾" dia. = 1,275 sq.ft*; 1,272 sq.ft**
  Total - 1,407 sq.ft*; 1,398 sq.ft**
Grate Area: 19.6 sq.ft*; 19.4 sq.ft**
Ratio of grate area to heating surface: 1 to 71.78*; 1 to 72.06**
Boiler Pressure: 170 lb/sq.in
Wheel diameters:
  Engine - 3' 9" and 6' 6"
  Tender - 3' 9"
Wheelbase:
  Engine - 6' 6"+ 7' 3"+ 9'3" = 23' 0"
  Tender - 6' 0"+ 6' 0" = 12' 0"
  Total = 43' 9"
Length over buffers: 54' 0¾"*; 54' 1"**
Height to top of chimney: 13' 2"
Tractive Effort @ 85% of Boiler Pressure: 16,485 lb
Ratio of blast nozzle to cylinder diameter: 1 to 3.60
Tender water capacity: 3,500 gallons
Tender coal capacity: 5 tons 5 cwt
Axle Loads:
  Engine:
    Bogie - 9 tons 15 cwt + 9 tons 12 cwt
    Driver - 18 tons 0 cwt
    Rear - 17 tons 17 cwt.
  Tender:
    Leading - 13 tons 15 cwt
    Middle - 13 tons 12 cwt
    Rear - 13 tons 3 cwt

Weights in Full Working Order:
  Engine 55 tons 2 cwt
  Tender 40 tons 10 cwt
  Total 95 tons 12 cwt
* Dimensions as given on last H&BR Diagram; those for the boilers correspond to dimensions given by the Yorkshire Engine Co. for Class L engines Nos. 157-161.
** Dimensions as given on the first LNER Diagram: the differences probably arose due to different methods of calculation.

Dimensions for LNER Class D24, Rebuilt with Diagram 58B Domed boilers.
Boiler: Domed
Max. diameter outside: 5' 0"
Barrel length: 11' 0⅛"
Firebox length outside: 6' 0"
Pitch: 8' 7½"
Heating Surface:
  Firebox 128 sq.ft
  Tubes 227 @ 1¾" dia. = 1,181 sq.ft
  Total 1,309 sq.ft
Grate Area: 19.6 sq.ft
Ratio of grate area to heating surface: 1 to 66.78
Boiler Pressure: 175 lb/sq.in
Tractive Effort @ 85% of Boiler Pressure: 16,970 lb
Weights in Full Working Order:
  Loco - 55 tons 0 cwt.
  Tender - 40 tons 10 cwt.
  Total - 95 tons 10 cwt
These boilers actually contained 234 tubes, but seven of these were used for staying purposes. Although the use of stays through tubes was done away with in Darlington boilers from 1933, it is unlikely that the tube stays were removed from the Class D24 engines before withdrawal and scrapping.

"A watched kettle never boils". 2426 and three of Springhead's worthies test out that particular theory. Judging by the state of 2426's paintwork, its days of coming to the boil are drawing to a close. *Ron Copeman collection.*

2428 awaits departure from Scarborough late one summer afternoon in 1932. It would see only one more summer of work. *Ron Copeman collection.*

At least four of the five Class J's in store in Springhead works - 2428 (41) on the left and 2429 (42) on the right. Behind 2429 are 2426 (35) and 2427 (38), given away by the windjabbers on their chimney tops. To have such engines standing idle was anathema to any good railwayman, hence J.H.Smeddle at York wanting to put them back into good order for use on local passenger services. Someone had removed the front steam-heating hose from 2429, a minor matter which would have needed attention in any case. *Ron Copeman collection.*

The sad reminders of H&BR express locomotive power lingered on at Springhead until 1951 in the form of the boilers off 2425 and 2427, becoming stationary boilers 7030 and 7027 respectively. They are seen undergoing routine maintenance, as revealed by the ladders and lack of safety-valves on the left-hand boiler, plus the oval plate hanging on its backhead - presumably warning the over-impetuous against lighting it up. Quite what the graffiti on the bunker in the foreground refers to is uncertain; it may be an oblique reference to the musical, "The Showboat", although if so the author would have considered a reference to Don Quixote as more appropriate, in view of the years the H&BR spent in tilting against the giant North Eastern....!

CLASS L1 0-6-0 ENGINES. (LNER CLASS J28).
Introduced 1911.

The Hull & Barnsley's L, L1 and LS 0-6-0's have presented students of locomotive history with some confusion, for several reasons. Firstly, although invariably referred to in the above order by the H&BR and by earlier chroniclers of their history, the L1 engines actually appeared first, the LS engines coming last. Secondly, the twenty engines which made up the three family groups were actually built in four different albeit closely-related groups, for the ten L1 engines formed two groups (basically, superheated and saturated, with the latter having considerable affinities to the later Class L engines).

Even the LNER got into something of a muddle when classifying the three groups of engines, but gave up and referred to them all irrespectively as Class J28. Time was to reveal the weakness of this Procrustean approach, for when the Diagram 58B domed boilers were fitted from 1928 they found it advisable to add suffix numbers: thus all L/L1/LS engines with domeless boilers became J28 irrespective of their original H&BR classifications; the reboilered, domed L1 engines then became J28/2. Finally, 1930 saw them wake up to the fact that some domeless engines (formerly H&BR Class LS), had superheated boilers and this marked them out as somewhat different; thus the J28/3 classification was introduced for these engines. When three of them were reboilered with 58B boilers, the engines concerned joined the ranks of the J28/1's, along with rebuilt Class L's.

In an attempt to establish some semblance of order in the face of this impending maze of muddle and misunderstanding, your author has decided to treat the three (or four?!), groups of engines in chronological order; therefore we will begin this section with the superheated L1 engines of 1911, concluding with the saturated engines delivered the following year.

The processes which led to the L1 engines are more or less self-evident. The Class A engines left nothing to be desired as machines, but they had to be fitted into a form of traffic working specially created around them before achieving success.

Indeed, if they had been greatly multiplied they may have led to other factors coming into consideration: they were banned from several Hull branches and the full length of the Denaby branch; due to their heavier trains they were to be worked as far as possible with 20-ton brake-vans, and so on. Furthermore the "Tinies" were operationally limited - even if fitted with vacuum brakes they would still remain too slow to work passenger trains and probably fast fitted freights (in spite of any bonus schemes which might be devised to encourage their crews!).

Thus the well-tried and tested 0-6-0 type was returned to but much of the design work had already been done, for the L1's essentially married the Class A machinery with the Class J boiler, cab and tender. Thus, with cylinder diameters one inch larger, boiler barrel and firebox each one foot longer and re-use of the now well-established Allan straight-link valve gear with rocking levers driving open-backed, balanced slide valves on the cylinder tops, the L1's bore little if any resemblance to earlier H&BR 0-6-0's save for wheel and boiler diameters. Both of these were 5ft; hence the L1's would be as versatile as their predecessors regarding the work they could tackle. To imply, as other writers have on occasion, that the L1's were simply larger and modernised Class B engines is erroneous: the real contention arises when the question is considered as to whether they should be regarded as a form of "pocket Class A" or a goods version of Class J.

Whatever the truth of the matter, the first ten (all therefore to Class L1) were ordered from Kitson in 1909; their delivery was to be over a three-year period but in the event they appeared in two batches, in 1911 and 1912. This begs the question whether these engines were in fact designed before the Class J's or simultaneously with them, especially when their works numbers, 4705 to 4714, follow immediately on from theirs. Possibly consideration had been given to fitting them with Belpaire fireboxes as with the Class J's; if so, the possible disinclination of Kitson's to provide suitable flanging blocks would be harder to explain, although presumably they would have set the price of such blocks against the contract tendering price: if the H&BR were unwilling to pay the extra price necessarily called for, then this would serve to underline just how expensive these items actually were. (The five Class J's plus the ten L1's made up a substantial order, with the chance of further orders to

Class L1 No.17 at Springhead, as new. The ungainly Phoenix smokebox needs no further comment! *Hull Museums collection.*

No.29 represents the "normal" version of Class L1, as delivered in 1912. Note that Kitsons have provided another variation on the livery theme - the tender has full stops after each character. This was a unique feature of the Class L1 engines. *Hull Museums collection.*

come. In the event, Kitson's produced such flange blocks in 1912 for Great Central Railway Robinson 2-8-0's with 5 ft boilers and Belpaire fireboxes, the order being for twenty engines - only five more than the combined L1 and J orders).

The Class L1 engines had longer valve-travel and greater fixed cut-off than the earlier 0-6-0's, and a further indication of the revisionist spirit sweeping through the H&BR motive power department was evident in the balancing of the coupled wheels. Perhaps Matthew Stirling envisaged the new engines running at considerably greater speeds than their forebears, hence the need for increased balancing of the reciprocating parts.

One unfortunate aspect of the L1 design was the arrangement of the reversing gear. The reach-rod ran horizontally from the cab front to the weighshaft arm, with a slight curvature over the driving wheel splasher (reminiscent in a modest way of the more flamboyant arrangement as initially fitted to the Class J 4-4-0's). Entering the cab fairly low-down, connection to the reversing screw was effected by a rocking link - which had the unfortunate effect of reversing the action of the hand-wheel. Normally, winding the handle in a clockwise direction dropped an engine into forward gear, but performing the same operation on an L1 caused the valve gear to assume the positions necessary for setting the engine in reverse! The inevitable consequence of not noticing the different markings on the reversing screw scale did not apparently catch anyone out on the H&BR however - although without a doubt this was due more to luck than judgement! (The Class J engines also had a similar arrangement, which again underlines their close affinity with the L1's).

An innovation on the first five L1 engines was the fitting of superheating equipment. This was in the form of the Phoenix smokebox type, and very much in vogue at that time. Beyer, Peacock had fitted it in 1911 to a batch of 4-4-0's for the Irish Great Northern Railway, and the Furness Railway fitted it to two goods engines. These were 0-6-0's, had 18 x 26 inch cylinders and 150 lb/sq.inch boiler pressure, so were roughly comparable to the L1's. An enthusiastic *Engineering* reported in February 1910 that steam temperatures of 500 to 550 degrees F were found, and that the two engines were averaging a coal consumption of 40.5 lb per mile, in comparison to 53 lb per mile burnt by similar but unfitted engines. It was also noted that no extra attention had been found necessary regarding lubrication. (This points to the fact that the supposed "superheating" temperatures were in fact rather on the low side, and that the Phoenix equipment would have to demonstrate significant advantages in other areas to be worth retaining).

Basically, the Phoenix equipment consisted of two large cast headers set longitudinally in the bottom of the smokebox, one per side. They were linked by horseshoe-shaped elements, ends downwards in the headers, passages cast in which constrained the steam to make no less than five passages back and forth through the banks of elements in order to get from the main boiler steampipe to the cylinders. Two smaller headers either side of the base of the chimney also abetted this process. Due to the length of the main headers the smokebox had to be correspondingly extended, which led to the chimney being set much further forward than usual and also resulted in the exhaust pipe from cylinder to blast nozzle taking a somewhat convoluted course. To allow access to this plumber's nightmare, the smokebox was split horizontally and held together by a doubler-strip, riveted to the lower half but allowing the upper half of the smokebox to be secured by means of hexagonal-headed bolts. (This particular "dodge" was later re-invented and claimed as their own by the model engineering fraternity, being sometimes resorted to for similar reasons on small steam engines as on their full-sized brethren!).

The first five Class L1 engines (works Nos.4705-4709), rolled up at Springhead exactly a year later than the Class J's, despite their consecutively following works numbers. It would therefore seem that the order was in fact spread over three years, but the five J Class engines were included within it and actually made up the first year's delivery. The 1911 engines were quite eye-catching: the extended smokeboxes necessary for carrying the Phoenix equipment gave them an especially pugnacious aspect, exaggerated by the chimney being set so far forward on the smokebox. The hexagon bolt-heads on the upper smokebox segments spoilt the previously-smooth neatness of finish exhibited by all Matthew Stirling's earlier engines, giving the Phoenix L1's all the grace, style and perfection of finish of a tin bathtub.

The ugliness of these particular ducklings was highlighted with the passage of twelve more months, when the five saturated L1 engines were delivered - exhibiting an altogether more swan-like aspect!

All ten L1's were regarded as replacements for the old Kirtley 0-6-0's, but as with the 2-4-0's upon the appearance of

No.30, by way of contrast with its more pugnacious - looking brethren. Note that the engine is in back-gear, thus revealing part of the manhole under the boiler. Also, due to the cross-over link in the cab, the reversing-handle has been wound into what would apparently be forward-gear....! *Hull Museums collection.*

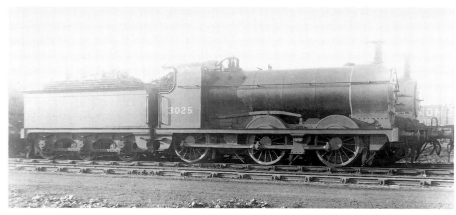

3025 at Springhead on 24th June 1923 with its North Eastern number although under LNER ownership. It retained its domeless boiler until withdrawn in September 1934 - first of the L1/L/LS family to suffer that fate.

2424 (32) outside Springhead's office block - its tender has been recently patch-painted with the LNER number, being cleaner than the LNER lettering. The wagon in the left background still proclaims its origins, although possibly not for much longer, for it stands in the wagon works' yard.

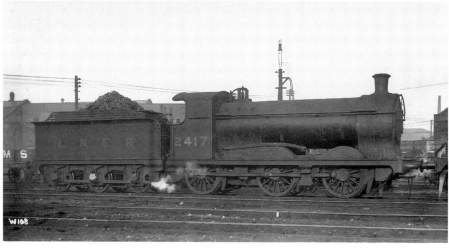

2417 paid the price for becoming the final domeless L1, it became the first to be withdrawn. *Ron Copeman collection.*

the Class J's this did not mean the immediate withdrawal of the older engines. The Phoenix engines displaced Nos.16, 17, 19, 24 and 31 to the Duplicate Lists, the 1912 delivery of L1's likewise meant continued existence on borrowed time for Nos.14, 25, 29, 30 and 32. Oddly enough, nobody seems to have ever pointed a camera at the old Kirtley 0-6-0's when they were running with the Duplicate letter "A" painted on their cabsides.

Two distinguishing features which all ten L1 engines had in common were round cab spectacle-windows and sandboxes beneath the footplating. These were also present on the Class J engines; unlike the Class B's, no alterations took place to the spectacle windows on any of these two classes of engines.

One alteration which was carried out was the removal of the Phoenix equipment from all five engines so fitted between November 1919 and February 1922. (It may also be recalled that Class B 0-6-0 No.133 had been the first H&BR engine to be given Phoenix equipment in May 1914, and was also the first to lose it, in May 1919). Despite the glowing reports of the two Furness Railway engines in 1910, it speaks for itself that their Baltic tanks of 1920 (mentioned in connection with the Class J engines), were turned out without any form of superheating. One should not be too critical of the H&BR and Stirling for use of a system which time and experience were to show was not worthwhile; even the mighty North Eastern was undecided as to the merits of superheating in 1911. That year saw them order 20 of their superb 3-cylinder 4-4-2 express engines from the North British Locomotive Co. Ten were to Class Z (saturated engines), and ten were equipped with Schmidt superheating to become known as class Z1 - a typical piece of North Eastern compromision! Clearly therefore, the jury could be said to be still out in 1911 on the matter of superheating.

One final twist was that the H&BR's final Diagram Book showed the dimensions for the Phoenix L1 engines with their longer frames and overall lengths, but the drawing showed them to have shortened smokeboxes. This, plus photographs of the engines whilst still domeless early on under LNER ownership would tend to suggest that the smokeboxes would have been cut back or renewed before the NER took over, probably at the same time as the superheating equipment was removed.

From 1928, by which date these engines had become Class J28, domed boilers to Diagram 58B type were fitted to all the class except for 2417 (25). Upon reboiling all the domed engines became Class J28/2, leaving their domeless brethren (of whichever branch of the family), to remain as Class J28. No.2416 (ex-Phoenix - fitted No.24), ended up with the second-hand boiler from D24 No.2428 (Class J No.41), after the latter's withdrawal in December 1933.

The last reboiling was done in August 1931, on 2411 (ex-Phoenix engine No.19). 2417 (25), a saturated engine delivered in 1912, retained its domeless boiler throughout its life, which came to an untimely end as early as September 1934 - the first of the L/L1/LS group to be scrapped.

The 58B type domed boilers had Ross "Pop" safety-valves, tallish North Eastern chimneys without windjabbers and twin handles for fastening the smokebox doors. NER twin whistles also appeared on the rebuilt engines, as did vacuum ejector exhaust pipes along the boiler side.

North Eastern replacement smokebox doors were of both large and smaller diameter types; generally, the smaller variety appeared as renewals on domeless engines after the original Stirling doors had corroded away, the larger pattern was usually fitted to the domed rebuilds. One ex-L1 received a small NER

2406 (14) in store at Springhead; sadly only the resident sparrows have paid it any recent attention. *Ron Copeman collection.*

Ex-Phoenix engine 2416 seen at Hull Dairycoates in the 1930's. The small lean-to built along the shed wall beyond 2416's tender were the latrines, which consisted of a row of stalls, each with a seat over a long, communal sluice. At the nearer end was a cistern which upon the periodic pulling of a chain, flushed away the accumulated deposits. Human nature being what it is, various individuals were occasionally known to sidle away and seek refuge within the sanctuary of a cubicle to the chagrin of their fellows, for absence did not necessarily make their hearts grow fonder in such instances. However, retribution was sometimes forthcoming - and merciless - taking the form of a small boat cunningly folded from old newspaper, being set alight and swept downstream upon the pulling of the chain. As the "fireship" passed below the nether regions of the occupant of a cubicle, the resulting screams of anguish when flames singed their more delicate anatomical parts may best be left to the imagination....

type door held shut by a wheel and handle whilst still domeless, but when photographed in this condition was so disreputably filthy that its number was indecipherable.

An upturn in the fortunes of some J28 engines (of whatever variety!), came from 1932 onwards when steam heat connections were fitted to both engine and tender along with screw-link couplings, in order to make them more suitable for passenger work. L1-type engines so affected were: 2406 (14) in January 1935; 2408 (16) in March 1934; 2409 (17) in February 1935; 2416 (24) in February 1934; 2422 (30) - October 1933; 2424 (32) - August 1933. Nos. 2408, 2409 and 2416 were ex-Phoenix fitted engines; likewise 2411 (19) and 2423 (31), but along with 2417 (25) and 2421 (29) they remained unequipped, retaining only their three-link couplings to the end. (2417, the first J28 withdrawn, was also the only ex-L1 to retain a domeless boiler throughout its life).

As with the J23 engines, Darlington altered the brake standpipes at each end from early 1924. The medium-height H&BR vacuum standpipes were replaced by hose connections below the bufferbeams, but a later change of heart saw things go to the other extreme with the fitting of tall standpipes. All engines which acquired steam-heat also received tall standpipes, as did 2411 (19), although 2417 (25) and 2423 (31) did not, going for scrap with the below-bufferbeam connections unaltered.

The L1's had been useful engines on the H&BR, appearing when the intensity of traffic working had reached a peak. They suffered none of the restrictions and prejudices inflicted upon

the Class A's, but despite being considerably bigger than the older Class B engines they were still rostered to take thirty 10-ton loaded wagons over the most heavily-graded section of the line from Sandholme to Little Weighton, although one may surmise that they did it faster and with greater ease than the Class B's! Any load greater than that mentioned resulted in double-heading being resorted to - a practice especially in vogue throughout the 1920's as we have already seen. During those years it was the accepted practice for permutations of any varieties of H&BR 0-6-0's to work in pairs.

As ever, the appearance of the Robinson O4 class ex-ROD 2-8-0's from 1929 affected the J28's drastically. Initially, they were transferred to lighter work from 1932 onwards - the Hull-Howden pick-up goods for example - but by 1933/34, periods in store became the norm for too many of the class. Then as older, ex-North Eastern 0-6-0's were withdrawn, J28's were transferred from store to resume active careers. This situation was especially prevalent at Dairycoates, which for many years represented virtually the North East's "condemned cell" in this respect. At their new home, the J28's assumed responsibility for all manner of workings around Hull, not infrequently going as far afield as Doncaster. One odd passenger working around Hull which was taken up by the J28's (or anything else with continuous brake equipment and a head of steam for that matter!), was a boat train, no less!

This particular exploit took place from Hull Paragon station to Riverside Quay via Dairycoates on ground-level tracks parallel to but mostly within and at an average of half a mile distant from the circuit of the Neptune Street-Paragon fish trains referred to earlier under Class J! However, the Riverside Quay boat train was no fancy affair of Pullman stock headed by Mr. Gresley's newest and smartest express engine, festooned with flags and headboards; nor was it some wondrously - clean spectacle like those arriving at Dover, looking as though Indians had ambushed it whilst traversing the "Badlands" around Ashford.....in no way!! Instead, a thoroughly disreputable-looking J28 (with copious steam leaks at the front end for good measure), made as great a show as it could of hauling whatever set of the dowdiest old North Eastern clerestories which could be found lurking in the carriage sidings at the back of Paragon yard! Just what sort of impression this spectacle made upon foreign visitors to these shores can well be guessed at - probably the firm resolution to sail to Harwich and take the "Hook Continental" next time! Still, at least the journey to Paragon was mercifully short, and the scenery (largely of trawler masts and smoke houses for kippers), left nobody in any doubt as to what the real business of Hull's Western docks actually was. It was as though the LNER was determined to make the point that it was doing all concerned a big favour by providing any sort of service at all; and those who didn't like it were welcome to walk over to Hessle Road and catch a tram! (It is also worthwhile pointing out that nowadays, with the North Sea ferry services well established, nobody has ever proposed attempting to try running a similar sort of service round to King George Dock, so maybe the LNER should not be too heavily berated: at least they provided a service).

Other ex-L1 engines were transferred much further afield than Dairycoates, however. At least one J28 (of the old L1 variety), ended up at Darlington, where that wickedly playful reversing screw arrangement caught out an ex-North Eastern driver. Winding the engine into forward gear, he must have been considerably dismayed and not a little alarmed to find the engine heave itself backwards and punch the tender through the wall of Darlington North Road shed! Unfortunately no correspondence between Stamer, Smeddle, Copperthwaite et al. appears to have survived regarding this particular escapade, although we can imagine that the crestfallen crew had some harsh words to say about Hull & Barnsley engines in general and that one in particular, as they shook the brick-dust and soot from their overalls and climbed shakily off the engine to survey the extra ventilation they had provided in the wall of the old roundhouse!

Meanwhile, others had gone a-wandering to the LNER Southern Area - 2408 (16) and 2422 (30) being transferred to Langwith (ex-LD&ECR territory), in May 1937; No.2411 (19) went to Frodingham soon after. Their stay away from Hull was of but a short duration - all three returned to Dairycoates in February 1938, to be withdrawn by October that year.

The last survivor of the J28's turned out to be 2409 (L1 No.17), withdrawn in October 1937. It was trundled on to a siding alongside Darlington Works, and by means of a pipe plumbed into the steam dome it was used as a stationary boiler until June 1939, but in view of the international situation it was not cut up until December 1939. It had started life as a Phoenix-fitted L1 and finished its useful existence with the most graceless, battered bit of old pipe stuck on the chimney - Stirling would have wept! So ironically, it began its life with an uglified front-end and finished it in similar fashion, too.

DIMENSIONS: Since the L1, L and LS engines were so similar, the Tables of Dimensions may be found at the end of the Section dealing with Class LS.

Summary: Class L1 0-6-0 Goods engines. LNER Class J28.

HBR No.	Built	Works No.	NER No.	LNER No.	Phoenix Equipment removed	Domed 58B boiler fitted	Withdrawn
16*	Dec. 1911	4705	3016	2408	July 1921	October 1929	October 1938
17*	Dec. 1911	4706	3017	2409	February 1922	June 1928	October 1937
19*	Dec. 1911	4707	3019	2411	November 1919	August 1931	September 1938
24*	Dec. 1911	4708	3024	2416	February 1921	June 1930	October 1938
31*	Dec. 1911	4709	3031	2423	August 1920	November 1929	May 1937
14**	Nov. 1912	4710	3014	2406	-	May 1929	July 1937
25**	Dec. 1912	4711	3025	2417	-	-	September 1934
29**	Dec. 1912	4712	3029	2421	-	February 1930	May 1937
30**	Dec. 1912	4713	3030	2422	-	January 1929	October 1938
32**	Dec. 1912	4714	3032	2424	-	November 1929	May 1937

Notes: * Built Kitson & Co. cost £3,020 each; ** Built Kitson & Co. cost £3,000 each.

(above) **With express headlamps up and a good head of steam, 2422 (30) heads "The Boat Train" out of Hull Paragon's excursion platforms towards Riverside Quay. No wonder the LNER gave services such as "The Hook Continental" far wider publicity!** *Laurie Ward.*

(left) **Matthew Stirling's last surviving tender-engine, 2409 (ex-Phoenix No.17), led a twilight existence as stationary boiler at Darlington works from 1937 until June 1939. The outbreak of war brought it a temporary reprieve from the scrapyard until December 1939; thus passed another suitable candidate for preservation, although at the time the LNER authorities (and most of Europe too), had more serious matters to attend to, of course.** *Ron Copeman collection.*

(opposite, top) **2409 in happier days at Springhead, by way of a contrast from the earlier view on this page.** *H.C.Casserley.*

(opposite, bottom) **Another aid for the modelmaker! The right-hand side of 2409 when in the same condition as the previous view. Springhead Works east end may be seen in the background.** *Ron Copeman collection.*

No.159 poses for Yorkshire Engine Company's photograph. These tenders had "Iracier" axleboxes, this being the only occasion when Yorkshire Engine used that type for an H&BR engine. They even lined out the axlebox covers for the works photograph, but not necessarily for the service livery.

CLASS L 0-6-0 ENGINES. (LNER CLASS J28).
Introduced 1914.

Next to appear in the long series of 0-6-0 goods engines on the Hull & Barnsley were the Class L engines. Externally, they were almost identical to the preceding saturated steam variety of Class L1 locomotives, but a few different features crept in, which serve to distinguish between the two types.

The distance from the leading axle - centres to the faces of the front buffers was 8ft 0½in on both Class L and the saturated L1's, in comparison to 9ft 2½in on the Phoenix L1 engines (their extra frame-length being required to accommodate the long smokeboxes).

Far more evident was the return of the sandboxes to positions above the footplating, being faired into the splashers as on the Class B engines, plus a change from round to shaped cab spectacles, similar to those on Class A and the proposed Belpaire Class J. Class L also had windjabbers fitted to the chimneys when new - no L1 being so fitted initially. The right-hand sides of the locomotives showed that someone had been having second thoughts regarding the idiosyncratic arrangement for the reversing screw on Classes J and L1, for this time the reach-rod was led directly down from the reversing-screw die-block to the weighshaft across the frames at approximately 20 degrees from the horizontal, emerging from the cab front just over half-way up from the footplating to the cab window.

Hardly noticed by anyone except possibly those drivers more "in tune" with the finer workings of the locomotives than the others, or those who took care to scrutinise the works drawings more closely, was the fact that Class L had undergone some alteration to the valve events - the L1's had fixed maximum cut-offs of 80% of the piston stroke, given by a maximum valve-travel of $4^5/_8$in, whereas the L Class locomotives appeared with 78% fixed cut-off and $4^7/_8$in maximum valve travel. On the face of it these were trifling alterations, but giving the valves longer travel and setting an increased maximum cut-off was part of the process used in enabling a locomotive to run faster. Thus Class L may well have had some advantage there over their immediate predecessors - had their drivers chosen to take advantage of it.

The order for these engines (a modest one, only five being ordered), went to the Yorkshire Engine Co., being worth a total of £17,750 to them. It was to be the last order which Yorkshire Engine received from the H&BR, for three days before the delivery of the first one on 7th August 1914, Britain had declared war on Germany, their troops having invaded Belgium whose neutrality Britain had pledged to defend. By the time the last of the five was delivered, (10th December 1914), the Western Front was well-established after the battles of the Marne and Ypres, and the British were still nursing their hangovers sustained after celebrating the resounding naval victory at the Battle of the Falklands. The engines actually appeared as follows:

H&BR No.	Y.E.Co. No.	Delivery dates
157	1182	7th August 1914
158	1183	27th August 1914
159	1184	9th October 1914
160	1185	10th November 1914
161	1186	10th November 1914

All were to Yorkshire Engine Co. Order E195

Several points are apparent from this: firstly, that the engines were regarded as additions to Capital Stock, and not as replacements for the Kirtleys.

Secondly, Yorkshire Engine Company's occasional streaks of bad luck when building H&BR engines had surfaced once again - presumably many of their workforce that August had rushed to throw away their jobs, joining the various "Sheffield Pals" battalions - ultimately to have their lives thrown away the following summer. Clearly though, this time Yorkshire Engine Co. could plead "circumstances beyond our control" as a perfectly valid reason for having their delivery dates made a nonsense of.

Thirdly, the L Class followed on from five of the F3 Class 0-6-2 tanks numbered 152-156, the other five of that class being regarded as replacements rather than additions. Although at the beginning of 1914 it was anticipated that the locomotive stock would rise to number over 200 engines, this was not to be - the total reached but never surpassed 186 engines, and no H&BR locomotive was to carry a number higher than Class L No.161.

Work patterns largely mirrored those for Class L1 under both the H&BR and NER and later the LNER, as did the life-history of Class L.

The first L (as LNER J28), to be reboilered with a Diagram 58B domed boiler was 2542 (161) in June 1928, followed by 2540 (159) in November 1933 and 2539 (158) in August 1935. Nos.2538 (157) and 2541 (160) were never altered, but this proved to be no handicap for all five were withdrawn between May and December 1937. Upon rebuilding with domed boilers the engines concerned joined Class J28/1; the two domeless engines remaining as Class J28. (The domeless ex-L1 engines were included in Class J28, the L1 rebuilds occupying Class J28/2. Just to confuse matters further, the Class LS engines were initially included in Class J28, but when reboilered joined Class J28/1 with the reboilered L's. The remaining domeless superheated engines were eventually classed as J28/3).

The inevitable detail alterations appeared on the five engines under the LNER and general points are as outlined for Class L1, although details applicable to Class L engines may be summarised as follows:

2540 (159) was probably unique among the domed rebuilds in having wheel-and-handle smokebox door fastening, and 2539 (158) was similarly the odd one out, in acquiring a windjabber.

2540 (159) acquired steam heat at both ends around 1924-1925, but still retained its three-link couplings. However, screw couplings were fitted to it in November 1933; two others received screw-link couplings and steam-heat connections in May and August 1935, being 2542 (161) and 2539 (138) respectively. The two domeless engines remained without the additional equipment.

The inevitable twin whistles appeared on the domed rebuilds, as did external vacuum ejector exhaust pipes alongside the boiler. Vacuum brake standpipes were also altered and probably re-altered, although the final position for 2538 (157) and 2541 (160) is not known.

Class L 3157 with its first LNER livery and NER number at Cudworth, probably in 1923.

Two small steps appeared on the smokebox fronts of probably all the domed rebuilds - 2538 (157) acquired them whilst still domeless.

Tender coal-rails (as with the Class L1 and J engines), were made up to four and plated behind by the LNER at a fairly early period under their ownership.

It would seem that the old Class L engines (whether in the guise of J28 or J28/1), were more popular than their immediate predecessors, for none appear to have been transferred far away from the H&BR Section. (It would seem that the Hull Area was playing the time-honoured game of letting older, worn and rather less-valued engines be transferred - hence the widespread distribution of the J23 engines across the LNER system. Needless to say, Dairycoates got its hands on odd ex-L class engines at times, to replace their old NER Class J21 engines).

Class L also provided something of a compliment for Matthew Stirling and the Yorkshire Engine Co., being chosen for additional building! The little Maryport & Carlisle Railway like the H&BR, the Welsh valley lines and the unfortunate Lancashire, Derbyshire & East Coast Railway was another system which made its living from coal, and in the case of the M&CR, a very good living it was, too. May 1919 saw them place an order with Yorkshire Engine Co. for two Class L engines. The M&CR, being but 42³/₄ miles in length, was really too small to bother with funding a locomotive design establishment (even one as efficient in manpower as the H&B's!), but were one up on Springhead having actually built a few engines themselves in their little workshops at Maryport.

One of these home-made products was an 0-4-4 tank, built in 1897 to drawings supplied by the North Eastern for the old Fletcher "BTP" Class. Another instance of the Maryport being on good terms with its bigger neighbours came in 1908, for they obtained an 0-6-0 which was virtually a carbon-copy of the Manson Glasgow & South Western Railway's "361" Class. Most of the Maryport's other engines were 0-4-2's or 2-4-0's; its engineers Hugh Smellie and J.Campbell, his successor, gave their locomotives a decidedly Stirlingesque appearance - in Smellie's case this was almost an apprenticeship for him, since he succeeded James Stirling on the Glasgow & South Western Railway! Consequently, there was nothing extraordinary in the Maryport company ordering a couple of Stirling locomotives for themselves!

2542 (161) was the first class L to be rebuilt with a domed boiler, in June 1928. This engine carried the highest number allocated to an H&BR locomotive; although the company's stock of engines totalled 186, twenty-five engines were put on a duplicate list, their successors being regarded as renewals rather than additions to capital stock. *Ron Copeman collection.*

2540 (159), outside the west end of Springhead works. Although given a small NER-type smokebox door, it still retains its Stirling chimney and identity as a "Class L (HB)". *Ron Copeman collection.*

2540 again, this time at York after reboilering, face-to-face with another ex-H&BR engine; a Sentinel steam railcar has also just managed to creep into camera-shot. The direct run of the reach-rod on these engines, from the screw reverser in the cab down to the wayshalf-arm can clearly be seen. *Ron Copeman collection.*

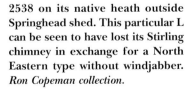

2538 on its native heath outside Springhead shed. This particular L can be seen to have lost its Stirling chimney in exchange for a North Eastern type without windjabber. *Ron Copeman collection.*

However, despite being described in the builder's Order Book as "Heavy Goods Engines & Tenders of the Hull & Barnsley Type", the two M&CR engines bore a distinct resemblance to Robinson's Great Central 0-6-0 goods engines, of the type classed as J11 by the LNER. This was due to the fitting of domed boilers with conventional regulators, Ross "Pop" safety-valves and cabs strongly reminiscent of those on the J11's. Tender coal-plates instead of rails further suggested Great Central practice. Other odd details were the replacement of the vacuum brake cylinder below the cab floor on the H&BR engines for a steam brake cylinder on the M&CR's pair; however, these two still had vacuum ejectors for train brakes, the exhaust pipes of which were led outside the boilers. The M&CR engines also had steam-heat connections, three-link couplings and a different arrangement of the sandboxes: the front two were below footplate level and none were fitted around the driving wheels, those for backward running being built into the cab along with the rear splashers to form seating. Driving and front coupled wheel splashers were also wider than on the H&BR engines, avoiding the need for coupling rod splashers, and as with the H&BR engines these wheel splashers were outlined with heavy, flat brass beadings, kept well polished. Two other H&BR features were evident on the M&CR engines though - the inevitable 20-ton jack on the left-hand footplating in front of the cab, and the "Iracier" shield-shaped tender axlebox covers.

The Maryport engines were also finished in green - but of a far lighter shade than the H&BR's, being nearly emerald in hue. Their two engines took up Nos.29 and 30, and although ordered in May 1919, it was 1st June 1921 before No.29 made its delivery run from Meadowhall under its own steam along the Midland Railway via the Settle & Carlisle, being followed exactly twenty days later by No.30.

They took Yorkshire Engine Works Numbers 1582 and 1583 - by coincidence exactly four hundred on from those of the first two Class L engines, but of course that is not to suggest that Yorkshire Engine Co. had turned out that many engines for Britain's railways (or indeed the World's), in the seven years intervening! (As related under Class A, Meadowhall gave works numbers in the same series to everything and anything they produced; in point of fact it was quite some time since they had built new locomotives although considerable repair work of such machines had come their way as a result of World War I).

An indication of how costs had rocketed in the four years of war lay in the fact that the two Maryport engines cost £24,000 - £5,250 more than the H&BR had paid for its five! (Some increase in cost may have been incurred in producing new drawings for the detail alterations, but that should have been wiped out by having the main drawings and patterns already available).

The Maryport engines earn their place in the history books for two reasons. Firstly, they were the last Stirling engines to be built, and secondly they represented the last of thousands of British goods engines to have inside cylinders and saturated-steam boilers, albeit they were not typical in having Allan rather than Stephenson Link Motion valve gear - the last British main-line application of the type, incidentally. However, the Great Western's Swindon works (ever a bastion of traditions and time-honoured custom), fitted Allan Straight-Link to six small pannier tanks in 1934, and continued to build inside-cylinder 0-6-0's until 1948 - albeit with piston valves and superheated boilers.

Sadly, the M&CR engines were not destined for long lives; although being renumbered by the London, Midland & Scottish Railway (who took over in 1923), they were withdrawn as LMS Nos.12513 and 12514 in December 1933 and March 1934 respectively - swept aside by hordes of Midland 4F's which the LMS continued to churn out until 1941. Thus the Maryport's engines didn't outlive their older cousins on the other side of the country.

After the withdrawal of 2540 (159) and 2542 (161) by the LNER at the end of 1937, both engines led a sad, lingering existence for a few months until the scrapman claimed them as his own in April and May 1938. Just four ex-L1's and two LS engines survived them; none were to remain in traffic at the year end.

DIMENSIONS: Since the L, L1 and LS engines were so similar, the Tables of Dimensions may be found at the end of the section dealing with Class LS.

Summary: Class L 0-6-0 Goods engines. LNER Class J28.

HBR No.	Built	Works No.	NER No.	LNER No.	Domed 58B boiler fitted	Withdrawn
157	August 1914	1182	3157	2538	-	June 1937
158	August 1914	1183	3158	2539	August 1935	October 1937
159	October 1914	1184	3159	2540	November 1933	December 1937
160	November 1914	1185	3160	2541	-	May 1937
161	December 1914	1186	3161	2542	June 1928	November 1937

Notes: Built Yorkshire Engine Company. Cost £3,550 each

Summary: Maryport & Carlisle Railway 0-6-0 Goods engines No's 29 and 30.

M&CR No.	Built	Works No.	LM&SR No.	Withdrawn	*Notes*
29	June 1921	1582	12513	December 1933	Yorkshire Engine Co.
30	June 1921	1583	12514	March 1934	Cost £12,000 each

2559 (158) near Springhead's coaling stage, below which can be glimpsed a "Tiny". 2559 remains substantially in H&BR condition, save for NER-type front vacuum brake connection, smokebox door and organ-pipe whistle. *Ron Copeman collection.*

2541 (160) out in the rain at the west end of Springhead shed, in more-or-less the condition Mr. Stirling intended. Its H&BR chimney has lost its windjabber, however. *Ron Copeman collection.*

CLASS LS 0-6-0 ENGINES. (LNER CLASS J28).
Introduced 1915.

Our saga of Matthew Stirling's Hull & Barnsley Railway locomotives can now be regarded as gradually drawing to a close, for the five LS class engines of 1915 represented the last design of locomotive built to order by a railway with a Stirling in charge. (As we have seen, they were not actually the last Stirling engines built; the two odd ones for the Maryport & Carlisle Railway had that honour). The LS class engines were also the only type of Stirling locomotive to be equipped in its entirety with superheating - all five being given the efficient Schmidt type, consisting of elements in flue-tubes, and introduced in Germany around 1900 and on the Great Western in England in 1906. With the delivery of the last LS, No.28 in February 1915, only the Great Western Railway was left as the sole producer of domeless locomotives, although as if to make up for that trait they fitted their smaller locomotives with domes of considerable size.

The Class LS engines were, in motoring enthusiasts' parlance, "tweaked" Class L engines; the letter "S" (for "Schmidt" as much as for "superheated"), could be regarded as being of similar significance to the letters "GT" or "Turbo" nowadays when applied to the rear ends of otherwise standard factory-saloons, denoting vehicles which possess the breathtaking ability to out-accelerate and out-perform more humble brethren as they dash from one traffic jam to the next. (Not that it should be imagined that Matthew Stirling was simply wanting goods engines to reach high speeds - it was simply that in the few years since Class L1 had appeared, superheating had come of age and the relative effectiveness of the various methods of its application had been fairly well assessed).

Curiously, no attempt was made to fit the Lytton superheater to Class LS; if it was considered at the design stage, then it has escaped record. Although the single Class B so fitted, No.60, was good enough to justify the retention of its equipment, it seems it was not sufficiently meritorious to warrant fitting it to other engines or to retain on No.60 after the superheated LNER boilers became available in large numbers. Possibly the joint considerations of accessibility and ease of dismantling told against Lytton's device; and probably considerations of the avoidance of Royalty payments prompted the H&BR and their canny Scots locomotive engineer to choose Schmidt's system - after all, there was little chance of Herr Doktor Schmidt chasing up his Royalty payments when his beloved Fatherland was locked in a life-and-death struggle with the British Empire!

Having thus settled the type of boiler, the machinery by means of which the locomotive would locomote was soon sorted out: Class L had given every satisfaction in service, so the same arrangement was re-used. The only alterations were the fitting of a mechanical lubricator between the leading splashers on the left-hand side and a modest forward extension of the frames by 5½ inches over Class L and the last five of Class L1. This allowed for the smokebox to be similarly extended, giving room to move the chimney forward and allow space behind there for the superheater header. This extended smokebox was a much neater and tidier design than on the Class L1 Phoenix engines, with the unfortunate "up and at 'em" appearance which they presented to the world.

The superheated LS boilers had 18 flue tubes of 5¼ inches diameter, containing elements of $1^3/_{32}$ inches in diameter. Boiler tubes were $1^3/_4$ inches in diameter and numbered 133. (The Class L and L1 engines carried 245 tubes of the same diameter when built). The superheater flues were arranged in three horizontal rows of six flues, each element making two double-passes back

No.20 in Kitson's workshop, posing for its official portrait in the usual place, by the manhole. *Mick Nicholson collection.*

2418 (26) outside Springhead's office block, in early LNER condition. The superheater header cover-plate may be seen behind the chimney, and the mechanical lubricator is prominent between the two leading wheel splashers. *J.B.Stork collection.*

and forth along each flue. Saturated steam from the main boiler steampipe gathered in the header to be led down any one of six openings to the first bank of elements, in the top row of flues. Having traversed them, the steam continued its passage back and forth along the next two elements directly below whichever one it had first entered, being constrained to follow this labyrinthine course by means of partitions cored into the header when cast. Thus the steam made six double-passes through the elements from the regulator valve to the steam-chest; all moisture content carried over with it being additionally evaporated due to its increased temperature. Lubrication problems due to the burning away or carbonising of oil by the hot steam led to the development of thicker, high-temperature oils. However, even the best steam oils were useless if their feeding methods were unreliable or erratic in any way - hence the LS engines were equipped with a mechanical lubricator. Professor Schmidt had been adamant in his view that only piston valves were suitable for use with superheated steam, but the H&BR found no problems arising with their balanced slide valves or even with the flat slide valves exposed to virtually full boiler pressure on their outer faces, as on No.60. For that matter nor did the LNER when they fitted their 18-element, domed superheated boilers. Had the number of elements been increased to say, 24 or 28 (which would in turn increase the temperature of the steam), then they could well have fallen foul of problems caused by lack of lubrication. Swindon and the GWR deliberately kept to moderate superheat temperatures for fear of incurring such problems until the early 1950's, by which time everyone else had long since demonstrated how to overcome them.

The advantages of superheating were immediate: less water consumption (a minor consideration in Great Britain but of considerable importance in other parts of the world), reduced coal consumption of the order of 12 to 30% according to the degree of superheat utilised, and an increase in haulage capacity of up to 50%, again depending on the degree of superheat employed. (Moderate superheat temperatures were from 50 to 100 degrees F., high superheat temperatures being above 200 degrees F). Such figures were produced on test and under favourable conditions: all that could be guaranteed in the rough-and-tumble world of daily locomotive operation were some savings in fuel and a more powerful and sprightlier performance. None of the foregoing should be taken as implying that goods locomotives could be suddenly transformed into express motive power by superheating no more than they would suddenly have the ability to haul much heavier trains, for superheating would do nothing to alter the behaviour of a locomotive as a vehicle, and if the initial adhesive weight was lacking then so was grip and therefore tractive effort. Sadly, for some designers the more fluid nature of superheated steam gave such immediate benefits when applied to older engines with more labyrinthine steam ports and passages, that they considered there was little more to be gained by paying closer attention to the design and layout of the steam circuit, both to and from the cylinders. Consequently, some very archaic practices were allowed to continue unchanged for another thirty years in a few cases; in this respect Matthew Stirling's later Hull & Barnsley tender engines with their open-backed, balanced slide valves were models of good practice.

The order for producing the five LS engines went to Kitson & Co., and represented the last of the many engines of all types which they had provided for the H&BR. They took H&BR numbers 20, 21, 22, 26 and 28 - completing the transfer of the Kirtley engines so numbered to the Duplicate List. (Five Class F3 0-6-2 tank engines delivered in 1913 - 1914 displaced the five Kirtley goods engines unaccounted for by the deliveries of Class L1 and LS). Kitsons charged the H&BR £3,600 apiece and allocated Works Nos.5010 to 5014 to the LS engines, which

Another way of cutting down on fuel bills was to simply not use the engines! 2412 (20) as rebuilt with domed, saturated boiler is in store with three other H&BR engines in Springhead works. It has been given tall LNER vacuum hose standpipe, screw couplings and steam heating, and still retains its mechanical lubricator. *Ron Copeman collection.*

2413 (21) at Dairycoates. This view shows the longer smokebox and greater length of frames in front of the leading sandboxes. 2413 is in H&BR condition save for steam heating, screw couplings, tall brake standpipe and whistle. The engine has ex-NER locomotives at both ends - that behind the tender is a T/T1 Class 0-8-0 (LNER Class Q5), with which the NER matched the H&BR's Class A engines when on loan during and after World War I. *Ron Copeman collection.*

Even reboilering with a domed, saturated boiler did not keep Stirling's LS class engines off passenger work. 2413, seen after rebuilding, leaves Driffield with a lightweight train on 24th August 1935. *Laurie Ward.*

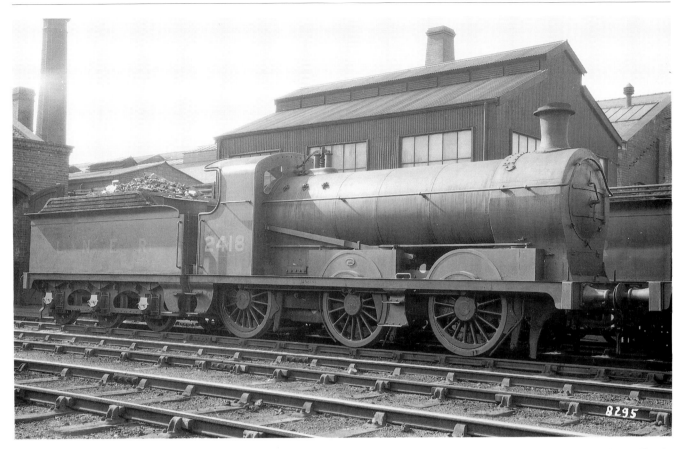

2418 (26) outside Springhead shed, with the boiler washout plant immediately behind. The small, round cover-plate immediately below the superheater header cover on the right-hand smokebox side is easily seen in this view. *Ron Copeman collection.*

followed close behind the Class L engines, arriving on the H&BR in January and February 1915. No.28 represented the last engine built for the H&B and was also the last domeless Stirling locomotive built; the end of a great tradition. Upon its completion, it left the GWR as the only company to be producing locomotives with domeless boilers - although that statement should be qualified by reminding the reader that they invariably fitted domed boilers to their pannier tank engines, and even turned out a batch of 4-4-0's for the old Cambrian Railways Section in the mid-1930's which really owed nothing to post-1895 GWR practices. At the same time as Swindon was indulging in its latterday feast of nostalgia, William Stanier (an ex-Swindonite), was introducing the LMS to domeless boilers along the lines of the GWR types, but that particular import to Crewe and Derby works turned out to be something of a false start.

The five LS engines were to serve the H&BR well for the final seven years of its existence, passing into the 1930's unaltered save for minor details.

Apart from the slightly longer front overhang, mechanical lubricators and superheating, the LS engines were identical to those of class L, even down to windjabbers, shaped cab windows and sandboxes above footplate level. Only the most observant would take note of the deeper-chested appearance of an LS engine, thanks to the rather longer smokebox. Latterly, superheater header cover-plates were more prominent behind the chimneys and these served to identify Class LS engines.

After Grouping under the LNER in 1923, No.2420 (28) became unique in acquiring two grab-handles-cum-footsteps up the right hand side of the smokebox to allow easy access to the

header covers. These grabrails hardly enhanced 2420 - they looked as though someone from Springhead Works had made a nocturnal foray down to the Fish Dock armed with a hacksaw and attacked the superstructure of a trawler! The same engine also acquired steam heat fittings around 1924 - 1925, although still retained its three-link couplings until November 1932.

The all-round usefulness of the five LS engines was recognised by the LNER in 1932, for the other four were fitted up in similar fashion to 2420 as follows: 2412 (20) and 2413 (21) in September, 2414 (22) and 2418 (26) in October, with steam heat and screw couplings.

The reason for this was that these engines were increasingly being rostered on lower-grade passenger workings, although they had been transferred to Hull Dairycoates by that time. Consequently at times of demand on Hull's motive power for the droves of summer Saturday excursion workings Dairycoates invariably fielded their LS engines; creditable performances on shorter workings along the Hornsea and Withernsea branches soon led to them being entrusted with workings over long distances, to Scarborough and Doncaster.

June 1934 saw 2412 (20) rebuilt with a domed, saturated boiler, as a result of which it joined the ex-L class engines as a Class J28/1. In February 1935 No.2413 (21) was treated likewise, followed by 2420 (28) in January 1936. Nos. 2414 (22) and 2418 (26) were never altered, remaining as Class J28/3 (a designation introduced in December 1930).

The domed boilers came with the same detail fittings as on the J28 and J28/1 engines - 2413 (21) acquired a windjabber and two steps on the smokebox front. The same boilers also had

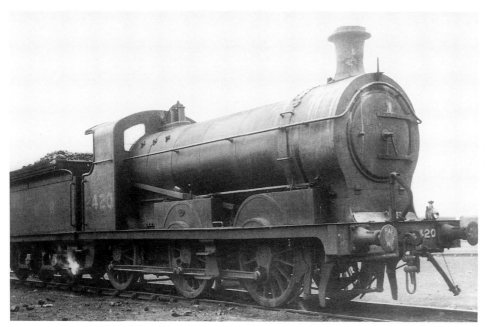

2420, in August 1935, still with its domeless boiler but carrying the ungainly grab-handles on the smokebox side.

After reboilering, 2420 clearly shows the hole in the front upper framing on each side, left unused when the shorter smokebox was fitted. *E.E.Smith.*

shorter smokeboxes, which despite being a snug fit lengthwise on the ex-L1 and L Class engines were shorter than the originals on the Class LS type. As a result the upper frames extended forwards at each side of the smokebox front, displaying one fixing hole unused each side as a reminder of their previous state; it would have been a rash move to have trimmed down this redundant frame section for the sake of neatness for there was always the possibility that one of the original boilers may have made its way back on to one of these rebuilds, which would have caused some headscratching if the frames had been altered.

Withdrawal of the LS engines came in May 1937 with J23/3 No.2414 (22) going first; J28/1 No.2413 (21) was the last survivor, being withdrawn in October 1938 along with all the other surviving varieties of Class J28 engines. Ironically, two of the older H&BR 0-6-0's, Class J23/3 No.2460 (79) and J23/2 No.2476 (95), built in 1898 and 1900, survived them - albeit by only one month.

In retrospect, the LS engines may be regarded as probably the best of the H&BR's engines thanks to their effective superheating. They could run well at speed but were equally at home slogging away on heavy goods trains. Like all Stirling's locomotives they were simple but solidly-built, having axle journals of 8 inches diameter by 9 inches long (generously-sized for 0-6-0's), and with driving wheel crankpins at $4\frac{1}{2}$ inches diameter; all these were bigger than on the Midland/LMS Class 4F 0-6-0's. On these latter engines, their crankpins (1 inch smaller in diameter than the H&B engines), were apt to snap off at the crank boss if the unfortunate engine concerned got into a slip; but in fairness to their designers the LMS insisted on grossly overloading them for they were rated as being able to haul 45 loaded wagons anywhere over the Midland system - including the gruelling climbs on the Settle & Carlisle or over Rowsley in the Peak District. The 4F's had the advantage of bigger cylinders at 20 inches diameter, with piston valves above. However, these valves were inadequately sized and had rather indirect steam passages; in contrast, Stirling's open, balanced slide valves were superior. Although frequently used on passenger work also, the 4F's were in some places heartily disliked on such work (the Midland & Great Northern Joint Railway for example), and at best were just about acceptable everywhere else on such turns, whereas we have already seen how welcome the LS engines were among the "first reserve" team at Dairycoates, being popular engines on passenger work.

Clearly, had the H&BR continued to produce Stirling-type engines, Class LS pointed the way forward for future developments into the early 1920's, but of course world events put an end to such prospects. It does seem to be a tale of lost opportunities that the LNER did not pursue the fitting of superheated boilers to the J28 and D24 engines rather than fit them to the J23's. As it was, the LS engines provided a pleasing finale to sixty-four years of Stirling locomotive design on four companies' metals - the LS engines unequivocally followed the family tradition, yet under the skin they were very much up to date.

DIMENSIONS: for Class L1, L and LS.

Cylinders: 2, inside 19" x 26"
Motion: Allan Straight-Link, driving open-backed, balanced slide valves on top of the cylinders via rocking levers.
Boiler: Domeless
Max. diameter outside: 5' 0"
Barrel length: 11' 0"
Firebox length outside: 6' 0"
Pitch: 7' $10\frac{1}{2}$"
Heating Surface: L1/L*/LS
  Firebox: all 122 sq ft.
  Tubes 245 @ $1\frac{3}{4}$" dia. = 1,263.8 sq ft.
  Tubes (LS) 133 @ $1\frac{3}{4}$" dia. = 690 sq.ft.
  Flues (LS) 18 @ $5\frac{1}{4}$" dia. = 280.7 sq.ft
  Elements (LS) 18 @ $1\frac{3}{32}$" dia. = 202.7 sq.ft
  Total: 1,385.8 sq ft. (LS) 1,295 sq ft.
Grate Area: 19.76 sq.ft.
Ratio of grate area to heating surface: 1 to 70.13; (LS) 1 to 65.55
Boiler Pressure: 170 lb/sq.inch
Wheel Diameters:
  Engine 5' 0"
  Tender 3' 9"
Wheelbase:
  Engine 7' 9" + 9' 3" = 17' 0"
  Tender 6' 0" + 6' 0" = 12' 0".
  Total 12' 0"
Length over Buffers:
  Phoenix L1 - 52' $2\frac{1}{4}$"
  L/L1 - 51' $5\frac{3}{4}$"
  LS - 51' $11\frac{1}{4}$"
Height to Top of Chimney: 13' 2"
Tractive Effort @ 85% of Boiler Pressure: 22,610 lb
Ratio of Blast Nozzle to Cylinder Diameter: 1 to 3.70
Tender Water Capacity: 3,500 gallons
Tender Coal Capacity: 5 tons 0 cwt

continued over/

Summary: Class LS 0-6-0 Goods engines. LNER Class J28.

H&BR No.	Built	Works No.	NER No.	LNER No.	Domed 58B boiler fitted	Withdrawn
20	January 1915	5010	3020	2412	June 1934	November 1937
21	January 1915	5011	3021	2413	February 1935	October 1938
22	January 1915	5012	3022	2414	-	May 1937
26	February 1915	5013	3026	2418	-	June 1937
28	February 1915	5014	3028	2420	January 1936	September 1938

Notes: Built Kitson & Co. Cost £3,600 each.

Weights in Full Working Order:

Class	Loco	Tender	Total
L1	50 ton 15 cwt	40 ton 10 cwt	91 ton 5 cwt
L	51 ton 3 cwt	39 ton 16 cwt	90 ton 19 cwt
LS	51 ton 6 cwt	39 ton 17 cwt	91 ton 3 cwt

Engine Axle Loads:

Class	Leading	Driving	Rear
L1	17 ton 13 cwt	18 ton 11 cwt	14 ton 11 cwt
L	18 ton 14 cwt	17 ton 18 cwt	14 ton 11 cwt
LS	18 ton 10 cwt 1 qtr	18 ton 15 cwt	14 ton 0 cwt 3 qtr

Tender Axle Loads:

Class	Leading	Middle	Rear
L1	13 ton 15 cwt	13 ton 12 cwt	13 ton 3 cwt
L	14 ton 4 cwt	12 ton 18 cwt	12 ton 14 cwt
LS	13 ton 17 cwt	13 ton 15 cwt	12 ton 5 cwt

*Note Yorkshire Engine Company gave the following different heating surface figures for Class L Nos.157-161 as built:
Heating Surface:
 Firebox 132 sq.ft
 Tubes 245 @ 1¾" dia. = 1,275 sq.ft
 Total 1,407 sq.ft
Grate Area: 19.6 sq.ft

These discrepancies may have arisen doe to different methods of calculation: it should also be noted that they correspond with the figures for the Class J 4-4-0's as quoted in the last H&BR Diagram Book, although curiously they were built of course by Kitson & Co., who gave different figures for their L1 class engines!

Dimensions for LNER Class J28, Rebuilt with Diagram 58B domed boilers.

Boiler: Domed
Max. diameter outside: 5' 0"
Barrel Length: 11' 0⅛"
Firebox length outside: 6' 6"
Heating Surfaces:
 Firebox 128 sq.ft
 Tubes 1,181 sq.ft
 Total 1,309 sq.ft
Grate Area: 19.6 sq.ft
Boiler Pressure: 175 lb/sq.inch
Tractive Effort @ 85% of Boiler Pressure: 23,275 lb
Weight of Locomotive in Full W.O: 51T 14C.
Maximum Axle Load: 18T 14C.

We conclude this section on Stirling's last 0-6-0's with a view of 2418 at Hull Paragon station on a passenger train. On the right stands ex-H&BR Class J 4-4-0 No. 2427 (38), a close relative of 2418. Whilst 2427 has rather come down in the world, no longer being regarded as an express locomotive, 2418 has come up in the world somewhat, having left mineral train working largely in the past. Both engines have 5 foot 0 inch diameter boilers, but the shorter chimney and raised footplating give 2427 a rather squat appearance from this angle. Finally, 2418 proclaims itself to be a "Class J28", whereas 2427 still harks back to earlier days, for it remains as a "Class J (HB)". *T.E.Rounthwaite.*

CLASS F3 0-6-2 RADIAL TANK ENGINES. (LNER CLASS N13).
Introduced 1913.

Although the F3's were not the last Stirling engines designed or built - the Class LS engines having that honour - the author has decided to follow the lead set by the LNER, which regarded the L and LS engines as developments of the earlier L1 design, and so lumped them all together under Class J28. The F3 engines although clearly derived from the earlier Class F2 0-6-2's, caused no head-scratching for the LNER authorities, which simply dubbed them as Class N13, following on after the F2's to which they gave the classification N12. Thus it follows that the F3's could arguably be regarded as the H&B's last totally original design.

Traffic requirements at the west end of the H&BR were well catered for, but 1914 would see the completion and opening of King George V Dock in Hull, built jointly by the Hull & Barnsley and North Eastern Railway - and the symbol of the mutual rapprochement between the two rivals after thirty years of antagonism. Since the new dock was to be the biggest on the East Coast, it was anticipated that it would bring about much increased traffic over the two companies' metals, therefore additional locomotives would be required by the H&BR. They also had to consider the imminent replacement of the old Kirtley engines, so clearly there would soon be a need for additional engines at the Hull end of the line.

With traffic workings becoming increasingly centred on the yards at Springhead, trip workings to and from the docks were well-established; these involved engines running back and forth on journeys of some 5½ miles each way - rather too far for 0-6-0 tank engines with their restricted supplies of coal and water, yet not really far enough to warrant the use of tender locomotives.

The F2 0-6-2 tanks had given every satisfaction in service but by 1912 were getting rather long in the tooth; hence Matthew Stirling probably considered some updating of that design would be advantageous.

The major alterations took place from the cab forward, and were clearly evident to the interested observer in the changed proportions of the F3's when compared with the F2 engines. The side tanks were lengthened, widened and deepened, their capacity increasing to 2,000 gallons. It was possibly due to this that the boiler pitch (its centre-line), was raised by five inches; had this not been done, the engines may have looked rather too slab-sided and ungainly. The side tanks were built right out to the outside edge of the footplating and the cab was widened also, but not to the same extent as the side tanks. Hence the cab and bunker were set in somewhat - a feature of all the other H&BR tank engines except the F2's (and of course the little Class K's). The cab spectacle glasses were the usual rather small 1ft 2in diameter, and remained set comparatively close together at the customary 3ft 7in between centres. This feature combined with the wider cab to give the F3's a rather cross-eyed look, more noticeably so than with Matthew Stirling's other tank engine types.

The F3 chimneys were visibly squatter and stubbier in appearance, the reason being that although shorter than the chimneys of Class C type which were carried by the F2's, they retained the same diameters at both top and bottom. The reasons for shortening are obvious; it was desired to keep the F3's overall height within a limit of 12ft 11in despite the fact that the F3 boilers had been set five inches higher.

Within the cab, the footplate level had been raised by nine inches due to wooden floorboards being built up to give the crews better vision - none of the problems with the Class A's were apparent in the F3's! The cab roof was raised in consequence, becoming 7ft 9in above the footplating level, compared with 7ft exactly on the F2's.

The raising of the floor level within the cabs also affected the bunker arrangements on the F3 engines, for the coal bunker

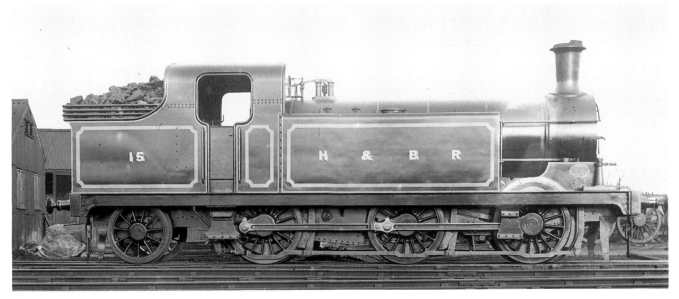

One of the engines which duplicated earlier Kirtley 0-6-0's was No.15, seen here at Springhead in immaculate condition. The much bulkier appearance of the F3 in comparison to the F2 engines is plainly evident.

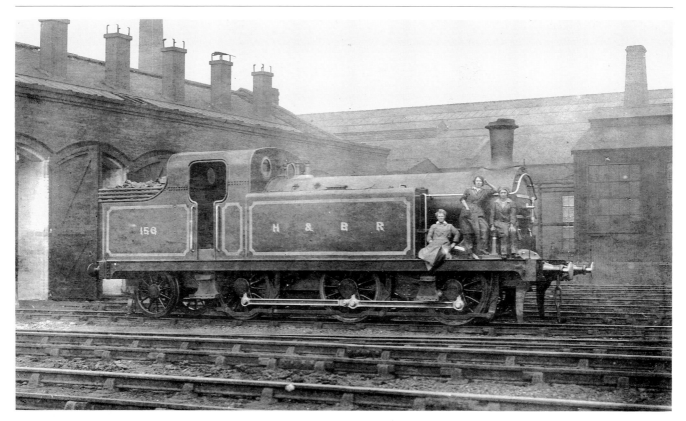

"They also serve...." No.156 again, but seen here at Springhead in World War I, evident by the three women cleaners, who have done as good a job as the men judging by the results seen here. The contribution made by women in the Great War in keeping the railways operating has been largely overlooked - working in a dimly-lit running shed could be as hazardous in its own way as working in a munitions factory: the risks there were so obvious as to hardly need pointing out! It is also often forgotten that cleaning was also in itself a form of inspection, and that it frequently included other duties, although how much simple fitting work or steam-raising was undertaken by Matthew Stirling's women staff is now probably gone beyond recall. At the end of the war, the women were unceremoniously paid-off, and banished to the offices once again. Finally, it may be seen that someone had found time to re-decorate inside the shed, although the roof was in need of some attention.

door had to be moved upwards also. The opportunity was therefore taken to re-arrange the interior of the bunker, its floor being raised to become level with the bottom edge of the coal door way, which was fitted with a vertical drop-door. The bunker floor sloped upwards towards the back before being levelled out, but at a slightly lower height at that point than on the F2's - measures which gained two gallons extra capacity on the F3 engines. No back tank filler was fitted to the F3 engines; presumably it had been found that the provision of such items on the F2's had not been worthwhile.

Below footplate level, the opportunity was taken to deepen the locomotive mainframes considerably at both top and bottom edges; for the rest, the machinery was to the same well-tried arrangement as found on Class C and all the other Stirling tank-engines, as were the boilers.

The order for the ten F3 tank engines went to Hawthorn, Leslie & Co., of Forth Bank, Newcastle. This builder was new to the H&BR, and represented only the fourth occasion in its 42-year history in which they went outside Yorkshire for an engine-builder. It was also the last occasion on which they did so. The F3's took up HL&Co's works numbers 3008 to 3017; the first five were regarded as being replacements of old Kirtley engines, being numbered 13, 15, 18, 23 and 27 by the H&BR, relegating the five Kirtley engines with those numbers to the Duplicate

List, whereas the last five were regarded as additions to Capital Stock and were therefore numbered 152 to 156 (falling between the last G3 tanks and the Class L 0-6-0's).

The F3's had steam brakes only, and hence were never to partake in hauling passenger stock (at least with passengers aboard!). Possibly by the time they were ordered, the sheer extravagance of having all fourteen F1 and F2 engines fitted with vacuum brakes was being appreciated - the H&BR themselves took the equipment off the F1's, and seven F2's were to lose theirs very soon after Grouping.

Before that date, all the F3's had been based at Springhead, but by 1922 Nos.3023 and 3152 (soon to become N13 Nos.2415 and 2533), were to be found at Cudworth. There matters rested throughout the 1920's and '30's: the bulk of the class were kept busy in Hull shunting the yards at Springhead, interspersed with trip workings to Alexandra or Kings George docks, or down to the yards at Dairycoates and Neptune Street. The two odd N13's out at Cudworth returned to Hull in May 1930 (2533), and January 1934 in the case of 2415.

World War II caused the greatest upheavals in the existence of the N13's, for early 1942 saw 2407 (15) and 2537 (156) sent to Newport (Middlesbrough), returning south - albeit to Selby - in March 1943, as a result of the mass reallocation of North Eastern Area engines in order to concentrate them at the smallest

3152 at Cudworth during the time of the North Eastern's ownership; it may be noted that a fourth coal-rail has been added.

number of sheds per class. As a result, 2405 (13) moved to Selby to join its two fellows, and 2419 (27) with 2533 (152) to 2536 (155) were sent to Leeds (Neville Hill) shed. This reduced the chances of damage to the locomotive stock, for Hull (the "North East Coast Town" so frequently referred to by wartime newscasters), was all-too-easy and inviting a target for the Luftwaffe. As it was, the war came perilously close to 2534 (153) during the night of 22nd February 1941. Proceeding southwards along the branch to Neptune Street, the unfortunate engine pitched nose-first into a bomb crater in the tracks just north of Dairycoates, nearly rolling over completely on to its left side. The engine received no lasting damage however; with Springhead Works only a mile or so to the north, 2534 was soon recovered and taken in for checks on wheel gauging, axlebox under-keeps and springs in the event of displacement, plus odd bits of deranged brake rodding and pipework being de-bent. The engine was duly sent back into service for another thirteen years before Darlington scrapyard achieved what Hitler's air force failed to do.

With the war over, January 1946 saw four engines - 2405 (13), 2407 (15), 2534 (153) and 2537 (156) - return to Springhead; thus Selby lost its allocation of three.

All ten entered Nationalisation in 1948, although 9110 (13) was unlucky enough to survive insufficiently long enough to get its British Railways' number in the 60000 series.

A few more transfers were made - 69111 (15) went to Alexandra Dock from May 1949 to November 1950, leading an alfresco lifestyle there since the shed had been demolished as far back as 1927 and never replaced! From there it returned to Springhead, where it finished its existence in August 1952.

69113 (23) had left Springhead in December 1952, going off to Neville Hill until withdrawn only five months later. It was then replaced by 69116 (153), and joined by 69119 (156) in September 1953. This latter engine had worked in Hull along with 69112 (18), which had spent its entire life at Springhead until its withdrawal came in November 1952. With 69119's transfer the following year, the last Hull & Barnsley locomotive to remain in Hull finally departed: none remained on their native system and none would ever return, thus the locomotive scene in Hull was so much the poorer for 69119's departure.

May 1955 saw 69115 (152) withdrawn from Neville Hill, to be followed two months later by 69117 (154) and 69119 (156); thus 69114 (27), was left as the sole representative of Hull & Barnsley Railway motive power and the final example of Mr Matthew Stirling's locomotive design work.

Sadly, the era of preservation was in its infancy, although interested enthusiasts tried to get the then British Transport Commission's Curator of Historical Relics to save 69114. Chief among the more aware enthusiasts was David R.Smith, who was doubtless dismayed to receive a letter from the BTC's Curator, the Late J.H.Scholes, dated 11th November 1955 in reply to his request that the BTC earmark 69114 for immortality. Mr. Scholes pointed out that considerable space would be needed to house the 46 locomotives already set aside, plus the more modern designs to be added in the fullness of time. Two paragraphs are worth quoting in full from Mr. Scholes' letter:

"Referring once again to your request, I feel its importance is local rather than national and that many similar engines of the same wheel arrangement have been used on many British railways and can be seen still in active service today especially on the Eastern and Southern Regions.

"I am fully aware, of course, that your suggestion has got a certain amount of merit, particularly so where it may encourage regional interest, but not-withstanding this, I feel that we must turn it down in favour of a specimen which represents a more important step in the development of the Steam locomotive."

The final NER goods engine livery appears on 2410 (18) in the form of letters "N" and "E" either side of the number. *Ron Copeman collection.*

2537 (156) at Springhead, carrying its first LNER livery (note the full stops), and number patch-painted on the tank sides. Single red lining is also evident, as is the removal of the original works plate and addition of the small LNER variety on the bunker. *Ron Copeman collection.*

Springhead plays host to 2419 (27), which is again in typical LNER condition, albeit with NER chimney and smokebox door. It still retains its identity as a "Class F3 (HB)" on the bufferbeam, and only three coal-rails. *Ron Copeman collection.*

2415 (23) at Springhead after receiving its domed boiler.

2405 (13) at Springhead, having just returned from Darlington with a new domed boiler. Lining-out has become too much of a luxury for goods engines by this time!

There are several points worthy of elaboration from this - firstly, of the "....many similar engines.....in active service.....on the Eastern and Southern Regions", only three were to survive into preservation, thanks entirely to the efforts of private enterprise. The rapid withdrawal of the remainder probably took everyone including officialdom by surprise: all the ex-LNER examples had gone by 1962, for instance.

Secondly, setting aside any North versus South acrimony, the view of 69114 as being of local importance was unfortunate, as was the decision to forgo its preservation "....in favour of a specimen which represents a more important step in the development of the steam locomotive...."; for the National Railway Museum's Collection today is woefully short of representatives of the most common workaday engines - namely 0-6-0 tender engines and 0-6-2 tanks, which by the nature of their work tended to be of local importance.

Thirdly, it has to be remembered that Mr.Scholes was working to a very restricted budget and having to deal with that most inflexibly monolithic and obtuse of organisations, namely British Railways: the progress which he did manage to make was in fact both remarkable and creditable.

Still not giving up on 69114, Mr. Smith tackled Hull Museums, but their reply dated 25th November 1955 was not hopeful, as the last two sentences revealed:

"I am interested to hear about the last H.&B.Railway engine, but I am afraid it is far too big for us to contemplate. Mr. Scholes, Curator of the British Transport Commission Museum is the only one I know likely to be in a position to deal with any object of this nature."

17th April 1956 saw J.H.Scholes writing to inform David Smith that Mr. Neville Stead was attempting to mount a concerted rescue bid to purchase the last survivor, but regrettably at the time Mr. Stead was stationed with the British Army of the Rhine, and thus remote from the proceedings: furthermore, the asking price at that time was too high at around £400. (This may seem ludicrously cheap by today's standards, but in the mid-1950's was approximately the same as a small terraced house). The idea also of individuals banding together to purchase an engine was then unheard of; although one Welsh narrow-gauge railway (the

Talyllyn), had been rescued from oblivion and was being worked by a preservation society, and another (the Festiniog), was well on the way towards becoming re-established; this had only been possible by the railway's owner virtually donating the line and its goodwill in the first instance, and by a wealthy enthusiast plus sympathisers buying up sufficient shares to gain control of and breathe new life into a moribund concern in the second. The age of purchasing redundant standard-gauge branch-lines and operating them on a voluntary basis lay in the next decade; sadly, had 69114 survived until then, it would have been extremely useful (with the addition of vacuum brake equipment), on virtually any and every one of those lines subsequently resurrected.

Only one engine had actually been purchased by a society for preservation, and that was Stroudley's London, Brighton & South Coast Railway 0-4-2 "Gladstone", which had been bought from the Southern Railway in the 1930's by the Stephenson Locomotive Society. They had no intention of ever restoring the engine to working order, being quite content to see it displayed on loan in the LNER's museum at York, as mentioned in John Scholes list. Even engines fortunate enough to be included among the 46 examples listed by him were not necessarily safe. No Gresley K3 2-6-0 was retained, and most tragic of all was the Highland Railway 4-4-0 "Ben Alder" of 1898. Although set aside and stored for some years, it was eventually broken up: the main reason for this being a factor which was also working against 69114 - it had been rebuilt with a completely different boiler type to that originally carried.

This rebuilding process had started on the N13 engines in September 1926 with 2405 (13), but not resumed until December 1930, for there was not the urgency to deal with the N13's as there was with the older Stirling tank engines, particularly the G2's and F2's. The reboilering process was completed by August 1934 with the alteration of 2537 (156).

The domed LNER replacement boilers were to Diagram 71B, which was as may be recalled, interchangeable between Classes N12, J75 and J80 as well as Class N13.

All the N13's got new 71B boilers except 2533 (152), which in October 1933 received that previously carried by 2405 (13).

2419 (27) receiving attention in Springhead Works on 3rd February 1934. Springhead's remaining fitters are giving it considerably more attention than is at first apparent, for the driving wheels have been removed (and also of course, the valve-gear eccentrics and connecting-rods). The odd, bench-like object in the foreground is in fact a radial axle-box (possibly off 2419, although its rear radial wheels are still in position). Other items worthy of note are the Ross "Pop" safety-valves half-hidden by their cover-plate; twin whistles; wheel-and-handle smokebox door locking; three coal rails only, and the frame slot and horn-blocks for the driving axle revealing the outward taper to the bottom for the adjustable axlebox wedge. 2419's buffers are ex-North Eastern (that on the left of the engine being bolted on out of square!), and the bufferbeam still announces it as belonging to "Class F3 (HB)". *Laurie Ward.*

2419 after a visit to Darlington works. The lack of a fourth coal-rail has gone unnoticed yet again, although the offending front buffer has been properly fitted, and the engine is now an "N13", according to the bufferbeam.

The change from LNER to British Railways numbers produced some interesting anomalies for a time - H&BR 155 is seen here at Neville Hill as BR E9118, whereas the Gresley D49 4-4-0 behind it can be seen to have received its proper number, 62775. E9118 has also been given LNER Group Standard buffers, and its number appears on the front bufferbeam due to the absence of a smokebox door number-plate. It also still retains only three coal-rails. *W.B.Yeadon collection.*

The boilers actually intended for Class N13 were built in three batches; four appeared in 1930 then came two batches of three each in 1932 and 1934 respectively. The opportunity had been taken to revise the design as compared with the twenty domed boilers built in the early 1920's. The boiler barrel was rolled in a single ring from one steel plate, rather than riveted up from three rings as in the earlier boilers; stays were re-arranged, flat-valve regulators were fitted and below-step injectors replaced the older backhead-mounted types. The three boilers constructed in 1932 were given washout plugs in the upper firebox sides to replace the hand-holes of the earlier types, but a return to handholes was made for the 1934 boilers. The 1932 boilers only ever appeared on the N13 engines, and of them only 2405 (13) and 2415 (23) never carried one of these plug-fitted boilers.

Another oddity was that the first LNER Diagram for the N13 locomotives showed one fitted with a 71B boiler and was dated 1924: yet it would be two more years before one was actually so treated!

As built, the Class F3 chimneys all carried windjabbers, but Darlington usually fitted taller chimneys of the Worsdell type at the first opportunity. No.2407 (15) was given one complete with windjabber when it acquired its new boiler in January 1931. The taller N12 type chimneys as fitted to the G3's and F2's when new also found their way onto 2535 (154) and 2537 (156) whilst they were still domeless, that on 2537 being retained until its reboilering in August 1934.

Ross "Pop" safety-valves on the 71B boilers replaced the original open Ramsbottom valves carried by the engines whilst domeless. The Ross valves had tall mountings on the earlier 71B boilers, concealed by a shaped, sheet-metal cover-plate, whereas the last ten boilers carried the safety-valves mounted directly on the boiler pads; consequently if the cover plates were retained, the valves appeared half-hidden by them. Most of the plates were understandably discarded in due course, but 69114 retained its cover-plate to the end of its days.

Organ pipe whistles appeared singly on domeless Nos.2533 (152), 2534 (153), 2535 (154) and 2537 (156), but twin whistles were placed in front of the cabs when reboilering occurred. Then from November 1940 No.2415 (23) ushered in a reversion to single bell-type whistles, thus putting the class back to where they started in that respect.

Several engines acquired NER-type wheel-and-handle smokebox door fastenings, including 2405 (13), 2407 (15), 2419 (27), 2534 (153) and 2537 (156); but all reverted in due course to twin handles. 2410 (18), 2419 (27), 2535 (154) and 2537 (156) were running at the time of Grouping with extended

smokeboxes eight inches longer than normal. The extended base was fully circular due to the extra clearance which was created by the higher pitch of the boiler on the F3/N13 engines - on Class F2/N12 No.2489 (108) which had been similarly treated, this extension had been given a flat base. It seems that these alterations had been instigated by the H&BR and carried out in the early days of the NER interregnum; the purpose was to provide more room for access to the smokebox regulator valve. Upon reboilering, all engines received the same shorter-length smokeboxes again.

Buffers originally had tapered stocks with square mounting flanges, 69112 (18) and 69119 (156) being withdrawn so fitted; 2419 (27) acquired the NER's similar type with circular flange, and the LNER's Group Standard type appeared on 2405 (13) and 2536 (155) in 1943. The re-railing jacks were soon removed by the LNER, being purloined for use elsewhere at the time of the first Darlington repair.

Coal rails were also not left unaltered, except for only 2419 (27) and 2536 (155) which retained the three rails as originally fitted throughout their lives. All the others received an additional coal-rail by 1923, and all ten of the class had the usual plating added behind the rails by Darlington works.

The fitting of domed boilers caused the handrails to be raised, that on the left side being extended as far back as the cab in order to run the blower control rod within it. The handrail on the right side was still left short, finishing adjacent to the tank front end. No handrails were fitted to the tank tops, unlike all other Stirling tank engines.

A further point of identification which served to differentiate between the N12's and N13's was the front splasher, which carried a heavy brass beading around the edge on the N13 engines, as opposed to the plain splashers of the N12's.

Originally, Hawthorn, Leslie's works plates were fitted on the front sandboxes but these were soon removed by the LNER which took a dim view of such things, preferring to fit their own cast-iron plates on the bunker sides. Under BR of course, the bunkers were once again required for displaying the engine's number in painted figures, so the plates were moved to the positions occupied by those originally fitted. However 69111 (15), 69114 (27) and 69118 (155) managed to achieve a touch of individuality here, for the first two had the plates in question bolted to the splasher itself (rather than the sandbox part), whereas the latter engine was to carry its plates on its cab sides. The same engine was also to achieve a further touch of

69114 (27) has acquired its BR number - which is more than ex-WD "Austerity" 2-8-0 No.63068, which is standing behind, has achieved. The scene is Neville Hill shed, Leeds, 3rd October 1948. *H.C.Casserley.*

69112 (18) at Springhead, displaying its final condition; the F3 engines and Class J 4-4-0's became the only H&BR locomotives to carry the current owners' armorial devices - even if in the case of the F3's it was only the small version of BR's odd little badge with the emaciated lion on a unicycle!

"customisation" by getting its British Railways' cast-iron smokebox numberplate fitted above the top door-hinge, rather than below it as on all the others.

Repainting also produced some oddities over the years, too. Among these was 3013 which emerged from Springhead in March 1923 in plain black, lettered "N.E.R." on its tanks, but sporting its number in H&BR shaded 6 inch numerals on the bunker. 3152 remained in full H&BR livery except for its new number, and the same style was displayed by No.154 as late as June 1923, the addition of its NER number in the 3000 series having passed it by. August 1923 saw Springhead turn out 3156 in black, but with single red lining, plus small cast plate on the bunker. Its tank sides proclaimed it as an "L.N.E.R." engine; its number being below in 12 inch numerals. (Darlington never used stops with the initials "LNER", having dropped them whilst still using Ampersand). July 1924 saw 3156 become 2537, its NER number being expunged with a patch of black paint and the new one put on top - thus it still remained the property of the "L.N.E.R.", since the painter didn't take the opportunity to obliterate the now-unfashionable stops at the same time! The first N13 to actually be renumbered was 3018, which received its LNER number 2410 between the smaller letters "N E" on its tank sides. This was in April 1924; presumably its NER goods-style livery had been applied in February 1923.

All lost the single red lining from June 1928 onwards in favour of plain black, and all became "NE" engines during World War II. No.9110 (13) was scrapped whilst still in this style, whereas 9111 (15), 9112 (18) and 9119 (156), if no others regained "LNER".

The first outward signs of Nationalisation appeared on E9118 (155), 69114 (27) and 69111 (15) in February and September 1948 and May 1949 respectively, in the form of the words "BRITISH RAILWAYS" painted along the tank sides. After that time, the smaller version of BR's emaciated lion-on-a-unicycle totem was applied to 69112-69119 inclusive.

So in that final form, Matthew Stirling's last few engines eked out their final years. Sadly, efforts to get 69114 preserved came to nought, as outlined earlier. Only its LNER worksplates survive in preservation as reminders of its existence, plus the memories of the dwindling numbers of those who worked on them in their prime. William Westoby recalled cleaning the F3's in the days when such activities were considered the norm rather than the exception. Their wide tanks left hardly any room for footplating, and the absence of handrails made any Tarzan-like attempts to get along the sides totally impossible. Consequently small, lad cleaners were unable to reach all the tank and invariably left a narrow, horizontal strip of dirt along them for someone taller to wipe off, unless they went to the extent of scrounging a trestle!

A BR Inspector, recalling some years ago his early days as a fireman at Neville Hill shed, enthused over the N13's and their accommodating cabs - like their predecessors the N12's, they offered the space to take forty winks in a measure of some comfort!

Regrettably, today's volunteer railwaymen on the preserved lines are unable to sample the comforts of an F3 cab for themselves or face the challenge of cleaning one, for the locomotive chapter in the H&BR's story of unequal struggles against overwhelming odds came to its sad conclusion in Darlington's North Road scrapyard in October 1956.

Summary: Class F3 0-6-2 Radial Tank. LNER Class N13.

H&BR No.	Built	Works No.	NER No.	LNER 1924 No.	1946 No.	BR No.	Domed 71B boiler fitted	Withdrawn
13	Nov. 1913	3008	3013	2405	9110	(6)9110	September 1926	June 1948
15	Dec. 1913	3009	3015	2407	9111	69111	January 1931	Aug.1952
18	Dec. 1913	3010	3018	2410	9112	69112	September 1933	Nov. 1952
23	Dec. 1913	3011	3023	2415	9113	69113	December 1932	May 1953
27	Jan. 1914	3012	3027	2419	9114	69114	December 1930	Oct. 1956
152	Jan. 1914	3013	3152	2533	9115	69115	October 1933	May 1955
153	Feb. 1914	3014	3153	2534	9116	69116	May 1933	Dec. 1954
154	Feb. 1914	3015	3154	2535	9117	69117	October 1933	July 1955
155	Mar. 1914	3016	3155	2536	9118	69118	September 1932	May 1952
156	Mar. 1914	3017	3156	2537	9119	69119	August 1934	July 1955

Notes: Built Hawthorn, Leslie & Co. Cost £2,740 each.
Rated Power Class 4F under BR, re-rated to 3F in 1953; also given LNER Route Avalability rating R.A.4.

Dimensions Class F3 0-6-2 Radial Tank:

Cylinders: (2, inside) 18" x 26"
Motion: Stephenson Link, slide valves back-to-back between cylinders.
Boiler: Domeless
Max. diameter outside: 4' 3"
Barrel length: 10' 0"
Firebox length outside: 5' 6"
Pitch: 7' 4"
Heating surfaces:
  Firebox: 104 sq.ft
  Tubes: 191 @ 1¾" dia. = 904 sq.ft
  Total: 1,008 sq.ft
Grate Area: 16.25 sq.ft
Ratio of Grate Area to Heating Surface: 1 to 62.03
Boiler Pressure: 160 lb/sq.in
Wheel Diameters: 4' 6" Coupled; 3' 9" Radial.
Wheelbase: 7' 3" + 8' 3" + 7' 6" = 23' 0"
Length over Buffers: 35' 10½"
Height to Top of Chimney: 12' 10⁵/₈"
Tractive Effort @ 85% of Boiler Pressure: 21,216 lb
Ratio of Blast Nozzle to Cylinder Diameter: 1 to 3.78
Water Tank Capacity: 2,000 gallons
  (600 gallons each side, plus 800 gallons in end tank).
Bunker Coal Capacity: 3 tons
Weights in full W.O.: L 15T 9C 12Q; D 16T 14C 0Q;
T 12T 12C 3Q; R 16T 13C 0Q.
Total: 61T 9C 1Q.

Dimensions for LNER Class N13, Rebuilt with Diagram 71B Domed boilers.
Boiler: Domed
Pitch: 7' 0½"*
Heating Surface:
  Firebox: 99 sq.ft
  Tubes: 205 @ 1¾"dia. = 972 sq.ft
  Total: 1,071 sq.ft
Grate Area: 15.48 sq.ft
Boiler Pressure: 175 lb/sq.in
Tractive Effort @ 85% of Boiler Pressure: 23,197 lb
Length over Buffers: 35' 11" (The half-inch discrepancy between the last H&BR Diagram and the first of the LNER ones may have arisen due to re-measurement - possibly an engine with new buffer springs may have been measured by the LNER!).
* The 3½ inch discrepancy in boiler pitch between the F3 in 1922 and N13 in 1926 may be compared with Class F2/N12, in which the boiler centre-line was at 6' 11". When rebuilt with Diagram 71B domed boilers, the LNER drawing for the new smokeboxes stated that the cylinder blocks on Class N13 engines had to be built up by 2" in height. The fitting of the taller Class N12 chimneys to some N13's by the LNER, whilst the engines concerned still carried domeless Diagram 71A boilers increased the height to the chimney tops on those engines to 13' 4¹/₁₆" - just over an inch more than the NER's Loading Gauge, but considerably more than the LNER Composite Loading Gauge, which was applied to the entire system in time. Yet there is no record of any H&BR locomotive coming into forceful contact with the underside of a bridge or tunnel!

69119 (156) remained in Hull as the last H&BR engine on its native system, being depicted here at Springhead on 24th August 1952. *John C.Wright.*

69119 at the west end of Springhead yard, whilst occupied as the C&W pilot. Beyond 69119's bunker can be seen Springhead waterworks - the tall chimney was soon to be demolished upon conversion of the pumps to electric power, from steam. The steady growth of housing to the south of Willerby Road may have been evident in the various photographs around Springhead - by 1985 they were to cover the site where 69119 stands for its photograph. *N.E.Stead.*

69115 (152) stands at Darlington North Road scrapyard on 21st May 1955. The message on the side-tank shows someone at Neville Hill shed appreciated Matthew Stirling's work, and was sorry to see "his" engine go for scrap. *Ron Copeman collection.*

H&BR LOCOMOTIVES - A SUMMARY.

H&BR No.	1908 Class	Type	Built	Builder & No.	LNER No.	Withdrawn	*Notes*
1	G1	0-6-0T	1884	B/P 2430	-	1922	
2	"	"	1884	B/P 2431	-	1922	Sold
3	"	"	1884	B/P 2432	-	1922	Sold
4	"	"	1884	B/P 2433	-	1922	Sold
5	"	"	1884	B/P 2434	-	1922	Sold
6	"	"	1885	B/P 2436	-	1922	
7	"	"	1885	B/P 2437	-	1922	
8	"	"	1885	B/P 2438	-	1922	Sold
9	"	"	1885	B/P 2439	-	1922	
10	"	"	1885	B/P 2440	-	1922	
11	"	"	1885	B/P 2441	-	1922	
12	"	"	1885	B/P 2641	-	1922	
13A	D	0-6-0	1885	B/P 2489	-	1922	
14A	E	"	1885	B/P 2490	-	6/1920	
15A	D	"	1885	B/P 2491	-	1922	
16A	E	"	1885	B/P 2492	-	1922	
17A	"	"	1885	B/P 2493	-	1917	
18A	D	"	1885	B/P 2494	-	1922	
19A	E	"	1885	B/P 2495	-	1922	
20A	D	"	1885	B/P 2496	-	1922	
21A	E	"	1885	B/P 2497	-	6/1920	
22A	D	"	1885	B/P 2498	-	1922	
23A	"	"	1885	B/P 2499	-	1922	
24A	E	"	1885	B/P 2500	-	1922	
25A	"	"	1885	B/P 2501	-	1922	
26A	D	"	1885	B/P 2502	-	1922	
27A	"	"	1885	B/P 2503	-	1922	
28A	"	"	1885	B/P 2504	-	1922	
29A	E	"	1885	B/P 2505	-	1922	
30A	"	"	1885	B/P 2506	-	1922	
31A	E	0-6-0	1885	B/P 2507	-	6/1920	
32A	D	"	1885	B/P 2508	-	1922	
33A	H	2-4-0	1885	B/P 2479	-	1922	
34	H1	"	1885	B/P 2480	-	1922	
35A	H	"	1885	B/P 2481	-	1922	
36	H1	"	1885	B/P 2482	-	1922	
37	"	"	1885	B/P 2483	-	1922	
38A	"	"	1885	B/P 2484	-	1917	
39	"	"	1885	B/P 2485	-	1922	
40	"	"	1885	B/P 2486	-	1922	
41A	H	"	1885	B/P 2487	-	1922	
42A	H1	"	1885	B/P 2488	-	1922	
43	K	0-4-0 WT.	2/1886	KIT. 2957	-	1922	
44	"	"	2/1886	KIT. 2952	-	1922	
45	"	"	2/1886	KIT. 2953	-	1922	
46	"	"	12/1888	KIT. 2954	-	1922	
47	"	"	12/1888	KIT. 2955	-	1922	
48	"	"	1/1889	KIT. 3128	-	1922	
49	B	0-6-0	3/1889	KIT. 3138	2430	2/1926	(1)
50	"	"	3/1889	KIT. 3139	2431	4/1925	"
51	"	"	3/1889	KIT. 3140	2432	2/1926	"
52	"	"	3/1889	KIT. 3141	2433	9/1928	"
53	"	"	3/1889	KIT. 3142	2434	4/1925	"
54	"	"	4/1889	KIT. 3143	2435	1/1929	"
55	"	"	4/1889	KIT. 3144	2436	9/1928	"
56	"	"	4/1889	KIT. 3145	2437	9/1926	"
57	"	"	8/1892	KIT. 3504	2438	6/1933	"
58	"	"	8/1892	KIT. 3505	2439	12/1933	"
59	B	0-6-0	8/1892	KIT. 3506	2440	6/1933	"
60	"	"	9/1892	KIT. 3507	2441	5/1937	" *
61	"	"	9/1892	KIT. 3508	2442	8/1926	"
62	"	"	9/1892	KIT. 3509	2443	8/1926	"
63	"	"	6/1892	V/F 1351	2444	6/1936	"
64	"	"	6/1892	V/F 1352	2445	1/1935	"

H&BR No.	1908	Type	Built	Builder & No.	LNER No.	Withdrawn	*Notes*
65	"	"	7/1892	V/F 1353	2446	3/1934	(1)
66	"	"	7/1892	V/F 1354	2447	1/1934	"
67	G2	0-6-0T	8/1892	R/S 2781	2448	9/1931	
68	"	"	8/1892	R/S 2782	2449	7/1931	
69	"	"	9/1892	R/S 2783	2450	8/1931	
70	B	0-6-0	9/1897	Y/E 547	2451	7/1933	(1)
71	"	"	9/1897	Y/E 548	2452	5/1937	"
72	"	"	10/1897	Y/E 549	2453	1/1936	"
73	"	"	11/1897	Y/E 550	2454	7/1937	"
74	"	"	11/1897	Y/E 551	2455	8/1935	"
75	"	"	12/1897	Y/E 552	2456	7/1937	"
76	"	"	12/1898	Y/E 560	2457	5/1937	"
77	"	"	12/1898	Y/E 561	2458	11/1935	"
78	"	"	12/1898	Y/E 562	2459	9/1933	"
79	"	"	10/1898	KIT. 3786	2460	11/1938	(2)
80	"	"	10/1898	KIT. 3787	2461	12/1933	"
81	"	"	10/1898	KIT. 3788	2462	7/1937	"
82	"	"	10/1898	KIT. 3789	2463	3/1928	"
83	"	"	11/1898	KIT. 3790	2464	5/1937	"
84	"	"	12/1898	KIT. 3791	2465	3/1934	"
85	"	"	3/1900	KIT. 3912	2466	11/1932	(3)
86	"	"	3/1900	KIT. 3913	2467	2/1934	"
87	"	"	4/1900	KIT. 3914	2468	12/1933	"
88	"	"	4/1900	KIT. 3915	2469	10/1937	"
89	"	"	4/1900	KIT. 3916	2470	2/1934	"
90	"	"	4/1900	KIT. 3917	2471	6/1934	"
91	"	"	5/1900	Y/E 604	2472	1/1936	"
92	"	"	6/1900	Y/E 605	2473	12/1933	"
93	"	"	6/1900	Y/E 606	2474	7/1937	"
94	"	"	6/1900	Y/E 607	2475	5/1937	"
95	"	"	7/1900	Y/E 608	2476	11/1938	"
96	"	"	8/1900	Y/E 609	2477	5/1937	"
97	F1	0-6-2T	1/1900	KIT. 3964	2478	1/1943	(4)
98	"	"	1/1900	KIT. 3965	2479	12/1944	"
99	"	"	2/1900	KIT. 3966	2480	5/1946	"
100	"	"	2/1900	KIT. 3967	2481	12/1945	"
101	"	"	2/1900	KIT. 3968	2482	8/1944	"
102	F2	0-6-2T	11/1901	KIT. 4070	2483	8/1938	
103	"	"	12/1901	KIT. 4071	2484	12/1936	
104	"	"	12/1901	KIT. 4072	2485	3/1937	
105	"	"	12/1901	KIT. 4073	2486	8/1948	Wdn. as (6)9089
106	"	"	12/1901	KIT. 4074	2487	9/1938	
107	"	"	12/1901	KIT. 4075	2488	10/1938	
108	"	"	12/1901	KIT. 4076	2489	2/1937	
109	"	"	12/1901	KIT. 4077	2490	12/1936	
110	"	"	12/1901	KIT. 4078	2491	10/1936	
111	G3	0-6-0T	12/1901	Y/E 655	2492	9/1937	
112	"	"	12/1901	Y/E 656	2493	6/1937	
113	"	"	12/1901	Y/E 657	2494	5/1937	
114	"	"	1/1902	Y/E 658	2495	5/1937	
115	"	"	2/1902	Y/E 659	2496	9/1937	
116	"	"	2/1902	Y/E 660	2497	5/1937	
117	A	0-8-0	2/1907	Y/E 899	2498	9/1931	
118	"	"	3/1907	Y/E 900	2499	8/1931	
119	"	"	3/1907	Y/E 901	2500	5/1931	
120	"	"	3/1907	Y/E 902	2501	8/1931	
121	"	"	8/1907	Y/E 903	2502	11/1931	
122	"	"	4/1907	Y/E 904	2503	10/1931	
123	"	"	5/1907	Y/E 905	2504	10/1931	
124	"	"	5/1907	Y/E 906	2505	8/1931	
125	"	"	6/1907	Y/E 907	2506	8/1931	
126	"	"	6/1907	Y/E 908	2507	8/1931	
127	"	"	9/1907	Y/E 942	2508	10/1931	
128	"	"	10/1907	Y/E 943	2509	10/1931	
129	"	"	10/1907	Y/E 944	2510	8/1931	
130	"	"	10/1907	Y/E 945	2511	9/1931	
131	"	"	11/1907	Y/E 946	2512	9/1931	

H&BR No.	1908 Class	Type	Built	Builder & No.	LNER No.	Withdrawn	Notes
132	B	0-6-0	2/1908	KIT. 4555	2513	5/1937	(3)
133	"	"	3/1908	KIT. 4556	2514	5/1937	" **
134	"	"	3/1908	KIT. 4557	2515	7/1935	"
135	"	"	3/1908	KIT. 4558	2516	7/1935	"
136	"	"	3/1908	KIT. 4559	2517	7/1937	"
137	"	"	3/1908	KIT. 4560	2518	11/1937	"
138	"	"	3/1908	KIT. 4561	2519	6/1935	(3)
139	"	"	3/1908	KIT. 4562	2520	2/1935	"
140	"	"	3/1908	KIT. 4563	2521	7/1936	"
141	"	"	3/1908	KIT. 4564	2522	5/1937	"
142	G3	0-6-0T	1/1908	KIT. 4545	2523	6/1938	
143	"	"	1/1908	KIT. 4546	2524	5/1937	
144	"	"	1/1908	KIT. 4547	2525	6/1937	
145	"	"	2/1908	KIT. 4548	2526	5/1937	
146	"	"	2/1908	KIT. 4549	2527	9/1937	
147	"	"	2/1908	KIT. 4550	2528	3/1939	
148	"	"	2/1908	KIT. 4551	2529	7/1937	
149	"	"	2/1908	KIT. 4552	2530	5/1937	
150	"	"	2/1908	KIT. 4553	2531	6/1937	
151	"	"	2/1908	KIT. 4554	2532	1/1949	Wdn. as (6)8365
33	J	4-4-0	12/1910	KIT. 4700	2425	8/1933	
35	"	"	12/1910	KIT. 4701	2426	12/1933	
38	"	"	12/1910	KIT. 4702	2427	1/1934	
41	"	"	12/1910	KIT. 4703	2428	12/1933	
42	"	"	12/1910	KIT. 4704	2429	9/1934	
16	L1	0-6-0	12/1911	KIT. 4705	2408	10/1938	(5)
17	"	"	12/1911	KIT. 4706	2409	10/1937	"
19	"	"	12/1911	KIT. 4707	2411	9/1938	"
24	"	"	12/1911	KIT. 4708	2416	10/1938	"
31	"	"	12/1911	KIT. 4709	2423	5/1937	"
14	"	"	11/1912	KIT. 4710	2406	7/1937	
25	"	"	12/1912	KIT. 4711	2417	9/1934	
29	"	"	12/1912	KIT. 4712	2421	5/1937	
30	"	"	12/1912	KIT. 4713	2422	10/1938	
32	"	"	12/1912	KIT. 4714	2424	5/1937	
13	F3	0-6-2T	11/1913	H/L 3008	2405	6/1948	Wdn. as (6) 9110
15	"	"	12/1913	H/L 3009	2407	8/1952	Wdn. as 69111
18	"	"	12/1913	H/L 3010	2410	10/1952	Wdn. as 69112
23	"	"	12/1913	H/L 3011	2415	5/1953	Wdn. as 69113
27	"	"	1/1914	H/L 3012	2419	10/1956	Wdn. as 69114
152	"	"	1/1914	H/L 3013	2533	5/1955	Wdn. as 69115
153	"	"	2/1914	H/L 3014	2534	12/1954	Wdn. as 69116
154	"	"	2/1914	H/L 3015	2535	7/1955	Wdn. as 69117
155	"	"	3/1914	H/L 3016	2536	5/1952	Wdn. as 69118
156	"	"	3/1914	H/L 3017	2537	7/1955	Wdn. as 69119
157	L	0-6-0	8/1914	Y/E 1182	2538	6/1937	
158	"	"	8/1914	Y/E 1183	2539	10/1937	
159	"	"	10/1914	Y/E 1184	2540	12/1937	
160	"	"	11/1914	Y/E 1185	2541	5/1937	
161	"	"	12/1914	Y/E 1186	2542	11/1937	
20	LS	0-6-0	1/1915	KIT. 5010	2412	11/1937	(6)
21	"	"	1/1915	KIT. 5011	2413	10/1938	"
22	"	"	1/1915	KIT. 5012	2414	5/1937	"
26	"	"	2/1915	KIT. 5013	2418	6/1937	"
28	"	"	2/1915	KIT. 5014	2420	9/1938	"

Notes:
(1) Built with 4' 3" diameter boilers.
(2) Built with 4' 9" diameter boilers.
(3) Built with 5' 0" diameter boilers.
(4) Ex-LDECR purchase.
(5) Built with Phoenix superheaters.
(6) Built with Schmidt superheaters.
* Fitted with Lytton superheater - ? 1912 to October 1925.
** Fitted with Phoenix superheater - May 1914 to July 1919.

Springhead shed and works from the west, shortly before the end of the H&BR. From left to right may be seen the coal stage of 1907; the reception roads for the wagon works; the new erecting shop (1914); the 1887 erecting shop, with the brick-based water tank of 1897 just visible in front. Above the right-hand line of locomotives may be seen the water softening plant; between it and the locomotive shed is the 70ft. brick chimney built for the 1901 stationary boiler/powerhouse. The two main running lines are easily made out, with the reception loop leading directly into the marshalling yard. The signal indicator on the right was a home-made H&BR item. *Author's collection.*

Cudworth in June 1938 with ex-GC types dominating the shed roads. The original timber shearlegs had been replaced earlier in the decade by the LNER with the steel girder structure on the left. Coal dominated the life of this shed and all around can be seen evidence of that once great industry. Just discernible below the left horizon is the LMS Royston engine shed. *B.Roberts.*

(previous page) **North Eastern 4-4-0 No. 115 of Class D22 is the odd one out amongst a collection of H&BR locomotives, including members of Classes Q10, J23, J28, N12 and N11. The N11 is obviously in for attention to its radial axleboxes, whilst the coupling rods on the ground near No.115 are clearly off the Q10 in front.** *Author's collection.*

JACKS.

Such items were unusual additions to British locomotives, but by no means confined to H&BR engines only. They appeared at times on locomotives belonging to the Midland & Great Northern Joint Railway, the London, Tilbury & Southend Railway, the Taff Vale Railway, Great Central Railway, Waterford & Limerick Railway, the Leek & Manifold Railway, the County Donegal Railway, the Londonderry & Lough Swilly Railway, Belfast & County Down/Northern Counties Committee, the Isle of Wight Railway, the Isle of Wight Central Railway, the Irish Great Northern Railway, the Colne Valley & Halstead Railway, the Stratford-on-Avon, East & West Junction Railway and the Midland & South Western Junction Railway! Not surprisingly, the Robinson 2-8-0's built to order of the War Department from August 1917 were also fitted with similar jacks - essential equipment for engines operating in a war zone.

Quite why Matthew Stirling decided that all his engines should carry jacks is unknown for they never appeared on Great Northern locomotives, but herein may lay the reason why! During his employment by the GNR as Shedmaster at various depots he would have had to take responsibility for breakdown and accident recovery work, and most of these incidents must have been of a minor nature. Maybe he realised that all too often there was no need for a full breakdown gang to turn out complete with packing vans and crane, and that an engine's crew (with assistance from local permanent-way staff for example), could sort out minor mishaps far more expeditiously themselves. As Locomotive Superintendent in his own right on the H&BR, he could order things more or less as he wished.

Under the LNER the jacks were removed from most locomotives, but continued in use around Springhead Works for many years. When the Carriage & Wagon Repairs and Outdoor Machinery Maintenance Departments transferred from Springhead to Dairycoates in 1971, the jacks went with the rest of the movable fittings.

A few odd ones were purchased by various preservation groups, and hence remain in occasional use today. Although much heavier and harder to use than modern hydraulic jacks, they have the advantage of never leaking off under load: of inestimable value when used in restoration tasks of a somewhat protracted nature.

In view of the reasonably widespread appearance of similar jacks, the author hopes that the accompanying drawings will be of assistance to the modelmaker.

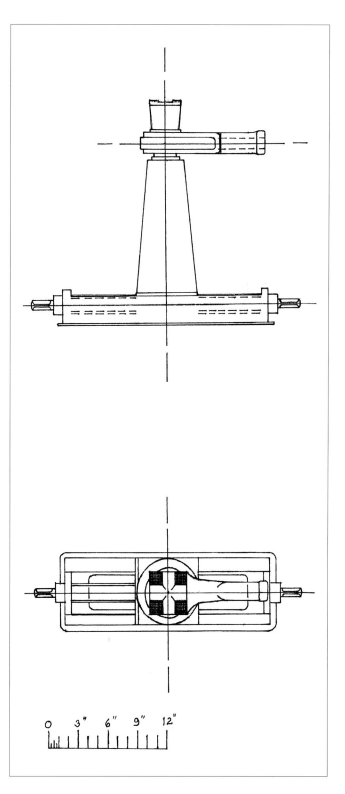

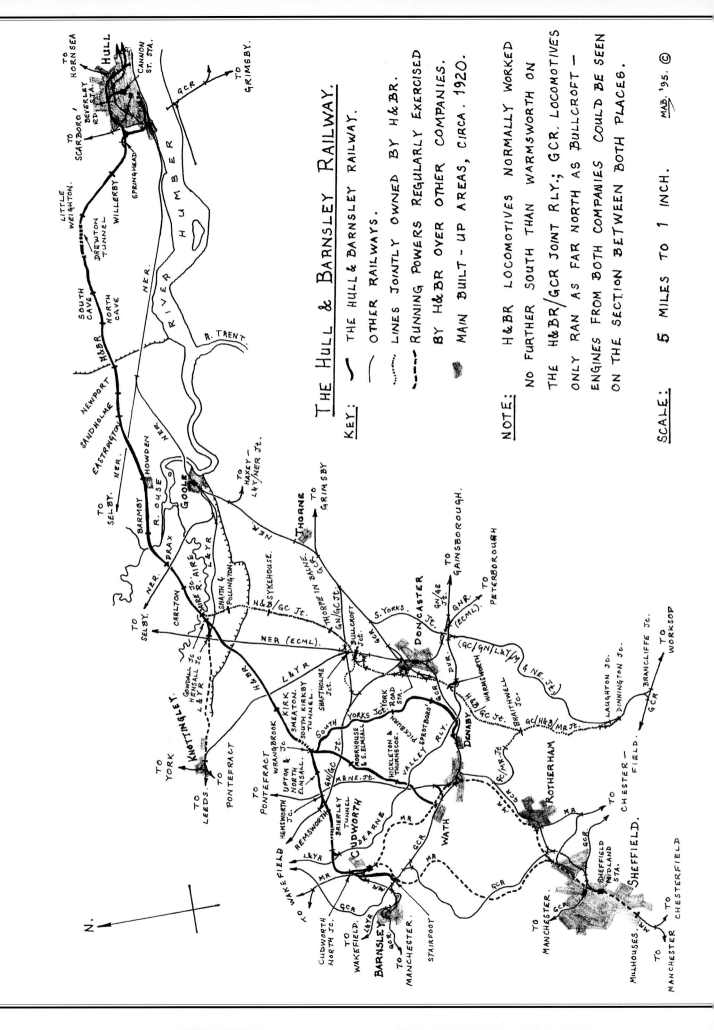

THE HULL & BARNSLEY RAILWAY.

KEY: ——— THE HULL & BARNSLEY RAILWAY.
 ——— OTHER RAILWAYS.
 .... LINES JOINTLY OWNED BY H&BR.
 — — — RUNNING POWERS REGULARLY EXERCISED
 BY H&BR OVER OTHER COMPANIES.
 ▓ MAIN BUILT-UP AREAS, CIRCA. 1920.

NOTE: H&BR LOCOMOTIVES NORMALLY WORKED
 NO FURTHER SOUTH THAN WARMSWORTH ON
 THE H&BR/GCR JOINT RLY.; GCR LOCOMOTIVES
 ONLY RAN AS FAR NORTH AS BULLCROFT —
 ENGINES FROM BOTH COMPANIES COULD BE SEEN
 ON THE SECTION BETWEEN BOTH PLACES.

SCALE: 5 MILES TO 1 INCH.

MAB. '95. ©

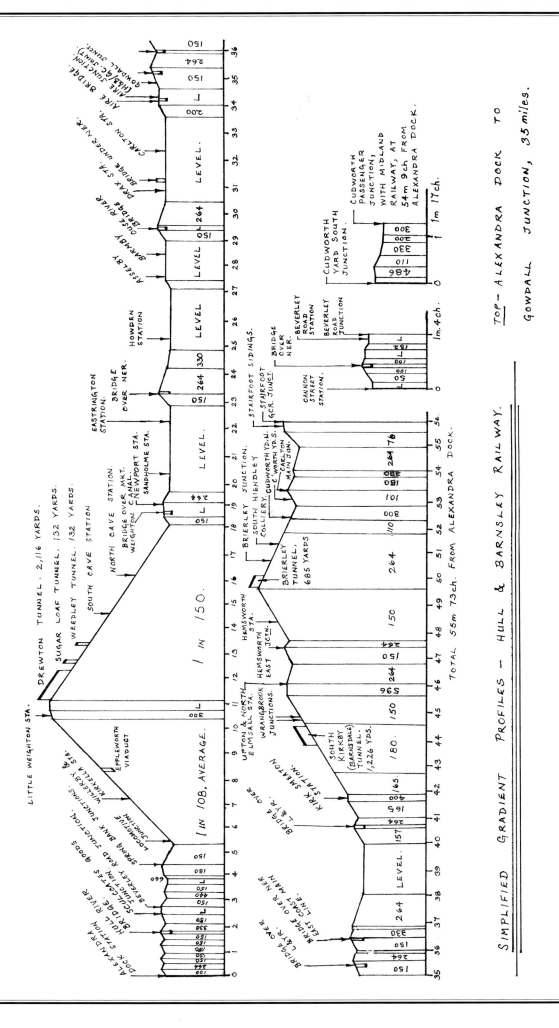

SIMPLIFIED GRADIENT PROFILES — HULL & BARNSLEY RAILWAY.

TOP — (L. TO R.) GOWDALL JUNCTION, 35 miles TO STAIRFOOT JUNCTION, 56 miles; CANNON STREET STATION TO BEVERLEY ROAD JUNCTION, 1 mile 4 chains; CUDWORTH YARD SOUTH JUNCTION TO CUDWORTH STATION, 1 mile 17 chains.

TOP — ALEXANDRA DOCK TO GOWDALL JUNCTION, 35 miles.

MAB. '95. ©

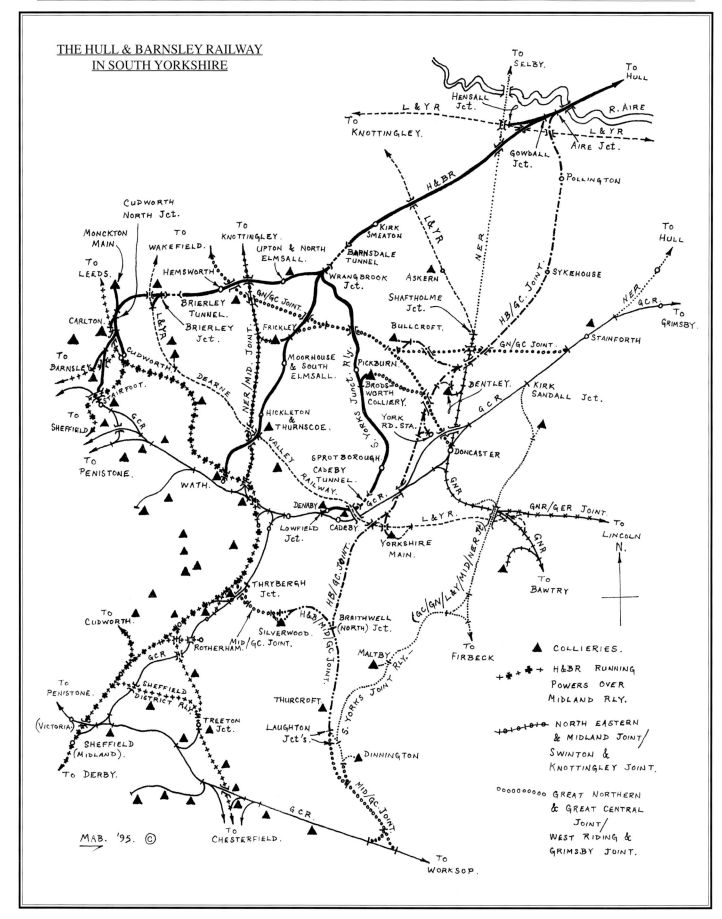

THE HULL & BARNSLEY RAILWAY
IN SOUTH YORKSHIRE

INDEX of main subjects. Volume 1.

BIBLIOGRAPHY / SUGGESTIONS FOR FURTHER READING.

AHRONS. E.L.	Locomotive & Train Working in the Latter Part of the 19th. Century. (Railway Mag.).
	The British Steam Railway Locomotive, 1825-1925. (Bracken Books, 1987).
BARNETT. A.L.	Railways of the South Yorkshire Coalfield from 1880. (RCTS, 1984).
BELL. A.M.	Locomotives - Vols. I and II. (Virtue & Co., London, 1948).
BOWEN-COOKE. C.J.	British Locomotives, 1894. (Facsimile edition, Gresham Books, 1979).
BRADLEY. D.L.	The Locomotive History of the London, Chatham & Dover Rly. (RCTS., 1979).
	The Locomotive History of the South Eastern Railway. (RCTS., 1985).
	The Locomotive History of the South Eastern & Chatham Railway. (RCTS., 1980).
BROWN. F.A.S.	From Stirling to Gresley, 1882-1922. (Oxford Publishing Company. 1974).
	Nigel Gresley - Locomotive Engineer. (1961).
COLE. THE REV.E.M.	Notes on the Geology of the Hull, Barnsley & West Riding Junction Railway & Dock. (1886).
COX. E.S.	Locomotive Panorama Vols. I & II. (Ian Allan, 1976).
CULPIT. J. & TAYLOR. W.	The Lancashire, Derbyshire & East Coast Railway Company. (Oakwood Press, 1988).
DODSWORTH. E.	The Train Now Standing: Vol I, Life & Times of Hull & Barnsley Rly. (Hutton Press, 1990).
"ENGINEERING".	Various issues from 1880's to 1920's.
FLEETWOOD. N.P.	Springhead Works of the Hull & Barnsley Railway. (Article "Railway World", April 1985).
GILLETT. E. & MACMAHON. K.A.	A History of Hull. (University of Hull Press, 1993).
GOODE. C.T.	Railway Rambles in East Yorkshire. (1984).
	Railway Rambles on the Hull & Barnsley Railway. (1985).
	The Railways of Hull. (1992).
HARESNAPE. B. & ROWLEDGE. P.	Robinson Locomotives - a Pictorial History. (Ian Allan, 1982).
HEWISON. C.H.	Locomotive Boiler Explosions. (David & Charles, 1983).
HILLS & PATRICK.	Beyer, Peacock, Locomotive Builders to the World. (Transport Publishing Co. 1982).
HINCHLIFFE. B. (as Editor).	The Hull & Barnsley Railway. Vol II. (Turntable Publications, 1980).
HODGSON. J.T. & WILLIAMS. J.	Locomotive Management from Cleaning to Driving. (London, 1920).
HOOLE. K.	Railway History in Pictures - North East England. (David & Charles, 1969).
	North Eastern Locomotive Sheds. (David & Charles. 1972).
	North Eastern Album. (Ian Allan, 1974).
	Railways in Yorkshire. 2 - The East Riding. (Dalesman, 1976).
	An Illustrated History of NER. Locomotives. (Oxford Publishing Co., 1988).
(As Editor).	The Hull & Barnsley Railway, Vol. I. (David & Charles, 1972).
HOOPER. J.	LNER. Sheds in Camera. (Guild Publishing, 1984).
HULL & BARNSLEY RLY.	Drawings; Annual and Half-Yearly Reports; Minutes.
LAKE. G.S. & REIDINGER. A.	Valves and Valve Gears for Steam Locomotives. (Reprinted T.E.E. Publishing, 1981).
LOCOMOTIVE MANUFACTURERS ASSOC. of G.B..	Locomotive .Manufacturers Association Handbook. (London, 1949).
L & N E R.	The Port of Hull. (LNER Docks & Overseas Dept., Fenchurch Street, London. 1935).
	Various Work's internal memos and correspondence.
THE LOCOMOTIVE MAGAZINE.	Various Issues.
NOCK. O.S.	Locomotives of the North Eastern Railway. (Ian Allan, 1974).
PARKES. G.D.	The Hull & Barnsley Railway. (Oakwood Press, 1970).
R.C.T.S./PANEL OF AUTHORS.	Locomotives of the LNER. (Multi-vol. history pubs by the R.C.T.S. from 1963 onwards).
REED. B.	150 Years of British Steam Locomotives. (David & Charles, 1975).
RUSSELL. J.H.	A Pictorial Record of Great Western Absorbed Engines. (Oxford Publishing Co.).
	A Pictorial Record of Southern Locomotives. (Oxford Publishing Co., 1991).
STIRLING. M.	Various notes and drawings, held by Hull Museums and in Hull Central Library.
STRETTON. C.E.	The Development of the Locomotive, 1803-1896. (Reprint by Bracken Books, 1989).
TUPLIN. W.A.	North Eastern Steam. (Allen & Unwin, 1970).
WEIGHT. R.A.H.	Great Northern Locomotives, 1847-1947. (The Gresley Society, 1970).
YEADON. W.B. & NICHOLSON. M.	An Illustrated History of Hull's Railways. (Irwell Press, 1993).
	More Illustrated History of the Railways of Hull. (Challenger Publications, 1995).
YODER. J.H. & WHAREN. G.B.	Locomotive Valves and Valve Gears. (1917; Reprinted by T.E.E. Publishing, 1993).

PUBLISHERS NOTE

The Appendix Volume of this two volume work will contain, amongst other items, General Arrangement and scale drawings of H&BR locomotives along with the various components and mechanical details to be found on those locomotives. A full description of the Locomotive Department, covering all aspects and including the works, sheds and the myriad of personalities who held office therein from cleaners to Locomotive Engineer. If you ever had any doubts about how a steam locomotive worked then look no further than this superb addition to the annals of steam locomotive lore.
